Modern Hungers

Modern Hungers

Food and Power in Twentieth-Century Germany

ALICE WEINREB

OXFORD
UNIVERSITY PRESS

Oxford University Press is a department of the University of Oxford. It furthers the University's objective of excellence in research, scholarship, and education by publishing worldwide. Oxford is a registered trade mark of Oxford University Press in the UK and certain other countries.

Published in the United States of America by Oxford University Press
198 Madison Avenue, New York, NY 10016, United States of America.

© Oxford University Press 2017

First issued as an Oxford University Press paperback, 2020

All rights reserved. No part of this publication may be reproduced, stored in a retrieval system, or transmitted, in any form or by any means, without the prior permission in writing of Oxford University Press, or as expressly permitted by law, by license, or under terms agreed with the appropriate reproduction rights organization. Inquiries concerning reproduction outside the scope of the above should be sent to the Rights Department, Oxford University Press, at the address above.

You must not circulate this work in any other form
and you must impose this same condition on any acquirer.

Library of Congress Cataloging-in-Publication Data
Names: Weinreb, Alice Autumn, author.
Title: Modern hungers : food and power in twentieth-century Germany / Alice Weinreb.
Description: New York, NY : Oxford University Press, [2017] | Includes bibliographical references and index.
Identifiers: LCCN 2016049608 (print) | LCCN 2016052906 (ebook) | ISBN 9780190605094 (hardcover : acid-free paper) | ISBN 9780190605100 (Updf) | ISBN 9780190605117 (Epub)
ISBN 9780190092481 (paperback : acid-free paper) |
Subjects: LCSH: Food supply—Political aspects—Germany—History—20th century. | Food industry and trade—Political aspects—Germany—History—20th century. |
Food—Political aspects—Germany—History—20th century. |
Food—Social aspects—Germany—History—20th century. |
Hunger—Political aspects—Germany—History—20th century. |
Hunger—Social aspects—Germany—History—20th century. |
Power (Social sciences)—Germany—History—20th century. |
Germany—Politics and government—20th century. | Germany—Social conditions—20th century. | Germany—Economic conditions—20th century.
Classification: LCC HD9013.5 .W38 2017 (print) | LCC HD9013.5 (ebook) | DDC 338.1/9430904—dc23
LC record available at https://lccn.loc.gov/2016049608

CONTENTS

Acknowledgments vii

Introduction   Modern Hungers in Modern Germany   1

1. The Geopolitics of Total War: Food in the First World War   13

2. Blood and Soil: The Food Economy and the Nazi Racial State   49

3. Hunger and the Remaking of History: Rationing, Suffering, and Human Rights in Occupied Germany   88

4. Fueling Reconstruction: Production and Consumption in Divided Germany   122

5. Kitchen Debates: The Family Meal and Female Labor in East and West Germany   164

6. Fighting Fat: Obesity and the Healthy Body in the Late Cold War   196

Epilogue   Yes, We Have No Bananas: Negotiating Past and Future in Reunified Germany   237

Notes   251
Bibliography   281
Index   305

ACKNOWLEDGMENTS

It is a pleasure to have the opportunity to thank the many individuals and institutions that have supported me and my research over the years spent working on this book. As a graduate student, I received research support from the Social Science Research Council, the Free University Berlin Program, and the University of Michigan's Rackham Graduate School. Just as important as this financial support was the help and inspiration provided by faculty and fellow students. In particular, I want to thank Kathleen Canning, Geoff Eley, and Scott Spector, who have not only supported this project since its inception, but have become mentors and friends in the years since graduate school. I consider myself lucky to have had the opportunity to work with them. Before Ann Arbor, my time in Berlin was deeply influenced by the intellectual generosity of professors Christina von Braun, Stephanie von Schnurbein, Renate Brosch, and Birgit Dahlke at the Humboldt University. My amazing friends Victoria Hegner, Slavo Szabo, Ines Koeltzsch, René Krüpfganz, and Florence Vittu made these years some of the best of my life—leaving Berlin was hard because of you.

After leaving Ann Arbor, I spent three productive years in Northwestern University's History Department. These years were so useful in large part thanks to the kindness of colleagues Deborah Cohen, Sarah Maza, Tessie Liu, and Ben Frommer. After an academically engaging and remarkably beautiful year at Utah State University, I was lucky enough to join the history department of Loyola University Chicago. I want to express my gratitude for having been welcomed so warmly into a department shaped by collegiality and amiability as well as curiosity and intellectual rigor.

Like all histories, this book was enabled by the generosity of countless librarians and archivists. With a topic as vast as food, I relied on the insights and creativity of the staff of the German Federal Archives in Koblenz and Berlin and the city archives of Berlin, Dresden, Leipzig, Cologne, Düsseldorf, and Dortmund to track down and interpret materials. In Munich, both BMW and Siemens generously granted access to their corporate archives; at a crucial early point in my revisions, the Wellcome Collection Library in London shared some thought-provoking material that became the core of chapter 3, and Stanford University's Hoover Institution Archive provided crucial sources for what became the book's first chapter. Particular thanks go to the librarians of the German Institute for Nutritional Research and the Dresden Hygiene Museum for providing both tremendous hospitality and sincere interest in this project.

I was fortunate to receive valuable editorial feedback as I wrote this book. Deirdre Mullane, with the support of the SSRC, provided helpful editing support at an early stage of the project. I want to express special appreciation to David Lazar at the German Historical Institute and to Loyola University for assisting with publication costs. My editor Susan Ferber was unfailingly generous with her time and energy and as a result tremendously improved this project; so did the very useful feedback from two anonymous reviewers.

Over the years, this project has profited from a number of wonderful historians; fellow Germanists Eli Rubin, Ulrike Weckel, Ari Sammartino, Jan Palmowski, Edith Sheffer, Uwe Spiekermann, and Monica Black generously provided feedback and advice at various conferences where I presented parts of this work. Atina Grossmann, James Vernon, Richard Tucker, and Roger Chickering expressed their support at key moments. A special thanks are due to Sue Levine, whose tremendous warmth and sincere interest in my work has made a real difference in my time in Chicago.

Over the many years of working on first the dissertation and then the book, I have relied upon the friendships of Carla MacDougall, Kelly Buckle, Emil Kerenji, Nina Wieda, Ema Grama, Lenny Ureña, Tania Munz, Kelly Summers, and Bertie Mandelblatt to help keep my head above water. Carolyn Zola and Sasha Rossman were my best friends growing up, and are still some of my very favorite people—I can't wait to read your books in a few years! Latha Reddy has been both an amazing friend and critical thinker since we first met on a trip to Cape Town in 2004. Since moving to Chicago, I have come to rely on the kindness and intellectual engagement of Tara Zahra as both a friend and mentor. My mom Andrea and step-dad David have unwaveringly believed that this book was not only wonderful but also finishable. More than anyone else, Edin Hajdarpasic has helped to make this belief a reality. His brilliance and his love have made my book, and my life, so much better. This book is dedicated to my baby sister Maddy and my baby boy Malik—watching you both get big(er) has been my favorite pastime over the past years; now that this book is done, I look forward to having more time for it!

Modern Hungers

Introduction

Modern Hungers in Modern Germany

In April 2007, the International Association for the Study of Obesity released the results of a recent study of European overweight. It unexpectedly revealed that Germany had become the "fattest country in Europe." The country was embarrassed to find itself second only to the United States in its percentage of overweight population.[1] The news attracted considerable attention in the German media and inspired both state officials and medical experts to suggest a plethora of interventions and policy changes.[2] The painful evidence of a so-called epidemic of fat adults and chubby children was suddenly everywhere to be seen. Especially upsetting was the fact that the Germans had surpassed the English, who had long held the dubious title of "fattest Europeans" in comparative weight tables. In rapid response to this new crisis, the German government promised a revamping of nutritional education in schools, increased promotion of physical activity, and a prioritization of healthy eating in workplaces and at home. Within weeks of the release of the study's results, Germany hosted what was billed as the first international conference on the "latest innovations and trends in weight loss and weight management," optimistically titled "Slimming Germany 2007."[3] Since then, several subsequent studies have produced similar results and similar reactions; yet despite countless interventions, Germany's fatness seems here to stay.

Although German bodies are today generally associated with stoutness, over the first half of the twentieth century Germans were far more frequently described in the international press as underweight, indeed, as starving. During both world wars and again in their aftermaths, Germany was the only European country to repeatedly alternate between impressive prosperity and dramatic hunger and collapsing public health.[4] Not until the Cold War did Germans cease perceiving themselves as underfed and instead embrace the joys and perils of a particularly modern sort of overeating. The growing size of the bodies of both East Germany (the German Democratic Republic [GDR]) and West Germany (the Federal Republic of Germany [FRG]), seemed to confirm a narrative in which economic growth, modernization, and democratization were embodied by steadily expanding stomachs.

However, the story of German bodies is not a simple narrative of increased prosperity and caloric intake wherein Germans gained weight as they grew increasingly removed from militarism, economic chaos, and even Nazism. Considered since the nineteenth century the most "modern" economy in continental Europe, Germany's industrial strength and vast wealth were interpreted by Germans and non-Germans alike as guarantors of satiety. Indeed, the general trajectory of European industrialization seemed to support an assumed opposition between modernization and hunger. Yet the country's much-vaunted modernity did not ultimately protect it against bread riots, empty stomachs, or even state policies of mass starvation. Rather than view the persistence of Germany's hunger in the twentieth century as a paradox, this book argues that it was in fact essential to global projects of economic, cultural, and political modernization.

During both world wars, assertions that German civilians were malnourished coexisted with claims that they were the best-fed people in Europe. After each war, Germans became the leading recipients of American food aid despite the existence of more severe food shortages elsewhere in Europe and the world. In wartime, the Allies accused Germany of deliberately causing the hunger of the rest of the continent and depicted the Germans as growing fat off of stolen foodstuffs—yet European and American publics also came to be haunted by heart-wrenching images of starving German women and children. These competing visions of German bodies continued to coexist even as the wars themselves became distant memories. During the Cold War, "Fat Germany" became associated with the capitalist West, whereas "Starving Germany" symbolized the communist East. By the end of the Cold War, when slimness rather than plumpness had come to represent modernity and prosperity, these corporeal categories were reversed yet again; the heft of the GDR's population symbolized Communism's inability to adequately care for its population, whereas West Germans' slenderness revealed the West's prosperity, good taste, and material abundance.

Such constantly shifting descriptions of German bodies and appetites represent more than changing aesthetics or health standards; they provide a critical lens onto the enduring political struggles and global conflicts that defined the short twentieth century, stretching from the outbreak of the First World War to the fall of the Berlin Wall in 1989. Throughout these decades, in Germany as well as across the world, food and its constant corollary—hunger—remained at the forefront of evolving state concerns over economic systems, political strategies, familial structures, and cultural norms.

Food, Hunger, and Governmentality

The 1880s and 1890s, a time when "Europeans were eating better, living longer and traveling with ever greater ease and speed," was also the age of what historian Mike Davis has termed the "late Victorian holocausts," massive famines that stretched across the globe, claiming millions of lives and remaking the landscape of the modern world by dividing it between spaces of food excess and of food shortage.[5] At the same time that the West was asserting itself as a global hegemon, Europe's reliance on overseas food imports caused the deaths of tens of millions of people living in the global South.[6] This imperial displacement of hunger from Europe to Asia, Africa, and Latin America proved unexpectedly short-lived. What this era actually signaled was not the end of European food crises, which reappeared with a vengeance during and after the world wars, but the emergence of a transnational food order that was shaped by late imperialism and the rise of industrial capitalism. To observers horrified by the explosion in human suffering during an era of unparalleled growth, globalization came to be recognized as a central cause of hunger at the same time that it seemed the only possibility for fighting hunger, be it by means of trade regulations, international agencies, or humanitarian food aid. As the British geographer David Nally noted in his analysis of modern food aid, "the regulation of scarcity . . . does not signal the end of hunger so much as its displacement in space and time."[7]

During these last decades of the nineteenth century, a time of intensive technological and geopolitical innovation, controlling food resources seemed to be the key to economic growth, national and moral health, and biological vitality. Nations strove to improve the bodies of their inhabitants through the new science of nutrition; various projects of bodily regulation occurred alongside and complementary to state efforts to optimize economic growth and realize military and political ambitions.[8] Modern states began to perceive food-related activities, ranging from shopping trends to cooking techniques to dieting habits, as methods for monitoring and controlling citizens. As a result, the nutritional sciences played an especially important role in states' efforts to document—and to improve—popular health.[9] Population sciences such as statistics, economics, demography, and social hygiene were all "used to inform the regulation of the law, property, healthy, life and conduct of subjects through the regulation and normalization of mundane activities."[10] Such "mundane activities" increasingly connected state power to individual bodies. As state institutions began to take an active interest in the diets and foodways of their populations, they also began to conceptualize hunger as a potential tool of modernization. The history of the twentieth century reveals hunger's singular importance to the political trajectories of European nation-states, which consistently emphasized the material link between land, food, and populations.

For new European nation-states, manipulating hunger and satiety became central strategies for regulating both local and global populations.[11] As philosopher Michel Foucault put it, "grains and scarcity ... was always the issue" at the heart of governmentality—his term for the systems of knowledge by which modern states attempt to manage populations. Food and hunger became central expressions of biopolitics, "the set of mechanisms through which the basic biological features of the human species become the object of a political strategy."[12] While power is always expressed both through bodies and on bodies, modern biopolitics cast the body as the primary expression of political ambitions. Although most scholars of biopolitics have focused on sexuality and reproduction, Foucault's insights suggest that the industrial food system is a key framework for conceptualizing and enacting modern forms of governance.[13] This book approaches the food system as a "political economy" in the sense invoked by Foucault in his lectures on the birth of biopolitics: "the organization, distribution, and limitation of powers in a society."[14] Such an inclusive model of political economy intersects with food in multiple ways. Scholarship on food, hunger, and biopolitics has generally focused on questions related to public health or famine relief, studying how states regulate populations by defining "healthy" and "unhealthy" bodies or by deciding whom and whom not to feed. Quite differently, this book sees the industrial food system in its entirety as definitionally biopolitical. Thus, alongside classically biopolitical issues like anti-obesity campaigns and military policy, it brings this Foucauldian approach to bear on new topics ranging from grocery shopping to racial identity to home cooking.

By revealing the variety of ways in which food brings modern bodies into contact with political strategy, hunger emerges as a concern for states in times of abundance as well as times of shortage, suggesting a new way of understanding peoples' bodies both as active agents in history and as targets of state policies. As a result, this book approaches hunger not as a simple biological fact, but as a cultural, economic, and above all political category. Perhaps the most striking aspect of hunger in the modern age is its contradictory and mutually reinforcing meanings. As many scholars have noted, the twentieth century was shaped by the seeming paradox of constantly increasing food production and recurrent and increasingly deadly food shortages.[15] These famines have often been represented as emerging in stateless contexts, crises that take place outside of the control of local governments and emerging during, or even because of, a power vacuum. However, far from being extraordinary or unpredictable acts of nature, famines, as cultural geographer Michael Watts has noted, are "rooted in the normal, in the prosaic, and in the everyday."[16] A critical sustained focus on food and hunger offers insight into the quotidian workings of modern states, which strive to make certain hungers seem exceptional, while others seem normal or natural. By analyzing the biopolitical functions played by food and hunger over the short twentieth century, this book explores why and how the food system has become so intimately intertwined with the making of modern states and ideologies and, especially, with the making of both war and peace.

The management of political bodies has always been an inescapably gendered project. Food is especially important to the regulation of gender politics, because it is one of the few commodities that conspicuously bridges the public and private spheres. Indeed, food is perhaps the most immediate intermediary between modern states and modern bodies. More specifically, feminist and gender scholars have noted that food-related activities are central to the performing and enforcing of gender norms. Food contributes to the regulation of bodies through societies' establishment of aesthetics norms, health standards, and cultural expectations—and gender is itself constructed through precisely such categories and experiences. Historical analyses of cycles of political interest in women have often emphasized issues of reproduction and sexuality; this book shows that the gendering of the modern food system has been just as important to modern states. While women have long been typecast as feeders of husbands and children, women's and men's food worlds are gendered in more far-reaching and layered ways. One of the key arguments of this book is that the centrality of "grains and scarcity" to modern governmentality made women matter to states in particular ways: as wage laborers; private consumers; instigators of food riots; and, most consistently, as home cooks whose work in the kitchen enforces both economic and familial relations.

Modern Germany offers an especially illustrative case study of these dynamics. Within the continually shifting borders of the German nation, the regulation of food and the management of hunger changed radically, in line with the shifting desires and fears of imperial, fascist, communist, and democratic governments. For Germans themselves, instigators and losers of both world wars, food resources not only determined individual human life but decided victory or defeat. During the First World War, Germany's inability to cope with the food shortages caused by the British Blockade has long been perceived as decisive to the country's collapse.[17] As a result, military defeat and hunger became linked in the popular imagination. Historians have rightly noted that during World War II, "food became a central and often all-consuming preoccupation for most of the world's population."[18] However, few political leaders relied as aggressively on the invocation and manipulation of the food supply as did Adolf Hitler, whose rhetoric of "blood and soil" linked bread to racial identity, justifying a global war and rationalizing the starvation and murder of millions of "racial enemies."

Just as Germany had been located at the center of Europe's total wars, it emerged after 1945 as the key battleground in the new struggle between communism and capitalism; after 1961, the Berlin Wall came to be imagined as a line that divided the free from the unfree, the satiated from the starving. Gradually, nightmares of collective starvation under the communists were replaced with more moderate, though no less deeply felt, concerns over inadequately stocked shops and a restricted consumer landscape. In the West, a new sort of "communist hunger" was defined in terms of political and, especially, economic restrictions instead of inadequate caloric intake or tortuous bodily sensations. This Cold War project of defining a kind of political or economic rather than corporeal hunger required recrafting narratives of prosperity and lack for both capitalist and communist states, ultimately shaping reunified Germany as well.

In a sense, the point that food has been a vital concern for the German state in all its twentieth-century iterations is obvious; no government in human history has failed to recognize the importance of food supply for maintaining social stability. Societies have always relied on the acquisition of foods and the ritualization of their preparation and consumption to structure intimate relationships as well as social hierarchies. For this reason, anthropologists have long focused on foodways as a central window for understanding culture in its most basic sense.[19] In the industrial, globalized economy that is the subject of this book, the interdependence of national food economies only underscores the extraordinary economic, political, and military power embedded in the world's food supply. At the same time, the German experience over the course of the twentieth century was historically distinctive, and it possessed unusual power. Germans were neither the most overfed nor the hungriest people within Europe, let alone in the world—yet the status of their stomachs mattered, domestically and internationally, in particular geopolitical ways.

In other words, it is important to note that this book does not argue that Germans are uniquely preoccupied with food or that food has been more important for German states or Germans' lived experiences than for others'. Instead, it focuses on Germany in order to break down various forms of state power with respect to the industrial food system while acknowledging the historically specific ways in which people reacted to, improvised on, and resisted this power. To do this, my book traces evolving state preoccupations during the twentieth century and analyzes the ways in which they were interwoven into the food system. This approach reveals modern food systems to be economic, cultural, and eminently political structures that exist beyond the seemingly simple biological need for nourishment. The management of these food systems provided a means for states to express their power; at the same time, food exposed the limits of this power. As wars were waged and governments rose and fell, peoples' tastes constantly proved an irresolvable problem for German governments as they struggled to control why, what, and how their populations ate.

This book explores the varied ways in which food informed governmentality across the various German nation-states of the twentieth century. Through recurrent experiences of war, defeat, occupation, and reconstruction, these states all relied on food supply as a crucial source of power. This insight inspired the structure of this book, which is based on a historically grounded analysis of specific political concerns with managing food, populations, and state building. Thematic chapters, organized chronologically, explore war, race, human rights, economic growth, the family, and obesity. These themes are not intended to be exhaustive; rather, they were selected because they were crucial transnational issues at particular moments and continue today to be central state concerns. Each theme represents both a political means and an end to achieving an optimal population. The individual chapters thus each explore strategies of organizing and shaping the bodies of German citizens. Taken together, the chapters not only trace shifting concerns over the food economy chronologically and comparatively—between different governments and, especially, between the socialist East and the capitalist West. They also reveal a common set of strategies for deploying food and hunger as a political tool. Ultimately, the book suggests that these core themes are neither isolated concerns nor issues confined to a single historical moment or particular kind of state. Instead, they are constituent concerns of the modern food economy, which has shaped daily lives and government policy not only in Germany but across the world.

This approach allows the book to make distinctive contributions to German and European history as well as to food studies. First, it allows the twentieth century to be considered as a whole, thus making visible key connections as well as divergences across different governments, and especially across the break separating the world wars from the Cold War.[20] Second, a study of food policies, nutritional norms, and everyday eating habits engages a diverse array of historical actors. Debates over the contents of school lunches, the relationship between racial identity and diet, and the marketing of reduced-calorie sweets all engaged scientific and economic experts, political and military strategists, and ordinary citizens. The book assembles rich archival materials to document German struggles over food and hunger, developing an integrative historical approach to analyzing the fluid relationship between modern state power and food provisioning. Cookbooks and military plans, canteen menus and monetary policies, dieting manuals and political speeches, supermarkets and soup kitchens are just some of the sources that bear witness to the biopolitical ambitions of the modern state. Such sources reveal the ways in which many of the key preoccupations of the modern age have been interpreted in policy and experienced by ordinary Germans. This approach opens up several rarely explored aspects of everyday life to historical analysis, ranging from workplace canteens to anti-obesity campaigns. By bringing such diverse issues into dialogue with one another, the book highlights questions of individual agency and lived experience under dictatorships and in democracies, over time and across the Cold War divide.

Surprisingly few scholars have explored Germany's role in the global food economy. Much of the best work on the political economy of hunger has focused on European imperial powers and their relationship to colonial food shortages; owing to the centrality of both the Irish and Indian famines in modern conceptions of hunger, the British Empire has received the most attention.[21] Focusing on Germany, however, reminds us that hunger was a twentieth-century European story as much as a nineteenth-century colonial one—but Germany's hungers were linked to military ambitions rather than imperial economic growth. Germany's strategic importance in the world wars has insured that many historians have explored the causes and consequences of the country's food shortages during and after these conflicts.[22] On the other hand, while German food shortages has been an important theme for political and military historians, historians of food have themselves rarely been drawn to modern Germany, which lacks the culinary cachet of France or Italy, nations that are often considered to have played a key role in the "invention of modern cuisine."[23] The country's identity has also not been shaped by the production or consumption of a specific or charismatic foodstuff, such as Ireland's potatoes or Honduras's bananas.[24] Consequently, Germany may seem an unconventional site for food history. Nonetheless, it is a profoundly revealing one. This book shows that Germany has had a central role in the formation of our global food system and in our modern understanding of hunger.[25]

Rather than offer the history of a specific cuisine or commodity, this book traces food's role in the evolution of government strategies, economic policies, and popular pressures as they developed in Germany. By approaching the food system holistically, as a knowledge-power network that bridges a wide array of social and political concerns as well as military conflicts, the book develops a novel framework for telling the story of the twentieth century. In turn, it approaches the nation-state itself as a site of analysis and as a transnational project in flux, challenging the nationalist framework that has shaped much food history.[26] Exploring food policies and food realities under various German states, through fascism and democracy, statelessness and state socialism, economic depression and economic miracle, this analysis undermines widely held assumptions that there is a natural link between culinary and national identities, suggesting instead that food is not simply a matter of individual choice or cultural preference but a deeply political concern with far-reaching social and economic consequences.

Much of the scholarly literature on modern food systems has explored the technological innovations and economic and geopolitical networks that have changed the ways in which foods were processed, transported, and consumed. For example, the remaking of peoples' diets was one of the first and most intimate changes brought about by industrialization and urbanization and the accompanying decline in small-scale farming with its requisite transition to a cash economy.[27] Social and economic historians have long linked the rise of industrial capitalism with innovations in ways of procuring and trading foods across the globe.[28] By exploring links between political and economic systems throughout the century, this book's focus on food offers a different perspective on both capitalism and socialism. Writing almost two centuries ago, Marx developed a materialist understanding of history that underscored the real physical conditions of labor—beginning, as Marx himself noted, with "eating and drinking."[29] Labor and bread, communism has always asserted, were interdependent and equally essential. Nonetheless, labor history has rarely addressed the subject of food directly, and scholarship on communism has generally remained similarly silent when it comes to food consumption.[30] This study draws attention to the continued importance of both hunger and bread to the Left throughout the twentieth century.

Historians such as E. P. Thompson and Charles Tilly have explored the relationship between food riots as traditional expressions of popular agency and processes of economic modernization. These scholars have generally seen the rise of industrial capitalism as signaling the decline and eventual disappearance of the food riot as a relic of preindustrial society.[31] In the words of British historian James Vernon, "[T]he story of modernization [has been told] as the conquest of hunger."[32] Contrary to such assumptions, industrialized societies continue to experience periodic and often unexpectedly violent food protests.[33] The case study of Germany undermines teleological models of modernity that assume an inverse relationship between processes of modernization and experiences of hunger. At the same time, studying hunger alongside food offers a critical corrective to a implicit division between those who study culinary culture in the context of a normalized state of prosperity, and those who explore hunger among impoverished peoples and regions in far-off lands. The simple fact that hunger has been so central to the history of twentieth-century Germany, the wealthiest nation in Europe and one of the world's most powerful states, challenges standard assumptions about the meaning of hunger and satiety. Germany's many hungers, real and imagined, celebrated and repressed, determined domestic economic and social policies as well as the course of global wars. In the process, these hungers were exposed as political and cultural constructions as well as bodily and potentially life-threatening realities.

**

Food's centrality to warfare is by no means a product of the twentieth century; Napoleon famously asserted that armies march on their stomachs.[34] Nonetheless, the rise of a global food economy was both constitutive of and shaped by the century's vast world wars. Chapter 1 reveals that one of the most important legacies of the First World War was its role in shaping the modern food economy. During this war, food became conspicuous for its mobility and utility; the war can be traced by the different paths that foodstuffs traveled around, across, and toward Germany—blockaded by boat, shipped as aid, and transformed by chemical processes into munitions. Warring nations struggled to harness this mobility as a crucial aspect of military strategy, efforts that inspired governments around the world to claim that "food would win the war." Two decades later, in the midst of the Second World War, the *International Herald Tribune* would note that "food is war, today, just as are bombs."[35] Food and war were again intertwined, but in distinctly different ways than had been the case in that first total war. Chapter 2 shows that the Nazi state relied on food to create racial identity; the genocidal violence that defined the Second World War was the result of the Third Reich's novel intertwining of the languages of race, food, and hunger.[36]

Following Nazi Germany's defeat in 1945, the occupied country emerged as a key staging ground for what political scientist Jenny Edkins has termed the "depoliticization" of modern famine.[37] Focusing on the four years of Allied occupation that bridged the Third Reich and Cold War division, chapter 3 argues that German civilians, doctors, and politicians fought to have their hunger recognized as a marker of collective innocence that superseded ideology or political background. Assertions that access to food was a basic human right found a receptive audience among the Western Allies, who promoted a discourse of universal human rights in order to rationalize their particular commitment to caring for the former enemy. Thus, despite the fact that—or rather, because—Nazism represented a profound violation of the "rights of man," Germans became the recipients of more food aid than any other European population, and their hungry bodies became a widely recognized cipher of suffering and misery.

These first three chapters trace Imperial, Weimar, Nazi, and occupied German efforts to harness the military, rhetorical, and political powers of hunger during the first half of the twentieth century. The second half of the century witnessed the rise of both East and West German states to positions of substantial, if unequal, status and influence within Europe and beyond; unlike in previous decades, this power was linked with economic rather than overt military might. The reconstruction of defeated Germany played a key role in the development of modern biopolitics; this was a place where economic policies and ambitions replaced older, often more overtly violent expressions of state power. Indeed, Foucault emphasized "the paradigmatic character of the German experience" after the Second World War in the evolution of neoliberal economic strategies.[38] As the only country in Europe to experience both socialist and capitalist reconstructions, divided Germany offers a window into the processes by which these economic systems were (re)made. The second half of the book comprises three chapters that analyze both socialist and capitalist food systems, tracing similarities, differences, and intersections in East and West German state policies and popular experiences.

Chapter 4 looks at the role of the industrial food system in postwar economic reconstruction in both the GDR and the FRG. Focusing on two key spaces within industrial economies—factory canteens and supermarkets—it reveals shifting political and economic drives toward optimization and rationalization during the 1950s and 1960s, tracing their failures as well as their partial successes in terms of both gender and class structures. Chapter 5 uses cooking to explore the particular significance of female labor in the industrial economy. Despite their radically different approaches toward women's wage labor—East Germany had one of the world's highest rates of female employment, while West Germany had some of Europe's most restrictive laws regulating women's right to work—both states insisted on women's responsibility for their children's diets. Focusing on the 1960s and 1970s, the chapter explores the construct of the "family meal," exposing it as a method for regulating women's labor power and, as a result, for shaping their private and public roles in German society.

During the final decades of the Cold War, as both the FRG and the GDR were experiencing economic stagnation and social unrest, they also confronted the disturbing fact that approximately a third of their adult populations was seriously overweight. Chapter 6 analyzes the so-called obesity epidemic that by the early 1970s had begun to dominate health discourse in both East and West Germany. For socialist and capitalist nutritionists, obesity represented a profound challenge to the ideal of an industrial economy, which defines prosperity as a perfect balance of consumption and production. The failure of both the GDR's "scarcity society" and the FRG's "economic miracle" to resolve the problem of obesity challenges widespread assumptions about both the causes and the consequences of fatness within the industrial food system.[39]

Taken together, these chapters on divided Germany suggest a new interpretation of the Cold War. Joining a small but growing number of historians who are exploring East Germany and West Germany as intertwined or entangled states and populations, *Modern Hungers* uses these comparative case studies to challenge conventional narratives of abundance and dearth and to suggest novel ways of understanding both the gendering and "embodying" of economic systems.[40]

These Cold War struggles, of course, should not be seen as a break from what came before. While any story of Germany in the twentieth century cannot help but fall into two halves—war and peace, poverty and prosperity—a major argument of this book is that food's biopolitical centrality remained a constant across eras and states.

Food, of course, was no more important in the twentieth century than in previous centuries. However, the specific nature of the century's many wars, alongside and dependent on a globalizing economy, made food and hunger central to governmental policy in ways that had not previously been seen. The resultant conflicts between states and within populations, in all their ideological and real violence, inspired new forms of optimism and new expressions of misery. They also suggested new ways of resolving the problems of the twentieth century. The end of the Cold War did not mean the end of these struggles. Concerns over food and hunger continue to preoccupy governments, influence economic policies, and shape everyday lives within reunified Germany and across the world. Although the decades of World War and Cold War are over, new threats of shrinking resources, ecological catastrophe, and increasing rates of poverty and population displacement ensure that the world's food system continues to be at the heart of global conflict, and thus central to modern biopower.

1

The Geopolitics of Total War

Food in the First World War

In 1917, Herbert Hoover, the first head of the just-created US Food Administration, announced that "food has gradually, since the war began, assumed a larger place in the economics, the statesmanship, and the strategy of the war until it is my belief that food will win this war—starvation or sufficiency will in the end determine the victor. The winning of the war is largely a problem of who can organize this weapon—food."[1] In the same year, the German economist and statistician Ernst Wagemann, in an essay titled "The Foreign Food Economy," reported:

> The war has had a three-fold impact on the world's food supply. It has weakened the productivity of agriculture through the requisitioning of labor and draft animals: it has created the massive food demands of million-strong armies; and, most dramatically, it has destroyed the international division of labor, it has separated the global economy, which made up a single economic entity, into three distinct productive regions—Russia, the Central Powers, and the rest of the world ... [resulting in] a dramatic decline in crops.[2]

Despite the radically different wartime experiences of America and Germany, both men recognized that the war was remaking the international food economy. Both also believed that food had become the decisive weapon of the war.

During the decades immediately preceding the outbreak of the war in 1914, Europe's imperial powers had developed elaborate webs of resource extraction, transportation, and processing that stretched across the globe, ensuring that nations' wealth and power were linked to their dependence on international trade, not on their autonomy from it. This was especially true when it came to agriculture, which connected continents and hemispheres in unequal relationships of dependence based on such commodities as grain, beef, and sugar.

Between 1850 and 1913, innovations in transportation and processing technologies allowed the global trade in foodstuffs to grow at a rate of 3.44 percent annually.[3] While these expanding networks allowed some countries to accumulate massive wealth, they also ensured that any restrictions in transportation and international exchange would profoundly affect the world's food supply.

For these reasons, food's functions in the First World War diverged radically from all prior conflicts. Military conflicts had always had severe consequences for people's food supply; for thousands of years, war had been associated with food shortages caused by the increased demands of armies, widespread pillaging, and war-related disruptions of agriculture. The first "total war," however, completely redefined the relationship between waging war and making food. The war ushered in a far-reaching militarization of food that inspired new social and economic policies and led to the rise of particular actors and organizations that mobilized around these new transnational networks. Military food-processing technologies, chemical innovations that bound agriculture to munitions production, and propaganda that linked consumption on the homefront with the destructive power of the military, all reflected the centrality of food in a new "political economy of war"—defined by military historian Paul Koistinen as the interplay of economics, politics, the military, and technology.[4] This particular economy of war had multiple components, but three developments stand out as particularly important. First, the British elevation of the Hunger Blockade into a central weapon of the war encapsulated the extreme militarization of food; second, a transnational economy of food aid developed under American leadership that relied on the distribution of food as a method of political control; and finally, wartime food crises provided fertile ground for political radicalization across Europe and especially in Germany, spawning new organizations and party platforms that coalesced around the experience and anticipation of hunger.

Historians have usually analyzed these developments separately. This chapter, however, argues that they all were distinct components of a single innovation: the creation of a food economy of total war. Exploring these multiple developments alongside one another reveals that Germany played a pivotal role in this vast food-war system; the rise and fall of imperial Germany was intimately tied to the country's food supply. The trajectory of the conflict made manifest the inseparability of food aid and food blockades, as the war both created and resolved hunger by redirecting the global flow of foodstuffs first away from and later toward hungry Germans. In consequence, the politicization of hunger found its most extreme expression in the radicalism of the early Weimar Republic.

The German population was forced to learn early on that modernization remade rather than eliminated hunger. The country's workers produced vast quantities of the most modern weaponry, yet they lacked access to basic dietary staples. The protests and food riots that swept the country during and immediately after the war were not, as many believed, a return to "older" forms of political expression. Instead, they were an eminently modern voicing of new expectations on the industrial state.[5] Indeed, the hungry population blamed their suffering on the things that had made the German economy so modern in the first place: transportation systems, state welfare programs, currency regulation and inflation, and international trade. Reflecting such criticisms, a postwar public lecture on Germany's food shortages, sponsored by the International Workers' Aid program, claimed that "a true solution of this serious crisis is only possible after a new organization of the German economy and in close connection with a new organization of European and global economic relations."[6]

During the war, Germany's modern economy had created a new kind of hunger, one that lasted well after the armistice was signed and the blockade was officially lifted. Over the course of these hungry years, stretching roughly from 1916 to 1924, tens of thousands of German civilians died of sicknesses that could be directly or indirectly attributed to inadequate nutrition, and countless more suffered physical and psychological distress because of the inadequate food supply. This very real suffering contributed to a radical remaking of the government, as the Wilhelmine Empire was replaced with the volatile political landscape of the Weimar Republic. Concerns over food and hunger played a crucial role in this transition, shaping both mainstream and radical goals, policies, and rhetorics. While the First World War is often remembered as a time of governmental collapse, the real power of states to control their populations—what Foucault called "biopolitics"—expanded dramatically, shaping everyday life across Europe through propaganda campaigns, rationing programs, and humanitarian projects. During these early decades of the twentieth century, the drama of an alternately hungry and sated Germany encapsulated the centrality of food in modern warfare and, ultimately, in the making of modernity itself.

Beans Are Bullets, Potatoes Are Powder

Several months after the start of the war, Britain formally declared that it would impose a blockade of foodstuffs destined for Germany, saying that food was "as essential to the forces as bullets and therefore equally seizable; there is really no difference with regard to the consideration of food as contraband of war."[7] This assertion marked the beginning of a new kind of war, wherein food became central to all aspects of the conflict. As historian Isabell Hull noted, following the announcement of the British blockade, "the interdiction of food steadily expanded as one of the main instruments of warfare for both sides."[8]

The British Blockade of Germany, popularly known as the Hunger Blockade, drew on extensive historical precedent. Since the eighteenth century, Great

Britain, relying on its naval supremacy, had become particularly adept at the use of trade blockades as a strategy for maintaining military and economic power. More generally, as the British themselves were fond of pointing out, the use of military power to regulate, and especially to restrict, the flow of goods into enemy territory was a common strategy of war. As a result, few initially protested the British decision to institute such a program against Germany, casting it not as an innovation but an "age-old" weapon of war. In a 1918 article defending the ethics of the blockade, the British journalist Margaret Jourdain approvingly cited "the antiquity and respectability of the [military] method of starvation and the parallel between siege and blockade."[9] The analogy was deliberately misleading—the trade relations and shipping technologies that made modern food blockades possible were recent innovations that had little in common with medieval sieges. Sieges had generally relied on physically surrounding a select area and entirely cutting it off from the outside world, with the aim of literally starving the enemy into surrender, a strategy that was inapplicable to an entire nation. In contrast, naval blockades relied on disrupting transnational trade relations, aiming not for the literal starvation of the population but for the collapse or total restructuring of the national economy.

Britain had been calculating Germany's potential vulnerability to a naval food blockade since the late nineteenth century. The country's rapid industrialization had made it Europe's leading industrial power within decades of unification in 1871. However, this remarkable economic growth had also entirely remade the country's food system, leaving the population dependent on food imports. Although prior to the war Germans consumed more calories than any other population in Europe, averaging almost 4,000 calories per head a day, imports made up almost half of these calories, and provided a full 50 percent of Germany's meat and fat consumption.[10] Almost three-quarters of these imports entered the country via shipping.[11] Germany's dependence on food imports was a strategic weakness that seemingly begged to be exploited by its rivals, and the outbreak of war provided a major opportunity to do so. As the *New York Times* put it in 1916, "Germany's food supply has all along been one of the great questions of the war."[12]

Well aware of their vulnerability, Germans were quick to condemn the British use of the blockade as a weapon of war. In an April 1915 speech, the German foreign minister invoked the suffering of the Boer in British concentration camps and the "thousands who have starved to death under the British flag in India" to prove that "hunger is England's favorite weapon in order to oppress and to keep peoples in subordination."[13] In fact, the Germans as well as the British had been long planning to use food blockades in future war efforts. England's small size and extreme dependence on food imports—it produced only 20 percent of its own grain consumption, for example, a much lower rate than Germany—made it a prime target for a hunger blockade of its own. Germany's U-boat campaign was in actuality a counterblockade aiming at starving out the English; German military experts had estimated that, if England were cut off from its overseas food supplies, it could last a maximum of five months before collapsing.[14] Based on such estimates, the U-boat campaign was expected to starve the English into submission within months of its initiation. German military leaders shared with their British counterparts the belief that hunger would win them the war. Echoing claims made regularly by its enemies, Germany's naval propaganda claimed that "England is about to starve ... in the near future England will lie on the ground: unconscious, hungry, beaten with the same weapon with which it attempted to defeat the dutiful German people."[15]

The introduction of submarine warfare did initially devastate British food supplies, as the loss of hundreds of thousands of tons of merchant ships greatly reduced the country's wheat and sugar stores.[16] But unlike Germany, England was able not only to increase its own food production but also to successfully remake its international trade networks. By 1918, England was receiving almost two-thirds of its food supply from the food-rich United States.[17] Indeed, the German submarine campaign indirectly improved British wartime food supplies and, as a result, public health. The relatively equitable rationing program that was implemented in England meant that the poorer segments of the population ate better than they had before the war.[18]

The ubiquity of food blockades during the war not only reflected changes in how states provisioned their citizenry. When the British had justified their blockade with the claim that food was as "essential to the forces as bullets," they were not simply making a striking analogy; they were invoking a radical new interdependence between the food supply and munitions. The shockingly intimate relationship between food and warfare was most dramatically evident in the case of the chemical element nitrogen, which supplied, in the enthusiastic words of an American economist, "fertilizer in peace and munitions in war."[20] In 1914, at the outset of the war, the vast majority of the world's—and Germany's—nitrates were imported from Chile.[21] The British Blockade immediately severed this supply line, and Germany's stores of munitions were desperately threatened as a result; finding a new source of nitrogen for weaponry was a far more pressing initial concern than food shortages. The threat seemed even more dire as it became clear that the new trench warfare required unprecedented amounts of munitions. This sense of urgency inspired the creation of an official Nitrate Commission in Germany soon after the war's begin.[22] German chemist Fritz Haber's new nitrogen-fixation technique, first used on an industrial scale in 1913, was expected to produce nitrogen for two major purposes—to manufacture fertilizers and explosives. Unlike older methods of synthesizing ammonia, Haber's technique, which essentially extracted nitrogen from the air, was remarkably efficient and near-limitless (it remains the preferred method of nitrogen fixing today). At the time, it meant that Germany's production skyrocketed, growing from about 7,000 tons in 1913 to about 215,000 tons in 1918.[23] The importance of the Haber process was immediately apparent. Wartime analyses estimated that without the new technology, Germany would have run out of munitions as well as food by the spring of 1915.[24] The Great War thus became the first war to expose the "absolute dependence of the modern fighting man upon chemistry," since, in the dramatic words of a 1917 article on the importance of chemistry in the war "the soldier at the front can be provided with neither munitions nor food by those nations which have not at their command large supplies of nitrogen. Nitric acid is essential for explosives, and nitrates for the fertilizer which produces food."[25]

Similarly, the skyrocketing production of explosives and military machinery caused surging demand for another key industrial compound—glycerin. This meant that fats suddenly became a key national resource, directly linking civilians' dinner tables with munitions factories. Noted British economist Sir William Beveridge explored this interdependence in his 1939 analysis of the First World War *Blockade and the Civilian Population*. He wrote that "fats are literally ... the favorite food of guns in the form of propellant ... in another respect also fats are more nearly munitions than are other foods ... fat is needed above all by soldiers and for heavy work in factories and in transport."[26] Wartime propaganda on all sides pressured civilians to reduce their fat intake; this was especially important for Germany because the population had been consuming steadily increasing quantities of fat for years, reaching levels that far outstripped the country's production capabilities. As a result, fats were the dietary component in which the German Reich was least self-sufficient. At the outbreak of the war, the country was importing 40 percent of its dietary fats, and fat shortages plagued the country throughout the war.[27] An American wartime cookbook promised its readers that "von Hindenburg's men will lose out on the basis of fat rather than on the basis of munitions or military organization."[30] The British proved more successful at maintaining national fat stores. In 1917, the British Ministry of Munitions assumed control "of all fats, oils and oil seed and their products, including oil cake, soap and margarine ... to supply glycerin for use in the manufacture of explosives."[28] The English campaign known as the "Bone and Fat Bucket" (see Figure 1.1) informed housewives that "bones and fat provide glycerin for making explosives, glue for making aeroplanes, fertilizers for food production. Save them for munitions." Such claims revealed not only that domestic food preparation was linked to national military operations, but that kitchen labor and battlefield violence were competing for the same limited resources.

The technological links between waging war and food production went even deeper, as new strategies of total war became inseparable from the industrial

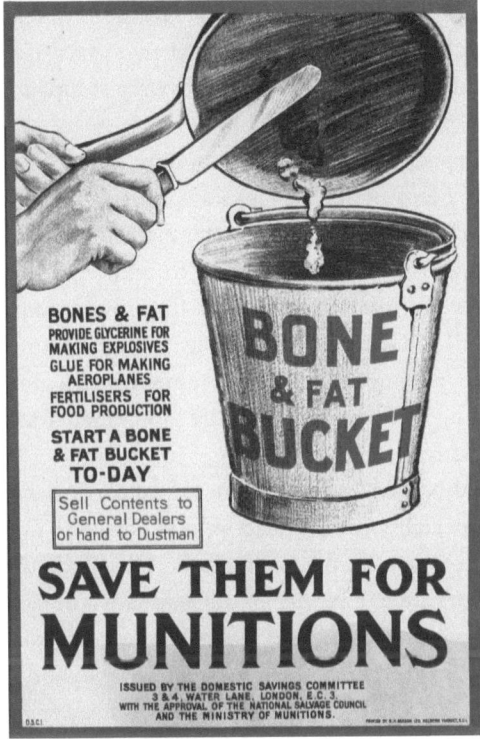

Figure 1.1 Bone and Fat Bucket. Save Them for Munitions. 1917. © Imperial War Museums (Art.IWM PST 13428).

food system. The development of poison gas, probably the most infamous chemical innovation of the war, was intertwined with work on insecticides.[29] Food waste was integrated into the war effort in multiple ways. Peach pits, for example, were used in the manufacture of gas masks, and children were encouraged to collect them by the pound.

The sheer numbers of soldiers involved in the fighting meant that transporting foodstuffs became a massive operation that resulted in important innovations in food packaging and shipping. Across Europe, mobile field kitchens were employed for the first time on a mass scale to feed soldiers across vast distances and under the new conditions of the trenches. These innovations literally made the war possible. Because trench warfare made the conflict essentially stationary, it not only dragged the conflict on interminably; it also was especially cost ineffective. Cut off from traditional wartime methods of food acquisition, including seizure, bartering, and foraging, soldiers in the trenches were dependent on whatever foods could be delivered directly to them. (Because trench warfare was especially destructive locally, it also had long-term impacts on food production. The vast swaths of fertile soil that had been transformed by these trenches into battlefields would take decades to recover their former levels of agricultural productivity.) In the first two years of the conflict alone, approximately eight billion tons of foodstuffs were shipped from Germany to the front lines.[30]

As the war reshaped the global food economy, countries around the world changed their diets. Many of the changes were driven by governments' attempts to modify civilian food consumption to better match the needs of the war effort. Those on the homefront were admonished to reduce their overall food consumption, and were promised that the food thus saved would go directly into soldiers' stomachs. The Georgia State College of Agriculture's poster claiming "beans are bullets—potatoes are powder" summarized a global move to naturalize the far-reaching idea that people's daily food intake was indistinguishable from modern weapons of war.

Unsurprisingly, this new kind of warfare placed particular demands on civilian populations, especially women, who were expected to uphold their prewar responsibility for domestic food consumption at the same time that they were told to enter the workforce in service of the war effort. In fact, the war dramatically increased women's food-related labor. In most European countries, and especially in Germany, the near-disappearance of able-bodied men from the homefront meant that rural women took on even heavier responsibilities for agricultural production. Urban women did not necessarily have it easier. Drawn into industrial labor to replace conscripted male workers, they struggled to balance caring for their families with performing demanding factory work under subpar conditions. Simply putting food on the table became an exhausting and sometimes near-impossible task. Constantly changing rationing allotments, unpredictable supply flows, and a growing reliance on the black market meant that food shopping and preparation demanded vast quantities of time, energy, and creativity. In both the city and the countryside, the very act of cooking changed as women grappled with limited fuel and cooking equipment. Some countries experimented with communal kitchens, which required that women learn new cooking techniques. An explosion of soup kitchens changed both what was eaten and how families ate together, shifting previously private activities into the public sphere.[31]

Most dramatically, the war changed what staples were available for consumption, requiring women to cook with new and often inferior foodstuffs. The *New York Times*, reporting on the domestic food situation in Germany in 1916, noted sympathetically that "the public continues to be imposed on by all sorts of inferior substitutes for food and by real food of poor quality."[32] German housewives were encouraged to bake with whole grains, especially locally produced rye, rather than imported white flour to reduce food costs. Germany developed a recipe for a rye-based "war bread," or *Kriegsbrot* (K-Brot), turning baking into an active display of patriotism. As the war dragged on and even rye came to be in short supply, bakers were required to incorporate a large percentage of potato in their K-Brot, creating a wetter and tougher dough that was more difficult to make and considerably less tasty. Rather than acknowledge the inadequacies of this bread, nutritionists recommended forgoing it altogether in favor of more economical options. Although bread had become standard breakfast fare by the turn of the century, women were now advised to "return" to the traditional, and much cheaper, breakfast soups as a way of further reducing grain consumption.[33]

In addition to modifying staples to enable lengthy storage and shipping— dehydrated potato flakes were created for this reason—new foods were developed to use up unexpected surpluses. For example, the military's demand for fats left many countries with an excess of skimmed milk and a need to find alternate sources of dietary fat. This inspired the massive promotion of peanut butter and cottage cheese in the United States and of sandwiches made with jam rather than meat in Germany.[34] Its difficult food situation made Germany especially innovative in the production of ersatz or substitute foods; over ten thousand different products of highly variable quality were produced for civilian wartime consumption, including modified breads and cakes; substitutes for honey, coffee, and chocolate; and over eight hundred varieties of meatless sausage.

As was the case for all wartime economies, the German government had hoped to maximize food production while restricting and optimizing food distribution and consumption. Unusually good harvests in 1913 had made leaders confident about the country's food supply, and encouraged them to emphasize controlling consumption through rationing and price regulation, rather than focus on increasing production. When the war began, in August 1914, the imperial government created the Wartime Raw Materials Department (*Kriegsrohstoffabteilung* [KRA]), which was charged with the organization and regulation of all war-related goods and products. The KRA initially focused on coal, metals, and the other resources traditionally needed in the production of munitions; it quickly grew to include the civilian food supply as well, in terms of both foodstuffs and the fertilizers and technologies needed to produce crops. Within weeks, cities across the country began imposing price ceilings on specific food items in an effort to regulate civilian purchases. The idea was that citizens would engage in rational shopping, purchasing cheaper foods and forgoing more expensive ones. However, fears of future shortages caused many Germans to purchase excessive quantities of staple products or to shop in otherwise idiosyncratic ways. Compounding these problems, farmers were outraged by the nonstandardized and highly variable price restrictions and consistently evaded them by withholding food from circulation or by selling it privately on the black market.[35]

This early policy stumble established a pattern of rural resistance to government intervention that plagued Germany throughout the war as the country's farmers struggled to maintain an adequate food supply. Labor was a major limiting factor. Most farms had to be worked by wives and mothers; the only available male laborers were usually foreign prisoners of war or forced laborers, who numbered in the hundreds of thousands on German farms by the end of the war. These men, most of whom came from Poland and Romania, played a crucial role in maintaining the country's harvests but still could not entirely replace the missing German farmers.[36] Moreover, blockade-caused scarcity of both fertilizers and fodder, almost half of which had previously been shipped in, led to a 25 percent decline in agricultural productivity and a 65 percent decline in the numbers of livestock available for both eating and farm work.[37] In the last two years of the war, the country's annual harvests of grain reached only two-thirds of prewar levels.[38] Even more dramatically, the availability of potatoes, which had displaced grains as Germans' primary calorie source, steadily declined throughout the war. The 1913 harvest had produced a crop of 52.9 million tons of potatoes, but in 1918 yields dropped to 29.5 million tons.[39]

Reductions in domestic food production impacted civilian diets more severely than military ones, since the rationing system allotted almost three-quarters of all officially available food to the German army.[40] During the final months of the war, as riots, strikes, and hunger protests spread through the country's cities, the German army consumed 30 percent of the country's total bread grains and 60 percent of the county's beef and pork, leaving little more than horsemeat for much of the hungry homefront.[41]

German officials had realized early in the war that price controls were an inadequate method of regulating the civilian food supply. Rationing was therefore introduced in January 1915; initially only bread was rationed, but eventually most staple foods were distributed primarily or exclusively through the rationing program. In the spring of 1916, the War Food Office (*Reichsernährungsamt*) was created to address food problems, particularly the growing supply gap between the city and the countryside. The office was intended to centralize regulation of the national food supply, ensuring that crucial munitions workers and other war workers received adequate nutrition. Eventually, as the demands of the war grew, the imperial economy expanded to regulate the entirety of the country's agricultural production. Not only were farmers no longer able to determine the prices of the goods they produced, but decisions about which crops to plant and to whom to sell them were also controlled by the government.[42]

These interventions in the food economy, along with a popular willingness to make short-term sacrifices for the war effort, prevented severe food problems during the first two years of the war. The British were initially surprised by the minimal impact of the blockade on the health of German civilians, who also benefited from the existence of abundant accumulated food stores, wartime food seizures by the German army, and from having been in a generally well-fed state at the beginning of the war.⁴³ Much of this early success was also due to the imperial government's rapid embrace of propaganda, which encouraged the homefront, and especially German women, to accept food restrictions and the increasingly draconian limits on their individual diets. Government publications framed the reductions in available grocery staples in a scientific language of optimal nutrition and public health, casting the war as a vehicle for improving and modernizing the German diet. The War Food Office, for example, claimed that official rations provided precisely the diet that "doctors and hygienists had been striving for in peacetime: limited consumption of meat, a reduction of fat intake, and an increase in vegetable consumption."⁴⁴

State propaganda regularly reinforced the idea that women's nutritional choices not only determined the health of their families but were also crucial to the success of the war effort. As feminist activist Käthe Schirmacher explained in 1918, "[T]he world war has taught us that cooking and homemaking are service to the country, defense of the country, and a form of citizenship. Not only is the sword a weapon—in the 'hunger war,' the cooking spoon is equally important."⁴⁵ This meant that women were required to recognize the adequacy of the country's food supply; in 1916, the *New York Times* cited a German study of the blockade's impact on civilian nutrition which affirmed that "no woman or child in Germany need go hungry even if no food can be brought in."⁴⁶ Posters compared the country's pork and grain production to that of England, picturing Germany's bacon pile and wheat stack towering over scrawny England's, graphically depicting the country's gustatory superiority. When it became clear that the war would last longer than expected and that the country's food supply was less secure than had been assumed, the KRA established a News Agency for Food Questions (*Nachrichtendienst für Ernährungsfragen*). Its purpose was to regulate and, especially, to censor information about the civilian food supply. None of these measures, however, was able to stabilize the food situation.

The first major food scare came in the spring of 1915, when the government ordered a mass slaughter of Germany's pigs in an attempt to free for human consumption the grain and potatoes used as pig fodder. This so-called pig murder (*Schweinemord*) resulted in a temporary glut of pork that was promptly followed by its near disappearance from the official market and reappearance at prohibitive prices on the black market; the misguided policy also became synonymous with the flawed leadership of the war's food economy. But while the sudden unavailability of pork, long the nation's favorite meat, was a source of great dissatisfaction, civilian nutrition initially remained adequate, if uninspiring. This fragile balance was undone in the winter of 1916/17, which came to be known as the Turnip Winter. By the end of 1916, cold weather had resulted in poor harvests across Europe, and an explosion of blight further reduced the German potato crop by almost half. The official recommendation to substitute rutabagas for potatoes not only lowered average caloric and vitamin intakes but also devastated popular morale, since the rutabaga had traditionally been reserved for livestock feed. Official rations dropped to their lowest levels of the war in February 1917, and actual food intake was often even worse than the paltry rations suggested, since many of the allotted foodstuffs were only partially available. Allied observers recognized the connection between the country's collapsing food system and its maintenance of the massively expensive war effort; the *New York Times* reported that "the many factories producing nitrogen from the air will not be able to produce enough nitrates by far, in view of the ammunition requirements, to replace the nitrates normally imported from Chile for agricultural purposes."[47] Indeed, the winter months of 1917 proved to be the turning point in civilian food consumption; they also marked the collapse of popular support for the war effort.

The country's propaganda machine ultimately worsened rather than stabilized popular attitudes toward the war. Despite shrinking rations and declining civilian health, state publications continued to insist that "Germany has become the model of its enemies especially in the area of the food economy."[48] In the middle of the Turnip Winter, Adolf von Batocki-Friede, the president of the War Food Office and the man called the "food dictator" of Germany, asserted that "if the war is to go on until Germany is starved out, then it will never end."[49] Just two months after Batacki had made this bold claim, in March 1917, a new set of regulations was distributed to all media outlets warning all those who make "public statements about food supply" to remember "the heavy responsibility that he takes on when, through thoughtless statements or publications, he endangers the safety and future of the fatherland."[50] Acknowledging that the food shortages were causing a "weakening of the resoluteness of the civilian population" and "a worsening of the atmosphere within the army itself," the bill forbade any public commentary on the food situation that contrasted the urban and rural populations or that compared regional nutritional situations. Newspapers were also prohibited from reporting on food protests or hunger riots.[51]

When the war began, the German national war effort was based on the much-celebrated *Burgfrieden*, or Fortress Peace—a negotiated truce between political parties and social classes to encourage them to come together in common support of the war, implying a shared acceptance of hardships and shortages. As the war dragged on, this rhetoric began to erode under the pressure from the blockade and in the face of growing scarcity and hunger. The dramatic rise of the black market represented the fraying of this consensus. The American media bitingly noted that the primary consequence of the imperial government's wartime food-distribution system had been "to convert Germans from a nation of law minders ... into whose minds a thought of violating a law or police regulation never came, into a nation of law breakers."[52]

The food crisis thus painfully exposed the growing divisions between classes, regions, and segments of the population. The wealthy, the rural, and those living close to agricultural regions consumed a different diet than did the urban working classes. Small towns usually maintained fairly stable health, and agricultural areas often showed relatively little reduction in food intake compared to prewar levels, whereas the urban populations suffered severely. Germany's densely packed cities proved particularly vulnerable to disturbances in the transportation and distribution of foodstuffs. Civilian food problems became a military concern when demoralized German soldiers realized how poorly their loved ones were eating.[53] Eventually, even the country's soldiers were impacted by the shortages. Allied POW camps attempted to exploit Germans' growing hungers by distributing letters written by German prisoners describing Allied rations as extraordinarily abundant; one German soldier in a French POW camp purportedly wrote, "We got bread with oil sardines and a good flask of wine, that was, of course, the best of all ... there stood two large bowls of soup, one plate full of meat, and two jibs of grape juice, which tasted excellently to us."[54] The French army even developed the innovative "sausage method" to weaken German morale; it smuggled Germans soldiers information on how to desert in a small vial embedded in sausage meat.[55]

Despite growing civilian dissatisfaction, the German government had maintained a fragile consensus by continually repeating that the end of the war would bring both victory and satiety. Defeat was ruled out as an option, and hunger was officially depicted as the exclusive fate of the war's losers and thus relegated to far-off enemy shores. Specifically, Germany's leaders vowed that the hunger would end as soon as the fighting ceased. A booklet titled "Daily Bread in War and Peacetime," written during the final months of the war, reminded readers that "victory and peace" would "ensure for everyone our daily bread for tomorrow and for all of the future."[56] In early 1918, the German military's unshakable confidence temporarily seemed justified when it forced Russia to accept a brutal peace treaty that ceded to Germany large parts of Poland and Ukraine. For a population sick of breadlines and empty stomachs, the situation was equated with abundant food; the Brest-Litovsk Treaty, signed on February 9, 1918 and popularly termed the "bread peace," obliged Ukraine to deliver to Germany the equivalent of a million tons of bread a year.[57] Many Germans assumed that they had won the war in the East and, with it, the war against hunger.

Although the population expected rationing to end and the food supply to immediately improve, newspapers filled their pages with sober reminders that it might take weeks, and even months, before food extraction could actually begin.[58] Nonetheless, everyone agreed, as an article titled "The Ukraine as a

Grain Export Land" explained, that "the peace with Ukraine is of profound value for the German grain supply."⁵⁹ The normally sober *Frankfurter Zeitung* rejoiced in the fact that "now that the encirclement from the East has finally been broken, our food supply land has expanded dramatically ... and what is the situation with our enemies? While our fertile fields grow, theirs shrink—insofar as their imported supplies become increasing unstable."⁶⁰ Figure 1.2 shows a cartoon from the satiric magazine *Simplicissimus* that was published two months after the treaty; it lampoons the obsessive food fantasies that surrounded the acquisition of Ukraine, depicting it as a land literally composed of food, with flying sausages instead of birds and fences made of pork chops and piles of wheat.

Of course, such gustatory fantasies and optimistic predictions were never realized. The German war effort ground painfully to a halt in 1918. The stalemate in the fighting on the Western Front and the failure of long-awaited floods of foodstuffs to arrive from the East dealt the final blow to the German people's support of the war. By the fall, it had become clear that Germany's defeat was inevitable. Most civilians, as well as soldiers, had lost faith in the

Figure 1.2 "How someone from Munich imagines Ukraine." 1918. Olaf Gulbransson: © 2016 Artists Rights Society (ARS), New York / BONO, Oslo. Courtesy of Klassik Stiftung Weimar.

imperial German leadership and with it any desire to continue fighting. A wave of strikes by industrial workers spread, and women on the homefront began aggressively demanding an end to the war. In response, a transitional government was created to negotiate the country's peace treaty with the Allies and ease Germany's transition out of the war. Nonetheless, the Imperial Naval Command, in willful denial of the inevitability of defeat, issued orders for a suicidal naval attack on the British in October 1918. The order inspired a mutiny among sailors stationed at the port city of Kiel, who rallied under the slogan "Bread and Peace." The revolt spread rapidly during the early days of November, leading to the formation of revolutionary workers' and soldiers' councils across the country. In the face of widespread popular demands for revolution, the transitional government collapsed. A spontaneous announcement of the abdication of the emperor on November 9 ushered in the country's first parliamentary democracy, initially dominated by the moderate socialists (the Social Democratic Party of Germany [Sozialdemokratische Partei Deutschlands or SPD]).

The first major responsibility of the government of the new Weimar Republic was the signing of the armistice on November 11, 1918. However, the long-anticipated end of war did not spell an end to the blockade, let alone an end to German hunger. Victorious Great Britain was committed to maintaining the blockade to compel Germany to accept the harsh terms of the Versailles Treaty. The 1918 armistice unequivocally stipulated that "the existing blockade conditions set up by the allied and associated powers . . . remain unchanged."[61] In February of 1919, a fact-finding commission organized by Winston Churchill recommended that as long as "Germany is still an enemy country, it would be inadvisable to remove the menace of starvation by a too sudden and abundant supply of foodstuffs. This menace is a powerful lever for negotiation at an important moment."[62] The blockade was thus transformed from a weapon of war aimed at destabilizing the German government and demoralizing the civilian population to being a guarantor of peace. It was not until Social Democrat Friedrich Ebert, the leader of the civilian government, signed the Treaty of Versailles, at the end of June 1919, that the blockade was lifted.

For the population at large, the continuation of the British Blockade into 1919 blurred the distinction between war and peace. Hunger became both normalized and depoliticized, severed from direct connection to the military (which refused to accept responsibility for the country's defeat), the imperial government (which was dissolved), or the German war effort itself. Instead, it seemed to be a deliberate punishment being inflicted on the defeated civilian population. This impression was only strengthened by the Weimar government's conviction that the best way to reduce the harsh reparation demands of the Versailles Treaty was to expose the poverty and, especially, the hunger of the German people.

Thus, in contrast to the state's wartime insistence that domestic hunger was practically nonexistent, early Weimar officials and public figures dramatically detailed the population's ineffective struggles to get enough to eat. The new German government actively encouraged voices of misery and suffering to address the postwar international community. A medical representative from Cologne wrote to the German chancellor to explain that there was a "new duty of doctors in this moment" to "let the voice of humanity, which we serve, ring out over our borders and through the world, speaking as well to our former enemies and declaring that our people are threatened with the serious and irreparable collapse of their health."[63] The Berlin Medical Association sponsored a convention in early 1919 to protest the continuation of the blockade, claiming that "we have already spent of our bodies as much as is possible; no other nation has ever quietly and patiently withstood such privations."[64] Meanwhile, the medical profession officially complained that the frequent reports issued by Allied visitors misleadingly emphasized the good physical appearance of the general population. The black market had been criticized during the war for causing hunger; now it was blamed for giving visitors a false impression of German prosperity: "The foreign visitors who descend upon us every day in vast numbers are unlikely to believe in our general misery if they are able to witness such celebrations of decadence as take place in countless hotels, inns, and ballrooms."[65]

As historian Gerald Feldman has noted, when the victorious nations had gathered together to determine the terms of the armistice, "had the Germans been visibly starving either during or at the end of the war, judgment would have been simple and arguments clear and to the point."[66] Instead, a lack of clarity about the nutritional state of the population—and a general impression that German civilians were in relatively good health—encouraged the French and British insistence on a punitive peace. The most drastic effects of the wartime food shortages had been seen among marginalized populations who were entirely dependent on official rations, especially the inhabitants of state institutions, homes, and prisons. The elderly also suffered elevated mortality rates because of their social isolation and inadequate access to social services and familial support. In contrast, scholars generally concur that for the population at large, the blockade and resultant food shortages did not directly cause starvation.[67] Nonetheless, civilian health was severely impacted by the wartime food crisis, an impact that is generally quantified in terms of "extra" deaths caused—that is, deaths in excess of what would have been expected based on prewar mortality rates.[68] Immediately after the war, Germany officially reported a total of 762,796 "extra" civilian deaths during the war years; ten years later, this number was revised to 424,000. A recent study estimated 300,000 people died due to the direct and indirect effects of the blockade.[69] The increased mortality rates primarily reflected deaths from illness, which was much deadlier when paired with malnutrition. Tuberculosis, aggravated by food shortages and inadequate heating, became both more common and substantially more fatal, claiming more than 160,000 lives during the war.[70] In 1917, tuberculosis death rates increased by more than 25 percent.[71] Dysentery, rickets, digestive and stomach problems, and other sicknesses directly linked to improper diet spread throughout the population, weakening the healthy and killing the most vulnerable. The most infamous and deadly illness was the global outbreak of the Spanish influenza. Influenza and related pneumonias ravaged a weakened Germany in the immediate aftermath of the war, killing up to 200,000 men and women in the winter of 1918, a higher civilian mortality rate than at any time during the military conflict.[72] In addition, the dramatic drop in birth rates, though typical of a country at war, was attributed to the nutritional deficits suffered by the country's women.

This landscape of wartime restrictions, deprivation, and death seamlessly merged with the misery of poverty and defeat; hunger linked the war and the postwar years, blurring the difference between total war and international peace and between imperial and democratic governments. The continuation of the blockade rendered irrelevant the fact that the German homefront had been relatively healthy until the hardships of the Turnip Winter; it also overshadowed the various European hungers that had been caused by the German military during the war.

Many German voices appealed to international humanitarian sentiment as they addressed their plight. Within weeks of the signing of the armistice, the president of the new Imperial Food Office, Emanuel Wurm, speaking before the Reichstag in November 1918, told the public that only foreign food aid could save the German people: "[W]hen we show to the entire world how destitute the German people have become due to the war, then we will be able to count on America's help in order to get the necessary foodstuffs."[73] What everyone in Germany was calling for were influxes of foreign food—a form of transnational charity that the war had normalized as a method of political control and population management.

Herbert Hoover and the Invention of Modern Food Aid

Between 1914 and 1924, international food aid for the first time played a key role in a global war effort and shaped the postwar food economies of both the United States and Europe. The new transnational economy meant that nations could imagine—and in some moments even realize—complete control over food distribution. Just as it became possible to cut a country off from food imports, it was now also possible to engage in mass-scale international provisioning of food supplies. Food aid was not the direct consequence of food's use as a weapon during the war; it was an extension and modification of a larger set of military strategies that had transformed hungry people into a source of political power.

The hungers of Belgium, France, Poland, and Germany during the war by no means represented the first time that industrialized Europe had confronted the horrors of mass starvation. In fact, the proliferation of famine across much of the globe during the decades immediately preceding the First World War had inspired moral outrage, as well as calls for international charity. Quite different from these colonial famines, when hungry bodies had been seen as a sort of collateral damage of industrialization, the food economy of the First World War had explicitly aimed at their creation. Thus modern food aid emerged alongside a new conceptualization of hunger as central to the landscape of total war. Shaped by the sweeping vision of Herbert Hoover, international food-relief programs flourished during the war and in its immediate aftermath. Germany, as both the primary target of the hunger weapon and the perceived cause of Europe's food shortages, found itself at the center of the emergent transnational economy of humanitarian food aid.

Despite the fact that the Hunger Blockade officially targeted Germany, the primary site of European hunger during the war was the small, landlocked nation of Belgium. In August 1914, the German army had invaded neutral Belgium, a highly urban nation with little capacity for domestic food production. What followed was a military operation that became infamous for graphic tales of mutilation, mass executions, and sexual assault inflicted by the Germans.[74] Yet it was Germany's control over the country's food supply, specifically the military's aggressive policy of food requisitions, that posed the greatest threat to Belgian civilians. The severe food shortages that quickly spread across Belgium and northern France inspired the creation, in 1914, of the first major international food-relief program: the Committee for the Relief of Belgium (CRB). Alarmed by stories of widespread civilian suffering, and aware of the potential benefits to the United States of providing relief, Hoover nearly singlehandedly conceptualized and established the CRB. The committee was designed as a nongovernmental aid project whose purpose was to distribute private charitable food donations, operating entirely separate from the wartime food economy, which was dominated by trade restrictions and various food blockades. Hoover needed to create a neutral, independent organization that could secure cooperation from all the main belligerents: the British government, which would have to allow neutral food shipments through the blockade; the German government, which would have to promise not to seize the food for its own population; and the American public, which had to approve the costs of the vast undertaking. After extensive negotiations, Hoover convinced both Germany and Britain to let the CRB organize the delivery and distribution of foodstuffs. In 1917,

Germany's declaration of unrestricted submarine warfare provoked the United States' entry into the war, but the CRB managed to retain its de facto neutral status. Eventually, the organization became an important channel of communication between Germany and England, giving the United States a particular kind of political power by means of humanitarian activity.

By the end of the war, the CRB was supplying about two-thirds of Belgium's civilian food needs.[75] In doing so, it had found a new market for America's massive wheat surplus, transforming an economic liability into a source of international influence and potential profit. The work of the CRB thus signaled the emergence of the United States as the breadbasket of the postwar world. The pattern of the Belgian crisis would repeat itself throughout the first half of the twentieth century as American and Allied war efforts created hungers that were, in turn, assuaged through American surpluses. The CRB was the only international food-aid program that functioned while the war was actually being waged. It should thus be understood as being part of the war, revealing the innovative military idea that the charitable provisioning of food could have as much strategic significance as the deliberate starving of enemies.[76]

Key to the CRB's success had been Hoover's ability to depict food aid as something that existed completely outside the political and diplomatic machinations of the various warring governments. At the same time, however, Hoover expected to wield food aid as a tool to shape postwar European political sentiments. In the wake of the war, food regulation was increasingly linked to global geopolitics. President Woodrow Wilson told Congress in January 1919, "[F]ood relief is now the key to the whole European situation and to the solution of peace."[77] Food had not only "won the war"; it would secure the peace and remake the devastated continent. Building on wartime propaganda that had urged civilians to restrict their food consumption to ensure victory, postwar debates depicted hunger as a profound threat to peace, economic stability, and even the very existence of the human race. In March 1919, the *New Republic* warned that "the whole structure of European pacification, of the reconciliation of peoples is conditioned on the prompt and complete extinction of the ghost of famine. Yet this ghost still stalks abroad more frightening and forbidding than ever."[78] Hoover, who continued to direct humanitarian efforts after the war's end, was especially adept at using the language of Christian brotherhood when talking about the problem, regularly describing to the American public "long lines of emaciated women and children" and insisting that "not only should this pull at our hearts, but beyond this it is a menace to our very safety."[79] This notion of the hungry as objects of both pity and fear was part of a postwar imaginary that visualized the world as divided between the hungry and the satiated.

This frightening vision inspired one of the most reproduced maps of the postwar moment, the Hunger Map of Europe (see Figure 1.3). This powerful

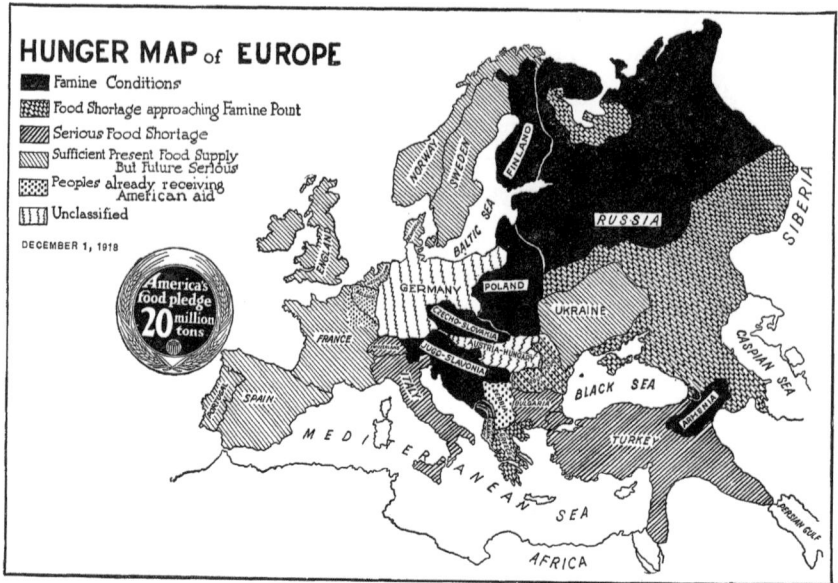

Figure 1.3 Hunger Map of Europe. 1918. Source: *World's Work* 37, no. 3 (1919): 256.

image, designed by the US Food Administration in December 1918, was widely circulated by Hoover's postwar relief programs to spread the message of a looming European food crisis and the need for continued American involvement.[80] According to the map, the stakes for Americans were high, nothing less than "our own safety ... the social organization of the world [and] the preservation of civilization itself."[81] The map was published in the *New York Times*, included as an insert in local newspapers, hung in public buildings, and reprinted in journals and periodicals throughout the country, ensuring that the entire nation became acquainted with its vision of hunger as geopolitical threat.[82]

The Hunger Map and similar depictions were important in establishing the scale and scope of the European food crisis and its larger ramifications. On the map, each nation's hunger was evaluated based on relative level of severity, making hunger comparative rather than absolute; the map's purpose was to make clear that some countries were more and some less hungry. Equally importantly, the map graphically cast European famine as existing in relationship to American food aid. The categories of the map—"famine conditions," "food shortages," and "people already receiving American aid"—suggested an opposition between receiving aid and hunger; the implication was that American aid was the only solution to hunger. This reflected Hoover's conviction that European hunger should be interpreted in relationship to American economic prosperity and political stability.

The vision of Europe as a territory composed of regions that all needed different levels of American food aid had economic underpinnings. During the war, American agricultural surplus had found a ready market in warring Europe, so that the disrupted food system of Europe greatly advantaged neutral United States. Not only occupied Belgium but also France and England had quickly come to rely on American food. These new markets were a tremendous boon for the American economy, especially for its farmers, whose real income rose by almost a third between 1915 and 1918 despite little change in production levels.[83] From an American perspective, the end of hostilities posed a real economic threat; Europe's resumption of its prewar trade patterns would mean that America would lose access to markets that were consuming millions of pounds of wheat and corn. Hoover's creation of global hunger maps suggested a potentially limitless demand for American food surpluses.

One of Hoover's basic arguments in favor of providing food aid was that it could be profitable—and America's wartime experiences seemed to prove him right. All of his aid programs required that recipient countries use credit to pay for the aid they received. Historian Helen Veit claims that it was this food-aid economy that "cement[ed] ... the US position as a postwar creditor to the empires of Europe."[84] It was this emphasis on further financial opportunities that won for Hoover President Wilson's support for expanded postwar food-aid programs. In a statement sent to Congress in January 1919, Wilson requested the appropriation of $100,000,000 "for foodstuffs [that] must be placed in certain localities within the next 15 to 30 days if human life and order are to be preserved." This aid was to be sent "to such populations in Europe, outside of Germany, as may be determined upon by me from time to time as necessary."[85] Congress approved the funding of what became the American Relief Administration (ARA) in February of 1919. The ARA ensured that American food became, in the words of Hoover himself, "the medium of exchange between the United States and the liberated nations of Europe."[86]

The food shortages that had ravaged Europe during the war had generally been blamed on the Germans: "Germany has not alone sucked the food and animals from all those masses of people she has dominated and left them starving, but she has left behind her a total wreckage of social institutions and this mass of people is now confronted with engulfment in absolute anarchy."[87] Even the Hunger Map placed Germany outside of its geopolitical vision of a hungry Europe. The accompanying caption explained that "the only nations about which there seem to be any doubt [about their hunger] are Germany and Austria-Hungary."[88] Wavy lines covered both territories, in contrast to the solid black lines of the famine areas, the stripes of the areas experiencing shortages, and the dots of the areas receiving aid. This lack of clarity about the former enemy was intended to reassure Americans that those lands were not the intended recipients of "America's food pledge of 20 million tons." While "the terrible conditions in Russia and other countries which Germany has plundered of their food supply are clearly shown,"[89] the map made a point of explicitly refuting German claims of hunger, noting that "the accounts sent by American correspondents with the American armies of occupation do not describe such a serious food shortage as the German government has described in its appeals to President Wilson."

Unsurprisingly, the American public initially viewed these German claims with skepticism. A November 1918 *Washington Post* editorial, provocatively titled "Let Germany starve first," wrote that "Germans are drawing a little too heavily upon American credulity and her magnanimity when they ask Americans to regard them as genuine converts to democracy, victims of their late rulers, and deserving of the fatted calf and forgiveness."[90] In debates in Congress in early 1919 over the distribution of food aid to Europe, many senators and congressmen expressed doubts about the level of hunger in Germany. One speaker reported that "just a few days ago I had a letter from a soldier who is in our army of occupation, written in a German house, where he said they were sitting down to one of the best meals he ever saw, where they had roast beef, port and so forth."[91] Wilson himself emphasized, in his initial communications to Congress, that

> the money will not be spent for food for Germany itself, because Germany can buy its food, but it will be spent for financing the movement of food to our real friends in Poland and to the people of the liberated units of the Austro-Hungarian empire and to our associates in the Balkans.[92]

Even more punitively, Britain's leaders and the British public generally agreed that a deliberately imposed hunger was an appropriate form of political discipline for the country deemed responsible for the horrors of the war. In July 1919, the London *Sunday Times* issued a warning lest "the sentimental folk who cry out for pity for the German children forget that Germany used most of her milk for munitions purposes."[93] German pleas for food were rejected outright as evidence of perverse and threatening appetites: "Big Bertha whoops and shrieks in ever wilder fits of hysterics. Feed me at once, she screams, or I will kill myself. Stay me with lard, comfort me with pork, or I will bring the roof down."[94] The Cambridge economist C. W. Guillebaud visited Germany's capital in the spring of 1919 and wrote, in a much-publicized letter, that he

> was surprised by the good external appearance of the vast majority of the persons whom I met about the streets. There are very few fat people in Berlin to-day, but equally there is no obvious expression of hunger and exhaustion on the faces of the people. The bulk of the middle

and upper classes looked in quite normal health, and their faces did not appear sunken or pinched. The poor certainly showed the influence of privation to a greater extent, but although lack of food and the depressing influence of defeat have taken the desire and the capacity to work hard from the majority of people, the bulk of adults are, in appearance at least, a long way from actual starvation.[95]

Even advocates of aid to Germany admitted that "the stories from Germany are very conflicting . . . from one section you would hear there was plenty of food . . . in another place where there was better control, food was more scarce."[96] After the armistice, during the transitional months before the blockade was finally lifted, the ARA did send gradually increasing amounts of food aid to Germany. However, ARA distribution in Germany was restricted by recently passed legislation stipulating that no enemy adult or child could be fed with Congress-appropriated money. As a result, Germany lagged far behind most other European nations in receiving food aid.

This widespread skepticism about German suffering was eventually replaced by a growing international discourse that emphasized instead the distinct tragedy of German hunger. The country's privileged role as symbolic center of European culture and its great wealth and economic power made the suffering of Germans uniquely disturbing. Humanitarian reports from the field tended to emphasize the suffering of those whom the aid workers believed were "well-educated, refined people." This meant that there was particular interest in the men and women of the German middle class, who had long been admired in the United States for their industriousness and cultural sophistication.[97] American relief worker Robert Hotson, for example, had seen hunger across the continent but was particularly affected by the suffering of the Germans because it represented the collapse of the "standard of living [of what was] once the highest and most civilized and complex [people] on the continent."[98] The hunger of Russian peasants, Polish orphans, or French laborers was recognized as tragic and regrettable, but it was the "slow deterioration and decay" of the once powerful Germans that troubled American visitors the most.[99] In the United States, this empathetic identification with German civilians was framed in a Christian rhetoric of helping the weak. As the birthplace of Martin Luther, Germany had special significance for predominantly Protestant American activists, who quickly began to identify the hungry women and children of Germany as victims of "worse atrocities than even were perpetuated by Turks."[100] The focus on women and especially children victims—reflected in the names of many of the new humanitarian programs—underscored hungry peoples' basic innocence. In these ways, hunger was stripped of its wartime context at the same time that it was valorized for revealing the humanitarian instincts beneath seemingly brutal global politics.

The widespread conviction that Germany was indispensable to the economic reconstruction of Europe also contributed to a particular valuation of German lives. American and British relief workers sent to Germany to organize feeding programs were convinced that "much more than Germany is involved, for Europe cannot live with a non-producing, starving and desperate Germany in her midst."[101] Germany might not have been the hungriest country after the war, but well-fed Germans were the most potentially productive of all the hungry populations of the continent: "no doubt starvation is not confined to Germany, but it is the German people who are expected to reconstitute Europe by their industry. How is a half-starved nation to fulfill such expectations?"[102] The *Nation* cynically predicted that a hungry Germany would only increase England's expenses; were Germany to succumb to famine, "all the benefit we will get from our expected bondsman is the trouble of burying him, and even the expense of the funeral will not be covered by the few battered halfpence we may find in his pockets."[103]

Still, a powerful thread of fear existed alongside the empathetic and pragmatic interpretations of German hunger. Germany had been the most prominent enemy nation during the war, and citizens in the Allied nations had been trained for years to fear the German people—a fear that was exploited by linking hunger with a crazed and uncontrollable violence. In a radio essay titled "The Starving German Nation," a Professor Forster warned that the hunger in Germany was capable of producing "an entirely new type of terrible degeneration in which the individual becomes scarcely responsible for his words and actions."[104]

More specifically, especially in the aftermath of the unexpected success of the 1917 Russian Revolution, there was a widespread fear that hunger would push Germany into the arms of the communists. A 1919 British report on the situation in Germany found that "in their present state they [the Germans] are fit for subjection to any forceful personality and would accept willingly any sort of dictatorship if it were combined with provision of food."[105] An officer stationed there in the winter of 1919 warned succinctly that "hunger will lead to rioting and Bolshevism."[106] Journalist Henry Brailsford published a dramatic report of his travels in the lands "across the blockade" in 1919, warning that Germany

> is not merely half-starved; it is in a state of nervous ill-health, that varies according to temperament from dull apathy to neurotic overexcitement . . . thinking is active, feverish and destructive . . . the whole current of political thought is "to the left."[107]

These fears were not simple empty words but rationale for policy. The signing of the Versailles Treaty in June 1919 had finally opened up Germany for international aid, and Hoover once again intervened to radically increase food imports. Although the process might have seemed agonizingly slow to the increasingly hungry Germans, in fact, the transition to prioritizing German hunger happened with impressive rapidity. Between December 1918 and May 1919, Belgium received by far the greatest amount of US food relief: a remarkable 768,443 metric tons. Germany was a distant second, receiving 313,001 tons.[108] After the signing of the treaty, American aid to Germany expanded exponentially; by the end of June, Germany had skyrocketed to the top of the list, receiving in that single month 207,353 tons of relief, followed by Austria with 121,004 tons.[109] These numbers reflect the fact that the food situation in Germany, unlike that of Belgium, had been worsening rather than slowly improving since the war's end. At the same time, Austria and Russia were suffering from more severe food shortages than was Germany, and much of Europe found itself with a more damaged infrastructure after the war, especially in terms of agriculture, than the relatively untouched German nation. Nonetheless, of all the European nations facing massive food shortages after the war, Germany was to receive the largest quantity of American food aid, a total of 1,215,000 tons.[110] US food aid to Germany was also long-lived. The Quakers, with the resources and backing of the German government and the European Children's Fund, provided over three million dollars' worth of food donated by the American public to German children for five full years, not leaving the country until October 1924.[111]

The year 1924 marked the stabilization of the German economy and the end of hyperinflation, as well as the cessation of the country's international food relief. With the closure of both German and then Russian relief programs in 1924, the era of Hoover-led international relief projects came to an end. These programs had a legacy that reached beyond full bellies and grateful children. Hoover's elaboration of a new kind of international food-relief project, developed alongside the Allied wartime blockade policy, transformed hunger into an effective political weapon that was economically beneficial for the Allies, especially the United States. These programs also established Germany's centrality in discussions of the future of European, even global, food security and hunger. Additionally, Hoover's remarkable propaganda success institutionalized an image of the United States as the main global provider of food relief, which in turn became an effective, even necessary, weapon in the fight against Bolshevism.

Having famously dismissed the Bolshevik Revolution as a "food riot," Hoover, like President Wilson, and other US policymakers, conceptualized Communism not as a coherent ideological or economic platform but as an expression of chaos, degeneracy, and material hardship. The unexpected success of the Russian Revolution seemed to confirm the idea that communism almost automatically arose wherever there were widespread food shortages; for these men, it became, above all, a collective reaction to hunger. During the Russian Civil War that followed the 1917 revolution, the ARA had organized food aid to the anti-Bolshevik Whites, in direct violation of its mandate to distribute food regardless of the political affiliations of recipients. Since the summer of 1918, American diplomats had been advocating food relief to the USSR as a way of strengthening American influence in the war-torn country. Indeed, Hoover's relief programs, the ARA and its affiliates, managed to deliver large amounts of foodstuffs to millions of starving Russians during the severe shortages of the early 1920s. Nonetheless, this aid failed to achieve the anti-Communist victory that Hoover had hoped for, ironically resulting in the stabilization of the Soviet government rather than its collapse.

Germany alone thus became the success story proving the political efficacy of food relief. As early as December 1918, Hoover had warned Wilson in a personal letter that "[v]iewing the German empire from a food point of view, there will be no hope of saving these people from starvation if bolshevist activities extend over the empire in a similar manner to Russia."[112] In the wake of the failed Spartacist uprising in Berlin, in January 1919 Wilson, echoing Hoover's warning, explained to Congress, "Bolshevism cannot be stopped by force, but it can be stopped by food."[113] The numerous left-wing and revolutionary activities that took place in Germany during the chaotic end of the war were held up as evidence of the need for an influx of American food. Years later, Hoover confidently asserted that "there can be no question but that the delivery of these supplies to Germany saved that country from the fate of Russia. . . . It is significant that soon after the first food ship arrived the political situation made a decided change and, after that time, steadily improved."[114] A retrospective ARA report from 1931 depicted this humanitarian intervention as an almost otherworldly force:

> It was hoped that the effect of food arriving suddenly from a distance, by an unseen hand, without price or compensation, would do much to develop their [the Germans'] ideals of justice, altruism and citizenship and perhaps obliterate in a large part the influences of the degrading environment of the war.[115]

In this context "altruism" and "citizenship" were not humanitarian or economic values but deeply political ones. Hoover's ambitious food-aid programs encouraged both Americans and the recipients of American aid to equate democracy with an abundance of food.[116] Food would win support for democracy and capitalism, systems that were conflated and then placed in opposition to Communism. Weimar Germany was upheld as an American foreign policy success, its not turning Communist seen as inarguable proof of the efficacy of Hoover's agenda.

Hoover's ability to present hunger as a universal humanitarian concern that transcended local politics shaped subsequent aid projects, as well as a new vision of global security that saw scarcity as a threat to American peace and prosperity.[117] Food aid's power derived from its use in managing the economic and political development of hungry states. More specifically, the expansion of American-led humanitarian projects in Germany turned the defeated country into an internationally recognized illustration of the consequences of the militarization of food, as well as of the politicization of hunger.

German Hunger and Political Radicalization after the War

To the profound disappointment of the German population, food shortages and food protests continued for several years after the end of the blockade. The economic instability of the early Weimar Republic ensured that many Germans would continue to struggle to adequately feed their families.[118] However, the continued existence of hunger should not obscure the fact that Weimar hunger was quite distinct from its wartime counterpart. Despite dramatic political rhetoric blaming the British for German suffering, the hunger that Germans experienced after the end of the war and after the signing of the Versailles treaty was not simply the result of the blockade. German agriculture was in bad shape, and it took years for the country's farming communities to recover from the psychological and material impact of the war. During the war, labor scarcity had been a major factor limiting harvests; as a result, after the war millions of demobilized soldiers were expected to make themselves available to work in the fields. What sounded good in theory was a failure in practice, however; most soldiers refused to become farmers, and the government was forced to deal with both inadequate crops and massive unemployment among veterans. Farmers had still other reasons to be angry. The last remnants of the wartime government's interventions in the food supply, including price regulations and restrictions on food production and delivery, did not disappear until 1923. This both guaranteed the continuation of the black market as well as active and passive resistance by farmers and other food producers, who felt unfairly burdened by government regulations.[119] The war impacted agriculture in other ways as well. The massive depletion of the country's livestock, especially its horses, meant reduced labor power and, especially, inadequate fertilizer, a shortage that had been exacerbated by the military's vast appetite for nitrogen.[120] The terms of the Versailles Treaty meant the loss of much of the country's fertile farmland in the east. For all these reasons, Germany's first postwar grain harvest was just under half of the yield of 1913; harvests did not exceed 75 percent of that initial prewar bumper crop for the first postwar decade.[121] As a result, the country continued to be heavily dependent on food imports.

Economic problems after 1919 compounded ongoing problems with the domestic food supply; the early years of the Weimar Republic were shaped by catastrophic economic collapse, peaking in the infamous hyperinflation of 1923 that brought about the near total collapse of the Deutschmark. High unemployment, increasing government expenditures on social-welfare programs, and Germans' loss of personal savings, all deepened the grave preexisting problems. High prices and poor quality often made postwar groceries little better than the loathed ersatz foods that had been ubiquitous during the war. In general, both the quality and quantity of food in working-class diets took an especially long time to return to prewar levels; in 1925, the per capita consumption of meat had still not reached its 1912 levels, and potatoes continued to provide the bulk of calories for many of the urban poor.[122] As had been the case during the war, women and the unemployed bore the greatest burden in this dysfunctional food economy; women often sacrificed their own portions to feed their husbands and children. The unemployed simply lacked access to affordable foodstuffs. The most distinctive component of Weimar-era hunger, however, was the particular importance it acquired within the country's diverse political landscape.

During the war, the domestic food situation had been a central topic for Germany's fragmented Left. Communists and Socialists had believed that widespread experiences of hunger would increase their appeal to citizens searching for an foothold in a time of economic and political instability. As the shortages worsened and public discontent increased, a range of radical voices began to seize on the atmosphere of crisis, casting hunger as proof of capitalist-militarist exploitation. The war and hunger were described as intertwined and interdependent, so that ending one was inherently seen as ending the other. In June 1916, deputy of the Independent Socialist Party Adolf Hofer announced to the parliament in a widely quoted speech that "the people now know that they must starve at home and be slaughtered at the front in the interests of a small clique of capitalists."[123] Underground publications, such as the nationally circulated pamphlet *Hunger!*, called on the populace to demand "fair" food pricing and distribution.[124] The Independent Social Democratic Party, a left-wing splinter party formed out of the SPD in 1917, relied on reports of working-class hunger to illustrate the general evil of the war and the incompetence of the government.[125] The illusory victory achieved after the Brest-Litovsk negotiations on the Eastern Front further alienated the Left, which saw the "annexationist peace" as further evidence of the insatiability of the German military and proof that war meant hunger abroad as well as at home. Indeed, it seemed that the severity of malnutrition and the fear of hunger among the German working classes were setting the stage for revolution. In 1917, as a wave of industrial strikes swept the country in reaction to reduced bread rations, the Communists predicted that the "basic human desire to satisfy hunger" would ultimately cause "a political and social will to break free, to force peace with its own strength, something that is kept from us by a criminal system of war."[126] During the final months of the war, underground socialist literature had celebrated the fact that "hunger riots are ... preparing fertile ground for the stimulating agitation of the Socialist elements."[127]

This wartime discourse continued in modified forms in Weimar Germany. In the new republic, given the tremendous diversity of parties and political agendas that made up what could be termed "the Left," a common interest in hunger often seemed the only unifying factor. Historian Alf Lüdtke has noted that the German Communist Party (KPD), founded in December 1918, based its political vocabulary upon popular fears of war and memories of hunger.[128] As late as 1932, a KPD poster (see Figure 1.4) invoked starving children to appeal for votes. This rhetoric was prominent within the Left more generally. The more moderate SPD also relied on the imagery of hunger to attract votes and mobilize the masses. A cartoon from the early 1920s in support of striking dock workers in Hamburg claimed that "the last weapon of the German capitalists against the fighting worker is starvation" depicting an overweight capitalist wielding a "club of starvation."[129] The radical anarchist Theodor Plievier defined hunger as the existential state of living in oppression, "the opposite of excess, of property," casting it as "the crystallization of pure misery, the greatest expression of the miseries and afflictions of all those who have been cast out, who die lonely in the streets and who are locked in factories, prisons, and bordellos for the duration of their lives."[130] In 1923, as skyrocketing inflation increased popular suffering, the socialist Central Committee for International Workers' Aid predicted in a propaganda booklet titled *Hunger in Germany* that this hunger would provide the "fresh breath of revolution" that the country needed. SPD activist Max Wurm believed that it was in the struggle against hunger that "the solidarity of the world proletariat" was becoming "a new powerful force of action," serving as "proof of the interconnectedness of all the exploited of the world, uniting them all in the struggle."[131]

The prevalence of hunger in German left-wing political rhetoric during the early Weimar years represented continuity with wartime trends among activists and agitators. However, after the war these radical voices were joined for the first time by individuals and parties across the political spectrum, all of whom saw the food supply as the country's most pressing problem as well as a uniquely effective topic of propaganda.

The highest echelons of the German government relied on hunger as a core political strategy. Politicians and public figures deliberately exploited international fears of a Bolshevik Germany in making their pleas for increased food aid.

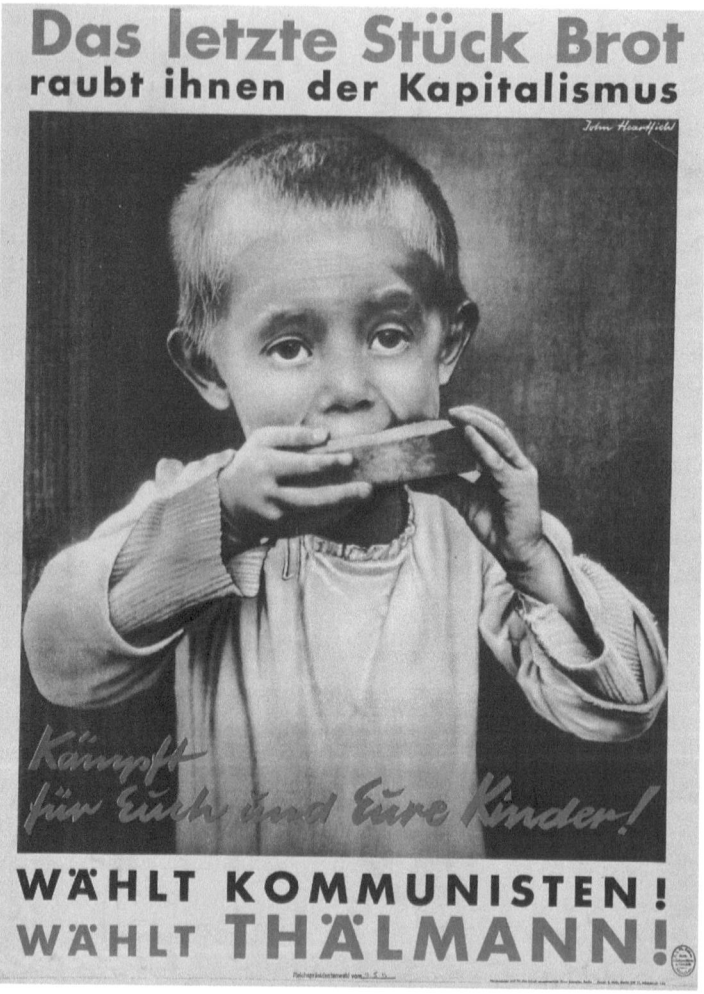

Figure 1.4 "Capitalism is stealing their last piece of bread. Fight for you and your children! Vote Communist! Vote Thälmann!" 1932. BArch Plak 002-016-079 / John Heartfield.

During the early years of the Republic, the American media sent periodic questionnaires to high-ranking officials in the Weimar government asking whether the Quaker feeding programs had "been an aid against Bolshevism or against a desperate reversion to monarchy."[132] The German government, well aware of the consequences of its answers, always assured the American press that the proffered food was all that had prevented the country from turning to violent revolution, promptly following up this information with requests for further food aid to continue the struggle against Communism. In a widely circulated publication titled *Hunger! The Effects of Modern War Methods*, Max Rubmann warned the international community that recent occurrences have made a different danger abundantly clear, namely that the German people, devastated by undernourishment, would no longer be capable of putting up a defense against the dangerous nervous disease of Bolshevism, something vital to the security of Europe.[133]

Although German officials strategically described food protests as Bolshevik to convey a sense of destitution and to persuade the Allies to reduce the country's massive reparations debt, in point of fact the country's food riots usually lacked any explicit political agenda.[134] Most bread riots and hunger marches tended to be consumer initiated, and focused on restoring "fair" food prices rather than achieving political change. These short-lived popular protests only indirectly and occasionally intersected with actual left-wing activism, although, in their frequency and high drama they did make the Left seem more politically menacing.[135] In reality, riots and plundering were more frequently instigated by the Right than the Left, which generally advocated organizing and distributing foodstuffs rather than vandalizing and seizing them.[136] To the relief of some and the disappointment of others, poverty and hunger frequently discouraged political engagement; even the extremities of the hyperinflation did not create a revolutionary atmosphere.[137] Indeed, contrary to the expectations of both international and domestic observers, the food crisis of the war years seemed to have explicitly discredited Communism; many Germans associated their wartime deprivations not with the military or conservative imperial structures, but with the rationing system, which had been popularly though inaccurately described as "wartime socialism." A resultant rejection of the Left was especially widespread among the country's farmers, who became increasingly conservative, perceiving themselves to be pitted against a voracious and unappreciative class of urban, industrial, and often left-leaning consumers.[138]

Indeed, the hunger of the early Weimar years seems to have pushed many people, especially young men, to the Right rather than to the Left. In response, writers and activists from the political Right increasingly invoked hunger as a symbol of national or racial oppression. Because the military claimed that domestic collapse rather than armed conflict had brought about Germany's defeat, many patriots blamed the civilian population for not being able to withstand the pressures of the food shortages. Such accusations had begun early. In March 1918, the amateur economist Warte Briester sent the War Food Office an analysis of the wartime food situation in which he blamed civilian hunger for the country's ongoing military failures: "[O]ur inner front lacks the preparation for a hunger-war, the system of self-discipline, the strict control, the self-awareness, that would make us unconquerable."[139] Such accusations were at the heart of what became the myth of Germany's "stab in the back," the idea that the German military had remained undefeated, but the civilian homefront had caved to the pressures of the war—and especially the pressures of hunger.

While army officers had been little interested in the suffering of the homefront during the actual war, once that war was lost, they became obsessed with it. Former General of the Infantry Hermann von François wrote an analysis of Germany's situation in 1919, titled *Germany's Hunger: How Did It Come About? And How Is It to Be Overcome?*, in which the controversial war hero claimed that "the complete misery that has spread itself throughout Germany is rooted in the hunger crisis."[140] Asserting that the British Blockade had been the sole cause of the country's defeat, von François was convinced that naval food blockades would "continue to be a hunger screw that the enemy will apply at will. For he knows that a weakened and demoralized *Volk* will not be able to break free of the chains of slavery."[141] Such graphic imagery of enslavement and dire predictions of future hunger were common in Weimar political rhetoric; while the Communists blamed the capitalists and military greed, the military and conservative voices blamed both foreign and internal enemies for Germany's suffering. Ultimately, however, no one proved better able to mobilize the population around a particular vision of hunger and satiety than Adolf Hitler and the fledgling National Socialist Party (Nationalsozialistische Deutsche Arbeiterpartei or NSDAP).

Founded in 1920 as one of countless splinter parties that proliferated during this time, the NSDAP was born out of the chaos and political extremism of the postwar hunger years. Hitler regularly invoked his own early experience of hunger as an impoverished youth in Vienna as a way of explaining the extremism of his ideology. While hunger was a key political trope across the political spectrum, the emerging radical right-wing movements developed their own distinct imagery. Early Nazi rhetoric described hunger not as the sign of working-class exploitation at the hands of the wealthy but as an expression of racial oppression at the hands of the Jews, who were working alongside their comrades the Communists. An anonymous NSDAP article from the early 1920s, titled "The Pogrom on the German and Russian People," described the impact of the Volga famine on the large community of ethnic Germans in the region. In heartwrenching detail, the author lamented the innocent men, women, and children who were suffering at the hands of the intertwined forces of Soviet Judaism and Bolshevism:

> Now, when the Jewish government calls, the hungering people of Germany should help again, when already here the marrow is being pressed from the bone, even though everyone who is clearheaded knows that the sent bread never will reach the starving 25 million

Russians, let alone adequately feed them, but rather will strengthen the Jewish government.[142]

A 1923 General State Commissioner report from Bavaria reported that students in particular were attracted to the fledgling Nazi party because of their own poverty and bodily suffering:

> Many do not know how to still their hunger, and even less whether they can continue to study next month. Naturally, it would be a form of salvation for them to be enrolled in an army where they had regular meals and could eat their fill. The local authorities believe that this is a not to be underestimated factor in the entire Hitler movement.[143]

For the bulk of the population, the experience of hunger did not change political affiliations or voting patterns. Instead, recurrent food crises and anticipated hungers encouraged a rhetoric of Allied cruelty and German suffering that reached beyond the musings of defeated military leaders or the rants of obscure Nazi propaganda to pervade the food economy of the struggling country and thus the activities of daily life. A 1922 guide to frugal cooking, *Economic Eating Based on Research Done in War and Peace*, claimed that the imperative to economize in the kitchen was the result of vindictive Allied policy toward Germany:

> The creators of the so-called peace treaty of Versailles, the same men who forced us into war and who viewed the horrific hunger blockade as a justifiable tool of war, refuse to admit that the peace treaty only serves to keep us enslaved ... The only thing that can help us is twofold; internationally we need to win back our rights and our freedom, something we can only do when we are united again. Domestically we need to rebuild our utterly destroyed affluence—in order to do this we need to work more and consume less. Since approximately half of our total consumption is in the area of food, it is precisely here that economizing would have the greatest effect.[144]

Cookbooks like this one expressed the fears of many ordinary Germans during these years, as political expectations became linked to food supply. Nutrition and citizenship became intertwined, and having political power was equated with the demand for adequate food. Despite its lack of an explicit political framework, the themes that run through this cookbook—becoming independent from food imports, economizing in the kitchen, revitalizing "Germanic cuisine," increasing agricultural productivity, and territorial expansion to increase the country's grain production—were embraced primarily by the far Right. Detached from the specific context of the Weimar moment, they would become core rationales for the Nazis' initiation of the Second World War.

*	*	*

As food shortages became less frequent and less extreme, the atmosphere of crisis that had defined the early Weimar years gradually dissipated. In 1925, the signing of the Treaty of Locarno, which symbolized Germany's readmission as one of the Western powers, corresponded with the end of Hoover's food-aid projects in Europe. Both events signaled the stabilization of the continent and the end of mass hunger. A new desire to integrate Germany into Western Europe meant that reparation demands steadily decreased. Even in previously hostile Britain and France, punitive voices were replaced by "a new, skeptical narrative of the war," wherein no nation, not even Germany, bore responsibility for it.[145] The Weimar state successfully suppressed talk of culpability in favor of a narrative of the German people's senseless suffering.[146]

In the face of this international recognition of the significance and tragedy of Germany's hunger, the British Blockade became a shameful chapter in a senseless war, a weapon that had targeted innocent women and children instead of an acceptable strategy for compromising a militarized homefront. A 1919 British National Labor pamphlet, *Family Life in Germany under the Blockade*, claimed that "if a vivid imagination could set before the eyes of the mass of the people in every detail the results of the English-American blockade in Europe, it would even during the war have been banned, condemned by the loathing of the whole world as the most horrible of all methods of war."[147] Indeed, an abiding international concern with the health of the German population and the state of the country's food supply was an unexpected legacy of the blockade. Throughout the interwar years, Allied studies carefully documented German popular diets and expressed concern over the population's nutrition.[148] Over time, the reported harms caused by the blockade grew rather than diminished. Both American and European newspapers and public speakers regularly cited German reports claiming that up to a million civilians had starved to death due to the blockade.[149]

Within Germany, the legacies of the First World War's food economy were far-reaching. An overwhelming fear of hunger suffused the public sphere, intensifying the country's economic instability and the misery of unemployment. In this fragmented social landscape, parties across the political spectrum used a common vocabulary of hunger to express grievances, inspire particular visions, and form bonds of community and cohesiveness. Individual memories, experiences, and expectations of hunger continued to provide fodder for the explosion of radical political parties for years after the blockade was lifted. By the mid-1920s, both the SPD and the centrist parties attributed the country's hard-won stability to its crackdown on the Left; they continued to perceive communists as the state's greatest threat and to link hunger with popular radicalization. Although the Weimar government was firmly committed to international trade, the drive for "food autarchy"—ending food imports in favor of producing all foodstuffs domestically—became entrenched among many members of the military and those on the political right.

Collective and individual identities were remade in terms of suffering—specifically suffering at the hands of the Allies. The continuation of the blockade during postwar negotiations and the harsh terms of the armistice violated the population's assumption that the end of the war would mean the end of hunger. As a result, much of the German public perceived their hunger as having been deliberately created, inflicted upon a nation that had surrendered and that was inhabited primarily by women, children, and the elderly. The official report on "current nutritional conditions in Germany," released within weeks of surrender in December 1918, claimed that the defeated country's suffering was "one that is without parallel in the history of the world."[150] The report singled out the centrality of the blockade for the collapse of public health, concluding that "the symptoms of gradual decline are better known to us [Germans] than to anyone else in the world."[151]

This sense of suffering was woven into the larger denial of defeat that saturated the early years of the Weimar Republic. It allowed some German leaders to deny their responsibility for non-German wartime misery. In 1919, the conservative former chancellor Theodor von Bethmann-Hollweg countered widespread accusations of German wartime atrocities in Belgium with a reminder that German suffering was still ongoing:

> [A]re we forever to talk of nothing but our own sins, even those consisting in the violations of international law, we who stand face to face with an anomaly of international law like England's blockade through which . . . our people have been relegated to an existence of misery for generations.[152]

Agricultural chemist Paul Ehrenberg warned in 1920 that "if we do not in some way defend ourselves against the most terrifying enemy, hunger, then there is no doubt that within a few years this painfully purchased so-called peace will demand more victims than did the war."[153]

After several years of relative stability, the 1929 Wall Street Crash signaled the beginning of a global depression, and with it a new wave of German hunger caused by skyrocketing unemployment. Harkening back to the tumult of the early Weimar years, local officials expressed their concern that the food crisis of the early 1930s would incite revolution. A rural economist warned in 1932 that a new butter tax would push the population over the edge: "[E]very day I receive letters of desperation ... and now I hear that the butter tax is finally arriving. ... I watch with horror the radicalization of our farmers ... every day there are corpses."[154] This time around, Germany's food crisis did inspire a populist revolution—but one quite different from the Communist uprising that had been feared a decade earlier. While the Communist Party did see a tripling of its membership in response to the catastrophic economic situation, the KPD's traditional promise of "bread and work" ultimately could not compete with the lure of the NSDAP's graphic invocations of starvation and racial degeneration.

The success of the NSDAP in the final years of the Weimar Republic is a product of its success at manipulating German memories of the food economy of the First World War. In the face of looming political defeat and increasingly vicious harassment, many German Communists recognized this fact early on. From his self-imposed exile in the United States, Communist agitator Bernhard Menne dedicated himself to proving that hunger rhetoric was an intrinsic part of the country's military ambitions: "the 'hunger of the German people' represented an integral part of all Germany's war plans from the beginning of the present century onward."[155] By harnessing the anxieties and desires caused by popular experiences with food blockades and food aid, Hitler based his platform on a constant invocation of what Menne termed the "lying legend that Germany, after the last war, was deliberately starved by the Allies."[156] In its embrace of this "legend," the Nazi movement developed a vast transnational food economy that was framed not just by the violent reality of war but by the even more violent fantasy of race.

2

Blood and Soil

The Food Economy and the Nazi Racial State

During the run-up to the series of elections that brought Adolf Hitler to power in 1933, electoral posters for the Nazi party claimed that a vote for Hitler was a vote "against hunger and despair." This simple, generic slogan had tremendous resonance. Indeed, both Socialists and Communists were also recruiting voters with similar promises of bread and work. Such political strategies made sense. By 1932, the Great Depression had left eight million of Germany's 20 million workers unemployed, and many of these men and women had not worked for several years. The situation was so severe that a 1932 public health report on European nutrition by the League of Nations singled out Germany for particular concern, as the available data suggested that "serious malnutrition" existed "among millions of unemployed in Germany today."[1] NSDAP food sloganeering was explicitly targeting impoverished industrial workers, hoping to lure them away from their traditional affiliation with the KPD. However, despite such focused propaganda, the Nazi Party enjoyed its greatest popularity not among hungry urbanites but in rural communities.[2] Indeed, without the votes of Germany's farmers, the NSDAP would never have achieved 37 percent of the popular vote in 1932, its strongest results ever at the ballot box. Farmers voted for Hitler because of their own food-related fears. The years 1930 to 1933 had seen dramatic drops in the prices of almost all agricultural commodities, as farmers struggled to meet skyrocketing interest rates while their profits evaporated.[3] In 1932, the year that marked the NSDAP's electoral breakthrough, the country's agricultural income was at its lowest point since 1913.[4]

This agricultural crisis had a major impact on Hitler's early economic policies. One of his first acts as Führer was to establish the Reichsnährstand, or National Food Estate, which centralized the country's food economy in order to optimize state regulation and control. The Reichsnährstand proved successful because of its nearly unlimited power. An American wartime analysis of the German economy noted that "the agricultural sector was the most tightly knit part of the Nazi economy, completely dominated by government agencies. There was not a single agricultural product that was not rigidly controlled by some section of the Reich Food Estate."[5] Hitler marketed this intensive remaking of the country's food economy as a way to protect against the mistakes of the First World War. As Wolfgang Clauß, a leading official in the Ministry for Food and Agriculture, explained in 1938, Hitler's policies promised to "render a starvation of the Volk impossible."[6] Indeed, the incredible reach of the Reichsnährstand had enabled the stockpiling of a six-million-ton grain reserve by 1939, far more than Imperial Germany had possessed at the outbreak of World War I.[7]

The vow to eliminate hunger was one of the NSDAP's first and most important promises, more important for many Germans than ridding the nation of its Jews. Crucially, however, both promises—eliminating Germany's hunger and its Jews—frequently overlapped, eventually becoming synonymous. The Nazi food economy proved to be inseparable from notions of racial difference that pitted disparate groups against one another in a lethal struggle over scarce resources. Nazi theorists defined constant struggle between racial groups as the basic state of human existence. Food, in neo-Malthusian terms representing a "natural" limit on population growth, provided the primary motivation for that conflict while also playing a crucial role in defining the races themselves.

The racialization of hunger was not Hitler's innovation but was rooted in longer traditions of European race thinking. Indeed, the NSDAP's reliance on the modern food system to popularize, rationalize, and "make bodily" the modern fiction of race could be traced back to the foundational logic of Western imperialism. At least since the European discovery of the New World, racialized colonial spaces had promised to satisfy the Old World's insatiable appetites. The race sciences of the nineteenth century, including not only eugenics but also anthropology, anatomy, and archaeology, were predicated on the idea that diet determined racial development, offering an ostensible rationale for imperialism. For Western nutritionists, the colonies provided access to bodies to observe and on which they could experiment, formalizing the link between nutritional sciences and race sciences.[8] In the segregated United States, by the early twentieth century, it had become a commonsensical notion that different races ate differently and that these dietary differences were constitutive of racial identity.[9] Such ideas and the biopolitical sciences that supported them—such as statistics, demography, and medicine—were widespread, ultimately playing a vital part in the ambitions and abilities of modern states to regulate diverse populations and territories.

In Germany, the new sciences of anthropology and nutrition were especially well-developed, inspiring many researchers to explore the link between race and diet. These theorists focused attention on the skull, especially the teeth and lower jaw, in the process developing the "interesting field of comparative nutritional studies" to create hierarchies of cultural sophistication and social development. One such study, for example, traced racial development "from fossilized remnants of the moors to contemporary Bavarians" based on the size of molars and the relative quantities of grains, fruits, and meat in a given diet.[10] A turn-of-the-century German anthropologist explained that the consumption of gelatinous foods by the Chinese explained their weak physical strength, while the predilection among Jews for "blood-drained meat has resulted in a poor ligament quality ... causing flat-footedness and the characteristic non-elastic stride." He asserted that in contrast, the Germanic tribes had traditionally enjoyed "the fruits of the forest, roots, dandelion greens, oats, rye dishes, and an occasional roast." These appetizing foods made German bodies not only strong but beautiful: "the oat straw yellow color of their hair and beards ... is connected to their preference for oats, while there is a striking similarity between the seed case of a ripening rye corn and the blue color of their eyes."[11]

During times of prosperity, this linking of diet with racial characteristics could easily be manipulated to justify imperialism and to rationalize social inequality. However, in times of shortage or escalating societal tension, this logic also meant that hunger could be easily translated into a racial threat. As early as 1921, German medical experts had warned that childhood malnutrition due to the First World War's British Blockade was resulting in "an intensive racial worsening of the growing generation," as inadequate nutrition for "the majority of growing children results naturally in a degeneration of the race."[12] This eugenicist discourse was common across the political spectrum, as activists on the Left as well as the Right shared these fears; a Weimar-era study by several socialist doctors and social workers determined that hunger among the country's working classes "ruins the race, demoralizes it, increases its misery; this [inadequate diet] is the defining feature of our new age, the truest, the most visible, the uncontestable."[13]

Nazi propaganda consolidated and magnified these fears by describing hunger as a weapon wielded by the racial enemy, an enemy who was almost always described as the Jew. As a result, battling hunger became a racial project; slogans like "against hunger and despair" were ultimately as much about race as the statement that "the Jews are our misfortune." Such a personification of hunger appealed to many Germans grappling with both real and anticipated hungers, as it gave them an easy target to blame for their suffering, and implied a simple solution. If the Jew, who was made to symbolize both limitless financial power and excessive appetites, was responsible for Germany's hunger, then removing the Jew would also end hunger—an appealingly simple calculation that proved especially attractive in the face of the seemingly unresolvable hungers of the recent war and postwar years. In 1937, an American journalist interviewed a German woman who claimed that she had gone hungry while "Jews were drinking costly wine and shaking paunchy stomachs to American jazz"; she described watching as their bodies "waxed fat and overbearing while her own people starved in misery,"[14] an experience that she credited with her passionate support for Hitler. She did not need to explicate the connection between Jewish satiety and German hunger; it was self-evident precisely because it was rooted in racial identity, not individual actions. This chapter explores the ways in which food linked Nazi domestic policy with its racist military ambitions, arguing that in this context food served as a fundamental expression of race. An obsessive regulation of what individuals ate provided both the means and the ends for the Nazi assignment of racial identity as well as the management of racial threats. As the American-Jewish activist Boris Shub noted in his 1943 book *Starvation in Europe (Made in Germany)*, "[I]n the hands of the German state, the science of feeding . . . is the race theory in action."[15]

During the Third Reich, food inscribed Nazi racial categories into daily social interactions as well as onto the flesh of individuals, becoming the glue that held together the *Volksgemeinschaft* (people's community). Race shaped diets not only in concentration camps and Jewish ghettoes, but also in German munitions factories, in the villages of occupied Poland and Russia, and on the pastoral farms of Bavaria. Political theorist David Theo Goldberg has argued that the modern state creates and shapes the bodies of its subjects through the penetration of "everyday social life"—the deeper this penetration, "the greater the hold of race over the social horizons of the conceivable."[16] The horrors of the Second World War and the Holocaust reveal that total control over the food economy can push the "horizons of the conceivable" to previously unimaginable extremes. Nazi Germany played a crucial part in the historical development of modern biopower—the ability of states to define and regulate life. By fusing ideological imperatives with biological truisms about bodily needs, the Nazi state transformed food into a constant, everyday reminder of the materiality of the racialized body.

The archives of Nazi Germany are replete with the minutiae of a government that obsessively regulated and re-regulated the consumption of food. Every trip to the grocery store, every factory canteen, every home-cooked meal was transformed into a site for racial performance, assigning collective racial identity at the same time that foodstuffs themselves remade individual bodies in racially predetermined ways. Although Nazi strategists insisted on the inseparability of the acquisition of Ukraine's grain fields, the annihilation of the Jewish race, and the regulation of German bread consumption, these different levels of food production, distribution, and consumption have rarely been analyzed together. This chapter shows how at the individual and collective levels, locally as well as internationally, a highly modern food economy became suffused with race, rather than existing as a separate and supposedly apolitical space of exchange and consumption.

The Food Economy and the Construction of a Racial State

In the fall of 1935, German chancellor Adolf Hitler gave a speech promoting his extraordinarily successful charity drive, the *Winterhilfswerk*, which aimed to feed and clothe the poor during the cold winter months. In his talk, Hitler focused particular attention on one of the oldest and most popular of the drive's programs, the "casserole Sunday" (*Eintopfsonntag*). Admonishing men and women who were reluctant to participate in the program, the Führer explained passionately:

> Don't tell me: "yes, but it will be a hassle" ... you have never known hunger yourself or you would know what a burden hunger is. You have never experienced having nothing to eat, or, even worse, having nothing to give your loved ones to eat. And when someone says to me: "but don't you know, this *Eintopfsonntag*, I'd like to give something, but my belly, my belly is already giving me constant trouble" ... Oh no, no, my dear friend ... whoever does not participate is a characterless parasite of the German people.[17]

The *Eintopfsonntag* was created in October of 1933, just months after Hitler's rise to power. It called for every German man, woman, and child to replace their traditional Sunday cut of meat with a cheaper *Eintopf*, or one-pot meal. The money thus saved was to be donated to the *Winterhilfswerk* organization, where it would be used to care for hungry and impoverished veterans of the First World War. (Later the funds were used for the poor and needy more generally.) The Sunday *Eintopf* was quickly normalized in households and public dining facilities throughout Germany. Restaurants were legally required to offer an *Eintopf* at a reduced rate every Sunday, and these cheap and filling meals became staples in factory canteens. A new genre of *Eintopf* cookbooks flourished, and newspapers and women's magazines popularized a variety of regionally specific and particularly economical recipes.[18]

The *Eintopfsonntag*, in the words of one of the many German publications celebrating Nazi charity, was "the best and most successful socialist component of the German *Volk*."[19] The significance of the *Eintopf* was its ability to consolidate two key aspects of the Nazi food economy: food's potential ability to represent, reflect, and create racial identity, and the *Eintopf*'s celebration of sacrifice, self-denial, and hunger as central to racial health. These two strands of Nazi racial thinking shaped the Third Reich's food economy in crucial ways, as Hitler and other leading National Socialists struggled to align state policy with the inconsistent and often contradictory premises of Nazi race thinking. Thus the *Eintopf* can be seen as an early and remarkably successful attempt to embed Nazism's particular form of racism in everyday food habits.

Until the rise to power of the NSDAP, the *Eintopf* was not a prominent part of the German culinary repertoire. The dish, usually an assortment of vegetables and cheap cuts of meat cooked together in a single pot, was associated with poverty cooking and found primarily in North Germany.[20] Although stews and casseroles were common throughout central Europe, they were not necessarily known as *Eintopf*. The Nazi appropriation of this culinary genre was rooted in both ideology and practicality. The dish was based on indigenous German food products, primarily root vegetables, dried fruits, beans, and pork. These "native" foods were cooked together, without hierarchy or individual preparation, in a single pot, so that ingredients as well as cooking technique expressed the direct link between food and race. Cooking in one pot (*ein Topf*) was supposed to symbolize the Nazi creation of "one people" (*ein Volk*), the crafting of a delicious casserole by combining diverse ingredients analogous to the uniting of the various native German peoples into a single and self-sustaining whole. The ritualization of the consumption of the *Eintopf*, linked as it was to a specific time and day, further underscored its performative power. Nazi nutritionists' assertions that "a strong bond unites people of the same race and same diet" were made real and public every Sunday when the nation consumed the *Eintopf*.[21]

Perhaps the most important aspect of the *Eintopfsonntag*, and what made it so important to the Party while ensuring its remarkable popularity, was the way in which the *Eintopf* allowed the NSDAP to frame eating as, in the words of a 1935 celebration of Nazi charity programs, "a common burden ... [and] collective sacrifice."[22] A regional report on the *Winterhilfswerk* highlighted the sacrificial nature of the *Eintopf*:

> [T]he monthly casserole-eating bring us together to form a community that knows no hierarchy of class or birth ... the casserole is the fast-meal [*Fastmahl*] of the German nation. Just as faithful Christians unite in the holy sacrament of the last supper in service of their lord and master, so too does the National Socialist Germany celebrate this sacrificial meal [*Opfermahl*] as a solemn vow to the unshakeable people's community.[23]

When German housewives agreed to go "a little hungry" in order to feed even hungrier veterans, the German Volk was strengthened and fed. When, however, individuals chose to eat more than their share, they were "stealing" food from the collective, revealing themselves to be leeches, ticks, or "characterless parasites" sucking resources from the Volk.

Such religiously inflected rhetoric of sacrifice was by no means a Nazi innovation; a similar discourse had been invoked during the First World War by Germans, as well as most other belligerents, as they attempted to link civilian wartime deprivation with future victory. In particular, participants in that war had consistently justified homefront rationing as a form of "shared sacrifice," claiming that women's deprivations at home enabled more food to be sent to soldiers at the front. This discourse, however, was existentially different from the Nazi veneration of the *Eintopf* and, more generally, the Party's embrace of self-abnegation. During the Third Reich, sacrifice was in the service of the Volk; the collective racial body purportedly thrived because of the voluntary hunger of individual Germans. Race scientists used their research to justify national policies of austerity when they proclaimed that too much and too rich food was as dangerous to the race as too little. A 1938 analysis of the country's epic "Struggle for Bread" claimed that

> the German people is accustomed from days immemorial to the difficult battle to acquire its daily bread. We do not regret this fate, for this mighty struggle for bread has made the German people, over the course of centuries, tough and hardworking, thus enabling the German people to achieve accomplishments that have been admired around the world, allowing us to gaze with pride upon the great history of our nation.[24]

Even more explicitly, Hugo Hertwig, dietary expert and a leading figure in the German natural foods movement, explained in 1938 that eating a racially appropriate diet—one based on native German foods rather than imported ones—ensured that all members of a given community would remember that food was "originally and by necessity always associated with self-sacrifice."[25]

Amid this rhetoric of self-abnegation and racial health, Hitler's vegetarianism and spartan eating habits were the subject of substantial media coverage. Reports on the radio and in newspapers encouraged families to eat less meat and to consume more local vegetables and brown bread "like the Führer." Hitler's vegetarianism was described in a 1936 guide to healthy living as the source of his "wonderful freshness and liveliness."[26] This alternative dietary regime supported Nazi rhetoric both because it represented abstinence, self-sacrifice, and modesty, and because it reflected Hitler's belief in the mystical power of diet over the individual human as well as the collective body of the Volk. Crucially, the rise of the *Eintopf* and, more generally, the indoctrination of this discourse of gustatory self-denial, took place in the prewar years, between 1933 and 1939. Conceptualized by Nazi leaders as part of the general preparation for war and for austerity, the German public ironically associated this new way of eating with peace and prosperity.

During the early years of the Third Reich, German men, women, and children were compelled to adopt a racially appropriate diet that demanded self-denial in terms of both the quantity and the kind of food consumed. Nutritionists claimed that native foods nourished the Aryan body better than enervating imported foreign foods. Housewives were expected to insist on food grown in Germany; a true *Eintopf* could not be made from imported potatoes. A cookbook titled *Housewives, Now You Must Use What the Field Gives You! Healthy, Nourishing Meals from Native Soil* encouraged every German wife and mother to "design her cooking plan from the products of our home soil, and in so doing include almost no meat, very few eggs and only the necessary amount of fat," a form of abstinence that would ensure the health of the Volk.[27] Even food names and cooking terminology mattered; the Aryan canteen chef was reminded to

> always show that you are a German not only in thinking and acting, but also in speaking, so that when you are working you should always use your German mother tongue rather than the countless foreign words that are as unnecessary as they are outdated. We do not need to imitate the cuisine and language of foreign peoples; rather we are willing and able to shape and refine our own cuisine and kitchen language ourselves.[28]

While this new culinary imaginary stretched to encompass all members of the *Volksgemeinschaft*, it primarily targeted women as those responsible for regulating civilian food intake. The Nazi state dedicated tremendous energy to educating housewives; regional centers distributed millions of posters, board games, and pamphlets teaching new cooking skills and promoting particular commodities such as whole-grain bread, quark, potatoes, fish, and homemade preserves, all to support Nazi goals of autarchy and restricted food intake. As the "gatekeepers" of familial food consumption, women were responsible for controlling their husbands' and children's appetites, and ensuring that the family's tastes matched state requirements.[29] These new demands dramatically increased the amount of work required of Germany's mothers and wives. For example, experts recommended that women replace the traditional cold supper of bread and sliced meats with a warm cooked dish (usually based on potatoes) in order to reduce consumption of both bread and fats. Women were supposed to not only cook different, often more labor-intensive recipes, but also to substitute homemade products, such as jams and vegetable conserves, for their store-bought counterparts. Gardening and the gathering of wild comestibles were heavily encouraged by the state and carried out primarily by women and children.

As the Nazi state ramped up for war over the 1930s, food propaganda aimed to prevent women from complaining about the increasingly restrictive food situation. Nazi officials often emphasized to women the need to accept regulations and embrace new recipes without complaint. A 1938 publication, "Nutritional Politics and Schooling," dedicated to improving German girls' understanding of nutrition, agriculture, and racial hygiene, ominously warned that "in the long term it is not viable that portions of our Volk, out of ignorance of our farmers' hard labor on German soil, are totally uninterested in their [i.e. the farmers'] concerns, but are nonetheless eager to speak up when any sort of food desire or habit is for once not entirely satisfied."[30] Food shortages under the Third Reich were transformed into tests of will as well as expressions of racial allegiance; the vitality of the collective relied on the austerity of the individual. As early as 1934, when the country's food supply was relatively stable and rationing still years away, women were sternly warned not to purchase more than their "fair share": "should, atypically, temporary difficulties [with the food supply] emerge, the most important issue is to maintain discipline when shopping, rather than allowing a lack of discipline, fear-based hoarding, or the spreading of rumors to make this unpleasantness even worse."[31] A 1940 cartoon suggests that the only real food shortages in Nazi Germany were of luxury products; consumer complaints were thus an expression of greed rather than need. The cartoon depicts an overweight woman complaining that she is "starving" while literally drowning in domestically grown staples like cucumbers, plums, and carrots (see Figure 2.1.) Indeed, Nazi pundits informed the population that within the new racial state, it was impossible for a true German to experience hunger; "there is no German comrade and no German housewife who is not able to acquire on the market what is necessary to feed the family."[32]

Past German hungers always were blamed on the twinned forces of Jews and industrial capitalism, evils which had seduced Germany into the trap of "global economic thinking."[33] For example, the British Blockade was blamed on Germany's dependence on the international food economy. In a not entirely inaccurate retelling of the recent past, agronomists and economists complained that the country's growth over the nineteenth century had been caused by the industrial revolution and the pressures of growing rates of urbanization; in contrast, agriculture had been sorely neglected and was shrinking in both size and political power. This, in turn, had caused low levels of food productivity and a related dependence on cheap food imports, the factors that had insured that the blockade would have devastating consequences. In the opening speech of the 1936 agricultural exposition *Grüne Woche* (Green Week), the minister of food and agriculture Walther Darré explained that "German agriculture was, as a

Figure 2.1 "Help, I am starving! There are still no bananas!" 1940. BArch Plak 003-023-071/Fuchs.

result of being bound to the world market, unfree and abandoned to the game of global speculation and the stock market . . . our task therefore was to liberate the food supply of the German *Volk* from this slavery."[34]

Traditional anti-Semitic tropes linking Jews to global capital merged with this narrative of national hunger, revealing that "the will of international Jewry had the goal of making Germany absolutely unfree in the realm of food supplies."[35] In 1937, Darré published his study of the "pig murder" of the First World War, in which he blamed the ill-fated decision to slaughter the country's pig holdings to reduce the need for animal fodder on a Jewish conspiracy to decimate Germany's fat supply.[36] Eliminating the country's Jews thus became equated with the autarchic economic policy of separating Germany from the global market by eliminating food imports. The country's food supply thus contained the promise of both economic stability and racial health. Konrad Meyer, an agricultural scientist who held the post of Commissioner for the Consolidation of German Ethnicity and was responsible for the "resettlement of the Eastern Territories," explained in 1938 that

> in National Socialist state building, agriculture fulfills not only the economic function of producing food and thus existing as a core basis of the peoples' economy, but ultimately it is the nation's reserve of biological

strength. And this biological purpose is of the same importance, yes even more important, as the economic.[37]

Seen in a longer historical context, these Nazi policies marked a significant shift from nineteenth-century notions of sustenance and prosperity. Earlier visions of the ideal German diet, modeled on the policies of leading imperial powers such as England, sought to feed Germany through a network of global commerce and colonial extraction. Before and even during the First World War, the country's scientists had dreamt that

> in the future we will not only produce great harvests of healthy, long-lasting potatoes from German agriculture, but also in German Africa we will produce valuable sweet potatoes and excellent eggs, and both German farm houses and African negro-huts will be lit with German oil lamps, a healthy light, unlike the unclear light of American petroleum ... [in Africa] government-run bakeries will serve as training schools, spreading knowledge of German baking skills and food preservation techniques, while travelling teachers trained in food science could improve poultry breeding.[38]

In the wake of the country's defeat in 1918, however, Germany's goals changed from overseas colonial extraction to the principles of economic self-sufficiency and the simultaneous expansion into Eastern Europe.

The Nazis' own interpretation of autarchy was that it was not simply an economic or agricultural project. Leading nutritionist Hans Glatzel reminded his readers in 1939 that

> the battle for food autarchy affects everyone: the doctor and the nutritionist, the botanist, the geneticist and the chemist, the farmer and the gardener, the baker, the butcher, the housewife and the family father. There is not a single member of the *Volk* who is not affected by food and nutrition.[39]

Self-sufficiency in foodstuffs was seen as necessary for racial survival; being well-fed did not mean simply having enough to eat, it meant having the right sorts of foods grown in the proper locations. In the words of a 1939 nutritional guide,

> a healthy diet is the same thing as a diet that is connected to the soil. That which the German land can produce is healthy for the German body. Foods that are specific to this soil have kept the German people

strong for thousands of years; it would be foolhardy to deny or ignore this fact.[40]

German foods were thus by definition healthy, authentic, and vital, in contrast to flavorless, non-nutritive, and enervating foreign foods. With true Nazi zeal, the manufacturer of the culinary product "Prittlbacher Herb Mixture with a 'Pepper' flavor" protested the directive to label his mixture a "pepper substitute," "since in my opinion our peppery herb mix cannot be seen as a 'substitute,' since it is made from processing the purest German herbs. Basil and marjoram and paprika are after all not replacement herbs—they are pure herbs."[41] Nutritional chemist Max Winckel vowed that turning exclusively to grains grown in German soil to produce the country's breads would be enough to "counter hunger [and] eliminate scarcity."[42]

In the imagined riches of the "traditional" German diet, the single most racially charged food was bread—more specifically, *Vollkornbrot*, translated literally as "whole-grain bread" but generally meaning bread made from rye rather than wheat flour. Germans' particular predilection for dark rye bread had been accepted as a defining characteristic since the nineteenth century. During the Third Reich, Germany's historic identity as a "rye land" was contrasted with the effeminate, wasteful, and weak "white bread lands," particularly France and Great Britain, where, German nutritionists claimed, the artificial vitaminization of bread flour was necessary to maintain popular health.[43] In contrast, dark breads—pumpernickels and ryes—made with barley and native seeds rather than costlier and less healthful wheat berries, nourished German uniqueness as well as intellectual and physical vigor. *Vollkornbrot*, made from the entire grain, expressed the German affinity for wholeness, naturalness, and purity, and "native" *Vollkornbrot* became an ideal metaphor for a healthy, independent, and uncontaminated *Volk* that was strong in its isolation: "In the battle for bread freedom [i.e., independence from wheat imports], the entire German *Volk* has unified itself insofar as it follows the Führer. . . . [T]he new ethos of bread finds its most beautiful expression in the words of a young poet: we are the grain!"[45] Indeed, German bodies were often depicted as being mystically composed of rolling rye fields (see Figure 2.2.)

As the foundational food of the *Volk*, bread was also deeply racialized. According to a 1939 analysis of the global Jewish wheat monopoly, "the Jewish race reveals its core difference nowhere more clearly than in the issue of bread."[44] By linking Jewishness with wheat flour, the Nazis aimed to reverse the general European trend to value white wheat bread over dark rye; nutritionists cast rye bread as not only healthful but as sacred, warning mothers to "teach your children to honor bread, and not tolerate that they let even one piece dry out and be thrown away!"[46] Ominously, in 1936, Hermann Göring, Commander of the Air

Figure 2.2 "Eat vitamin-rich whole-grain bread. It contains all the nourishment of the grain, it strengthens bones, blood, and nerves, prevents cavities, is easier to digest, satiates, and is regulated by the State." Courtesy of the Stadtgeschichtliches Museum Leipzig.

Force and close confidante of Hitler, warned that "whoever misuses the holiest product of a nation, the bread grains of the German people, is a traitor and must be destroyed."[47] This threat explicitly targeted Jews. While a true Aryan man, woman, or child "senses the godhead and the deepest sense of existence" when he sees rye fields, "for [the Jew] grain and bread are not something holy ... the Jew sees [in grain] only an outstanding opportunity for making profit, for speculation and for exploitation."[48] Two years later, a school nutrition textbook celebrated the people's embrace of rye bread rather than wheat by proudly declaring that "the world market no longer delivers the German *Volk* its bread, but rather the German farmer and agriculturalist."[49] Already in 1934, the Nazi Party had declared a "battle for production" to increase agricultural yields and to change the make-up of domestic food production in order to better substitute for imports. Specifically, German farmers were tasked with ending the country's dependence on foreign markets for both fodder and fats. The NSDAP hoped to achieve these goals through an increased use of fertilizer and technologies, especially tractors, changes which did initially improve yields; the first year of Nazi rule saw a record harvest. However, the subsequent year saw substantial drops in both rye and wheat crops. Despite all efforts to the contrary, the country could only achieve modest improvements—about 10 percent—in its total food production. In fact, Nazi Germany actually increased the country's fat deficit, largely due to the demands of rearmament and then of the war itself; by 1936, more than half of the country's fats still had to be imported.[50] Nonetheless, "nutritional freedom" remained the official goal and was continually invoked as a guarantor of racial health and, after 1939, of military victory.

Attracted by these ambitions, German farmers were among the Party's most passionate supporters. The rhetoric of "blood and soil" (*Blut und Boden*) suggested a way out of their social and material crisis and implied a restoration of a perceived loss of prestige. In the March 1933 elections, peasant communities in Northern and Eastern Germany had been the only segments of the population to give Hitler an absolute majority. During the first five years of Hitler's rule, the largest and most impressive Nazi celebration, larger even than the vast national Party rallies in Nuremberg, was the annual harvest festival, the *Erntedankfest*. First held in October 1933, the festival, which at its peak was attended by over a million visitors, celebrated the spiritual and biological advantages of eating indigenous food products, and served as a public display of the symbolic significance of peasants and the rural population for the Nazi Party.

Further confirming the centrality of the peasantry to the country, one of the first major laws passed under Hitler's new regime was the September 1933 Reich Farm Inheritance Law, which regulated and radically restricted the inheritance of midsized German farms; nonethnic Germans were prohibited from owning these farms, and they could only be inherited by a single son. The law's primary function was to make explicit the link between racial and agricultural law, since "the fate of our *Volk* depends decisively upon whether . . . a healthy farming element can be maintained as the base of national existence."[51] Walther Darré explicitly prioritized the racial function of the farmer above his practical role as "feeder of the nation." In a 1938 speech, he proudly noted that he had

> always emphasized that farmers have a dual task: on the one hand to ensure the feeding of the *Volk*, on the other to be the blood source of the German *Volk*. In this day and age, guaranteeing the food situation is so much at the fore of our concerns that people often . . . only see this task, and believe that farmers are only important because they ensure the food supply. They are not always aware of the far more essential task of the farmer, his life's mission: to be the blood source of the nation.[52]

The Austrian journalist Anton Zischka, registered NSDAP member and internationally best-selling author, claimed in his 1938 book *Bread for Two Billion People*, "No *Volk* can endure as long as it does not recognize that only one thing is eternal: blood and soil . . . [H]e who produces food is thus as earthshaking as hunger itself."[53]

Nazi propaganda depicted the country's rural communities as bastions of racial purity as well as authentic German traditions. By casting farmers as preservers of a mythic German past, this rhetoric placed them in implicit opposition to modernization and its associated harms. Thus, in accordance with the embrace of so-called "traditional" dietary habits, German peasants provided a gustatory model for the Nazi state. Nazi food innovations were always described as a return to former foodways rather than as modern innovations or new ways of eating. The far-off past was linked not with hunger and poverty but with health and abundance, and citizens were encouraged "to match their diet to products that can be produced naturally and that are rooted in the soil, as was the case in earlier eras."[54] Hitler sponsored various projects to gather, preserve, and disseminate "native" foodways among the various "native" German races. Disappointingly, such studies rarely confirmed the sort of authenticity and anti-modernity idealized by the NSDAP. A 1935 study of rural communities in Westphalia, for example, required local communities to submit a detailed report on traditional cooking among the peasantry. Many communities simply did not answer the survey on first and even second requests, and a surprising number of respondents denied the existence of any sort of authentic culinary culture. As one frustrated official stated, "I must report that in this area there are no traditions that are related to special foods or dishes. In this area on St. Martin's Day in prosperous circles a goose is consumed. However, this custom is generally widespread and by no means a special habit of the peasantry."[55] Nonetheless, the NSDAP continued to fetishize the imagined German diet of an imagined German farming community.

In addition to celebrating food producers themselves, the NSDAP dramatically increased funding for food- and nutrition-related sciences. The transition from the Weimar Republic to the Nazi dictatorship was marked by impressive growth in state support for agriculturally related research projects. Both the German Research Foundation (*Deutsche Forschungsgemeinschaft*) and the Reich Research Council (*Reichsforschungsrat*) shifted their priorities toward funding projects in biology and agriculture. There was particular support for projects aiming to increase agricultural productivity in order to reduce imports and increase grain stores, as well as for projects to develop domestic ersatz products, especially fats. Nazi scientists also explored ways to optimize animal and plant breeding and to develop varieties of food crops that were resistant to climactic vagaries and disease. Spending further increased with the outbreak of war in 1939. Between 1937 and 1943, the agricultural and nutritional sciences made up about a third of Germany's total science spending; in every year except for 1942 agriculture received more funding than any other branch of scientific research, including military research and medicine.[59] Thus, at the same time that farming and food consumption were reified as timeless, traditional, and "anti-modern," scientific innovation shaped the agricultural and nutritional sciences.[60]

Unsurprisingly, nutritionists basked in the new importance placed on their discipline, embracing the Nazi state's support of dietary research and accepting without complaint the total removal of Jews from their professional ranks.[56] An American assessment of Nazi agricultural policy noted the irony of the country's anti-Semitic policies, which resulted, among countless others, in the resignation of Fritz Haber, the man whose discovery of nitrogen fixing was "in a measure responsible for Nazi achievement in agriculture."[57] Nonetheless, most German experts affirmed the racialized understanding of nutrition advocated by the NSDAP and eagerly deployed their expertise in the service of what they saw as a battle for racial survival. In the same year that Germany invaded Poland, the internationally renowned vitaminologist Arthur Scheunert affirmed the explicit link between the country's very existence and food supply in a letter to the Ministry of Food and Agriculture: "Diet is the foundational concern of every *Volk*. A people can only have permanence if its diet is correct. If through social, climactic or other causes changes happen that lead to [dietary] mistakes, then degeneration and ultimately extinction are the unavoidable consequences."[58]

The prioritization of farming and food production by the Nazi state reflects the inseparability of food concerns from military goals. A year before the invasion of Poland, the *New York Times* interpreted Nazi investment in the food system as part of the country's buildup to war, reporting that Germany's "success in winning a war depends as much on food as on high explosives or airplanes."[61] During the early years of the war, the seeming invincibility of the German army was attributed to its outstanding diet; a 1941 study in an American medical journal noted that "the great efficiency of the German Army has been ascribed not only to its excellent arms and the best of training but also to its use of special methods of nutrition," noting with admiration that "the science of nutrition had progressed at a rapid pace when the new German government began with the upbuilding of its conscripted army."[62] Certainly, the army was the primary beneficiary of the state's nutritional research; soldiers' rations benefitted from the various innovations in food processing technologies developed by Nazi scientists, especially in the areas of food dehydration and freezing. According to a *Harper's Magazine* exposé published in 1946, Nazi food scientists had developed techniques that bordered on the miraculous, including new forms of butter and cheese, a near-limitless method of producing a high-protein yeast, and "new, advanced refrigeration techniques." The confidential report was especially impressed by a new way of preserving food based on "a secret plastics mixture"; according to the report, when bread "fresh from the oven was dipped, dried, redipped, then heated half an hour at 285 degrees," it was found to remain "unspoiled and good to eat eight months later."[63] Certainly, such products bore little resemblance to the traditional *Vollkornbrot* advocated by the Führer; they were nonetheless authentic products of the Nazi food economy.

Far more significant than its innovations in food production, however, were Nazi Germany's innovations in the production of hunger. In the attempt to reserve "real food" for Aryans, German scientists developed pseudo-foods for racial inferiors that proved more damaging than no food at all. As a 1943 article published by the American Academy of Political and Social Science summarized: "the great blessings which the modern science of nutrition has to offer to mankind, the demonical scientists of Germany now turn on upon mankind as instruments of torture."[64] German nutritionists claimed that a sort of juice made of pine needles could serve as "a supply of vitamin C for the protection against diseases of malnourishment among [Soviet] POWs"; they noted that, due to its indigestibility, "distribution [of the tonic] is only an option when rations contain very few foods with vitamins."[65] In an especially well-documented example of this sort of non-feeding, in the summer of 1943, minister of the interior, head of the SS, and trained agronomist Heinrich Himmler enthusiastically described a new form of "celluloid-sausage" recently developed by German scientists and immediately incorporated into prisoner rations at Mauthausen concentration camp. Hundreds of inmates in Mauthausen suffered horribly and ultimately died from being served this inedible "ersatz-food," which had a 75 percent death rate among consumers.[66] As the science of food was harnessed to serve the ambitions of a race war, a wave of nutritional experiments and feeding innovations linked the fates of Aryans and non-Aryans through deadly acts of food acquisition and food deprivation.

War, Land, and Grain

Since Hitler's earliest writings, it had been clear that his plans for Germany's food economy were in the service of a massive war effort. He rightly predicted that this future war would demand that Germans produce more food and eat differently. Most importantly, it would require that millions of non-Germans starve to death. The Nazi veneration of whole-grain bread was not simply a matter of taste or custom; it was the food that epitomized the state's racial fantasies and military ambitions. According to Nazi ideology, grain cultivation was the ideal form of land use, a belief that provided the rationale for their obsession with the embattled soil of the East. Not coincidentally, the German drive for autarchy focused primarily on grain production, a platform that was inseparable from the outbreak of the war. The Nazi Party promoted a program of agricultural reform that demanded the acquisition of massive amounts of new farmland as it simultaneously claimed that German soil should only be owned and tilled by German people. On the opening page of *Mein Kampf*, Hitler had articulated the inseparability of racial war from the acquisition of food-producing territory:

> Only when the boundaries of the Reich include even the last German, only when it is no longer possible to assure him of his daily bread within them, does there arise, out of the distress of the nation, the moral right to acquire foreign soil and territory. The sword is then the plow, and from the tears of war grows the daily bread for generations to come.[67]

In this rhetoric, grain cultivation becomes the justification for expansion and invasion—in other words, for the war itself. Within Germany, what was termed the "battle for rye" melded domestic agricultural policy with brutal military policy by linking the desperate push for increased food production with the seizure of the croplands of eastern Europe. Grain here became a shorthand for "land": it both symbolized and was produced by fertile soil, which, in turn, nourished the Aryan race. In the words of Hugo Hertwig, "If we are to approach the food question as a question of perfecting the race, then we must understand it as intimately intertwined with the question of land."[68] As a result, the cultivation of the soil was transformed into an act of racial war. Max Winckel programmatically declared that "the battle for existence is the battle for fertile soil, for food, it is the battle against hunger, it is the source of all war and revolution."[69] Invoking this merger of bloodshed and grain production, the minister of propaganda Joseph Goebbels explained the 1941 invasion of the USSR as the drive "for grain and bread, for an overflowing breakfast, lunch and dinner table . . . we finally want to be able to claim what is ours."[70]

The interdependence of food, land, and race gave rise to the brutality of the Second World War, which the Nazis officially waged under the banner of "blood and soil." Food linked individual racial identity to physical space, a belief that explains both the unimaginable violence of the war and the appeal of the Nazi racial community within Germany. The imagined threat of Aryan extinction through hunger inspired the country's contradictory ambitions. On the one hand, Germans were required to feed themselves exclusively with the products of their "native soil." On the other hand, they needed to radically expand the borders of this "native" soil by seizing huge sections of Eastern Europe that had long been cultivated by racial enemies: Slavs and Jews. What connected these goals was Germany's natural right to *Lebensraum*, or "living space"; if it did not acquire this land, then it would perish.

Both soldiering and farming were projects to protect and invigorate "blood and soil." A 1935 analysis of the German farmer asserted that the desire to "return to simplicity, to a diet based on rye grown on the meager German soil as the model," represented "a race war that is not fought by men with their weapons but a fight wherein all of the strength of the family and the race is brought to the fields."[71] Such metaphors grew increasingly militant as war grew closer; territorial expansion was continually equated with food acquisition. The annexation of Austria in 1938 inspired the sixth edition of a Weimar-era dietary reform book that advocated the consumption of rye bread, *Truths about Bread*. The newly composed preface noted that "the happiest of facts can be stated with this edition: we are making energetic progress on the path to the necessary reform of our bread habits in this new and now larger Germany!"[72] Months later, as the invasion of Poland signaled the beginning of the war, the Whole-Grain Bread Committee (*Reichsvollkornbrotausschuss*) was founded in Germany under the leadership of nutritionist Franz Wirz.[73]

The linking of race with land cast the racial struggle between the Aryan and his enemies in terms of land and agriculture. One of the most pervasive tropes of European anti-Semitism had been that there was an intrinsic opposition between Jews and agricultural labor: the Jew was, by definition, not a farmer. During the Third Reich, this long-held prejudice explicitly slated Jews for annihilation. Herbert Backe, an influential figure in the Ministry of Food and Agriculture under Darré, stated that "racially and historically, Jews had proven themselves incapable of agricultural labor, and any attempt to train them to become farmers was bound to fail."[74] The anti-Semitic rhetoric that claimed an opposition between Jews and healthy rye crops underpinned Nazi visions of *Lebensraum* in the vast plains of Poland, Belarus, Ukraine, and Russia. The populations of the East, generally referred to as "Slavs," were singled out for their slovenly and ineffective farming techniques; indeed, Poles and Russians were often described not as farmers at all, but as scavengers or as modified hunter-gatherers.[75] Backe, who had been born and raised in Russia, had originally specialized in Soviet agricultural science; his dissertation, written in 1926, argued that the backward grain economy of Russia was an intrinsic expression of the flawed character of the Slavic race.[76]

Since the First World War, German military strategists had been declaring Germany's "right" to acquire farmland in the East, complaining both that "Russia is over-rich in land" and that "the Russian population is not so firmly rooted in the soil as is that of western and central Europe."[77] The Nazis adopted this particular vision of the East. It was the drive for grain in the East that allowed the NSDAP to describe the invasions of Poland and later the Soviet Union as necessary for collective survival and as defensive responses against powers that were aiming to starve the German people. By linking (Aryan) blood with a natural claim to specific tracts of land in Central and Eastern Europe, racial and cultural survival became synonymous with having "enough to eat," something that was allegedly only possible with access to the soil of the Soviet Union, especially Ukraine.[78] In 1942, when Nazi Germany controlled vast portions of the western Soviet Union as well as central Europe, newly appointed minister of food and agriculture Backe confidently declared that

> the reconstruction of this space is currently underway. Clearly it is not possible to overcome the consequences of war and decades of Bolshevik mismanagement in only a few months . . . [however] the vital energy of the many thousands of German farmers and agrarian workers who have been sent to the east since the last summer will achieve a steady increase in the food surplus produced in these regions beginning next year.[79]

As late as 1944, Nazi officials defined military victory and defeat above all as matters of satiety and hunger:

> A victory of the enemy would officially damn all of Europe to becoming barren steppes, to waste away and to hunger. Germany's victory, which after all we are certain of, will preserve the European continent in its agricultural productivity and its internal strength and vigor for eternity.[80]

In the short term, the war did bring about an increase in Germany's food supply. However the foodstuffs that the German people acquired from the East were the result of violent military seizure rather than the products of skilled Aryan cultivation. Soldiers did not win foreign land for future food production; they were officially encouraged to seize local foodstuffs and consume them personally or to send them to their families. To facilitate such transfers, postal restrictions on international food shipments to Germany, as well as traditional limitations on wartime food seizure, were officially lifted; soldiers thus fought for the actual foods that they and their wives and children ate.[81] As a result, during the early years of the war, the pleasures of unlimited access to local foodstuffs enabled invading German soldiers to connect their fighting with their loved ones at home, and implicated those on the home front who consumed these foods. German civilians were well aware of the military's rapacious policies of seizure. When domestic rations increased, German housewives were told that it was because of the "sacrificial bravery of our soldiers," who had successfully conquered "the fertile eastern regions" so that they could "deliver food surpluses to the German homeland."[82] The eggs, butter, sausages, and grains seized from occupied Europe thus ensured support for the Nazi war machine by feeding the population. In this way, the abstract rhetoric of a war being fought for racial survival became comprehensible and meaningful to ordinary Germans.

By the time the Nazi army invaded the Soviet Union in June 1941, however, Germany's grain surplus had been decimated, profoundly destabilizing supplies for the German homefront. Underpinned by this pressing need, Operation Barbarossa (the code name given to the invasion) connected the acquisition of vast swathes of Soviet territory with the death by starvation of entire populations. According to the minutes of a Nazi army organizational meeting held just prior to the invasion: "1. The war can only continue to be waged if the entire army is fed from Russia. 2. As a result, x million people will doubtlessly starve, if that which is necessary for us is extracted from the land."[83] Nazi policy in the East perceived the interests of the local peoples as incompatible with German ones: the grain of the East could feed either Germans or Slavs, but not both. This was not simply rhetoric; between 1941 and 1943, the occupied Soviet territories provided Nazi Germany with 7 million tons of grains, 2.7 million tons of potatoes, and 325,000 tons of edible fat.[84] Strikingly, despite these merciless seizure policies, the war with the Soviet Union did not profit the German food economy; Germans had received more grain from the USSR through legal trade in the two years prior to the invasion than they took by force between 1941 and 1944.[85]

Brutal policies of food theft, rather than Aryan agricultural skills, thus made up the heart of the much-vaunted Nazi food system. German historian Lochar Burchardt has calculated that without these vast amounts of stolen foods, Nazi Germany's food supply was actually below the levels maintained during the First World War.[86] A recent analysis found that the Third Reich extracted about a third of the food it needed from occupied Europe.[87] For German civilians, the steady flow of foodstuffs from occupied territories helped establish a vast transnational economy of rationing and starvation along racial lines. As of 1942, when Nazi control over Europe was at its peak but domestic food supplies were shrinking under the tremendous weight of the war effort, all food deliveries from Germany to soldiers in the field were called off. Troops in the East were thus required to feed themselves entirely from the land they occupied, regardless of the consequences for the local population. Thereafter, the vast majority of food seized from Eastern Europe went directly to soldiers, with little trickling into Germany for the hungry homefront.[88] The year 1942 also marked the first use of dedicated death camps to murder Jews and other racial enemies. From the Nazi perspective, killing millions of Jews across Eastern Europe would free up vast quantities of "surplus" foodstuffs; this new surplus would be added to the spoils of unlimited food seizure. Ultimately, especially for poorer regions of the continent, these policies meant starvation not only for Jews but for all local populations.

As a result, hunger was the dominant experience of the war for most non-German Europeans; all countries except for Axis powers Austria, Italy, and Germany, and neutral Portugal, Sweden, and Switzerland, faced major food crises, if not downright famine. The *New York Times* wrote in 1942 that food deprivation played a key role in the shockingly high levels of collaboration seen throughout occupied Western Europe:

> Next to the firing squad, food is Nazi Germany's most powerful weapon in forcing collaboration from the captive peoples of Europe.... [T]he loyal Frenchman, Hollander or Dane who so far has been able to keep body and soul together may weaken and take a job in Germany this winter when the Nazi bleeding of his country's already meager foodstuffs is pressed to the point of starvation and he sees his family, already undernourished, emaciated and suffering the anguish of slow death.[89]

Figure 2.3, taken from Shub's *Starvation in Europe*, graphically depicts the hierarchies that defined Europe's food economy in 1943. The image measures each country's allotted rations against the German norm; at the bottom of the ranking are the Greeks and the Jews, receiving respectively 31 percent and 21 percent of the amount received by the average German. The image makes clear that in southern and Eastern Europe, Nazis used hunger not to pressure and control populations but to eliminate them.

German soldiers, especially those on the Eastern Front, experienced starvation as something intertwined with, and indistinguishable from, military conflict. Shooting local inhabitants and starving them were simply different means

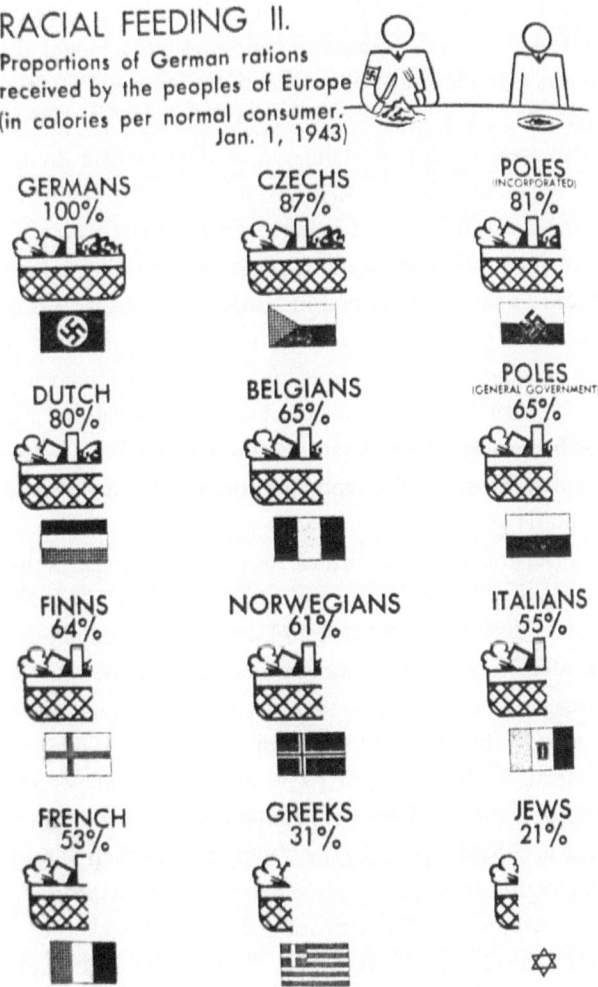

Figure 2.3 Racial Feeding II. From Boris Shub, Zorah Warhaftig, and Institute of Jewish Affairs, *Starvation over Europe (Made in Germany): A Documented Record, 1943.* New York: Institute of Jewish Affairs of the American Jewish Congress and World Jewish Congress, 1943, 48.

to the same end. Military policy in the East called for the starvation of whole cities and regions, so that many German soldiers literally watched as thousands of men, women, and children starved to death. More people died in the besieged city of Leningrad—most of them from a lack of food—than British and American soldiers combined during the entire war effort.[90] Nazi food seizure was especially devastating in Ukraine, the "breadbasket of Europe" and a region that was still reeling from a devastating famine caused by Stalin's brutal collectivization policies. Large percentages of the populations of the cities of Kiev and

Kharkiv perished from hunger.[91] A German soldier serving in Belorussia wrote home in July 1942 that "if the campaign continues much longer, they will have to make sausages of the Jews and offer them to the Russian POWs or the skilled Jewish laborers."[92]

The German army's defeat at Stalingrad in 1943 marked the turning point of the war. As the German army was forced to retreat, the Germans themselves began to starve alongside their intended victims. As was the case with Soviet civilians, the majority of German soldiers who died at Stalingrad perished from hunger and cold. A soldier described in his diary a diet that was eerily evocative of the starvation meals reserved for Soviet POWs by the Nazi nutritionists: "morning and evening two thin slices of bread, for lunch a thin soup, absolutely no potatoes . . . Today there was horsemeat—a very special day."[93] German soldiers who had been lucky enough to survive the actual fighting were either taken to poorly supplied Soviet POW camps or continued to fight in an army that increasingly could not feed its own.

Given the inseparability of Germans' food provisioning and the war effort, it is unsurprising that the country's food situation rapidly worsened as its military approached defeat in 1944 and 1945. Although guidelines distributed to military leaders continued to explain that "the readiness to fight and the force of an engaged troops are more than anything else dependent on the feeding of the troops,"[94] the dire food situation rendered such recommendations purely theoretical. In the spring of 1944, new regulations were passed that eliminated the previous privileges of occupation. Because of the devastation inflicted on the occupied regions by the war effort, "the then-abundant surplus supplies of the regions occupied by the German army" had disappeared, and as a result "we must prohibit the removal of flour, meat, and fat from the occupied regions and the General Government"[95] to prevent the complete collapse of local food production. It had became obvious that food theft was not a sustainable strategy for maintaining the war effort and that the Nazi state could no longer able ensure that its fighting men received an adequate diet.

Soldiers' rations rapidly shrank until they were little better than standard allotments to German civilians on the home front. Complaints about inadequate supplies and requests for supplemental rations were dealt with by "clarify[ing] to soldiers that the food situation of the civilian population is much much worse than the troops, and excessive demands come at the cost of the civilian population, including his own relatives."[96] However, such appeals backfired, demoralizing soldiers by encouraging rumors of severe food shortages at home. In August 1944, an SS soldier named Lange was court-martialed for reportedly complaining that "our women and children have no more to eat and yet, though our army has been retreating in the east for a year, they put stores of grain to the torch."[97] Surveys conducted by the Allies with German POWs revealed a widespread belief that their wives and children at home were "getting only a few potatoes and a few grams of bread."⁹⁸ By the winter of 1945, Goebbels was warning German soldiers that complaining about the food situation "is an area where stupidity and carelessness become a crime, and punishments are appropriate that deviate from the typical scale."⁹⁹ In 1944, Backe frantically reminded the civilian population that "upholding the soldiers' confidence in the German food economy is a crucial responsibility of German farmers. Confidence in the future of our food economy will be maintained."¹⁰⁰

Since the beginning of the war, the Allies had recognized the importance of food for explaining Nazism's allure. The British, Americans, and Soviets bombarded the German civilian population with pamphlets guaranteeing them abundant food, especially long-restricted luxury items like chocolate and coffee, if they abandoned the war effort. In an attempt to undermine the Nazis' claims of abundance and prosperity, illicitly broadcast Allied radio programs reported German malnutrition on a vast scale, suggesting that Hitler had created rather than ended the German people's hunger. In response, the NSDAP published articles and delivered speeches casting such Allied propaganda as lies, a "gleaming façade . . . out of which ring constant false promises to feed the entire world after the war," but which actually "conceals only a single massive expanse of ruins."¹⁰¹ An article in a trade journal for canteen workers claimed not only that the Allies wanted Germans to go hungry, but that the Allies themselves were perilously close to starvation:

> All the promises of the British, Americans and Bolsheviks, all supposed stores of foods set aside, have proven to be empty words . . . not only has none of the promised food aid materialized [in the liberated countries], but the Allies insist on feeding their troops off of the occupied territories, and they have opened the door to the black market, usury, inflation, in short to the exploitation of the masses.¹⁰²

Throughout the war years, Nazi newspapers published frequent reports about starving workers in Britain and the United States and exposés meant to counter the belief in the "supposed inexhaustible food reserves of the United States"¹⁰³ by announcing that "a third of all Americans are without adequate food supplies."¹⁰⁴ In 1940, Göring had assured female farm workers that "while our grain reserves are being kept in silos as safe as in a vault, England's supplies—for excess they don't have!—are resting 'safely' on the bottom of the sea, thanks to the clever attacking spirit of our bombers and submarines."¹⁰⁵ Even as the war effort grew increasingly beleaguered, Nazi newspapers continued to report that "the provisioning of the Axis lands has improved more than expected while that of the enemy has gotten worse."¹⁰⁶ The leading nutritional journal of the Nazi years, *People's Nutrition and Cooking Science* (*Volksernährung und Kochwissenschaft*), ran a regular series on the dietary status of countries across Europe and in North Africa, Asia, and the Americas, reviewing changes in domestic rationing and food production as well as predicted crop yields. The reported statistics invariably mapped perfectly onto Allied-Axis lines, with the Allied countries always allegedly suffering from poor crops, decreasing rationing allotments, and rising rates of malnutrition, while the opposite was true for the Axis powers and their allies.

Even during the final weeks of the war, Nazi authorities depicted Germany as a land of satiety and abundance, one that was giving rather than taking food. As the Allied forces gradually liberated lands previously under German occupation, Nazi nutritionists reported that "the past two years have proven that only Germany has selflessly ensured just and adequate food distribution in those areas which stood under its influence and rule." Recently liberated countries, including Italy and France, were portrayed as longing for the Nazis as they learned firsthand that "the lowering of the German-set level of food rationing is one of the first policies of the Soviets."[107] An August 1944 article published in a food-trade journal described Nazi food plans in Greece, Finland, Norway, Italy, France, Belgium, Holland, and other countries as "examples of German selflessness against which our enemies have nothing equivalent to show." The author boldly asserted that it was food supplies "approved and largely provided by Germany that protected the Greeks from starving to death."[108] In a brazen retelling of Third Reich food policy, a few months later the same journal published an article titled "Germany Gave Europe More to Eat: UNRRA Means Starvation," which claimed that "in the parts of Europe that were occupied by Germany there was admittedly no excess of food, but there was enough so that everyone could live. The black market was inhibited, and a relatively equitable distribution was ensured."[109] In a jarring display of solidarity with the peoples of the Third World, Nazi nutritionists harshly condemned the

> seizure of grain and cattle by the Anglo-Americans in Algeria and Morocco, which placed the entire population in a state of emergency. Not to mention the starvation and inflation in Tschungking China ... or the new famine in Tanganijka, the former German East Africa.[110]

Along similar lines, Backe announced, in the fall of 1944, that "owing to German influence during the war, other European countries have got back on their feet agriculturally, and some have even produced a surplus."[111]

Propaganda contrasting Nazi abundance with Allied deprivation proved relatively effective in persuading the general public that they should cast their lots with Hitler rather than the Allies. Since Hitler's appointment as chancellor in

1933, the population of Germany had been bombarded with reminders of the pleasures and anticipated rewards of nutritional self-abnegation. "Aryan" men and women had become accustomed to increased work demands along with lower wages and lower caloric intake. This embrace of austerity was accepted by the public as both racially advantageous and as a guarantor of future satiety. As a result, the Allied forces noted with dismay that, despite growing domestic shortages, German morale remained strong.

Dr. Howard Fishburn, an American doctor living in Germany during the Third Reich, reported in 1943 that though food and medical care were scarce, public morale was "surprisingly high." But he also noted that "although the German authorities have tried to assure the people that their wartime diet is adequate, there has been a steady and gradual loss of weight and of the sense of well-being among the entire population," pessimistically predicting that "Germany might expect to keep her civilian population above the starvation level until the autumn of 1943." He, consequently, admitted to being "at a loss to explain the apparent efficiency of the German workers and the high level of public morale."[112] Indeed, the vast majority of the German population remained at least passively cooperative with the war effort to the bitter end. In contrast to the situation in Germany during the First World War, efforts to stir up popular revolt or military mutiny during the Second World War remained marginal and unsuccessful. The "high level of public morale" was one of the results of the successful propagation of the idea of a racial community, or *Volksgemeinschaft*, by the NSDAP's relentless state apparatus. Popular acceptance of the ideals of the *Volksgemeinschaft*, in turn, was one of the most striking consequences of the Nazi food economy. Food was not simply a rationale for racist policies; the state relied on food to construct and "make real" its paradoxical and genocidal racial economy—deliberately linking Nazi plans for genocide with the everyday meals consumed by "ordinary Germans."

Categories of Identity and States of Starvation

By reframing hunger and satiety as racial categories rather than individual sensations, the Third Reich's system of food distribution—especially the elaborate rationing program that began immediately before the invasion of Poland in September 1939—transformed food into one of the most important methods of delineating belonging and exclusion. An analysis of the ways in which food was distributed and acquired shows that the everyday activities of "ordinary Germans" in their kitchens and gardens, shopping and baking, were as crucial to the maintenance of the Nazi racial state as the killing fields of Poland or the gas chambers of the concentration camps. Access to specific kinds of foods, and ultimately the right to any food at all, was determined by the state's assignment of racial categories; as a result, regulating the food supply proved one of the most immediate and powerful methods of enacting the modern fiction of race. Because food determines the physical form of bodies, it allowed the state to create raced individuals and collectives as it used varied levels of sustenance to differentiate bodies along racial categories. Quotidian acts of food acquisition and consumption compelled individuals in the Third Reich to continually confront their new social reality as raced beings, identities that determined their position in the hierarchy of Nazi racism.

Nazi leaders relied on foodstuffs as an effective and popular method of gaining support, rewarding good behavior, and cementing popular commitment to the war and the government. At the same time, the domestic food system was regulated with brutal severity; many violations, from forging or stealing rationing cards to illegal buying and selling of foodstuffs, could be punished with the death penalty. Even those who did not directly break the law were vulnerable; because of food's tremendous significance stores, restaurants, and markets were carefully monitored and thus especially dangerous public sites. Germany's rationing program should thus be seen as the most mundane expression of Hitler's vast racial fantasies, as it was inseparably intertwined with the violence of the country's military project. Nothing expressed as clearly the state's "routinization of race silently in social life."[113]

Strikingly, the Nazi rationing program proved far more popular amongst Germans than the much-loathed wartime rationing system of imperial Germany. Especially during the early years of the war, the Nazis' rationing scheme, which divided the population by age, gender, and labor assignment, included manifold ways in which participants could receive extra allotments and have more flexibility in the foodstuffs distributed. The greatest innovation of the Nazi rationing program, however, was its reliance on race as its definitive structural base, ensuring that it shaped the lives of both Aryan and non-Aryan Germans by regulating all aspects of food circulation for all individuals living in the country. The ramifications of living in a racial state had become painfully obvious to Germany's Jewish population long before the rationing program formalized them. Beginning as soon as the Nazis seized power, Jews were gradually removed from the public sphere and thus found it increasingly difficult to purchase foodstuffs. In 1933, the Nazi government officially banned kosher slaughtering as an act of animal cruelty, making it impossible for observant Jews to legally purchase meat for private consumption. Years before laws legally required shopkeepers to restrict sales to Jewish customers, voluntary discrimination in stores and restaurants was encouraged. The seizure of Jews' personal property, and laws prohibiting Jews from owning land, further limited their ability to feed themselves. The institutionalization of rationing in 1939 formalized these experiences. The ration card itself became a visual display of racial identity that shaped everyday interactions like entering a grocery store. Two years before Jews in Germany were required to wear the iconic yellow Star of David to mark their bodies in the public sphere, their rationing cards (see Figure 2.4) marked them as "other" every time that they tried to purchase food. These cards were strictly regulated. Detailed rulings determined the angle of the word "Jew" ("such that it covers each individual segment") as well as the color of the ink ("a color must be chosen that is easy to distinguish from the base color of the card") used to produce them.[114]

As the foodstuffs available to the populace changed in accordance with the shifting economy, so too did the specific consequences of being Jewish in Nazi Germany. When rationing was first initiated in 1939, *Vollkornbrot*, as the

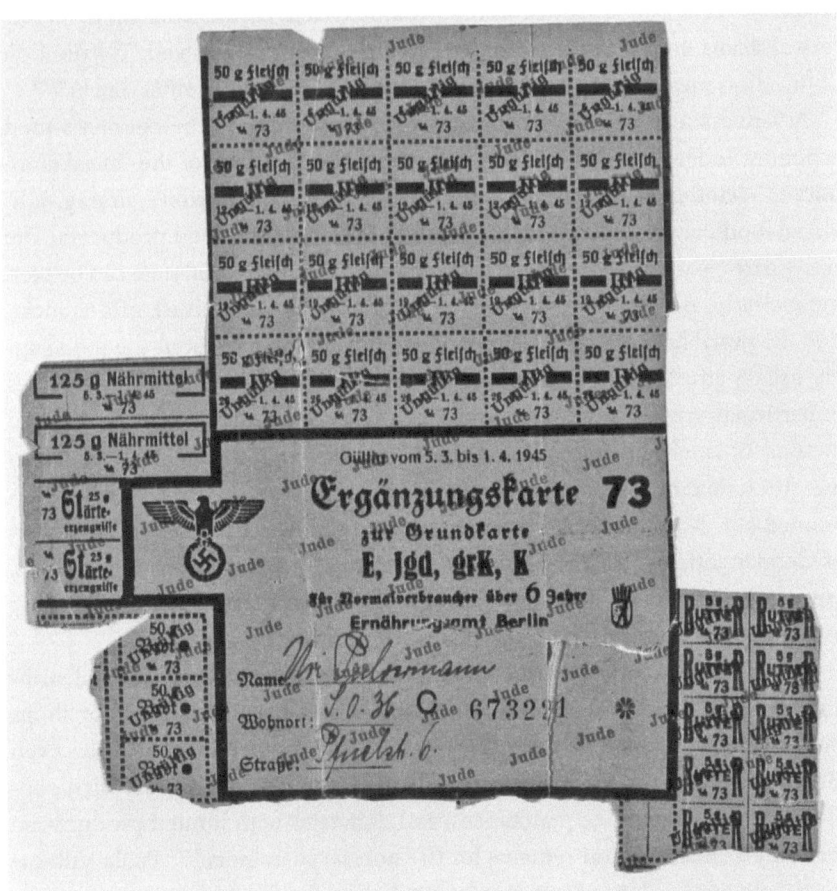

Figure 2.4 A Jewish rationing card from Berlin for March 1945. Jewish Museum Berlin. Photograph by Jens Ziehe. Gift of Paul Norbert Pulvermann. Courtesy of the Jewish Museum Berlin.

most sacred of foods, was officially restricted to members of the Aryan racial community.[115] Two years later, the high cost of imported wheat meant that official regulations stipulated that "the bread cards given to Jews can only be used to receive rye flour products."[116] In 1940, the Berlin nutritional office announced that "consumers whose ration card is marked with a 'J' cannot receive apples or pears."[117] A few months later, it confirmed that "Jews naturally receive no oranges or mandarins."[118] In the late fall of 1942, national law prohibited Jews from receiving the following groceries: "meat, eggs, wheat flour products (cake, white bread, cookies, flour etc.), full-fat milk or reduced-fat fresh milk." Their access to "turnips and cheap varieties of cabbage" was left to the discretion of local nutritional offices, which were also advised to "determine special shopping times for the Jewish population" in order to "avoid discomfort with the provisioning of the Aryan population."[119] A few months later, in February of 1943, the few skilled Jewish workers who remained in the workforce were barred from eating in factory canteens since they were prohibited from eating meat; instead, "distribution of [meatless meals] to Jews will take place separately from the other diners."[120]

Aryanness as much as Jewishness was created through the country's food economy. Indeed, food-based tensions within the members of the "racial community" reinforced the racial hierarchy by normalizing hostility among individual food consumers and between food consumers and food producers. The active participation of the "Aryan" population in the Nazi racial state can be seen most clearly, and at its most banal, in the country's rich culture of denunciation. Regional headquarters were flooded with complaints about the food supply, usually attacking shop owners for illegal or suspicious behavior. Housewives in particular saw these denunciations as a meaningful and socially condoned method of asserting both their societal importance and their general suffering. These letters of complaint reveal that, as historian Robert Gellately has pointed out, Nazi racial policy was contingent on the "continuing cooperation of German citizens."[121] They also reveal the ways in which individual citizens, especially German women, internalized and enacted their racial responsibility to regulate the country's food supply.

The most frequently voiced complaint was that food was not being distributed "fairly." Letter writers often reported that particular restaurants or shops were violating race laws by serving Jews or other enemies of the *Volk*. Even more frequently, angry women complained that local shopkeepers "first supply all of their friends, acquaintances, and deliveries with limited products, so that only a small amount remains for the normal customers."[122] Paula Villnow from Cologne, in a letter from August 1941, described her struggle to purchase beans from a local shopkeeper, who "ripped the red cabbage from me and also tried to take away the potatoes." She claimed to have filed her complaint "in order to reveal the ways in which housewives in our grocery stores are being treated."¹²³ By calling upon the Nazi state to crack down on this sort of mistreatment, Villnow sought to display her adherence to the *Volksgemeinschaft* and her acceptance of her role as enforcer of the racialized food economy. The Nazi state took letters like this seriously. Haunted by the bread riots of the previous war, which had been dominated by women frustrated by the country's food situation, many Nazi officials believed that dissatisfied housewives posed a problem that, as the Cologne police department explained in 1941, "simply for political reasons urgently demands a solution."¹²⁴ Complaints about rationing generally sought not to challenge Nazi policy but to optimize it to better achieve the twinned aims of material abundance and racial purity.

Food consumption racialized society far beyond the relatively limited confines of shops and restaurants, as the act of eating brought different races into contact with each other even as it distinguished them from one another. By the end of the war, a third of all Germans categorized as Aryans, as well as the vast majority of forced laborers and camp prisoners, depended on collective feeding programs rather than private kitchens for their daily meals. These meals, prepared by professional chefs for public and collective consumption, played a key role in enforcing racial identities. Even at the front, German soldiers were fed differently from their allies-in-arms, who received separate and inferior, meals. Factory canteens across Germany used different recipes and cooking styles for the various ethnic categories of forced and voluntary laborers. A radical expansion of collective meal programs, the consequence of the dramatic increase in collective living and working facilities, meant that the Nazi state directly regulated the individual food consumption of populations beyond the traditional confines of the military and prisons. The NSDAP promoted the shift from private to communal food consumption for Aryans in particular as a way of reducing food waste and private energy consumption and of strengthening the bonds of the *Volksgemeinschaft*. Canteen chefs became national heroes as their normally unglamorous profession was cast as central to racial survival: "practical labor in the service of our food situation and the biological assurance of the future of our people are inseparable from one another."¹²⁵ Left unspoken was the fact that German canteens were as important for their role in starving racial enemies as for their nourishing of racial comrades.

Indeed, state-dictated food allotments had catastrophic, often deadly consequences for non-Aryans. Most infamously, Nazi concentration camps distributed meals based on a strict racial hierarchy.¹²⁶ In the larger camps with large-scale killing facilities such as Auschwitz, camp rations were often augmented by the seizure of foodstuffs from newly arrived Jewish prisoners; high-quality products were reserved for guards and the camp staff, while contaminated and spoiled foods were served to the lowest ranks of inmates. Generally camp inmates were subject to elaborate systems of categorization; Western European prisoners were favored, while "Gypsies" and Jews were conceptualized as distinct populations that received the worst food in the camp. Nutritional analyses carried out by German nutritionists to ensure that camp meal programs were following Nazi regulations found that the meat served to Jews "was in a condition of general rotting," and that the sausages produced for prisoners were composed of up to 78 percent water with a smattering of fillers.[127] Contrary to the government's officially publicized announcements, the actual calories consumed by Jews in these camps ranged from 700 to 1,150 a day. The consequences of this diet were predictable. Camp staff regularly placed rat poison in trash cans to prevent starving prisoners from eating discarded food waste.[128]

Wartime rations outside the camps also enforced racial differences in extreme ways. At the beginning of 1940 in German-occupied Poland, Germans were allotted a daily ration of 2,600 calories; urban Poles received 609 calories, and Jews, forced into cramped and isolated ghettos, were officially granted 503 calories. By the end of the year, this impossible number had been further reduced, to 369 calories per Jewish adult.[129] As the *New York Times* succinctly reported in 1943, "[I]n Poland, a sharp distinction is made in rationing between Germans, on the one hand, and Poles and Jews (of whatever nationality) on the other . . . actually, many Poles and Jews are being starved as part of a deliberate and consistent German policy."[130] This rationing system was not an attempt to feed populations but an expression of the ambition of racial annihilation. Since the Nazis deliberately pursued a program of mass starvation, Jewish hunger seemed a problem only insofar as it threatened Aryans. In 1942, German nutritionists who were considering a further reduction in rations for the few remaining Jews living in Germany wondered whether the "planned reductions might be going too far, and whether, through a too-great starvation of the Jews, the Aryan population would be threatened due to danger of infection by epidemics and plagues."[131] Even such mild expressions of concern implicitly challenged the racial economy, which demanded equating the Jewish race with absolute hunger; a bill describing the "Provision of Food for Jews in the Workforce," passed in February 1943, outlined in meticulous detail the vast array of foods that Jews were not allowed to eat rather than what they could eat.[132]

The production of food was similarly racialized. Since the early years of the Reich, domestic food shortages had made clear the need for additional agricultural workers to meet Hitler's ambitions of autarchy. Nazi military plans had therefore included plans for the seizure of hundreds of thousands of slave laborers to work the nation's farms. Even though the "Slav" was officially conceptualized as incapable of tilling the soil, prewar economic analyses had suggested to the Nazis that the war effort would depend on a massive influx of agricultural workers. After war broke out in 1939, German food thus largely ceased being produced by German hands. Since almost the entire male population was drawn into the military, between 40 percent and 60 percent of German agricultural labor was performed by "foreign workers," the majority of them slave laborers and POWs from Poland and the USSR. By the summer of 1944, at least eight million foreign workers and 400,000 concentration-camp workers labored within German borders, making up more than a quarter of the German workforce.[133] This uncomfortable fact meant that farms became some of most racially diverse spaces within Nazi Germany.

German farms, the ideological core of the Aryan race, thus became sites of racial conflict. Indeed, the Nazis were tremendously concerned about the potential dangers of having German farmers, especially female farmers, eating meals with the forced laborers who were replacing their missing sons and husbands. The first rule set down in the Reich's "Regulations for Handling Foreign Workers" stipulated that

> in opposition to German members of the workforce, who belong to our society without limits, the foreign workers are to be shut out of our society. [Their] meals must principally be consumed at separate tables from us. Through the preservation of a great distance from the foreigners, the unlimited authority of the German people is created and preserved.[134]

German women were warned not to share food with Italians, Poles, Russians, and others, or even to witness them eating; mixed-race "table-communities" (*Tischgemeinschaften*) were seen as analogous to mixed-race sexual contact. The Nazi legal system spent a substantial amount of energy prosecuting Aryans who ate with, sold food to, or served foreign workers; restaurants were shut down for offenses as minor as selling lemonade to Polish farm workers.[135]

Despite the fact that these foreigners had often been forcibly brought to Germany to work, the German public vocally expressed its outrage over having to feed them. Communities near large factories and worker barracks complained that these unwanted mouths were eating more than their allotted share.[136] A 1940 report from Württemberg noted "a steadily growing bitterness over the 'Polish invasion' due to the local ammunitions factory." Enraged by "this Polish rabble" descending on city shops "like a swarm of hungry locusts," the local inhabitants claimed that these workers were being paid too much for their "poor-quality work" and were disgusted to see the "scallywags" "purchas[ing] foods and groceries out from under the noses of the population." Locals were especially angered by Poles' purported predilection for "everything that is good and expensive," especially fresh fruits, breads, and cakes, foods that should be reserved for Aryan consumption.[137] Any increase in foreign workers' rations was met with anger and incomprehension by German co-workers as well as locals; likewise, any reduction in German rations inspired calls for a parallel reduction in the rations of foreigners—especially Soviet and Polish workers. One factory manager found that it was "necessary to send an expert to give a presentation on the labor of prisoners to the different economic categories [of German civilians]" in order to convince resentful neighbors of the need to feed foreigner workers at all.[138]

The Nazi racial hierarchy thus shaped the country's economy in far more complex ways than a simple Aryan versus non-Aryan division. Factories and camps became massive laboratories for studying the relationship between food, labor, and race. Nutritionists and economists struggled to determine the optimal diets for the great variety of workers that they were confronted with "not because of false sentimentality, but because we need them with their arms and legs, because they thus must play a part in ensuring that the German *Volk* achieves a great victory."[139] The eugenicist logic of animal breeding was applied to labor camps. A Nazi educational ditty explained: "In order to run things thriftily / you should only keep those animals / who best utilize / whatever they eat / so you must constantly control / your animals' performance / and in no case should you feed / animals that are performing poorly."[140]

Foreign workers often received no wages or were "paid" with inadequate food and housing, and were subject to draconian punishments, including restrictions on their movement, physical and mental abuse, and even death. The 1943 League of Nations report on health in wartime Europe singled out the "mass of some twelve million foreigners, prisoners and civilian workers at present in Germany" as a population of particular concern:

> [T]his foreign population, moreover, does not form the subject of any published health statistics. Information concerning them (clandestine correspondence, accounts given by escaped and repatriated persons and their condition, deaths reported to the Red Cross) shows that their health situation is definitely bad.[141]

Unsurprisingly, in letters sent home by these unfortunate people, the abysmal food situation was a recurrent theme. The Psychological Warfare Division of the US Army excerpted some of these intercepted letters in a June 1945 report, depicting the misery of these men and women's lives:

> With 12-hour work they receive very little to eat. They don't demand good food, no, they are very humble, but there is so little that the last ones to come to the table don't get anything at all! And when they tearfully plea that they give them something, (since in the kitchen there is still an entire pot full of soup—for whom?) they are cursed. The word "pig" they hear constantly.[142]

Economic concerns inspired several "reports from industry about poor health and inadequate performance of foreign workers because of inadequate diet." They confirmed that Italians experienced particularly high weight loss when starved, and noted that "an increase in performance was observable" with increased rations.[146] Industrial giant Siemens submitted several reports advocating improving the rations of workers they deemed racially and ideologically superior: "Baltic Germans," "Ethnic Germans from the East," and "Dutch National Socialists."[147] Within German factories the universal reality of an inadequate diet coexisted alongside elaborate and carefully reinforced racial hierarchies. Regional nutritional offices were repeatedly warned to avoid grouping together different, and thus differently fed, categories of non-Aryans. While Western European employees received vitamin-rich conserves in the winter, there was an instruction that "foreign workers, Jews and Poles do not receive preserved vegetables."[143] At large factories with diverse workforces made up of POWs, camp inmates, slave workers, and volunteers from the Scandinavian and Baltic countries, workers attempted to strategically exploit the Nazis' racial vocabulary to improve their food situation. In late 1942, "Dutch and Flemish workers were very disturbed that in newspaper articles which announced special Christmas rations for the German *Volk*, they were placed on the same level with the Jews and the Poles as not permitted to receive them."[144] One report pointedly claimed that "the situation whereby prisoners at the institution at Werl collapsed at the machines is just as worrisome as the appearance of several cases of hunger edema in Bochum," but immediately clarified that it was troubling because "almost all of these cases involved Dutch people."[145]

While requests for improved prisoner rations relied on racial affiliation as a rationale, a 1943 Siemens report on the company's "experiences with foreign workers" noted that Slavs were especially cost-effective because they required less food than other prisoners; the author praised their hunger-induced docility (what he termed an "undemanding nature"), making them "especially appropriate for heavy labor."[148] Many experts believed that Slavs carried out physical labor best when they were in a state of semistarvation. A German officer who had served in Russia and thus claimed particular knowledge of the Slavic body and mind wrote to the SS in 1944 to recommend a radical reduction in the already extraordinarily low rations allotted to the *Ostarbeiter* (workers from the East). Warning of the dangers of overfeeding rather than underfeeding, he claimed that the Slav "will only reach his best productivity when he is handled appropriately . . . he who performs well, receives much to eat, who produces less, receives less, and who does not work at all or who does not want to work, will be destroyed as a parasite."[149]

Indeed, the Soviets were the population most consistently targeted for starvation. Nazi military strategists planned to annihilate the civilian population of Russia by depriving them of access to food, and their vast

Hunger Plan called for the deliberate starvation of Soviet POWs in direct violation of international norms.[150] Only a few months after the invasion of the USSR, in November of 1941, Göring issued official guidelines for dealing with Russian laborers. He confirmed that

> the Russian is easy to satisfy, and thus easy and without complication to feed without substantial impact on our food balance. He should not be spoiled or allowed to become accustomed to German food, but he must be fed and maintained in a condition necessary for him to achieve the necessary level of productivity.[151]

This statement was deeply euphemistic; in practice, the only way to feed millions of prisoners "without substantial impact" on German food supplies was to not feed them. By the end of the war, Nazi policy had starved to death millions of Soviet citizens.

Adapting earlier fantasies and fears of the East, the Nazis described Russia as a land of limitless and timeless hunger.[152] Newspapers regularly reported cases of starvation-induced cannibalism in the USSR. In letters sent from the Eastern Front, German soldiers described Russians as both ravenous and greedy—condemned for being too hungry, despised for eating in a bestial, inhuman manner. German farmers who received Russian forced laborers to work their fields were warned against feeding them too well, since "the Russian has lived with poverty, hunger, and submission for centuries. His belly is elastic, so no false sympathy."[153] German chefs developed a standardized recipe for so-called *Russenbrot*, "Russian bread," which was initially set at 72 percent rye and 28 percent sugar-beet peel, with the addition of fillers including leaves, grass, or straw. Even this grotesque recipe eventually needed to be reserved for more racially valuable prisoners. German army leaders quickly realized that "a large portion of the severely undernourished Soviets found in the prisoner of war camps" could not tolerate "normal food," which in this case meant the nearly inedible *Russenbrot*. So as to not waste foodstuffs, they recommended that these starving men be exclusively served "flour soup," a dish so entirely lacking in nutrition that it was sure to finish them off.[154]

The institutionalized mistreatment of Soviet prisoners extended throughout German-controlled Europe. In the summer of 1942, a General Reinhardt compared the "resilience" of his Russian farm laborers favorably to the French POWs who were also working his land, again emphasizing the cost advantage of using workers who do not "need" food:

> [O]nly one [of the Russians] has died so far; the rest are continuing their work in the fields. Their provisions cost us nothing, and we don't

have to suffer under the fact that these animals, whose children are killing our soldiers, are eating German bread. Yesterday I was forced to kill two of these Russian beasts, as they had secretly gobbled up the milk that had been reserved for the mother sow.[155]

In a letter to his lieutenant, the German soldier Otto Essmann described with horror Soviet POWs who "gobble up earthworms, and throw themselves at the dirty dishwater. I watched as they ate dirty grass. It is hardly believable that they are human."[156] Such images of disgust and perverse appetites were common in, for example, the memoirs of former members of Hitler Youth, who recalled organized tours of local Russian POW camps meant to show the children the inhumanity of the Slavs as they devoured bugs and chewed soil in desperate attempts to stay alive.[157] Countless German civilians remember the sight of starving Russian POWs eating grass and leaves inside prison yards, collapsing from hunger as they marched through towns and cities, and snatching potato peelings and rotten foods from garbage piles at the risk of being beaten or shot by their guards. The devastating hunger of these racial enemies was not kept secret from "ordinary Germans," but was integrated into their everyday food economy. In this way, food production and consumption bound social, economic, and military ambitions together in a racialized vision of a "new Empire" that claimed the lives of tens of millions of men, women, and children.

* * *

In June 1941, on the eve of the invasion of the USSR, Hitler proclaimed that he "had never heard of a German eating a loaf of bread and worrying whether the land that produced it had been conquered by the sword. We also eat Canadian wheat and don't think about the Indians."[158] This haunting analogy, though suggestive of both the ubiquity and invisibility of race within the modern food economy, denies the distinctiveness of the Nazi racial imagination. In the Third Reich, land and the food that it produced were inseparable from race, and they were thus directly implicated in projects of population displacement and genocide. As a result, across Europe, starvation was central to the experience of the Second World War. Of the 14 million civilians and POWs who died in Central Europe between 1933 and 1945, more than half starved to death.[159]

Despite Nazi fantasies of creating a new world order, the agricultural lands of Eastern Europe that were seized and repopulated by Germans consistently underperformed; in particular, Ukraine, the mythic solution to German hunger, did not come close to fulfilling the Nazis' expectations. Replacing local inhabitants with ethnic German farmers did not increase productivity, and the foodstuffs that were extracted from occupied Europe for German consumption were almost exclusively produced by non-Aryans. Not only were Slavic and

Jewish farmers across Eastern Europe dispossessed and killed, but their land was destroyed, falling victim to the scorch-and-burn policy of the German army as it retreated westward in the final months of the war. Indeed, after the collapse of the Third Reich, it took almost a decade for the soil of occupied Europe to reach the productivity of Germany's nearly untouched farmlands.[160]

Despite constant promises of future abundance, the Nazi regime actually decreased Germany's available food supplies both by diverting food to industrial and military segments of the population and by reducing food imports. The state's claim that it was achieving food autarchy was a sham; an American agricultural evaluation of the German food economy summarized the situation in 1939 as follows: "Our survey of Germany's attempt to attain agricultural self-sufficiency has shown that on the whole agricultural production has not been substantially increased and imports have not been substantially reduced."[161] What the Nazis termed "nutritional freedom" was largely a shifting of import strategies. In 1942, Germany actually imported 50 percent more food than it had in 1938, but it was all from within Europe, and primarily from countries under the control of the Third Reich—thus nominally "domestic."[162] Even more important, wholesale theft of the continent's food supply was more important for the success of the NSDAP's food policy than regulating fertilizer distribution or improving farming techniques.

Contrary to both contemporary perceptions and Germans' individual memories, recent studies have suggested that Hitler's reign resulted in an overall decline in quality of life for the average German. Although severe hunger did not become part of daily life for non-Jewish Germans until the end of the war, and overall civilian mortality rates stagnated during the Third Reich, mortality rates actually increased for children and the ill because the removal of Jews and other "undesirables" from the medical profession weakened already overtaxed health services.[163] Employment increased dramatically thanks to the expansion of industry and the military, but wage value dropped, and the situation of those who could not work declined even more precipitously.[164] Increased spending on the military was balanced by decreased public-welfare spending, leaving the unemployed and destitute entirely dependent on voluntary charities like the *Winterhilfswerk*. In 1936, the average German consumed less of all major food groups except for fish than he or she had in 1929.[165] Per head caloric consumption had declined steadily during the prewar Nazi years, and the outbreak of war only worsened the average German's diet.

For the German working class, the impact of salary freezes, price regulations, and the dismemberment of welfare projects was especially devastating. Even German workers in heavy industry, despite receiving extra rations, suffered. Their official caloric allotment at the height of the war was only half of what the 1936 regulations had stipulated as the minimum necessary to maintain optimal performance. The standard German consumer, the so-called normal user, also received 36 percent less than he or she had initially been promised.[166] Indeed, as economic historian Jörg Baten has pointed out, "if biological aspects are taken into consideration," the economic success of domestic Nazi policy did not improve the welfare of the majority of the population but produced instead a "major crisis in health and mortality."[167] And of course for the Germans who were excluded from the racial community, the Third Reich was an unmitigated catastrophe. The handicapped, elderly, imprisoned, and the poor suffered unprecedented levels of distress alongside racial enemies like the Jews and Gypsies; thousands of "useless eaters," many of them children, were deliberately starved to death by their doctors in asylums and hospitals. Many other racially pure "undesirables" were given inadequate food as a method of quiet and cost-effective elimination.

Still, it was not until the final weeks of the war that pervasive hunger reached most German civilians. The bitterness of having lost the fields of grains promised by Hitler framed the fear, anger, and disappointment with which the population of defeated Germany greeted Allied feeding plans during the postwar occupation. Twenty-five years earlier, the hunger caused by the British Blockade had defined both the war and postwar experiences of the German population. After the Second World War, the situation would be quite different. As Germans found themselves again defeated and again under occupation, they again experienced the pain of empty stomachs. In response, they began to depict their food situation under Hitler as a paradise compared to the deprivations they suffered during the so-called Hunger Years (*Hungerjahre*) from 1945 to 1949. While Germany had ostensibly been defeated in the First World War by the "hunger weapon," the Second World War had been waged to get Germans enough to eat. This time around, defeat could be interpreted as the cause rather than consequence of hunger, ironically confirming the racialized hunger discourse of the NSDAP. Nazi propaganda predicted and shaped many Germans' experiences and memories of hunger, ensuring that, although far more Germans starved to death during the war than after it, the Third Reich became a time of imagined abundance. In this new postwar narrative of German history, true hunger began not with the rise of the Third Reich in 1933, but with its collapse in 1945.

3

Hunger and the Remaking of History

Rationing, Suffering, and Human Rights in Occupied Germany

Over the course of the Second World War, the Allies had developed various plans for reconstructing a devastated Europe, all of which anticipated that food would emerge as the world's most valued commodity. Months before the end of the war, Nobel Peace Prize–winning biologist and politician Sir John Boyd Orr predicted that a hungry Europe would find itself deprived of the ability to feed itself: "[W]hen the Nazis are driven out they'll . . . leave the peasants with burned out villages, no seeds to sow, no ploughs or other machinery, no crops to feed themselves or their children or their animals."[1] More optimistically, given the vast scale of the hunger being experienced around the world at the time, some experts claimed that "there never has been a greater opportunity in history to make progress toward the great goal of freedom from hunger and malnutrition for all."[2] American economist and future Nobel Prize–winner Theodore Schultz, in his 1945 book *Food for the World*, espoused his belief that "along with its legacy of starved bodies and warped minds . . . the war has disciplined people and governments in matters pertaining to food."[3] Others were not so hopeful, anticipating that "whole populations will be in acute distress and will need quick and effective help if we are to avoid the breakdown of civilization in many parts of Europe and Asia."[4]

The United Nations Relief and Rehabilitation Administration (UNRRA) was founded in 1943 to aid the hungry populations of war-ravaged countries. The same year the UN announced that it would hold a conference in Hot Springs, Virginia, to consider "the world problems of food and agriculture," declaring "its belief that the goal of freedom from want of food, suitable and adequate for the health and strength of all peoples, can be achieved."[5] Describing both Europe and Asia as places where "hunger is the general rule, starvation is commonplace, and . . . the area enslaved by the Axis is a breeding place for all the diseases of the body and of the spirit that are born of starvation, suffering, and death," the conference formalized the Allies' interest in international food distribution and the management of global hunger.[6] Plans were drawn up for what was to become the UN's Food and Agricultural Organization (FAO), which held its first session in October 1945. In Great Britain, concerns over the spread of hunger during the war led to the formation of the Oxford Famine Relief Committee (later renamed Oxfam) in May 1942. Originally created to provide aid for the devastating famine in Greece, the organization rapidly expanded to organize wartime famine relief throughout Europe.

Given the vast scale of global hunger, European and American experts agreed that international food relief would be one of the most important components of postwar reconstruction. The United States expected to emerge from the war as one of the world's few food-surplus regions, making food aid seem a significant economic opportunity. Wartime propaganda promised American farmers that after the war had ended they would "provide the food—boatload after boatload—to feed the conquered people of Europe and put them back on their feet immediately after liberation."[7] These early plans for food relief were shaped by American experiences during the First World War. Indeed, in the aftermath of his unpopular presidency, Herbert Hoover again rose to public prominence because of his food-aid projects. In 1940, he had founded the National Committee on Food for the Small Democracies, which advocated delivering food relief to several especially worthy countries under Nazi rule: the "small democracies" of Norway, Finland, the Netherlands, Belgium, and Poland. In 1942, already looking ahead to the end of the war, Hoover announced to the American public that "we'll have to feed the world again,"[8] framing these ambitions in terms of the hunger experienced during the prior world war. In a nationwide radio address titled "Can Europe's Children be Saved?," Hoover invoked memories of "brave little Belgium," where, he claimed, American food aid had prevented "a holocaust of death and stunted bodies and minds."[9]

In fact, such simple historical analogies between the two world wars inadequately prepared the Allies for the realities of the Second World War. The radical differences between the two conflicts meant that the triumph of Hoover's Belgian relief program could not be easily re-created, as the failure of his Committee for Small Democracies made clear. The terrifying military success of Nazi Germany, as well as its aggressive seizure of foodstuffs across the continent, rendered British attempts at another hunger blockade similarly ineffective.[10] Indeed, the wartime food economy of Europe had little in common with its earlier incarnation. As a result, the face of hunger that defined the Second World War was not that of a frail Belgian or French child who, in Hoover's dramatic language, had "been ground between the millstones of German requisitions and the British blockade."[11] Instead, the hunger of World War II found its iconic victims in the starved concentration-camp inmates who were liberated by the Allies during the final days of the war.

The particularity of this sort of wartime hunger had not been immediately apparent to the Allies. Initially, doctors were completely unprepared for the extremity of camp survivors' needs. Starved, abused, and traumatized camp inmates were often neither grateful nor even treatable. The largest camp liberated in the British zone of Allied-occupied Germany, Bergen-Belsen, was a typically demoralizing example. Belsen inmates continued to die by the thousands long after medical aid began pouring in. Some 13,000 corpses were found at liberation; within the next month, that number had more than doubled, as 14,000 more inmates died of starvation, disease, and hopelessness. A British doctor remembered with shame and frustration that "only a fraction of the men and women who lived and died in these camps were seen by Allied personnel."[12] Another doctor reminded his readers that "the figures [for medical treatment statistics] do not on the whole represent the most severe cases. The thinnest patients died earlier and had been too ill to be weighed."[13] Aid workers were especially traumatized by the fact that initial relief was often literally deadly, as patients' starving bodies proved incapable of digesting the suddenly available foodstuffs.[14] Expecting to address treatable issues of malnutrition, not incapacitating starvation, doctor after doctor noted that "the first impression that these patients made on us was simply devastating."[15] One of the earliest articles about Belsen to appear in the British press, published in May 1945, described a world in which starvation had destroyed humanity and individuality: "[W]hen they began to carry round the bowls of soup a horrible animal-like clamor broke out. Skinny arms were held out, blankets fell back, and naked, scarecrow figures flung themselves forward in their beds."[16] It was these nameless and starving bodies that rapidly became the universal symbol for the catastrophic hunger of this war.

Many scholars have noted that initial contact between the Allied forces and concentration-camp inmates resulted in a misleading impression of the victims of what came to be known as the Holocaust. The inmates who greeted the liberators were usually those few who were so ill that they had been abandoned by fleeing camp personnel. Their frail bodies were falsely assumed to be the norm in all Nazi camps and for the duration of the war. In fact, camp life had been characterized by a wide variety of lives, and thus an array of causes of death, including beatings, shootings, gassings, and hangings. This was especially true for the Jews of Europe, the majority of whom were killed in mass shootings outside the camps or were gassed immediately upon arriving at the camps. Thus the piles of emaciated corpses that the Allied forces saw when they entered camps in 1944 and 1945 represented an atypical and fairly small percentage of the total victims of Nazi persecution.[17] Nonetheless, the liberators, confronted with the sight of the skeletal bodies of tens of thousands of starving inmates, came to see hunger as the most immediate form of suffering and primary cause of death in Nazi camps. Allied documentaries from these years consistently described

Nazi camps as "hunger camps," and inmate life was generally summarized by reference to the painfully inadequate rations.[18] Contemporary medical studies reported that German concentration camps were "the theater of the greatest starvation tragedy in Europe."[19]

In their attempts to revive these devastated bodies, both medical and lay observers noted that the most striking feature of starving former prisoners was the uniformity of their symptoms and appearance; experts frequently invoked a sort of universal camp inmate whom they equated with a generalized "hunger victim."[20] British doctors reported that "the emaciation of the corpses in the camp [Bergen Belsen] showed that starvation had been almost universal among them also when alive."[21] First-person accounts overwhelmingly emphasized that "nearly all the patients presented the same picture both mentally and physically."[22] Hunger seemed to destroy individuality, creating "a general familial similarity" among an otherwise diverse assortment of peoples.[23] These hungry bodies were defined by their sunken eyes, jutting cheek bones, apathetic expressions, hunched postures, and stilted movements; in turn, "these extreme changes made all the patients look alike, so that it became difficult to distinguish one from another. The difficulty was accentuated by the fact that all patients had had the bulk of their hair shaved off."[24]

Unlike the crimes committed by the Japanese in Asia or the suffering of the populations of Hiroshima and Nagasaki, it was Nazi concentration camps that were to become touchstones for postwar conceptions of collective suffering and human rights violations across much of the world.[25] In the devastated landscape of postwar Europe specifically, hunger quickly became equated with suffering at the hands of the Nazis. The association of the evils of Nazism with mass starvation inspired the 1948 Universal Declaration of Human Rights. The Declaration, which noted that a "disregard and contempt for human rights have resulted in barbarous acts which have outraged the conscience of mankind," specified, in Article 25, that "everyone has the right to a standard of living adequate for the health and well-being of himself and of his family, including food, clothing, housing and medical care."[26] This "right to eat" would become an important value in the wake of the war. In 1952, a Danish medical report on the long-term consequences of starvation among former concentration-camp inmates hoped to use its data to underscore "the primary right of man, the right to have enough to eat."[27]

This new way of framing hunger meant that postwar Germans' hunger not only shaped their daily lives; it brought them into the fold of global humanity. Almost immediately after the collapse of the Third Reich, German civilians appropriated the pervasive discourse of the inhumanity of hunger to craft powerful demands for human rights, particularly the right to food. They did this to remake themselves into a new community that was distinct from the Nazi *Volksgemeinschaft*. During the four years of Allied occupation, hunger became a crucial strategy by which Germans redefined themselves as victims of a Cold War instead of perpetrators of a World War.

Immediately after the war, Germans, because of their association with Nazism, were implicitly excluded from initial Allied efforts to articulate a human rights agenda.[28] Despite the early reluctance of many human rights advocates to extend their new "rights regime" to defeated Germany, Germans themselves rapidly learned to express themselves in this new and particularly modern vocabulary. As Cold War divisions deepened, the occupation authorities in all four of the zones of divided Germany, and especially in the British and American zones, expressly encouraged this rhetoric, seeing the adoption of a human rights vocabulary as foundational to the values of democracy and antithetical to those of Nazism. As Germans became more sophisticated advocates of their own suffering, the distinction between the suffering caused by the Nazis and the suffering of former Nazis lost any significance. As a result, the starving German rather than the starving Jew became the focus of postwar human rights discourse. This fact not only shaped the Western Allies' policies toward the occupied country but also played a key role in shaping the Cold War. Feeding hungry Germans became an act of both defending human rights and battling communism.

The evolution of this postwar discourse of hunger was a crucial component of what historian Mark Mazower has described as the "strange triumph of human rights" after World War II.[29] In the landscape of postwar Europe, hunger became a primary mark of victimization, corporeally exposing a violation of the "rights" of the sufferer. Given the severity of the food shortages facing the world after the war's end, the seeming legibility of the hungry body made starvation an ideal vehicle for integrating human rights into projects of reconstruction and re-education. In the face of international opprobrium, Germans asserted their right to have adequate food, not as Aryans, Germans, or even Europeans, but as humans and "citizens of the world." Constant appeals to the "conscience of the world" and addresses to the "hearts of our fellow human beings" displayed German proficiency in the language of human rights and in international norms of political behavior.

Managing German Hunger after the Second World War

Quite differently from World War I, it had not been expected beforehand that German hunger would become a major problem at war's end. In a starving Europe, Germany had always been described as a land of ample food: "the diet is adequate and any idea that the Germans are starving or are likely to starve in the near future must be dismissed as foolish."[30] Thus the issue of feeding civilians had received little attention in Allied planning for postwar Germany. The Allies had not only assumed that Germans were not hungry but had held them directly responsible for the starvation surrounding them across Europe. During the war, British prime minister Winston Churchill had warned that "the Germans cannot starve the peoples of Europe during the war and immediately afterwards expect to live in luxury."[31] In 1949, the Jewish American businessman Ira Hirschmann, special inspector for the UNRRA in Germany, reflected on his travels in Germany immediately after the country's surrender. In his memoir, he openly equated guilt and innocence with specific levels of body fat:

> [T]he contrast between the normal, healthy life of the German and that of their neighbors was overwhelming. Who won the war, I asked myself as I saw obviously well-fed Germans . . . the plumpness of the German Hausfrau in her tailored black suit was the healthy plumpness of the adequately nourished; that of the Jewish women in the camps, in their shabby cotton dresses and ragged sweaters, was the unhealthy bloatedness of the ill-fed.[32]

In May 1945, Britain's *Daily Mirror* reported gleefully that several dozen "fat SS girls" would be receiving a "more restrictive diet as they awaited trial, and if they are going to do a little slimming for a change, at least it will improve their appearance."[33] Such skepticism and hostility toward German appetites shaped early policy toward the defeated country.

While the war was still being fought, US president Franklin Roosevelt had entertained ideas for a punitive approach to postwar Germany. The Morgenthau Plan, proposed by his secretary of treasury Henry Morgenthau Jr. and briefly supported by Churchill and Roosevelt in the fall of 1944, proposed deindustrializing Germany and remaking it as an agricultural region. This proposal, which was consistently referred to in the Nazi press as the "Jewish Murder Plan," continued after the war to symbolize to German civilians an ill-concealed desire on the part of both Jews and Americans for the "decimation of the German people."[34] In fact, though the plan was in many ways a horrified reaction to the excesses of Nazi strategies of food seizure and mass starvation, the plan's supporters had insisted that "hardworking farmers would never starve."[35] They claimed that the plan would ultimately transform Germany from a consumer to a producer of Europe's foodstuffs. However, even before the war ended, America had abandoned the plan as unrealistic, punitive, and counterproductive.

Initially, the August 1945 Potsdam Conference determined the parameters of the defeated country's division and delineated the Allies' shared goals for occupation. Preoccupied with preventing a resurgence of Nazism and convinced that a unified German nation presented a threat to European peace, the Allies divided the defeated nation into four distinct occupation zones. Each occupying power was largely free to do what it wished in its zone, but they all committed to maintaining relative equity in terms of quality of life across the different zones—and they all agreed to base their rule on the common objectives laid down in Potsdam: demilitarization, denazification, decartelization, and decentralization. More specifically, the Potsdam Conference directly addressed the Nazi food economy that had placed Germans at the top of the racial hierarchy by de facto inverting this order; the Allies declared that Germany should experience "average living standards not exceeding the average of the standards of living of [other] European countries."[36] More than anything else, this statement was intended and experienced as a policy of regulating Germans' caloric intake. During the final days of the war, both the French and the British press had regularly expressed outrage over the rations allotted to German POWs being detained abroad, which were reportedly more generous than standard civilian rations at home: "Hun prisoners—even SS men seized at death camps—get twice as much rationed food as British civilians," reported the *Daily Mirror* in April 1945.[37] US president Harry Truman put it even more bluntly in an August 1945 speech to the American public: "Europe today is hungry. I am not talking about Germans." As a result, he explained that "the Germans are not to have a higher standard of living than their former victims, the people of the defeated and occupied countries of Europe."[38]

This ranking of the German people below the level of Europe's other populations proved short-lived. The Potsdam agenda quickly collapsed in the face of mounting tensions between the two superpowers, the United States and the USSR.[39] In a way that was reminiscent of the debates over German hunger during the early Weimar Republic, the initial Allied consensus that the Germans were the cause of Europe's hunger rather than its victims was gradually replaced with diverse and divisive interpretations of the occupied country's hunger. As the United States and the USSR attempted to woo Germans within their respective zones, the food-distribution programs in the different zones acquired both political and economic significance. Occupation authorities swiftly abandoned their commitment to keeping Germany at average or even below-average food levels; the harm that might be done by a hungry and angry German population outweighed the perceived ethical dilemma of feeding the former enemy more than its former victims. Provisioning German civilians thus became a project that served varied agendas over the occupation years, ranging from punishment to reward, shifting from reparations to reconstruction, inspired by denazification and democratization.

The country's varied rationing systems clearly represented the combination of sincere feelings of victimization and cut-throat competition that defined postwar life. The severe food shortages throughout the postwar world, the collapse of Germany's economy and infrastructure, and the massive increase in the country's population due to the temporary presence of countless survivors (forced laborers and displaced persons [DPs]) as well as millions of ethnic German expellees, all seemed to guarantee inadequate food supplies. Rationing had been practiced by all of the Allies on the home front during the war. The premise of most wartime rationing programs had been a common valuation of shared sacrifice and solidarity, what the British termed "fair shares" and what the US government promoted with the slogan "rationing is good democracy." This belief in the egalitarian goal of rationing was crucial in getting populations to cooperate; when citizens ceased to believe that the system was "fair" and that common sacrifice was in fact "common," rationing inevitably lost its popular support.[40] However, despite the official promotion of solidarity, wartime rationing policies has always been based on hierarchies—changing political necessities as well as unavoidable fluctuations in the quality and quantity of food available for distribution. Although rationing implicitly assumed similarity—common needs and identical supplies—across populations and regions, even within individual countries difference was more conspicuous than sameness. This proved especially true in occupied Germany. This was in many ways a simple material fact. For example, as a 1947 Cologne report explained, "since in different parts of Germany different ratios of flour and water are used to make bread, bread is not always the same bread; nonetheless, rationing boards assume a constant value."[41] In occupied Germany, such differences assumed profound significance, becoming a primary expression of the relationship between the German people and the occupation authorities.

In the face of the complex and contested inhabitants of occupied Germany, Allied rationing programs divided the population into distinctive and unequal categories in order to regulate food allotments. When crafting their rationing plans, the Allies assumed that nationality and political affiliation were interchangeable, a view that was intended to simplify caring for the remarkably diverse population then living on German soil. Initial feeding plans, developed in the fall of 1945, specified that all citizens of Allied nations, "including the Chinese," regardless of age or gender, were to be granted an elevated ration level, while specifying that "Italians do not belong to the Allied nations and thus do not enjoy any special privileges."[42] Determining who was in fact an "Ally" proved complicated, as almost all national identities included both fascists and antifascists of one sort or another; in October a clarification was therefore issued explaining that unless otherwise indicated, "all Dutch, Belgian, Luxemburg, Norwegian, Danish, Yugoslav, Greek und Polish people should be temporarily assumed to be 'allied.'"[43] The arrival of Allied rationing thus reversed Nazi rankings, privileging the Allies and former victims of the Germans while treating Axis civilians as second-class subjects.

More specifically, the Soviet zone's rationing scheme was modeled on an earlier system developed in the USSR wherein there was no single, standard "normal consumer." Instead, the population was divided into several categories ranked according to calculated value for society. In occupied Germany, Soviet policy favored heavy and industrial workers, particularly those in steel, mining, and transportation. Artists, intellectuals, and some professionals were also included in the highest rationing level. A person's "value" was thus not exclusively based on physical labor or economic contribution. Communists were automatically assumed to have been anti-Nazi during the war and thus also received the highest rationing level; former Nazis, regardless of their employment, received the lowest.

This system of determining food allotments based on past political affiliations was unfamiliar and disturbing to most German citizens. The implicit goal was to insure that the better off one had been in Germany during the Third Reich, the worse one fared after its collapse. Equally importantly, the hungrier one had been during the war, the better fed one was after it. This deliberate desire to invert the Nazi hierarchy inspired the creation of the new category "victim of fascism" (*Opfer des Fascismus* [OdF])—a catch-all rubric that in the Soviet sector was automatically granted to members of the Communist resistance and to Jews, but could also be granted to camp survivors more generally. Recognition as an *OdF* did not guarantee a specific ration level; "victims of fascism" were instead allotted supplemental foods that augmented the standard rations of whatever category they had been assigned initially, as determined by their profession or training.

All high-ranking NSDAP members, regardless of their postwar employment or social status, were officially allotted a Card V, which meant they received the lowest rationing allotment (though, in practice, exceptions were made for highly skilled or powerful individuals if it suited the needs of the authorities). They shared this dubious distinction with those members of society who were considered economic liabilities: the unemployed and housewives.[44] This controversial policy, historian Donna Harsch has shown, had lasting consequences for the attitudes of German women toward the Communist government, creating a rift that would never be fully mended.[45] The many women who were expected to make-do with Card V dubbed it the "trip to heaven" card, as their allotment was supposedly inadequate to sustain life. Thus the Soviet rationing policy grouped those directly responsible for the evils of the war together with civilians whose labor was unvalued, punishing "the guilty" while simultaneously pushing civilians out of the home and toward the industrial fields deemed most valuable for reconstruction.[46] In the face of intense popular protests the Soviet authorities eliminated the hated Card V in February 1947, as part of a larger reconstruction of the relationship between labor and food supplies.[47]

However, the harm done to the Soviet zone's leadership—especially in the eyes of German women—could not be undone.

Departing from the Soviet model, the Western zones' rationing plans eliminated Nazi racial categories but maintained most of the standards established by the Third Reich's wartime rationing programs. This was deliberate; the decision to maintain rationing categories of the former enemy was seen as providing a key form of continuity for Germans in the West—something evaluated favorably, especially when looked at in contrast to the alienation produced by the ostensibly more punitive Soviet system. Thus in the Western zones rationing continued to be based on a standard adult "normal consumer," who received a set allotment of foodstuffs. This barely adequate diet was augmented by an array of supplements (*Zulagen*), which could be awarded based on a wide array of criteria, some of which repeated Nazi categories (performing intense physical labor) and some of which did not (being a former camp inmate). As a result, in the American and British zones, *Zulagen* shaped individual diets as much as the official "normal" rationing allotment. A British medical study of dietary intake in Nordrhein-Westphalen between 1946 and 1949 explained the surprisingly few cases of serious malnutrition by noting that "few people were living only as normal consumers. So many scales of supplementary rations existed that a great many persons managed to qualify for one or other of them."[48]

Ultimately, these quite different models of rationing—one that ranked all people in society at different levels, another that awarded every inhabitant identical minimum rations and then distributed highly variable individual supplements—produced roughly equivalent levels of food intake. But regardless of where one received his or her foodstuffs, there was a persistent conviction among Germans that "the other zone" had it better. The Allies indirectly encouraged this belief as common occupation goals receded, to be replaced by geopolitical strategizing wherein all four zones used rations to compete for popular support. Widely circulated reports of ration increases at home and ration reductions in neighboring zones were used both to still voices of complaint and to lure workers and citizens into that nation's zone. Although most movement tended to be away from the French, Soviet, and British zones and toward the more prosperous American zone, the Soviet zone also used food supplies as a form of propaganda. For example, the manager of a steel plant in the American zone warned that a "week-long released announcement in the FDGB [socialist trade union] paper the *Tribune*, which included descriptions of the special allotments" (sugar, vegetables, fresh milk) and free hot canteen meals in Soviet-contracted factories had already lured numerous metal workers to move to the East."[49] In the summer of 1946, a report from the American zone warned that "widespread radio news that the rations have been improved in the Russian zone due to the decision of the Socialist Unity Party, that is to say the Communists" was "quite dangerous for the political attitude of the population."[50] Soviet authorities also chose to report extensively on food crises in the Western regions, highlighting "hunger demonstrations" in the Ruhr region and corruption among the food authorities of the French zone.[51] Countering such claims, the American media reported ration declines and widespread starvation, depression, and political apathy resulting from inadequate rations in the Soviet sector.[52]

The comparison and competition between East and West only encouraged Germans' perceptions of their own victimization. In 1947, American military surveys found that "probably the most discussed problem among German people today is the food situation . . . and there is no likelihood that the situation will be radically changed over the next years."[53] Germans' obsession with monitoring their rations not only implied a belief that the occupation authorities were causing their hunger but also passively denied the fact that many other factors outside Allied control were determining the food situation in Germany. As an American military report noted, former Nazi officials and postwar German authorities, not the Allies, were responsible for "such notably mishandled matters as the allocation of planting quotas, the collection of foodstuffs from the farms, the distribution of food, the allotment of farm tools or machinery, the movement of workers from city to country,"[54] yet all such problems were consistently attributed to Allied mismanagement. The Allies developed educational programs that they hoped "should aid the German people in assuming their own responsibilities" for "the real shortages of food in Germany."[55] However, attempts to explain that "not only Berlin, but all of Europe hungers" fell on deaf ears.[56] For example, German civilians in the French zone, which generally had the lowest rations, were little interested in hearing that bread rations in France were the same as or lower than their own, a fact that had inspired protests in hungry France.[57] In the British zone, posters explained to angry German civilians that

> More than 50% of the bread and flour consumed in the British zone was covered by imports. . . . No foodstuffs were exported from the zone and almost the entirety of the food needs of the British occupation troops was covered by imports. Over this same time, the food rations in England were reduced . . . 93% of the food for the deported peoples in Germany has been imported, although the German population bears the responsibility for feeding these mistreated peoples.[58]

Such careful explanations fell on deaf ears. Rather than increase a sense of collective solidarity or shared responsibility, these sorts of zonal and national rationing comparisons reinforced a widespread belief that the "bad Germans" were growing fat while the "good Germans" starved. In many ways,

Allied rationing programs in occupied Germany had much in common with the rationing programs of the First World War because they reinforced existing societal divisions along gender, occupational, class, and regional lines. As had been the case during World War I, hungry city dwellers claimed that the rural regions were overflowing with food as the cities starved, a belief that seemed confirmed by city-dwellers' desperate trips to farms to acquire extra provisions. While urbanites accused farmers of hoarding food in anticipation of future profits, farmers perceived themselves as the main victims, complaining not only about the authorities' unrealistic demands, but also the waves of German expellees from Eastern Europe whom they were frequently compelled to house and feed.[59]

There were many German food producers who exploited the widespread hunger for their own profit. Adulterating food was a popular way of stretching resources and increasing returns. It was quite common, for example, to sell flour that had been "mixed with portions of sand, plaster and other substances."[60] In Thuringia, several local companies were turning vegetables that had frozen due to improper storage into prepackaged salads "by first cooking them in order to make them edible," forcing the regional Nutrition Board to "prohibit all production of vegetable salads" due to serious health concerns.[61] Inspectors in Saxony discovered that a shipment of more than 600,000 kilograms of butter had been inadequately refrigerated for over a year and was subsequently covered in mold; nonetheless, it was still marked for consumption.[62] Hungry civilians also frequently accused shopkeepers, like farmers, of hoarding foodstuffs. An anonymous letter from Cologne, for example, singled out a grocery store where pickled carrots "without onions and scarcely any vinegar" were being sold for "one hears and gasps—1 RM." The shop owner, a Ms. Vinken, was described as "an overfed red-haired woman" and accused of being "more power-hungry than Adolf Hitler" in her "dictatorial" pricing schemes, profiting from the hunger of her desperate customers.[63] Of course, German consumers themselves used a variety of extralegal means to obtain more and better food. Everyday efforts to acquire food expanded to include illicit activities ranging from participation in the black market to acts of prostitution and theft and even to the murder of milkmen.[64] The occupation years thus saw a dramatic rise in illegal or semi-legal activities connected to food acquisition and distribution. These so-called crimes of scarcity shaped immediate postwar life for the majority of German civilians and were part of their larger experiences of collective hunger.

Public opinion across all four zones singled out the Allies as cruel masters indifferent to German suffering. Rationing programs that punished former Nazis or that reduced "normal consumer" allotments enforced the perception of many German civilians that they were being stigmatized and mistreated. These feelings of discrimination and undeserved hunger were interpreted as distinctly postwar sensations, giving rise to a peculiar narrative of abundance and deprivation in which Hitler's rise to power in 1933 was officially commemorated as the beginning of prosperity, employment, and proper German eating. It was only when Germany began to lose the war—a reversal that is usually dated to Germany's defeat at Stalingrad in 1943—that German civilians claimed to have begun experiencing any sort of privation. And it was only after the war, most Germans agreed, that "true" hunger became a reality for most of the population. Long-time Berlin inhabitant Joseph von der Acht wrote repeatedly to the city magistrate to request that vegetarians be allowed to exchange their meat rations for pulses or fruit juice, something, he noted, that had been generously granted under Hitler but that was not possible under the Allies; these unaccustomed dietary restrictions inspired him to morbidly wonder whether the occupation authorities intended that "the *vegetarians* should be the *first* to die out?"[65] A March 1947 article in the newly created weekly news-magazine *Der Spiegel,* bitterly titled "Jubilee of Hunger," commemorated the hundredth food-rationing period since rationing first began in Germany in 1939. Claiming that "even anti-Nazis remember with pleasure the 700 grams of meat and 420 grams of fat per week" allotted to German civilians by the Nazi government, the article waxed openly nostalgic: "as long as the swastika sun was in the ascension, the food distribution held steady." Hunger, the article claimed, "marched in with the Allies."[66] By casting hunger as a distinctly postwar phenomenon, thus severing it of its connection to the policies of the Third Reich, such discourse was part of a larger transformation of German hunger into a staging ground for the elaboration of new models of human rights and of humanitarian ideals.

After the war's end there had been a general consensus that hunger would be Germany's "fate." Allied government officials saw German hunger as an unavoidable consequence of the economic and physical destruction of Central Europe; former victims of Nazism and German Communists saw hunger as a just punishment and an unavoidable reality. Many German civilians, doctors, and politicians cast their hunger as a redemptive and constructive expression of collective identity. Demanding the right to not only get food but also to express their suffering, German civilians staged countless public protests across all four zones that successfully transformed international opinion and also affirmed a distinctive sort of collective self-awareness. According to these protesters, the Allied forces needed not simply to satisfy basic food needs but to acknowledge the humanity of the German people. Or, as a placard from a 1947 protest expressed it, "We want bread, not calories" (see Figure 3.1). Ultimately, such demands framed a larger shift in ways of conceptualizing the category of human rights in the wake of Nazism.

Figure 3.1 "Hunger demonstration in Munich in 1947: Munich protesters demand "we don't want calories, we want *bread!*" *Süddeutsche Zeitung*, March 1947.

Hunger, Human Rights, and the Dilemma of German Suffering

In their rationing and food-distribution systems, both the Germans and the Allied authorities drew associations between the food economy and moral categories of guilt and innocence. As historian Atina Grossmann has convincingly shown, rations "calibrated new (and constantly shifting) standards of victimization and entitlement and, importantly, recognition" on the part of the Allied powers.[67] German civilians in all four zones initially relied on anti-Nazi rhetoric in their pleas for increased food. In letters to the Allied authorities, they frequently complained that "supporters of Nazism are being favored" in food distribution, implicitly asserting their own status as dual victims: opponents of Hitler during the war and starving innocents after it.[68] One German's appeal to the Quakers for supplemental food packages, for example, condemned the general populace while praising her own family: "Today most Germans deny having been a Nazi, which is of course generally not true. We three, on the contrary, have always been anti-fascist."[69]

A new way of conceptualizing the category of innocence, however, supplanted the initial assumption that guilty Germans should be worse-fed than innocent ones. This change was encapsulated in the American decision, in 1946, to distribute food relief to Germans regardless of race, religion, or past political affiliation. This policy, cast as a response to the open discrimination against former Nazis of the Soviet rationing system, extended benefits to the general population of Germany while implicitly disadvantaging former victims of Nazism. Western rationing policies thus began articulating an idealized "equality of suffering." This egalitarian approach to food distribution was suffused with a new language of rights that was becoming increasingly popular in occupied Germany. While Germans petitioning the Allied authorities for food continued to make generic assurances that they had been "opponents of Nazism from its very beginning," they could now also openly complain of their postwar persecution as former Nazis.[70] Given the relatively small number of Germans with unblemished records, the German press in the Western zones quickly took to championing the "principle of the equality of all sufferers, without disadvantaging the politically persecuted, nor former National Socialists, all of whom might find themselves in equivalent states of suffering."[71]

Emerging German voices countered accusations of collective guilt with cries of collective suffering. While individuals could assert any number of specific harms they had experienced during or after the collapse of the Nazi state (bombing raids, rape by occupying soldiers, expulsion, etc.), their collective suffering hinged primarily on a shared and ubiquitous hunger. Hunger alone transformed them from the racialized *Volksgemeinschaft* of the Third Reich to a pitiable *Notgemeinschaft*, a "community of need."[72] These German voices documented in painful detail the degeneration of their individual and collective bodies to display their innocence and powerlessness; at the same time, these performances of suffering forged new bonds of shared victimization. In the words of a prominent German doctor, writing in 1948, "[T]he hunger disease today has attacked our entire *Volk* and knows no social distinctions."[73] Similar claims were advanced by German politicians, lawyers, public figures, and civilians, who repeatedly affirmed that "we hunger all together [*wir hungern doch alle gemeinsam*]."[74] Remarkably, these cries for the recognition of German suffering made their case by explicitly comparing German hunger with that of the victims of Nazism, and especially that of the Jews.

The idea that, as a regional newspaper claimed, the German people had "all fallen into the same state of misery due to the total collapse" built upon ubiquitous Nazi propaganda that had claimed that all Germans would experience a "common fate" at the hands of the Allied forces.[75] Having been inundated during the war with NSDAP stories about Allied plans to starve them to death, German civilians had not been surprised to find themselves with empty bellies in 1945.

In addition, earlier portrayals of the bestial and terrifying appetites of the Jews and the Slavs in particular continued to shape popular perceptions in occupied Germany. Bavarian housewife Irmgard Kiepenheuer, for example, penned in stilted English a personal appeal to the justice officer of the American zone to protect her family from acts of retribution on the part of recently liberated Polish slave laborers. Asserting that she had been "from the first day (1929) hostile to Hitler," Kiepenheuer alleged that these Polish laborers were carrying out "criminal acts of revenge," above all the stealing of pigs, thefts which made life even worse than "the bomb times." She reported that she had heard that "in English zones, Poles have been punished sharply, and even are shooted [sic] . . . and now there [is] peace, and people can work quietly." She requested permission to do the same in her region (permission was denied).[76] Other letters to local government offices frequently complained that Jews, Russians, DPs, and Gypsies were stealing food from Germans, crimes attributed to their base nature rather than their desperate hunger. A German civilian interviewed several months after the liberation of Bergen-Belsen recalled with loathing the just-freed "Gypsy women," depicting them as "the very worst" of all the former prisoners because they had dug the bulbs out of local flower gardens and devoured them greedily. These women, he claimed with open disgust, ate flower bulbs because "they were their favorite [food]," invoking Nazi-era stereotypes to deny other peoples' hunger while confirming his own.[77]

Nazi representations of Jews as fat leeches or ticks had implied that their corpulence was the cause of German thinness; Jewish bread was by definition snatched from the mouths of German children. After the collapse of the Third Reich, this sort of imagery continued to provide Germans with a vocabulary for expressing both the extremes of their hunger and their hostility toward the large numbers of foreign Jews on the soil of occupied Germany. To many, the idea that Jews were responsible for German suffering seemed more real after the war than it had during the years of the Third Reich.[78] Many German civilians believed that Jews who had fled Nazi Germany for the United States had returned as members of the American army to exact personal revenge; reassert ownership of property that had been seized by the Reich; and, most of all, to simply enjoy watching the Germans suffer. Local political leaders did not shy away from voicing these sorts of paranoias. Josef Baumgartner, the Bavarian minister of agriculture, famously complained in a 1947 speech that the hunger afflicting the German people could be directly blamed on the fact that "the majority of the important Americans here [in occupied Germany] consist of freemasons and Jews." Full of hatred for the "many Jews from the East here in Bavaria," Baumgartner was enraged at having been required to attend the Jewish congress at Bad Reichenhall; he declared that "the only pleasant thing during this congress was the unanimous resolution [by the Jews] to leave Germany."[79]

Local German populations voiced their outrage at programs designed to feed the DPs, especially Jewish DPs, who remained in German territory. The vast majority of Jewish DPs were located in the British and American zones, where they became the objects of both tremendous fear and jealousy. More than three-quarters of German civilians living in the American zone felt that Germany should not be responsible for feeding DPs at all.[80] Local Germans often assumed that these few isolated survivors wanted to inflict the sort of suffering on Germans that they themselves had experienced at the hands of the Nazis. (In fact, although these communities of mostly Central European Jews did include some former concentration-camp inmates, they were primarily made up of young men and women who had survived the war by fleeing to the USSR or by going underground.[81]) Some Germans saw the care packages sent to Jewish DPs by Jews from other countries, acts of charity organized by UNRRA and the American Jewish Joint Distribution Committee, as proof that Jews were getting more than their fair share of food. Such claims ignored the fact that the official rations of German civilians differed little from those of DPs, Jewish or not.[82] The rations that were officially allotted to DPs changed over time, between zones, and between the different categories of people who made up the DP population, but they were never extravagant.[83] And in any case, in 1947 the American zone officially canceled all supplemental food allotments for Jewish DPs in an attempt to resolve a long-standing concern that American policies would be perceived by Germans as discriminating "in favor of the Jews."[84] From this point onward in the Western zones, Jewish Holocaust survivors officially received standard rations, and international Jewish donations became the only major source of additional foodstuffs.

Throughout the occupation years, many Germans remained convinced that these unwanted foreigners were receiving excessive quantities of food; ironically, many singled out Holocaust survivors, and especially Jewish former concentration-camp inmates, as being especially egregiously overfed. A local inhabitant from the region surrounding Bergen Belsen vigorously insisted that the former "concentration camp Jews [*KZ-Juden*]" were "really quite well fed. Especially when they began to get extra rations, they started to burst at the seams. If they didn't like their food, they would scream: what kind of food is this! We ate better in the camp."[85] Jewish overeating was not only attributed to the pro-Jewish bias of Allied rationing; Jewish survivors continued to be associated with both greed and criminality, attributes which had been central to Nazi anti-Semitism. For example, a German farmer struggling to provide his family with satisfying food expressed his anger over the fact that the Jew "E," a former camp inmate "always had a lot of bread, he still had the [rationing] cards of all of his murdered relatives, he had four of them. Therefore he could bargain with the extra supplies, he had 4–5 extra bread loaves."[86] The perceived unfairness of his bread surplus rendered entirely moot the fact that his entire family had been murdered. If the postwar German hunger discourse borrowed from earlier Nazi tropes, especially those defining German hunger against the threatening hunger of the Jews, it also allowed Germans to identify themselves explicitly with the victims of Nazi violence. The postwar moment, the German peoples' first collective reckoning with the meaning of the Holocaust, saw hunger being used to bridge the seemingly unbridgeable divide between the languages of Nazi racism and of postwar human rights.

According to postwar German leaders, topping the list of the "laws of humanity" was the right to satiety. They claimed that European civilization depended on the West's ability to adequately feed this defeated population. Taking up the language of new postwar hunger-relief programs, an amateur economist living in Dresden wrote to his zonal authorities claiming that eating to the point of being full (*das Sattessen*) is "the most basic, natural and self-evident right that any human being can demand; it comes before even that most democratic of rights, the right for personal freedom."[87] A public resolution issued by the German medical profession in mid-1947 informed the world that "the majority of the German population lives currently from rations that are only equivalent to a third of the internationally recognized minimal requirements."[88] A Düsseldorf article from a year later applied the language of the Nuremberg trials to claim that "what the German *Volk* has been forced to endure for the past several years is, in the truest sense of the word, a crime against humanity."[89]

Emerging German activists and politicians exhorted their compatriots to reveal their desperate plight to the world. As one dramatic letter to the Dresden city government began: "I belong to the people, not to the satiated, but to the hungry ones, and I know that my suffering is that of all the others, my thinking is the same as theirs."[90] Despite often contradictory or unclear results, German medical studies on the nutritional state of the country's civilians consistently concluded that "all levels of society are now succumbing to hunger."[91] Turning their accusatory gaze on a world they felt was letting them starve, German men and women wrote letters to the occupation forces voicing their fears that they had been "condemned to die out."[92] The food crisis, a group of leading German doctors and nutritionists claimed, was so extreme that "everyone in the entire world bears the guilt if he does not do everything in his power to give aid."[93]

German doctors and nutritionists used their medical expertise to explain the importance of the country's hunger and to warn of the threat that it represented. For doctors, empty bellies became an explanation for all kinds of psychological and moral problems, which they deemed "purely biological in nature, rooted in inadequate protein supplies."[94] If Germans seemed hostile, selfish, depressed, racist, and reluctant to work, still glorified the Third Reich, and displayed traits "otherwise not present in their character," these were not responses to the war or the internalization of Nazi values, but rather symptoms of the postwar "hunger-disease."[95] Hunger was blamed for the disintegration of familial relationships and friendships and the abandonment of "traditional" German values. Lack of food was responsible for the destruction of "all sense of mutual help and trust; in some cases family members have even stolen from one another, or burgled their neighbors."[96] Inappropriate, problematic, or downright dangerous behavior by Germans was thus always interpreted as reactive rather than causal.

When Germans chose to cite the facts of life and death in Nazi concentration camps and ghettos, they showed how well they had listened to, and learned from, the Allied occupiers. Economist Karl Brandt confidently claimed that "for prolonged periods the food rations in the Western zones fell to or below the rations fed the inmates of the Nazi horror camps."[97] Relatively few civilians claimed that "we didn't know anything"; instead, they openly asserted their knowledge of the camps—but only to compare and highlight the level of their own suffering. Within just months of capitulation, a report from the city of Görlitz unfavorably compared the population's weekly ration of 250 grams of bread to the daily rations of prisoners at Monowitz, a sub-camp of Auschwitz that had especially high mortality rates.[98] In 1948, an article published in the Rhineland compared rations in Buchenwald to those of the French zone (purportedly 1675 calories versus 805), leading a local politician to claim that Germans have "for three years been forced to bear a level of hunger such as that known in no concentration camp in the world."[99] *Der Spiegel* quoted the much-celebrated resistance fighter and pastor Martin Niemöller in a letter addressed to the "Emergency Committee for German Protestantism" in which Niemöller asserted that the current calorie allotment of 700 calories a day was less than the

> lowest rations in the concentration camps. Since the conditionless surrender of the German people, at least six million Germans have perished. One cannot help but believe that the total effect is nothing other than the attempt to annihilate an entire nation to its very roots.[100]

Such comparisons between Nazi concentration camps and the civilian rationing program had little basis in fact. Although the Nazis' standard caloric allotment for inmates was officially set at around 1,600 calories, scholarship has shown that in practice this number remained a fiction for the vast majority of prisoners.[101] Moreover, comparisons of quantities of Allied food provisions with those provided by the Nazis in the ghettoes and camps assume they were commensurate; in reality, much of the "food" that the Nazis provided to inmates was rotten, inedible, or deliberately contaminated. Yet the fundamental difference between the food supply of German civilians after the war and that of concentration-camp inmates during the war in terms of basic nutrition remains the fact that German civilians were free to acquire and to cultivate food. Thus bartering, stealing, and both producing and gathering foodstuffs across all four zones were ubiquitous; combined with the almost universal participation in the vast black market, it is clear that the rations allotted to German civilians were not their only, or even primary, source of sustenance. Nonetheless, analogizing the Nazis' genocidal food policies to the Allies' rationing programs was not just acceptable; it became a crucial symbol of the new postwar model of human rights.

Among the Allied forces, sympathy for hungry Germans acquired political traction for a variety of ideological and pragmatic reasons. British and especially American concern over German hunger reinforced the Western consensus that hunger was the greatest political threat facing the postwar world. The international empathy for hungry Germans in particular had a practical rationale; the defeated country's economic and cultural significance within Europe made the larger project of postwar reconstruction impossible to imagine without a prosperous German state.

Scholars Hoyt Price and Carl Schorske, hired by the US Council of Foreign Relations to write a report on postwar Germany, made the claim that "there will not be economic or political health in Europe until we have faced and dealt with the German problem."[102] The émigré German-Jewish economist Gustav Stolper warned, in his 1947 publication *German Realities*, that "the future of Germany is the future of European liberty. In Germany it will triumph or die."[103] Remarkably, a growing number of Western philanthropists relied upon the emerging evidence of the Nazis' genocidal persecution of Jews in framing their pleas to increase the rations for the German civilian population.

Influential British Jewish publisher Victor Gollancz was one of the first Westerners to explicitly invoke the Holocaust as a rationale for feeding German civilians and, especially, German children. In 1946, he published a booklet pleading for the provision of aid to Germans which relied on visual tropes and linguistic rhetoric that referenced the Nazi genocide of Europe's Jews. *Is It Nothing to You?* consisted of a series of photographs of young, malnourished children staring blankly at the reader or shown in profile, with their gaunt limbs and swollen stomachs painfully apparent (see Figure 3.2).[104] Such stark depictions of German hunger drew on older humanitarian imagery that employed children as symbols of innocence. Similarly, a postwar Swiss publication, *On the Provisioning of the European Continent in 1945*, described the streets of Germany as full of starving children, reduced to "skeletons, barely covered by paper-thin skin stretched tightly ... faces hollowed out by hunger ... a picture of boundless suffering ... a heartwrenching accusation against humanity."[105] Vowing to ensure that "nobody will be able to say: I did not know," the book warned readers that "we are not allowed to wait until the hunger-skeletons are pictured yet again in the newspapers."[106] An insistence on the distinctiveness of German hunger, on the particular suffering of children, and on the broader imperative that the global

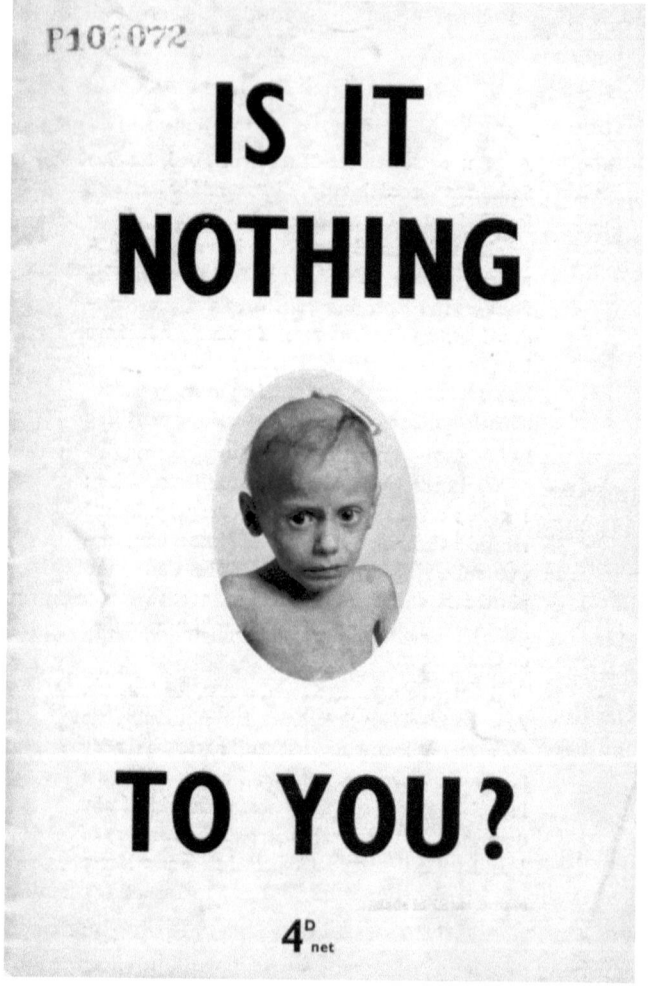

Figure 3.2 Victor Gollancz, *Is It Nothing to You? Photographs of Starving German Children*. London: V. Gollancz (currently, the Orion Publishing Group), 1946. Attempts to trace the copyright holder were unsuccessful. Courtesy of Charles Deering McCormick Library of Special Collections, Northwestern University Libraries.

community not "stand by and watch" as millions starved, implied an analogy between the Holocaust and the German Hunger Years.

The novelty of such portrayals was the juxtaposition of just-published photographs documenting horrors of Nazi camps with the ongoing suffering of German citizens. William Langer, a prominent US congressman, claimed that American rationing policy in Germany was making the country "an accomplice in one of the most staggering crimes ever committed against humanity."[107] Speaking before Congress in 1946, he reminded his listeners of the grim pictures of the piled-up bodies uncovered by the American and British armies, and [how] our hearts have rung with pity at the sight of such emaciation.... Yet now, to our utter horror, we discover that our own policies have merely spread these same conditions even more widely.... I hold in my hand absolutely authentic photographs which have been taken at the beginning of the winter in the city of Berlin. These photographs are interchangeable for horror with the photographs with which we became familiar from Dachau, Mauthausen, Buchenwald, and other extermination camps. These are photographs of children between the ages of 5 and 14.[108]

Herbert Hoover, the head of the newly formed Famine Emergency Committee, demanded improvements in German rations since "we do not want the American flag flying over nation-wide Buchenwalds."[109] The British media, in an article titled "Feed the Brutes," demanded aid for "those pitiful ambling Belsens which move along the highways of eastern Germany."[110] Prominent intellectual Dwight McDonald went so far as to claim that "the Nazis were less hypocritical [than the Allies]. When they decided to kill the Jews of Europe, they organized mass executions by gas chambers."[111] German civilian deaths, he claimed, were "already on a scale comparable to Maidenek, Oswiecim [Auschwitz], and Belsen."[112] A report by the US Special House Committee on Post-war Economic Policy and Planning claimed that American policy in occupied Germany would cause a "considerable part of the German population" to be "'liquidated' through disease, malnutrition, and slow starvation for a period of years to come."[113] British Labor politician John Hynd asserted that German civilians in the British zone were being forced to get by on 700 or fewer calories a day, though "even in Belsen at its worst the skeletons seen on the films were being given 800 calories."[114] As German hunger during the Allied occupation became equated with that experienced by those persecuted by the Nazis, Germans became legitimate targets of international sympathy.

As Cold War divisions among the Allies began emerging, German POWs being held in the nations of Eastern Europe, and especially the USSR, became crucial ideological symbols. The trope of hunger transformed German soldiers, previously seen as icons of brutality and bearers of death, into figures analogous to concentration-camp inmates. Both populations were confined in camps and subjected to starvation, and both thus became "innocent" victims of larger forces manipulating them. A 1947 letter from a Hildesheim woman inaccurately claimed that

> one and a half to two million [German POWs in the Soviet Union] are believed to have starved to death and perished. Is this a better treatment than in the German concentration camps? In the concentration camps,

people were immediate[ly] anaesthetized in the gas chambers, even though it was not nice to treat human beings like this.[115]

This emphasis on the significance and scope of German POW hunger served to underscore and validate the suffering on the German home front as well.

This use of hunger as a sort of social glue to link "all" Germans together was not universally embraced. German Communists consistently rejected such rhetoric, attempting to sever the affective relationship between the suffering home front and former soldiers held in internment. In 1949, the readers of the East German women's magazine *Für Dich* learned that German soldiers in a Polish POW camp were receiving a king's ransom in food supplies. After his release, one man reminisced about his "3038 calories per day [in the camp]. I couldn't even manage to finish off all of my daily serving of bread, since we received 800 grams every day, and in addition 40 grams of bacon, 50 grams of sugar, 125 grams of packaged foods."[116] That these former Nazi soldiers were thus substantially better off than their wives and children at home was an irony that the communist magazine belabored in an unsuccessful attempt to woo the female population in the Soviet zone. The communist press often explicitly demonized German POWs, linking them to war crimes rather than the deprivations of postwar German civilians. For example, a shocking two-page spread with the headline, "How It Is in Rüdersdorf: How It Was in the Concentration Camps," detailed the relatively high quality of life in a Soviet POW camp. Alongside photos of starved corpses at Maidenek and an image of famished German women standing in a bread line is a photo of the smiling and plump Alfred Müller, "who was a violent participant in the notorious *Kristallnacht* . . . no one could ever claim that he was suffering hunger pangs."[117]

Unlike the majority of German civilians who saw their hunger as especially distinctive and tragic, Communists in Germany categorically rejected claims of German uniqueness. A 1948 booklet aimed at recruiting German farmers to the KPD criticized the fact that

> the most widespread opinion seems to be that there has never been a people anywhere in the world who has experienced anything similar to that of Germany, and there is no place in the world where there is "such a hunger" as currently in Germany . . . Our poor memory for history is no longer acceptable . . . if only we didn't always think exclusively about our bellies.[118]

Those on the Left did not believe the hunger of the postwar years was caused by Germany's defeat; rather, it was rooted in the country's initial desire to go to war. Condemning a "century-long German tradition of crafting weapons for the conquest of foreign soil rather than tools to till the native fertile ground," left-wing activists linked hunger to German militarism, not the Allies' cruel negligence.[119] Predictably, Communists were outraged by the countless assertions by German citizens that "we ate better under Hitler"; in turn, they compared Allied rations favorably with those of Nazi camps and ghettoes.[120]

But these voices were in the minority in Germany and rapidly fell out of favor internationally. Even the Soviet Union, though deeply suspicious of German POWs, stopped denouncing German civilians' hunger claims. The desire to gain legitimacy and to overcome the association of Communism with hunger made the Soviets surprisingly sympathetic to German hunger pleas. Demonizing German POWs and blaming Germans for Europe's hunger was a poor platform for establishing a new, socialist German state. By the end of the Allied occupation in 1949, German hunger would prove to be as central to the new Cold War as it had been to the two world wars that had preceded it.

Starving Berlin

As noted earlier, the new language of human rights cast concern over German hunger as emblematic of a new, modern, and progressive valuing of all human life regardless of political activity or personal history. Cold War rhetoric in the West argued that Communism both arose out of hunger and created new hungers. The socialist East, in turn, rejected these accusations, striving instead to link capitalism with social inequality, poverty, and inadequate food supplies. Occupied and divided Germany became the major site for the postwar elaboration and enactment of these sorts of global visions.

Regulating food resources seemed a crucial power lever in the postwar world. The global food crisis, and the intimate relationship between Nazism, the war, and mass hunger, made resolving hunger a central issue in reconstruction efforts. Both within occupied Germany and across the globe, the former Allies vied to establish themselves as both unbiased and all-powerful food distributors. The London *Economist* complained in the 1946 article "Wheat in World Politics" that "there is at present no body capable of distributing the world's inadequate supply of wheat on a basis of sheer need and without taint of politics."[121] As the four powers debated the best way to feed the various populations all declaring their "right to be satiated," the Allies used food to represent the promise of their respective political systems—while monitoring each other's food policies with paranoia and growing suspicion. The American magazine *Fortune*, in a 1946 exposé on the "food scandal" in Europe, despaired that

> the political aspect of the food crisis is heightened by tension and suspicion between Russia and the US and Britain. Charges and countercharges of the use of food as a political weapon have been hurled back

and forth.... Russians demand that UNRRA stop feeding anti-Soviet refugees who refuse to return to their native countries. The US and Britain retort that UNRRA food is being used to bolster Communist regimes in the Russian spheres.[122]

In Western Europe and the United States, human rights discourse rapidly became more concerned with the struggle against communism than the causes and consequences of Nazism and genocide.[123] As had been the case after the First World War, the hunger protests in occupied Germany were watched more closely than those of any other population. Papers across Europe and North America, for example, were full of vivid descriptions of a "wild, two-hour demonstration" in Düsseldorf, when 100,000 people "stoned British-occupied buildings and attacked British military cars as they protested the shortage of food." Whereas German reporting described these marches as motivated "only by hunger" and thus "apolitical," the American press claimed that "the Communists were likely behind the affair."[124]

This growing association of German hunger with communism provided an ideal context for the re-emergence of Herbert Hoover on the global stage. After a tour of postwar Europe, the former US president expressed particular concern for the suffering German population. Lucius Clay, military governor of the US zone, recorded in his memoirs that

> Hoover was convinced that our needs were real and that the food shortage in Germany was more acute than elsewhere in Europe. He recognized the menace of communism and the possibility of its growth in a desperate Germany. Above all, he believed that there was no place for starvation where the American flag was flying and that with the raising of that flag we accepted the responsibility to maintain human values.[125]

The growing hostility between the USSR and the United States enabled Hoover to convince both his government and the American public to back his food aid projects, which were reorganized under the auspices of a new Famine Emergency Committee. The committee was established by President Truman on March 1, 1946, and had the elderly Hoover as honorary chairman and figurehead.

This committee was just one of a multitude of American aid programs that emerged after the war to address hunger across the world; however, the tremendous amounts of American aid sent to Germany overshadowed parallel relief projects targeting famine-stricken central Europe and Asia. The Cooperative for American Remittances to Europe (CARE) instituted the new CARE package in 1945 as a way to use surplus US army food packages; the parcels were initially sent to a destitute France. The prohibition against sending CARE packages to Germany was lifted within a few months of the program's beginning, and Germans rapidly became the largest CARE recipients. About a third of the program's total budget, approximately 85 million dollars in aid, went to West Germany, and five of every eight CARE packages sent to Europe were addressed to Germany.[126] The US-based Council of Relief Agencies Licensed to Operate in Germany (CRALOG) shipped more than 55 million pounds of food to Germans in 1948 alone.[127]

In 1946, a group of American intellectuals and businessmen "warned the American people ... that they must assume the responsibility of feeding the Germans if democracy is to compete with communism in Germany."[128] In this rhetoric, fighting communism became synonymous with establishing a healthy capitalist market in the West. Allied occupation officials admitted that

> it would probably be too much to say that an adequate food supply will guarantee the establishment of a democratic system of government in Germany. Contrarily, it is not likely that the seed of democracy will take root and thrive amid hunger, flagging energy and failing health. . . . The importance to the peace of the world of adequate food now [in occupied Germany] is tremendous.[129]

Hoover's 1948 publication *No Reconstruction without Food* made both economic and fear-based arguments for feeding Germans: "A half-starved people in cities and industrial areas, without direct access to farm surpluses, cannot work hard and assume civic responsibilities, and may easily be enticed or driven to desperate forces."[130] In 1949, CRALOG published a report that proudly claimed, "CRALOG's gifts, extended with love and compassion, will be the deciding factor which will tip the German political balance in favor of democracy and peace."[131]

Not surprisingly, German civilians embraced this prioritization of their hunger. Hoover's push to increase American aid to Germany was heralded by the *Tagesspiegel* as "the embodiment of a practical humanity."[132] Many Germans were especially enthusiastic about the involvement of Hoover, whose 1947 Nobel Peace Prize officially affirmed the value of his particular style of food aid. Between 1946 and 1948, Germans of all stripes penned letters of thanks and made personal appeals to Hoover. In one letter, Peter Gast from Bamburg claimed that the food-aid programs of the First World War had done "more for a better understanding between peoples and for democracy in Germany than any newspaper article or education course." Gast, a self-declared "former member of the Nazi party," had "lost all [his] property in the Russian and the Polish zone of Germany," as well as his job, due to denazification. In his appeal, Gast linked his plight, particularly his struggle to get supplementary rations as a former

Nazi, with the need to protect "our children from severe undernourishment."[133] Other letter writers openly celebrated Hoover's well-known compassion toward Germany. Anneliese Hartmann-Kempf, writing from Hessen, claimed that "all Germans who consciously lived through the First World War and the postwar years remember your generous aid program.... With thankful hearts we think of you as one of the greatest Samaritans of human history."[134] A Bavarian man, speaking for the "37 million antifascists in Germany" who had all been "subjected to the chicanery of the Nazi regime," claimed that Hoover "during [his] term as president [was] a German American, and I therefore feel that you will have a better understanding of the character of Germans."[135]

Hoover's extensive history of activism on behalf of German civilians not only endeared him to the population, it also shaped the evolution of international humanitarianism. However, Hoover played no role in the era's most spectacular food-aid program. The Berlin Airlift of 1948–49, perhaps the most celebrated food-aid program of the twentieth century, solidified food's role as a key method of transforming politics into humanitarianism, while establishing Germany as the geopolitical and symbolic heart of the Cold War.

The airlift, which began on June 26, 1948, was an American military reaction to the Soviet blockade of the western sector of Berlin. The Soviet government in the city's eastern sector, angered by the recent currency reform in the Western zones of Germany, decided to force the economic consolidation of the divided city by severing most of the land transport lines linking West Berlin to the other Western zones. The personal travel of West Berliners was not limited, and they were able to move freely, but goods could no longer be delivered to the western sector by truck or train, a move intended to compel citizens to seek out food and supplies from Soviet sources. The American Air Force, later joined by Britain, developed the idea of an airlift, or *Luftbrücke*, as a way of delivering supplies to the population, dubbing the project "Operation Vittles." Given the limited amount of food that was actually flown in by the West and the consistent availability of food in blockaded Berlin from Soviet and private sources, it is unlikely that the airlift actually prevented famine. However, it ended up serving important political goals.[136]

The nearly year-long airlift, which provided both coal and food to Berliners, was, like the Soviet blockade itself, intended to make food consumption an ideological issue. An individual's choice of what to eat became not just representative of his or her political identity but constitutive of it. Immediately after the blockade began, West Germans and American observers inaccurately described it as a Soviet plan for "mass starvation." Since then, the idea that the aim of the Soviet blockade had been to starve the people of West Berlin has become a trope in Cold War historiography. As late as 1998, an American military historian described the airlift as "a brutal method to change

Western policy by starving 2.5 million West Berlin civilians."[137] In fact, the Soviet blockade was aimed at centralizing the distribution of food more than preventing its consumption. As the communist media emphasized throughout the blockade, both the Soviet government and the city leadership of the Eastern half of the city "repeatedly offered to supply the entire city with food and coal."[138] The Soviets had accumulated extra stores of food and coal before initiating the blockade in anticipation of increased demands, though these stores could not realistically have met the demand of the entire Western sector of the city. West Berlin media acknowledged the Soviet offers, but waged an extensive political campaign to discourage citizens from taking advantage of them, inspiring the East Berlin newspaper *Berliner Zeitung* to claim that "one cannot speak in honesty of a blockade by the Russians, rather of a self-blockade."[139] It was not difficult to dissuade West Berliners from taking up the Soviets on their offer. Germans and Americans shared a suspicion of Soviet foodstuffs. Rumors of poisoned and rotten groceries along with innumerable Western news reports describing the lives of Germans in the Eastern sector as miserable, filthy, and always hungry, made Soviet food seem, at best, unappetizing and, at worst, downright dangerous.

Of course, some West Berliners remained unconvinced that this was true, or they simply proved weaker at withstanding hunger pangs. A small group of men and women, about 5 percent of the West Berlin population, chose to travel across the zonal border, register for the communist rationing card, and receive supplies of Soviet foodstuffs and coal. These West Berliners were subjected to tremendous public hostility and censure in the West German, American, and British media. Several months into the blockade, the West Berlin *Sozialdemokrat* newspaper ran a lengthy article titled "Now They Want to Come Back! Discussions with West Berliners who shop in the Eastern sector." The article included interviews with West Berliners who had "defected" to the East by choosing to register for rationing cards in the Soviet zone. Documenting the moral and physical degeneration that resulted from this behavior, the article detailed shifty personalities, a lack of political values, and a missing commitment to local community. Mocking those who "want to enjoy both the rights of a democracy and the bait of the dictator simultaneously," the article concluded with the charge that these people needed to learn "that grocery shopping is not simply a question of household economy, but rather something that one has to answer for with his political and human conscience."[140]

The West Berlin media negotiated a delicate balance between its emphasis on the "betrayal" of Berliners who ate Soviet food and the insistence that almost no one fell for this Communist trap. In the words of one article, "The Eastern Bait Seduces No One," "the Soviet plan to feed all of Berlin has failed. In November only 78,000 West Berliners—that is 3.7 percent of the population of the western sectors—registered for food distribution in the Soviet zone."[141] The reporter quoted these numbers with pride, proof that

> the people of West Berlin—with a very few insignificant exceptions—resisted all the threats and blandishments of the Soviets, accepted the serious privations that the blockade entailed, and remained loyal to the democratic government of Berlin and the representatives of the western powers who stood behind it.[142]

For 96.3 percent of the West Berlin population, the decision to go hungry rather than accept "Communist bait" could be upheld as a sign of political courage and an expression of commitment to Western values. Rather than being forced to starve, this time Germans could "choose" their hunger—and they chose a hunger that miraculously linked them with Western abundance instead of Soviet austerity. In this sense, it is striking that tens of thousands of West Berliners chose to consume both Soviet and Western food. As historian Paul Steege has reminded us, the decision to refuse the offered foodstuffs was not "motivated solely by some sort of moral or ideological opposition to the Soviet Union."[143] Moreover, the very ability of West Berliners to reject Soviet food for political or practical reasons contradicts countless claims of imminent starvation, revealing the permeability of the blockade and the resourcefulness of German citizens in the face of a hunger that they simultaneously despised and celebrated.

By resisting Communist blandishments, the people of West Berlin claimed, in the dramatic words of mayor Ernst Reuter, to have "given the world an example," not of tyranny or the "weapon of death" but of "the will for freedom, for social justice and for peace."[144] With its connotations of voluntary suffering and even martyrdom, the airlift linked German civilians, particularly the housewives responsible for acquiring food for their families, with hunger strikers and freedom fighters, similarly seeking to transform self-imposed hunger into a weapon against oppressive forces. The lifting of the blockade in May 1949 was described as "a success of female self-sacrifice [*weiblicher Opferbereitschaft*]," reinforcing both a general German narrative of victimization, and the particularly gendered nature of food-related suffering after the war.[145]

In the context of the Cold War, the suffering and perseverance of the Berlin population linked (West) Germans with the rest of the "free world" and especially with freedom-loving Americans, defying those powers "who could not achieve their goals through democratic means, whose allies are hunger and cold, disease and misery."[146] The successful marriage of German hunger and American abundance solidified both Germans' status as victims and their integration into the prosperous West. Along with raisins and chocolate, American planes also delivered tens of thousands of CARE packages to the beleaguered population of West Berlin. This proved to be the beginning of a long relationship; West Germany continued to receive CARE packages until 1962, a fact that reflects the symbolic and geopolitical importance that feeding Germans had for Americans more than it does the real needs of the German people. Ultimately, the airlift proved to Berliners that the Western world sympathized with and even admired them. Their rejection of Soviet bread and margarine, and their gathering of the candies and raisins distributed by American pilots, existentially transformed them in the eyes of the Western world from former Nazis into victims of Communism. The airlift thus offered West Germans an opportunity to create entirely new identities as heroic soldiers in the Cold War, freeing themselves of the baggage of the Second World War.

East German propaganda attacked this Western vision linking the United States with both abundance and sympathy for Germans, claiming that the Americans (rather than the Soviets) had been Germany's primary enemy during the just-past war. Reminding the people of Berlin that the "English and American military pilots fly today on the command of the same gentlemen as during the war," the communist press asked if these pilots "think of the dead [German] women and children" whom they killed in wartime bombing raids as they flew over blockaded Berlin, "now attacking the working class."[147] However, such rhetoric found little resonance, quite different from German fears of Soviet "starvation plans," fears which had been planted in the popular consciousness by the Third Reich. The undeniable suffering caused by American bombings already seemed archaic in the emerging terms of the Cold War, which defined America not by its military prowess but by its consumer prosperity. As one West German author saw it in 1949, the airlift was the "entry to a better time and the beginning of the reconstruction of our much-suffering city," the "most impressive display of the commitment of the entire world not to abandon us to our fate." The planes flying over Berlin, dropping not bombs but chocolate, their pilots "no longer enemies, but friends," confirmed the intertwined threats that yet again faced Germans: hunger and Communism.[148]

The Berlin Airlift signaled not only the political but also the moral and emotional valence of German hunger. At this moment, capitalist America stood for generosity, deliciousness, and satiety, next to which its new opponent—the communist USSR—seemed a desolate space of tasteless food, widespread hunger, and arbitrary restrictions on consumers. In the subsequent decades these categories remained so strong and seemingly self-evident in the Western imagination that it is important to remember that they were postwar inventions. Immediately after the war, in the face of the global food crisis, mass unemployment and misery, and increasing food productivity in the Soviet Union, it was not obvious which of the two economic systems would better feed its respective populations. The *New York Times* reported in 1947 that "Russia's grain and other harvests are going to be so good that the Soviet Union will be in a position to make wheat and other products available to some other nations," threatening to destabilize the United States' assumed role as postwar food provider.[149]

For the German population, the airlift held additional significance. Many Germans had viewed all of the occupying powers as enemy forces; the Russians may have been more hated than the British and Americans, but all had been wartime enemies and all were held responsible for German suffering. The onset of the Cold War and the airlift erased this commonality, replacing it with a new dichotomy: the USSR versus the United States. The cover of an American cookbook that was produced in celebration of "Operation Vittles" depicted Berliners as helpless and hungry baby birds; American airplanes care for them in defiance of the Soviets, who are frantically try to destroy the Germans' nest (see Figure 3.3). Divided Berlin became an international stage, allowing America to emerge as the "leader of the Western world," as well as the leading enemy of totalitarianism. Starvation, now seen as a Soviet instead of a German or British weapon of war, became part of a plot that transcended national borders. An American air force propaganda pamphlet from 1949 warned that the Communists, if left unchecked, would use "a hunger weapon against the Americans, against the British, and against the French." In response, the decision to feed Germans was made in order "to keep Berliners alive—and to keep Americans and their families well-fed."[150] The struggle against Communism was transformed into not only a project to feed the hungry but also a struggle to protect their rights, and the rights of humanity at large.

* * *

In the aftermath of the Second World War, the German past was officially gutted of all positive force, leaving a population without a center and with empty bellies. This devastating emptiness also offered Germans a remarkable opportunity; their shrinking flesh became an embodied version of the *Stunde Null* (zero hour), encouraging Germans to define themselves in terms of absence and loss. Hannah Arendt, in her scathing 1950 evaluation of the "aftermath of Nazi rule," also felt that lack defined the German people—not a lack of community, but one of power: "it is as though the Germans, denied the power to rule the world, had fallen in love with impotence as such."[151] Historian Robert Moeller has noted that the postwar embrace of the victim status, especially for women, was a strategic method of avoiding "any direct confrontation with the horrors of the thousand-year Reich."[152] The misery of the postwar expulsions and Soviet soldiers' mass rape of German women acquired particular significance in this gendered narrative of suffering. Hunger played an equally important role in "erasing" the uncomfortable German past. Unlike acts of physical violence like rape or expulsion, hunger rarely had a clear perpetrator or finite scope, something

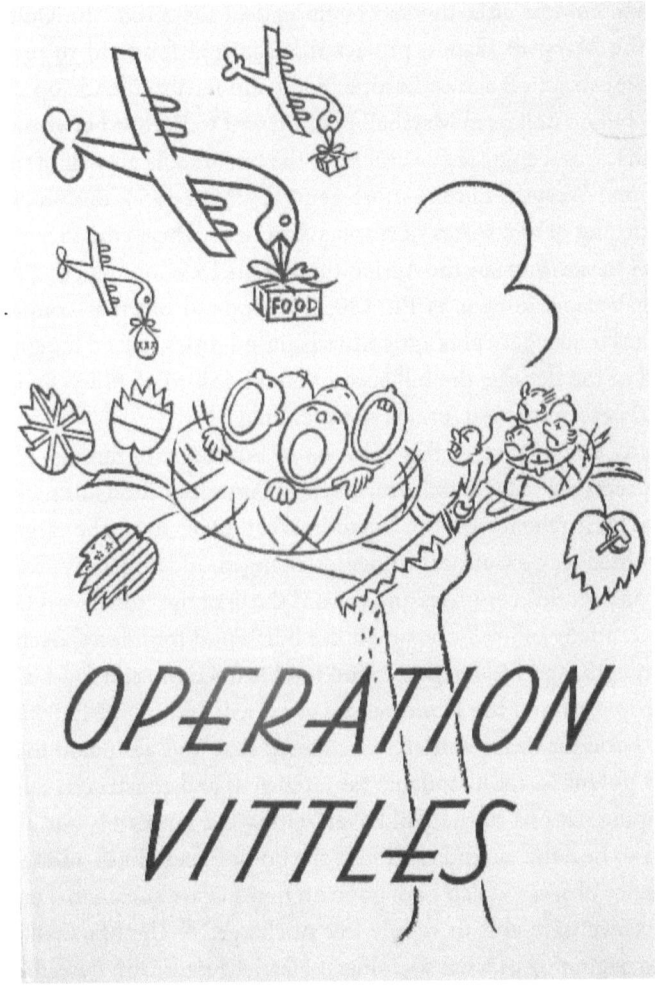

Figure 3.3 Cover of *Operation Vittles Cook Book: Compiled by the American Women in Blockaded Berlin*. Berlin: Deutscher Verlag, 1949. Private collection of the author.

that made it politically attractive at a moment when questions of responsibility and guilt were ubiquitous and unresolvable.

Bridging the transition from world war to the Cold War, the Berlin Airlift seemed to present proof of Western abundance and Western humanity—indeed, the two seemed equivalent—while confirming America's new mission to manage the world's food system. The US Air Force, whose reputation had been tarnished by wartime bombing raids on Europe as well as the horrors of Hiroshima and Nagasaki, declared in 1949 that the airlift "has conclusively proven a point of major concern to all American citizens—that American air power . . . is an instrument of peace."[153]

Just a few months after the successful end of the airlift, the United States launched the Marshall Plan, a project that married food aid to programs of national reconstruction across Europe. Food and fertilizer made up 29 percent of the 13.5 billion dollars in Marshall Plan aid sent to Europe between 1948 and 1952, aid that was recognized as crucial to the remarkable growth of the FRG in particular, and Western Europe more generally.[154] In 1954, the program's success at disposing of vast stores of surplus American wheat convinced President Eisenhower to sign into law the Agricultural Trade Development and Assistance Act, which became known as PL 480, the food-aid bill that committed the United States to using surplus agricultural commodities to feed hungry nations. By the end of the decade, the bill accounted for a third of all US grain exports and over 20 percent of total foreign-aid spending.[155]

In its early years, much of this aid went to Europe; for example, Poland and Yugoslavia received substantial quantities of American foodstuffs in an effort to decrease their reliance on the Soviet market. Over time, the targets of this food aid shifted as geopolitical priorities changed, moving away from the so-called "second-world" countries and toward those of the "third world." In 1961, President Kennedy officially renamed the bill "Food for Peace," declaring that "food is strength, and food is peace, and food is freedom, and food is a helping hand to people around the world whose good will and friendship we want."[156] In 1963, a Food for Peace conference claimed that "our abundant food supply is the most potent weapon available for intelligent and constructive use among the developing nations of the Cold War," citing the power of "our abundance of food . . . to heal the wounds and feed the bodies, reestablish and rehabilitate the economies of areas which have gone on to purchase substantial amounts of the products we were able to supply free of charge."[157] The Marshall Plan thus marked the beginning of what sociologist Harriet Friedmann described as "the rise of an international food order after World War II whose principal axis was food aid from the United States to formerly self-sufficient agrarian societies."[158]

This aid program, like its predecessor targeting postwar Germany, became intimately intertwined with discourses of human rights.[159] In Africa, Asia, and South America, the United States strove to repeat the success it had enjoyed in Berlin. But rarely did American food aid achieve as much political traction as it had had in post-Nazi Germany, where the humanitarian drive to feed the hungry seamlessly merged with the political project of battling Communism and the economic pressures of Cold War capitalist growth. This new form of food aid had allowed postwar states to fuse their far-reaching biopolitical ambitions, which aimed at the transformation of diverse bodies into distinct populations, with humanitarian projects and human rights concerns that were described as universal and ultimately apolitical. This is one of the reasons why, as Philip Alston has noted, "the right to food has been endorsed more often and with greater unanimity and urgency than most other human rights, while at the same time being violated more comprehensively and systematically than . . . any other right."[160] Probably one of the longest-lasting legacies of the Allied occupation of Germany is the trope of describing famine-stricken regions as analogous to Nazi concentration camps. Such facile analogies reveal the ways in which, over the course of the twentieth century, emergent languages of humanitarianism (after the First World War) and human rights (after the Second) transformed starving people into ideological currency, individuals whose political identity was waiting to be formed by donations of food. This way of conceptualizing the world's hungry in terms of their future political value assumes that the desire for food both precedes and supplants other desires and values, including political, economic, and moral ones. Or, as Bertolt Brecht succinctly put it in 1928, "First comes the feeding, then comes the moralizing."[161] Unlike most subsequent food-aid recipients, postwar Germans self-consciously used their status as "hungry victims" to remake their political identities. Indeed, during the Hunger Years, German civilians frequently cited Brecht's line in their pleas to the Allies for food. Men and women of all ages and political leanings described their sensations of hunger as simultaneously depoliticizing and politically revitalizing. By erasing their past, hunger forged bonds that simultaneously united Germans and, in the nascent Cold War, divided them from one another.

4

Fueling Reconstruction

Production and Consumption in Divided Germany

In 1949, just four years after the country's defeat and subsequent political and social collapse, the German nation was divided into two entirely new states: the socialist German Democratic Republic and the capitalist Federal Republic of Germany. The two countries faced similarly inauspicious beginnings; large cities had been reduced to rubble, their disaffected populations had grown dramatically with the arrival of largely unwelcome refugees, and their economies were in a state of crisis. During the Allied occupation, political activists had regularly complained that Germans did not care about anything except their stomachs; interest in larger political concerns had been replaced with an obsessive and exclusive focus on caloric allotments and rationing plans.[1] The founding of the two states, it was hoped, would gradually bring about an end to this all-consuming concern over the state of German bellies.

Remarkably quickly, formerly sworn enemies abandoned wartime agendas of punishment or revenge against the Germans, and instead began investing substantial amounts of energy and material resources into projects of German reconstruction. This was true for the GDR as well as the FRG. Although Marshall Plan aid to the West dwarfed Soviet aid to East Germany, and the Soviets continued to extract reparations for years after the war's end, Soviet leaders were nonetheless committed to an economically strong and industrialized German socialist state. Eschewing direct military conflict in the wake of the devastation wreaked by the past war, new political competition between the two postwar superpowers came to be expressed through economic—and particularly industrial—growth. Combined with an emphasis on the transformative power of work as a way to resolve the traumas of the war, this new Cold War competition meant that any serious attempt to denazify German industry by the Soviets as well as the Americans was quickly abandoned in favor of a commitment to increased industrial productivity.[2]

In the immediate aftermath of the war, the major constraint on Germany's industrial productivity was not limited resources, an inadequate labor pool, or even damaged infrastructure; it was the physiological requirements of its workforce. In the famous words of the American zone's military governor General Lucius Clay, "[W]ithout food we cannot produce coal; without coal we cannot support transport and industry; without coal we cannot produce the fertilizer necessary to improve future food supply. Only food can prime the pump."[3] In 1948, British general Brian Robertson similarly emphasized that "we all recognize that the food situation is the basic factor upon which [Germany's] economic recovery depends."[4] A report on industrial productivity in the American-British Bizone traced the impact of carefully calculated supplemental meals directly in terms of tons of coal produced (see Figure 4.1).

Inadequate food supply thus both symbolized and explained the country's economic incapacity, something that both Germans and Allied observers regularly emphasized. A German nutritionist noted in 1949 that "the reconstruction of our domestic economy is only possible when we have achieved an adequate

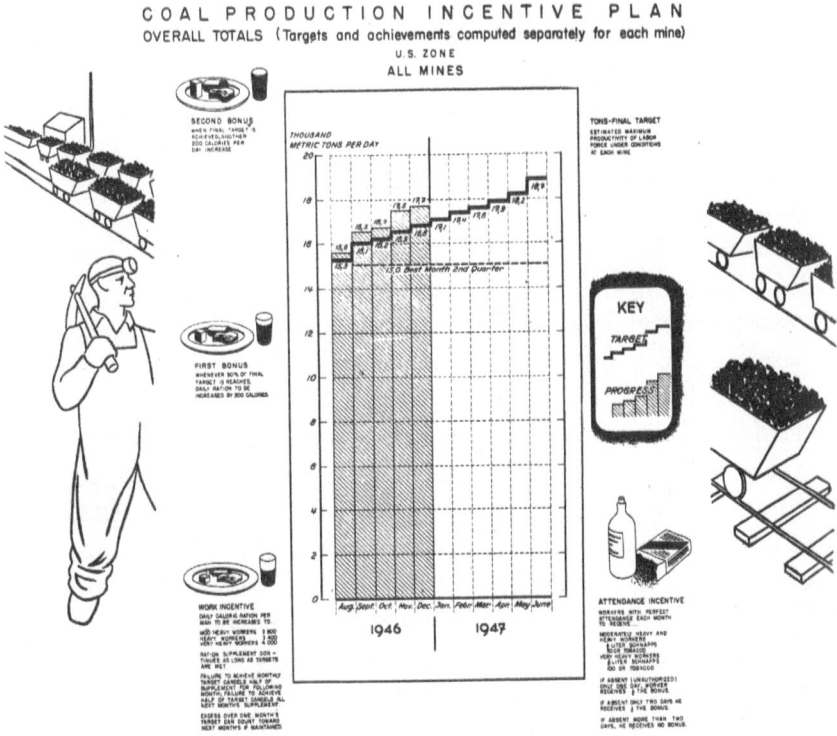

Figure 4.1 A coal production incentive plan. From U.S.-British Bipartite Food and Agriculture Panel, *Food and Agriculture, U.S.-U.K. Zones of Germany*. United States War Department, 1947, 46.

nutritional level."[5] During the harsh winter of 1947–48, industrial productivity decreased sharply; German doctors insisted that "increasing productivity is only possible by means of an increase of workers' calories."[6] The German newspaper *Telegraf* summed up the equation succinctly: "hunger grows, and productivity shrinks."[7]

The relationship between nutrition and industrial productivity had been the object of intense interest since the earliest decades of European industrialization, as economists, scientists, and social workers sought to calculate an ideal "optimization" diet for the working classes. This aim was part of a shift from the older idea of men "working in order to eat" to the idea of their "eating in order to work."[8] In 1896, Italian economist Francesco Nitti challenged governments around the world to recognize the "intimacy of the relation between the food and the labor-power of nations."[9] By the beginning of the twentieth century, new research on calories meant that food could be defined in mechanical terms, a sort of fuel analogous to coal or gas.[10] In this novel way of thinking, the individual body resembled the industrial machine—a "human motor"—that ran best on a perfect balance of "input" and "output."[11] Individual diets became incorporated into the larger project of scientific management that boomed between the wars in the search for, in the words of historian Charles Maier, "efficiency, optimality, enhanced productivity and expanded output."[12] Confronted with the need to incorporate large numbers of men and women into newly mechanized workplaces, factory owners and economic theorists linked industrial production with the regulation of nutrition, ultimately inspiring the creation and normalization of factory canteens.[13]

Just as canteens represented the industrial fantasy of totally controlling worker productivity, self-service grocery stores epitomized an idealized vision of private consumption and modern shopping. By the 1950s, supermarkets had become central to daily life across much of the industrialized world, as private consumerism became a key symbol of economic health and individual well-being.[14] Indeed, veneration of the supermarket as an emblem of free and unfettered consumption was as central to the rhetoric of the austere GDR as it was for the consumerist FRG. Despite such iconic status, the history of self-service stores makes clear that the concepts of "free choice" and "consumer freedom" have always been more fantasy than reality. Rather than reflecting a perfectible ratio of supply and demand, shopping was always shaped by limits of cost and supply. At the same time, individual shopping behavior has always proved impossible to regulate; the relationship between personal desires and the material objects available for consumption has consistently confounded the modern state, be it socialist or capitalist. At first glance, modern supermarkets seem diametrically opposed to factory canteens; the aisles of a well-stocked grocery store showcase free choice, freshness, and individual pleasure, in contrast to the monotony, drabness, and collective ethos of the workplace canteen. However, like these brightly lit, well-stocked shops, canteens have proved remarkably problematic over the course of the twentieth century. Despite decades of funding based on elaborate industrial calculations and careful nutritional research, they remained a major sticking point in the German industrial economy. Taken together, these twin spaces of industrialized food consumption reveal the aspirations, strategies, and limits of the biopolitical power of modern states.

Economic studies of divided Germany usually stress difference; this chapter uses canteens and supermarkets to develop a new kind of comparison that is focused on food's common functions in both socialist and capitalist industrial economies. An analysis of East and West German reconstruction during the 1950s and 1960s reveals that these functions are surprisingly similar across economic systems and class relationships. Moreover, exploring these sites together opens up the relationship between the politics of gender and the politics of food. Both the factory and the supermarket were highly gendered spaces. While the GDR struggled to align "traditional" gender norms with a revolutionary rhetoric of women's liberation, the FRG venerated the "shopping housewife" as a key figure in the country's economic recovery, developing what cultural historian Erica Carter has termed West Germany's "consumer-based model of citizenship."[15] Despite their clear differences, both of these models of femininity perceive women's economic power as uniquely bound to the production and consumption of food.

Factory Canteens and the Maximization of Labor Productivity

During the first half of the twentieth century, the incorporation of canteens and cafeterias into factories was an important part of German welfare policies that aimed to improve workplace conditions for the expanding population of industrial workers.[16] After 1914, the mobilization of industrial economies for war meant that many large factories in urban centers, particularly those in armaments, established canteens to provide employees with a hot meal during work hours. Factory meals were a crucial component of the Hindenburg Program, the military policy that aimed to double Germany's industrial output during the First World War. In the face of the economic pressures of total mobilization, industrialists increasingly saw factory canteens as a worthwhile investment that had the potential to ward off workers' protests and popular dissatisfaction.[17] The demands of the Second World War further encouraged the expansion of canteens within Germany and across the world. The 1943 Hot Springs Conference included in its list of human rights the requirement that "all industrial workers should be given full opportunities of obtaining a third of their total daily calorie required for maintaining health and efficiency in their respective employment at their midday meal."[18]

The Nazi Party had been particularly interested in optimizing the relationship between work productivity and the food economy, which inspired the rapid expansion of the canteen system. In 1938, on the eve of Germany's invasion of Poland, the NSDAP founded the National Committee for Communal Feeding, which centralized and supported research into new products and cooking methods for mass feeding. The committee's ultimate goal was to expand the country's underdeveloped canteen landscape; at the time, there were only 6,500 factory kitchens, serving 1.5 million workers, in all of Germany. It met with great success. Within three years, by 1941, the enormous size of the German army, along with an expanded workforce, meant that majority of adult males were eating in canteens. Labor Front leader Robert Ley, a tireless proponent of canteens, sent Hitler personal reports praising the Third Reich's canteens; for example, he claimed that "the factory feeding program was a major factor in the tremendous levels of armament production accomplished by male and female workers."[19] By 1944, tens of millions of Germans were eating in various kinds of collective eating establishments, and the country's 17,000 factory canteens were feeding the majority of Germany's workers.[20]

During the Third Reich, nutritionists had tried to establish a sort of "zero input" productivity. Experiments with feeding racial enemies on leaves, dirt, or grass reflected a brutal logic of optimization and annihilation. This research proved a troublesome legacy for the postwar nutritional sciences. Many of the scientists involved in Nazi research seamlessly continued their careers after the war's end. Dr. Heinrich Kraut, who had studied forced laborers' productivity under starvation conditions, was a founding member and early president of the German Nutritional Society (*Deutsche Gesellschaft für Ernährung* [DGE]).[21] Ernst-Günther Schenck, former Nutritional Inspector for the SS, and the well-known surgeon Heinrich Berning also had successful medical careers in the FRG despite having performed brutal experiments on starving Soviet POWs.[22] Arthur Scheunert, a prominent nutritionist who had researched alternative vitamin sources for the Nazi regime, was a founding father of East German nutritional science, serving as president of the East German Institute for Nutrition from 1951 to 1957. Thus the scientists who came of age during the Third Reich were the same experts who evaluated canteens and developed nutritional guidelines in both East and West Germany.[23]

The collapse of the Nazi dictatorship offered Germans the opportunity to reject collective meals, which had dominated popular food intake during the Third Reich—and many of them chose to do just that. Although canteens seemed an obvious solution to the food shortages of the postwar occupation, German popular opinion explicitly associated health, prosperity, and peace with private food consumption, turning away from the rationed, regulated, and collectively consumed meals of the prior decade. In all four zones, Germans wanted the freedom to select and prepare their own foodstuffs; popular opinion frequently linked state-run rationing programs with collective meals, seeing both as violations of their "free will."[24] Nonetheless, both the capitalist West and the communist East agreed that economic reconstruction required canteen programs in order to maintain a healthy workforce.

Both countries proved obsessed with distinguishing their canteens from those of their ideological enemies. According to the East German narrative, canteens could actually increase worker exploitation in the name of fascism or personal profit. A GDR report from the mid-sixties, for example, described the factories under Hitler as "degrading for the workforce," with canteens that were "expanded especially in the munitions industry. They were thus part of the preparations for war, rather than being in the service of the well-being of the working class."[25] The GDR also distinguished their canteens from those in the West, where canteens were described as a profit-driven business. The East German media, for example, excoriated West German businessmen like the wealthy hotelier Albert Steigenberger for transforming his workplace canteens into "a chain of cheap restaurants which ... exploit the working classes even more intensely."[26]

In contrast, socialist canteens claimed to maximize productivity both for the good of the individual and for larger society. Well-fed workers, the theory went, worked more and better not just because of their optimized nutritional input, but also because the consumption of these vital calories, proteins, and vitamins took place in a larger social milieu that encouraged collective bonding and worker solidarity, which in turn created a form of everyday legitimation of the East German state. Moreover, the GDR's canteens were intended to do away with the need for women's midday cooking, enabling them to join the full-time workforce and thus gain personal as well as economic freedom.

As a result, GDR economists of the postwar reconstruction years emphasized canteens as a crucial tool for strengthening the relationship between the working class and the state.[27] Throughout the 1950s, the socialist state repeatedly affirmed the value of the country's canteens, claiming that "of all the policies which were created to realize our goals since the construction of our entire society after 1945, the communal feeding program is particularly significant ... [because it] distributes a warm meal to workers in the factory, and not simply any meal, but a meal that, due to its always improving quality, preparation, and healthfulness, meets the requirements of the newest nutritional sciences."[28] Despite such optimistic declarations, however, from the outset East German canteens seemed to encourage not productivity and solidarity but divisiveness and competition, both between individual workers and, especially, between workers and the state that was feeding them.

A sincere conviction in the political and economic value of canteens meant that one of the first research institutes founded in the Soviet zone was the Institute for Nutrition and Food Science, which opened in 1946 and initially focused primarily on collective feeding programs.[39] The particular importance of feeding workers in the East was enshrined in the 1947 passage of Order No. 234. This bill was part of a larger project aiming, as its formal title indicated, for "An Increase in Work Productivity and the Increased Improvement of the Material Situation of Workers and Employees." By guaranteeing every factory worker a hot meal, Order 234 formally declared the state's commitment to providing worker canteens. The impact of the policy was immediate. The number of participants in factory canteens rose from 350,000 in mid-1947 to 1 million by the end of the year, eventually increasing to 1.5 million; accordingly, workplace productivity also rose.[29] Head of the Department of Labor and Social Welfare, Gustav Brack, declared that hot meals "had an educative function on work morale. Skipping out on work [Arbeitsbummlei] has been practically eliminated."[30] Alongside such gains, however, worker complaints increased as well, addressing issues ranging from expense ("about 400 colleagues chose not to eat a canteen lunch since its price is too high")[31] to poor taste ("workers scarcely touched the food and poured it down the drain").[32] The Soviet zone's Ministry of Labor fielded constant criticisms of its recommendation that the "removal of the warm lunch" be the punishment for absenteeism.

At the same time that Order 234 normalized canteen meals, it also established the use of food to reward exceptional workers and punish inadequate ones, transforming food into a tool of discipline, reward, and punishment that ironically echoed capitalist incentive strategies. The bill was intended to "encourage increased productivity" by allotting supply increases to the canteens of "the leading factories and transportation companies," which together served more than a million workers. These better-stocked kitchens were ordered to produce meals that would be divided into two categories: the A-meal, containing 634 calories made up of higher allotments of meat and fat, and the B-meal, with only 479 calories.[33] The ratio of A meals to B meals at each workplace was set at 40 to 60, and meal assignments were based on individual productivity.[34] State propaganda emphasized that even the B-meal was a dramatic improvement over postwar home-cooked meals and pre-1947 canteen meals. Nonetheless, factory workers loathed this hierarchical system. After its implementation, many factory organizers sabotaged the program by mixing the rations together and offering a single meal for all their workers.[35] Some workers would refuse to accept an "A" meal out of solidarity with their lower-ranked colleagues. Indeed, workers began to rely on canteens as a way of challenging socialist claims of egalitarianism; they claimed that inequitable food distribution within canteens and the hierarchically structured meal system contradicted the basic premises of socialism.[36]

When the GDR was founded in 1949, the new state affirmed its continuing commitment to collective feeding. Recognizing that Order 234 "no longer adequately fulfills current needs," the East German state called for the re-education of factory leaders and, especially, of workers to teach them to "feel responsible for these institutions [factory canteens] which were established for their own health and well-being, to ensure that they are no longer damaged or robbed" by the workers they were intended to nourish.[37] Walter Ulbricht, head of the Socialist Unity Party (Sozialistische Einheitspartei Deutschlands or SED) and future president of the GDR, asserted that "we must make it a priority that factory meals are improved to such a degree that a steadily increasing number of male and female workers take part in them," and he regularly backed plans to both improve and expand canteens.[38]

For Ulbricht and other party leaders, the establishment of an extensive array of collective feeding programs, especially workplace canteens and school lunch programs, was seen as essential to finding a permanent solution to the struggle to provide the population with adequate food supplies.[40] This was no easy task. In 1950, East German farmers only reached 70 percent of their 1936 productivity levels; two years later, this had increased to 91 percent. It ultimately took more than a decade for private consumption to reach prewar levels, and in 1958, it was still only 50 percent of West Germany's booming rates.[41] While the SED focused its energy on securing supplies of staple foodstuffs, especially meat, bread, potatoes, and dairy products, levels of which recovered fairly quickly, per capita consumption of luxury foodstuffs, such as tropical fruit, coffee, and cocoa, remained only a fraction of West German rates throughout division.[42] However, during the early postwar years, even basic staples were often only available in limited quantities, as the government struggled to predict and regulate people's shopping and eating habits. Not until 1958 were the GDR's last rationing coupons—for butter, sugar, and meat—finally canceled, and sporadic food shortages continued to periodically develop. In the early 1960s, for example, a modified rationing program was reintroduced to limit what was seen as "excessive" consumption of meat and butter.[43] These problems in supplying consumer goods were a source of constant complaint and popular protest; but it was the intimate connection between food consumption and industrial production that defined the GDR's first and last major public protest, the uprising of June 17, 1953.

On May 1, 1953—International Labor Day, the most important holiday on the socialist calendar—the SED had passed a bill to improve the quality of foods distributed to canteens. The decision to highlight canteen meals on May 1 reflected the importance socialists placed on collective feeding and was an attempt to address a key source of conflict between the population and the state. That year had seen a dramatic decline in consumer supplies, as well as price increases of up to 40 percent.[44] These increases caused enormous dissatisfaction, only compounding worker complaints about canteen meals. While the May 1 bill did improve the quality of factory meals, workers were outraged over the resultant increase in meal prices, which they did not accept as a "fair" trade-off. Surprised by the bill's failure to meaningfully increase canteen participation rates, nutritionists conducted surveys to determine the main cause of discontent; they unexpectedly revealed a total lack of interest in nutritional education and in the benefits of eating healthier, higher quality foods, and found instead that "discussions in the factory were almost exclusively focused on the increase in the price of the meal."[45]

Six weeks after the passage of this unpopular bill, long-seething tensions exploded into massive public protests, as tens of thousands of working men and women took to the streets. Initiated by construction workers in East Berlin and soon spreading to include marches in most of the GDR's large cities, the protest—which became widely known as the June 17 Workers' Uprising—had been triggered by an announcement of increased work quotas and further delays in the improvement of consumer goods. East Germans specifically complained about the generally inadequate consumer selection and poor-quality food provisioning.

Coincidentally, on the same day that protesters took to the streets, the GDR's chemical industry hosted a large national conference on workplace canteens, which was dominated by expert discussions attempting to pinpoint the reasons for canteens' lack of popularity. The final conference report recommended vaguely that canteens develop "collective cooperation . . . as well as encouraging critique and self-critique." In what proved painfully misplaced optimism, the authors stated that "this path will guarantee us not only the full support of all workers, but also win their trust, which is necessary to achieve the larger goals established by the five year plan."[46] Within a week of the conference and the protest, the Institute of Nutrition had proposed the creation of a centralized model canteen kitchen, which would be used to educate canteen cooks across the country. It was hoped that such centralized training would finally eliminate the "blind clinging to tradition of a majority of our trained staff," replaced by a "flexible, scientific approach to kitchen work, based on the newest developments of nutrition and the culinary sciences." In the institute's modern kitchen, cooks would learn that their style of cooking was a "critical and creative intellectual process" that allowed them to optimize worker health, satisfy economic requirements, and placate an angry workforce.[47] Although the June uprising was brutally crushed by Soviet tanks, becoming a long-lived symbol of the animosity between East German workers and the state that claimed to protect them, the GDR's official responses to the protests highlighted canteens' particular ideological significance.

In subsequent decades, East Germany consistently singled out workplace canteens as evidence of the superiority of the socialist economy over capitalist ones. Regional and national press regularly ran articles describing the country's factory canteens, not only celebrating success stories (the canteen at a television electronics factory reported impressive increases in participation rates due to "a varied canteen menu and a good supply of small snacks for breaks),"[48] but also pointing out areas in which improvements were needed (a construction site near Suhl-Döllberg, a remote area where the nearest canteen had shut down months earlier, required hungry workers to walk several kilometers when they needed "to buy breakfast or groceries"[49]). A 1961 report on the state of collective meals in the GDR, while bemoaning the fact that many of the country's workers chose not to eat at their workplace canteens, awkwardly asserted that the very existence of these canteens represented a victory: "the factory canteens created in our socialist factories are a great social success of the working class and document the political agenda of our party and government."[50] One needed only to look across the border to see

> how different it is in West Germany. A whole row of factories in West Germany also have factory canteens. However, these establishments help capitalists to extract the most possible from the people ... they help capitalists to continually perfect the exploitation of the working classes.[51]

In fact, not only did GDR workers generally express hostility toward rather than gratitude for their canteen meals; the early years of the Republic saw a large number of workplaces actually close their newly opened canteens because of flagging interest, high costs, or inadequate supplies. A report from the early 1950s found worker participation rates ranging from a high of 80 percent in Saxony to an embarrassingly low 47 percent in the capital city of Berlin; the author explained the poor results by highlighting the clash between an austere reality and growing popular expectations:

> With the successful carrying out of the two-year plan ... the workers in the factories have created the context for a substantial increase in the quality of life for the population. This development, however, is not reflected in the status of the factory canteen meals in a large number of our most important production and transportation companies. ... The consequence is that the workers eat this meal unhappily or simply reject it if they are of the opinion that the quality of the food is not in accordance with our economic development.[52]

In other words, canteens' low approval rates were actually the result of the coutry's impressive economic growth. This trend continued over the subsequent years; between 1955 and 1960, participation rates nationwide dropped another 15 percent despite rising general prosperity. Officials chose to blame "complainers who at home would eat the plaster from their window frames, and yet who complain about the best of meals served in the factory."[53]

The fact that East German workers did not want to eat at their canteens was a permanent obstacle to the establishment of a happy and productive workforce. Any price increase at a canteen led almost immediately to a drop in participation; an unpopular or badly cooked dish could cause surprisingly long-lasting hostility; and improvements in canteen meals were seldom acknowledged or appreciated. Increasing prosperity and the stabilization of the food supply by the 1960s only caused workers' gustatory expectations to rise, encouraging the abandonment of the collective dining hall in favor of now tastier home-cooked food. At the same time, nutritional analyses of canteen meals found that they almost never met the most stringent standards. In 1970, East German nutritionist Dr. Heinrich Haenel expressed his frustration with the situation: "The GDR could play a leading role in the realm of collective feeding from a societal, scientific, and social perspective. . . . But the current state of affairs no longer meets the increased demands of nutritional sciences, of the health industry, of the economy and production, and above all of the participants in these meals."[54] In 1967, Dr. Martin Zobel, head of the Collective Feeding Department at the Institute of Nutrition, was even harsher in his assessment, "Unfortunately, it has been repeatedly shown that the great majority of collective feeding programs do not in the slightest meet modern nutritional requirements. Even the flavor requirements . . . no longer fulfill expectations . . . . The consequences of this can be seen in the dramatic decrease in participants in canteen meals."[55] Nutritionists who visited canteens to evaluate performance had many complaints: kitchens had too few or too old machines, they were staffed by unqualified kitchen workers, and they worked with inadequate supplies of fresh fruits and vegetables.[56]

Despite the persistent problems, throughout the 1960s and 1970s, reports in East Germany continued to express the conviction that food quality and cafeteria atmosphere would improve under the guidance of scientific and enlightened staff. Canteens, not workers, were the main problem: "there are work canteens that are well equipped and provided with the highest quality ingredients, and yet that still prepare meals that eventually drive even the most positively disposed worker from the lunch table."[57] Nutritionists promised frustrated factory directors "that it has clearly been shown that all factories where the kitchen employees form a strong collective, where everyone supports one another and every individual feels personally responsible for one another, provide food that can fulfill the wishes of our workers."[58] Training programs encouraged canteen cooks to decrease their reliance on the *Eintopf* and to diversify their menus, recommending that individual dishes not be repeated within a standard 14-day cycle. The new mantra of the reformed East German canteen was to become shorthand for efficiency and thus that illusive worker satisfaction: "short preparation time, short cooking time, and a quick distribution of food."[59]

In the eyes of East German workers, the state's drive to improve canteens was not a sign of its devotion to their well-being but its obsession with increasing factory output and productivity. As one 1959 report put it, "[T]here are plenty of examples where those responsible for the factory only think in terms of production and treat the canteens and workers' meals as a fifth wheel on the wagon. In those places the food is poor."[60] Ashamed directors admitted that "in large part collective feeding is perceived as a necessary evil of the workplace, and we are happy as long as there are no active complaints about the food and the work of the kitchens, so that we can dedicate ourselves without any interruption to [increasing] productivity." Nutritionists despaired over the many factory leaders "who want to close factory canteens because they cause too much work," seeing mandatory provisioning of their workers as both a financial drain and a source of conflict.[61] Even more disturbing, questionnaires and surveys revealed a persistent aversion among workers to the collective nature of these meals. East German workers demanded "that the canteen-regime be brought to an end, they no longer want to simply have their bellies filled [abgefüttert werden], but demand that their canteen become a restaurant."[62] Such demands directly conflicted with official GDR doctrine, which explicitly conceptualized workers as "participants" in a communal meal rather than as "consumers" of individual commodities. Moreover, these conflicts revealed that the state's prioritization of collective meals conflicted with popular desires for private and familial food consumption. Many workers chose not to eat in the workplace canteen because "they claim[ed] that their wife would have to cook for the family anyway in the evenings"[63] or, as another report put it, out of a "desire to consume a warm meal together with the family."[64]

Canteen experts countered such "unenlightened" demands by affirming the need to awaken "the internal pleasure evoked by communal eating in the factory dining hall."[65] This was best done, they thought, through a proliferation of educational programs aimed both at improving the skills of the canteen chefs and teaching factory workers to appreciate the substantial investment in their well-being that the canteens represented.[66] By the 1970s, nutritionists, elaborating the themes of what has been termed "socialist consumerism," emphasized the importance of taste, comfort, and pleasure in popularizing canteen meals. A typical report from 1970 stated that

> as long as the food in many places continues to be prepared lovelessly and with inadequate culinary skill ... as long as the potatoes are overcooked, the sauces always identical ... as long as fresh vegetables are

offered only in the form of a limp salad leaf, when salt is the only spice mixed into the cooking pots—used by the handful—then we can only expect anger, complaints, a poor workplace climate, and grumpiness for all participants in the collective feeding programs, not to mention the reductions in productivity due to an inadequate nutrition.[67]

Such reports stressed that canteens needed to provide not only quality foodstuffs, but also a pleasurable environment for worker socialization.

Although the workers themselves rarely invoked the social pleasures of eating in canteens, participation rates did begin to slowly increase after reaching their nadir in 1961. The construction of the Berlin Wall did succeed, at least temporarily, in stabilizing the domestic economy. By 1970, a third of the country's workers ate at least one of their main daily meals in their workplace canteen. East German authorities continued to devote substantial energy and resources to expanding communal feeding programs despite shortfalls in state budgets and the global recession of the early seventies. This commitment gradually yielded dividends. By 1985, overall participation had reached its highest rate ever, with 66 percent of the working population regularly partaking. However, this impressive increase was as much a reaction to a worsening domestic food situation as a response to improvements in the canteens themselves. Many disgruntled employees complained that it was only the recurrent shortages in their local grocery stores that had convinced them to turn to their workplace canteens, which enjoyed privileged access to limited foodstuffs. By the end of the decade 22 percent of the country's total food production and sales ended up in collective feeding establishments, more than half of which were factory canteens.[68] Such numbers, impressive as they might seem, never lived up to the state's ideological commitment to canteens, nor did these spaces reflect the GDR's financial and material investments in them. Thus, nutritionists consistently saw canteens as a failure more than a success story, one that was ultimately more significant than the much more frequently discussed problem of keeping stores well stocked.

The long-term trajectory of factory canteens in the GDR offers insight into the difficulties in balancing the ideological and practical considerations of the socialist government with those of nutritionists, workers, and factory directors. Throughout the postwar decades, rates of participation in factory canteens ebbed and flowed with political crises and stabilization measures; certainly though, the fact that it took decades for participation rates to reach even 50 percent undermined on a daily basis some of the core assertions of East German socialism. Even when higher participation levels were achieved, GDR advisers reported growing rates of consumer dissatisfaction with the meals, as well as disturbingly high numbers of cases of food-borne illnesses; 1985 alone saw 281 incidents, involving 14,239 individuals, who missed at least one day of work because of canteen-caused sickness.⁶⁹ Studies to determine the cause of such discouraging statistics revealed a reduction in qualified staff since the 1960s; only a third of all canteen workers had received professional training.⁷⁰ By the time the GDR was dissolved in 1990, workplace canteens had been established as a central component of the industrial economy, but they were also consistently one of the most contentious components of the food system. Despite this problematic history, the GDR acquired an international reputation as a leader in the planning and execution of factory canteens in the Eastern bloc and beyond; collective feeding was one of the few areas of food supply where even West German experts looked to the East for lessons and strategies.

The relationship between food, labor, and economic reconstruction was quite different in the FRG, whose growth after 1945 made it a globally renowned case study for the "economic miracle." Hannah Arendt, writing in 1958, described West Germany's "booming prosperity" as reflecting an economy that "feeds not on the abundance of material goods or on anything stable and given, but on the process of production and consumption itself."⁷¹ Foucault argued, in 1978, that the remarkable postwar prosperity of West Germany represented the paradigmatic case study for how, in the liberal mode of governance, "the economy produces legitimacy for the state that is its guarantor."⁷² West Germany thus quickly emerged as the postwar model of the supposed primacy of the economy over ideology. Since the end of the Cold War and the resultant processes of reevaluation, historians have increasingly challenged the notion of the FRG's "miraculous" leap forward, pointing out that it was more gradual and less widespread than is often asserted. Nonetheless, it remains true that between 1950 and 1960, West Germany's GNP tripled, unemployment sharply decreased, and wages increased across the social classes.⁷³ This rising prosperity accompanied a decline in blue-collar work for Germans, as the country increasingly relied on temporary "guest workers" (*Gastarbeiter*), primarily from Southern and Eastern Europe, to take on low-paid and menial jobs. West Germany's postwar economic growth was thus associated with the creation of a middle-class society, as the German working class used their newfound prosperity to acquire the consumer products and leisure activities that had been traditionally associated with the bourgeoisie. The SPD, in response, shifted away from its traditional focus on industrial workers, revamping its political program around a reform of capitalist structures rather than revolution or a radical redistribution of wealth.

Although the rapid reconstruction of West Germany progressed quite differently from the slower and less steady growth of the GDR, efforts to optimize economic productivity followed a similar logic. In the West as in the East, the establishment of a healthy economy required a well-fed workforce. Thus, despite Cold War assumptions that associated collective meals with the communist East, the FRG's industrial economists also perceived canteens as crucial for economic growth. West German canteens represented the tantalizing goal of optimizing production, something that was primarily linked not with optimal nutrition or worker solidarity (as in the East) but with the transformation of the proletarian class into a pillar of middle-class society. This was a paradoxical project. At the same time that West German officials, businessmen, and media worked to deny the importance or even the very existence of "proletarian" canteens in the prosperous, individualist West, factory managers, as well as workers, relied on them on a daily basis. The FRG's industrial economists thus dedicated themselves to transforming canteens from traditional sites of working-class collectivity into centers of individual bourgeois consumption.

The social and economic value of canteens was tensely debated during the early years of West Germany's reconstruction, as their expansion during the occupation years had linked them with poverty and hunger rather than economic optimization and prosperity. Canteens' survival hinged upon their disassociation from welfare or charity programs aiming simply to most efficiently feed the greatest number of people. To this end, in 1954 the federal government slashed its canteen subsidies for members of the civil service, a decision that was greeted with anger in the poorer regions of the country, where a majority of lower-paid employees took advantage of the subsidized prices. A labor representative from West Berlin, for example, predicted that the loss of the subsidy meant that "lower earning workers will no longer be able, due to the financial burden, to eat a warm lunch during lunch break, and will instead have to satisfy themselves with bread brought from home."[74] Despite countless such appeals, however, the subsidies were canceled, and canteen participation dropped precipitously; this, however, was not interpreted as an inherent problem by the West German government.

Indeed, these subsidy cuts reflected the country's official aversion to collective eating, which was conceptualized as antithetical to a healthy family life and a contented workforce. The FRG's stance was rationalized by scientists and economists, who asserted an innately German "internal revulsion toward collective meals, toward the 'feeding,' or however else the workers tend to disparagingly name the canteen meal."[75] In 1959, nationally renowned nutritionist Joachim Kühnau blamed poor health among West German working-class men on the fact that "the family diet, earlier the exclusive concern of the housewife, has been removed from her control and increasingly handed over to the anonymous society of a canteen or mass kitchen."[76] Well into the 1960s, despite the fact that some 16 million FRG workers regularly dined at public feeding facilities, experts continued to describe collective meals as contrary to the German character, market relations, and even human nature itself.[77] Although critics argued that canteens inherently destroyed individuality and the cohesion of the family unit, they nonetheless wholeheartedly embraced restaurants as icons of modernity and prosperity. Restaurant meals, like canteen meals, were publicly consumed and professionally prepared. However, because they were consumed by individuals or, ideally, by nuclear family units, they seemed to reinforce normative social bonds, rather than striving to replace them with an artificial "working collective."[78]

Almost all West German experts believed that the "family meal" was inherently superior to the canteen meal. Even the nutritionists who were responsible for monitoring and improving West German canteens admitted that workers would never "truly enjoy" these meals because they did not "taste like mom's [nor could the canteen] replace the intimate sphere of the family table."[79] This deep-seated discomfort with collective meals inspired the creation of a less troublesome West German variant. A 1962 guide to work canteens by the renowned nutritionist Dr. Hans-Dietrich Cremer distinguished postwar West German canteens from all earlier incarnations by drawing a "clear dividing line" between "communal eating" [*Gemeinschaftsverpflegung*] and "mass feeding" [*Massenverpflegung*], which was linked with not only past poverty but with totalitarianism. Cremer argued that

> the very term "mass" is impossible to associate with the idea of a personality ... the situation is quite different with [West German] communal eating: within the [workplace] community, people do not exist as a mass, but rather as a large or small group of individual personalities, who must not simply be made full, but healthy and capable of peak performance.[80]

The term "mass feeding" was used to describe the "organized misery" of earlier fascist and postwar communist meal programs, which were described as entirely different from the "individualist" West German canteens.[81] From a West German perspective, the tendency of the canteen to subsume the individual into the working collective made it an especially meaningful symbol of communism; indeed, the canteen became one of West Germany's most frequently invoked images of the GDR. Depictions of life on the other side of the border relied on dystopic glimpses of eating halls where "a few hundred people sat ... hunched over their plates, shoving something boiled in their mouths," as both the actual food consumed and the way in which workers ate represented communism's simultaneous destruction of the individual and the family.[82]

Alongside this vehement condemnation of canteens as sites of revolting "mass feeding," however, a quiet but concerted economic push toward increasing productivity required the reinvention rather than elimination of workplace canteens, which were transformed into places of individualistic and solidly middle-class taste. Signaling the beginnings of this "normalization" of canteens, in 1957 the DGE opened the Advisory Board for Collective Feeding. The decision to reevaluate the state of the FRG's canteens stemmed from a commitment to maintaining and further increasing industrial productivity. The country's booming economy seemed to confirm, in the carefully chosen words of the Consortium of Work Committees of Federal Agencies, "that it is absolutely necessary, for the maintenance of health and the increase in work productivity, to have a lunch break during work hours in which the possibility of eating a warm meal exists."[83] Thus, the demands of reconstruction made canteen programs seem not only useful but necessary; as was the case in the GDR, West German economists argued that canteens were the most effective way of ensuring a healthy and productive workforce. Despite early West German policies designed to discourage canteen usage, by the end of the 1960s the booming economy had made "a meal at the workplace essentially mandatory".[84]

This process of "normalizing" West German canteens hinged on distinguishing them from their East German counterparts. As the GDR had done, the FRG vigorously denied any associations of military kitchens with workplace canteens. Whereas the East rejected these historical links on the basis of ideology (claiming that those earlier canteens had been in the service of "military-imperialistic" causes), in the West it was their collectivity and uniformity that was identified as the problem: "when one speaks today of communal feeding, one thinks of those huge soup kitchens of World War I, or the feeding station of an army unit during the past war. A long line of waiting men stand at a huge vat," one West German article reported, before remarking, "these times are over, and such memories belong to the past."[85] Even more important than rejecting militaristic overtones, however, was disassociating canteens from their proletariat or working-class roots. In 1969 the *Frankfurter Allgemeine Zeitung* reminded its readers that canteens had originated in nineteenth-century charity projects to feed malnourished workers in the Ruhr and other heavily industrialized regions, noting however, that "today it is different. Rather than being purely paternalist . . . collective meals in the factory cannot be run as they were 'back in the day.'"[86]

West German economists and nutritionists worked hard to present German industry's continued reliance on canteens as neither Communist nor Nazi, neither military nor proletarian but instead as staunchly middle-class. A West German vision of the canteen as a site for potentially transforming and even "taming" the working class built on early twentieth-century movements of scientific-industrial management.[87] After the Second World War, industrialists continued to advocate unlimited economic growth and constantly increasing profit levels; ideally, high profits would trickle down to the workers, who would then reject the rhetoric of class struggle in exchange for higher wages and standards of living. This conservative and paternalistic vision of industrial production was the ideal of Ludwig Erhard, West German minister of finance and the man known as the "father" of the economic miracle. Erhard famously advised the country's workers to strive not for a bigger piece of the pie, but for a larger pie altogether. This model was attractive because it correlated expanding industrial profit with decreasing labor discontent and social unrest.[88]

As part of this postwar vision of hierarchical prosperity, economists advocated transforming the canteen, a place of potential class conflict, into an apolitical space of individualized, bourgeois food consumption. This vision of the canteen inspired industrial psychologists to reflect on the "in-between situation of the factory canteen: it belongs to the factory like storage, sales, and production; nonetheless, it is more than any other region entirely removed from the purely productive sphere. It is a part of the factory and yet a world unto itself. Whoever crosses the threshold into the canteen leaves the sober sphere of labor."[89] Taking advantage of this liminal space, industrialists decided to focus on the canteen atmosphere, prioritizing the creation of a positive attitude and general good mood among canteen visitors as more important than an optimized worker diet or achieving universal accessibility. A Siemens report on workplace canteens reminded factory managers that "the purpose of canteen meals is not economic, but rather so-to-speak hygienic. After many hours of work, the human being requires a thorough renewal of his physical and mental strength," something that was best achieved through a meal "eaten in a pleasant atmosphere, separate from the work-world, with entertaining conversation."[90]

Generally, guides to canteen construction in the FRG emphasized the transformation of an industrial hall into an intimate, clean, and middle-class space, encouraging the creation of a familial atmosphere by means of quiet background music and the presence of "clean and efficient women serv[ing] the meal on beautifully arranged tables."[91] Having female staff serve male consumers was thought to be vital for achieving worker satisfaction. Thus, the best factory canteens promised to have "an entire army of sprightly and friendly women and girls [to] serve you," women who would "fulfill practically anyone's imaginable wish for relaxation and recuperation within a 30-minute break" by allowing visitors to "also enjoy those things that cannot be purchased: every visitor [to the canteen] receives individual attention that cannot be improved upon even in the most elegant restaurant."[92] When Siemens opened the new "skyscraper canteen" in its Erlangen factory in 1951, the local press admired its "real hotel atmosphere." One article's focus on "homey" details like white tablecloths and floral arrangements contrasted dramatically with the accompanying photographs of alarmingly modern technological apparatuses required to produce meals on such large scale (see Figure 4.2). These dual depictions encapsulate the tension inherent in canteens' status as an awkward bridge between the restaurant (a site of leisure and familial pleasure) and the factory (a site of obligatory, often unpleasant labor)

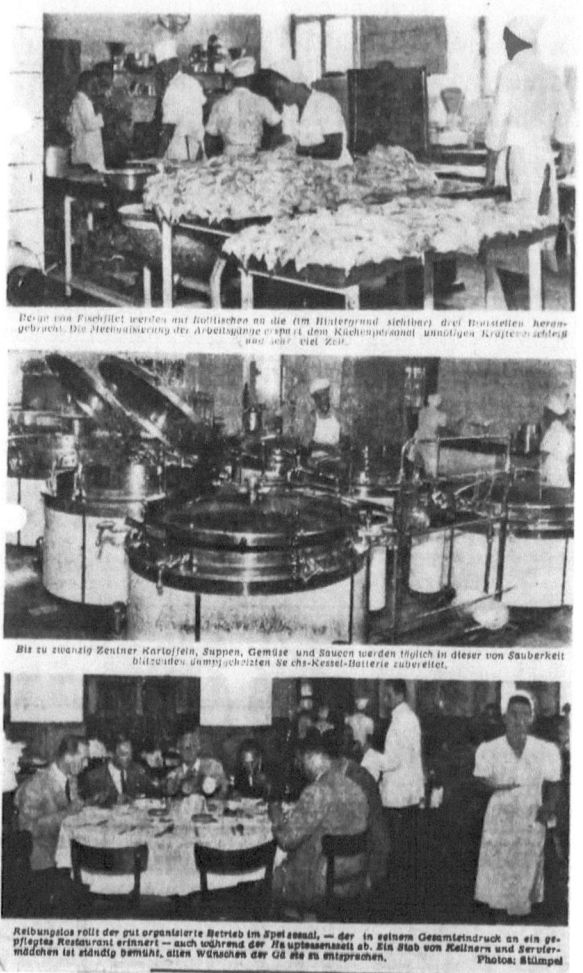

Figure 4.2 "The Technician Smiles—The Housewife Gasps." 1951. Siemens AG Corporate Archive.

Likening canteens to restaurants was part of a larger discourse that framed canteens as part of a free-market economy. By combining home-scale intimacy with public, purchased meals, the West German canteen became, in the proud words of the Association of Market Research for Grain Production, "a restaurant in which everyone can eat the same way that he does in his private kitchen."[93] Dr. Cremer suggested that "it is advantageous to see the member [*Mitglied*] of a canteen meal as a guest, not as a 'participant in the meal' [*Essenteilnehmer*] or, even worse, the 'recipient of food' [*Verpflegungsempfänger*]."[94] This emphasis on individual selection was supposed to give workers "the illusion of freedom" in their menu choices.[95] In this way, canteens claimed to "support the growing sense of individuality and rising sense of self-worth" among working men.[96] References to eating foods from a "private kitchen" or a "bourgeois home" were believed to implicitly empower male West German workers. Unsurprisingly, canteens proudly emphasized the so-called *gut-bürgerlich* dishes in their menus—a term that implies both "home-style" and "traditionally German" food but literally means "bourgeois" or "middle class."

Thus the reconstruction years witnessed the severing of canteens from any historical associations with the proletariat, associating them instead with white-collar workers and bureaucrats. Mirroring this change, by the end of the 1950s, Siemens' huge network of canteens was feeding twice as many clerical workers as manual laborers, and most branches reported that, in a reversal of prewar patterns, "the participation of white-collar workers is generally higher than that of the blue-collar workers."[97] A national survey from 1962 found that workplaces dominated by manual laborers tended not to have canteens at all due to difficulties in organization and the complications associated with shift work. Surveyors were further surprised to find that "even in workplaces that do have a canteen, it is the white-collar workers, rather than the manual workers, who take their main meal there."[98] By the late 1960s, more white-collar workers (33%) than physical laborers (27%) made up the approximately 15 million employees who ate daily at their workplace canteens.[99] This transformation of the canteen was part of an attempt to normalize and standardize middle-class values and lifestyles:

> [T]he worker of today is, like the white-collar worker and the civil servant, a citizen. He therefore expects to receive his meal at his workplace in an environment that corresponds to his private domestic conditions, in other words, looking like a middle-class home.[100]

Inspired by a profound fear of class conflict, West German economists hoped that these postwar canteens would confirm and strengthen, not challenge, social hierarchies. Nutritionists promised factory owners that "one of the central purposes of work feeding programs" was to inspire their employees to "show their thankfulness through increased worker productivity."[101] Workplace dining halls were advised to institute prearranged seating assignments for diners based on status. Many canteens had highly differentiated pricing, ideally insuring that better meals were eaten by higher-paid workers. (In contrast, hierarchies within East German canteens had been pervasive as well, but they were, at least theoretically, hierarchies of productivity rather than social or economic status.) A celebratory 1971 article about the canteens at a massive chemical plant noted several sets of distinct kitchens and dining halls, each serving a different social strata; the main factory operated "various eating rooms for company guests, conferences, celebrations, housewife coffee hours," which were totally separate from the "standard" worker canteen.¹⁰² Ultimately, the psychological and social value of canteen meals was seen as far more significant than their nutritional value or cost.

In the end, however, this "consumer-focused" approach to canteens struggled as much the GDR's centralized model. Popular dissatisfaction with canteen meals grew steadily over the postwar decades.¹⁰³ By the 1970s, the situation had reached a real crisis. The aftermath of the 1973 oil crisis, pressures of stagflation, rising unemployment, and growing feelings of societal instability, all produced a dramatic rise in workplace discontent and a related drop in canteen participation rates. In 1981, a speaker at the International Conference of Collective Feeding held in Cologne predicted that "due to the increased burdening of the individual in the workplace, in the future ever more attention must be paid to the tensions connected to the institutions for collective eating."¹⁰⁴ Despite such calls to action, workplace canteens continued to decline not just in popularity but in quality. As a result they were frequently blamed for health problems among the working population, and workers consistently expressed their preference for restaurants over canteens, despite higher prices and often lower nutritional value. A 1988 national Nutritional Report found that participation at the country's 20 thousand workplace canteens had steadily declined over the preceding decade, so that less than half of West Germany's workforce ate regularly in their canteens. Nonetheless, nutritionists had ceased advocating for the elimination of canteens, having grudgingly accepted them as "a necessary evil" of the postwar economy.¹⁰⁵

Both the capitalist FRG and the socialist GDR integrated canteens into their respective societies as standard components of an industrial economy. While in both states canteens represented the promise of increasing economic productivity through total control over workers' nutrition, the form that this optimization was supposed to take proved to be state-specific. Socialist planners consistently anticipated that canteens would strengthen the connection between the working population and the state. However history shows that collective meals consistently destabilized the socialist state rather than cementing its bonds with the people. Thus the GDR's commitment to canteens, seen in its ubiquitous rhetorical celebration of them and the high levels of funding and research they received, proved surprisingly ineffective if not counterproductive. In contrast, West German experts never managed to fully overcome their hostility toward collectively prepared and consumed midday meals. However, they reluctantly recognized the need for workers to eat outside of their homes during work hours. Rather than describe canteens as an expression of care for the proletariat, West Germans hoped that canteens could replicate and disseminate middle-class social norms, thus deferring rather than resolving social conflict. In both economic systems, canteens proved unexpectedly difficult to optimize, as conflicts over taste, eating patterns, and appropriate pricing consistently increased friction in the industrial workplace.

Shopping for Food as Labor and Leisure

Food shaped postwar Germans' efforts to achieve economic optimization and to regulate industrial productivity beyond the concerns over factory infrastructure. Even workers who enjoyed hot meals at their canteens continued to spend a substantial percentage of their wages on foodstuffs consumed privately and outside the workplace. For all citizens of both East and West Germany, food shopping was a vital component of a modern consumer culture. Indeed, foodstuffs were particularly important for postwar economies because, as the West German finance minister explained in 1957, "in contrast to other consumer objects, these [food items] are things with which the consumer comes into contact on a daily basis."[106]

West Germany's emphasis on food shopping as a barometer of economic health originated in the currency reform of June 6, 1948. This reform, which replaced the Reichsmark with the new Deutschmark, was intended to support the consolidation and expansion of the Bizone's economy; it was also supposed to celebrate the return of prosperity to a demoralized and impoverished population. The currency reform also signaled the end of mandatory rationing. In the Western zone, economists hoped that this radical loosening of the economy, with the increased potential for profit, would encourage food producers to sell their goods on the "free market." The assumption was that increasing the quantity of food in circulation would result in increases in individual food consumption—in other words, better-stocked shops would mean better-fed people. Initially, however, the opposite seemed to be true.

The cessation of rationing, paired with skyrocketing prices, decreases in wage value, and the loss of personal savings that had been held in the now-defunct Reichsmark, meant major increases in poverty. By December of 1948, grocery prices had increased by 20 percent and malnourishment was on the rise. Increased abundance only underscored the fact that the working class could rarely afford it. A 1948 trade union article described the troubles faced by housewives in the immediate aftermath of the reform:

> Never before has it been so difficult to feed the family, says Frau Schaefer. She puts the shopping bag on the kitchen table. She had bought potatoes, onions, and a large savoy cabbage. Nothing of the other pretty things one can see in the grocer shops: white firm cauliflower, long green cucumbers, dark juicy cherries, mushrooms which still give off

the aroma of the forest. None of these are in her shopping net. Those things are not for her.[107]

Erhard's commitment to eliminating price controls had radically increased possibilities for profit, which indeed meant newly overflowing shop windows. However, it also ensured, as British agricultural economist Werner Klatt noted in 1950, that

> nowhere in Europe is the inequality between the rich and the poor of such dimensions as in western Germany where, in spite of economic recovery, approximately every fifth family is still short of the barest necessities of life, such as a dwelling, some furniture, household goods, and a reasonable supply of foodstuffs.[108]

A 1951 survey revealed that a majority of the West German population felt that they were worse off than they had been a year earlier, and that few expected this trend to change.[109]

Even after they had weathered these early years of crisis, the West German population was not easily convinced of the benefits of an open market, especially when it came to foodstuffs. Despite Erhard's commitment to an unregulated market, West Germany's markets remained heavily regulated and many basic goods continued to be under federal price controls. Rationing of fats, sugar, and cigarettes was only gradually eliminated. A federal price council, mediating between the demands of housewife advocacy groups and West German businesses, regulated the prices of basic foodstuffs including rye, potatoes, and margarine, and price ceilings remained in effect for other key foods as well. Not until 1954 did the ruling Christian Democrats repeal such policies and cancel the last remnants of the wartime rationing program.[110] Even the increasingly prosperous middle class continued to practice various forms of austerity that were shaped by both individual and collective memories of hunger. During the 1950s, more than 75 percent of all private households in West Germany bottled or canned their own fruit,[111] and such individual food production was essential for many working-class communities. In 1955, *Die Zeit* published an article titled "Erhard's Miracle Cure Is Actually Working," which reported that industry was voluntarily lowering prices to ease burdens on the working poor. The newspaper explained that "the mechanism of the market allows room for individuals' free decisions," while implying that this "freedom" also encouraged the natural ebb and flow of prices in the interest of consumers.[112] Belying such confidence, however, a survey of Nordrhein-Westphalen from the same year showed that industrial workers still relied on their gardens for three quarters of their fruit and more than half of the vegetables consumed by their families.[113] Thus, following patterns that had been established over the previous half-century, even in the midst of the "economic miracle," West Germans continued to rely upon multiple avenues of food acquisition, displaying their reluctance to depend on the "free market" when it came to food supply.

In the newly divided country, both new German governments prioritized increasing food production, but the generosity of the aid provided under the Marshall Plan, as well as the relatively good condition of West Germany's farmland after the war, put the FRG in an especially favorable position. As early as 1949, dramatic increases in fertilizer usage and good weather meant that West German harvests exceeded prewar levels.[114] One of the first pronouncements of the new Adenauer cabinet was a promise to move away from the federal regulation of foodstuffs and toward to the more popular goal of increasing food production, a shift that symbolized a rejection of both wartime and East German economic strategies.[115] Above all, this shift had profound implications for the country's food manufacturing industry, which "experienced increasing capital intensity of production, increased plant size, and declining levels of employment."[116] During the early postwar years, West Germany quickly emerged as an international leader in both food imports and industrial food processing. Indeed, the growth of the West German food market inspired the Federal Republic's first major consumer explosion, the so-called *Fresswelle*, or "eating wave," of the early 1950s.

West German economists celebrated the postwar trend toward consuming expensive, highly processed, and imported foodstuffs. A new industry publication, *Die Ernährungswirtschaft*, gleefully reported in 1954:

> The consumption of products of a more elevated life style, specifically including high-end food stuffs, has steadily grown since the overcoming of scarcity, since the end of rationing, and with the currency reform. Everything seems to indicate that it will continue to rise as long as social services continue to expand and as long as general incomes, and thus the consumer capabilities of the masses, continue to grow.

The author predicted continued growth in purchases of "meat and meat conserves, butter, eggs and cheese, sugar and sweets, fruit, fresh vegetables, and tropical fruits including fruit juices and conserves."[117] Indeed, the early fifties saw striking increases in the consumption of ham, tropical fruits, and chocolate.[118] Even popular weight-loss regimes focused on luxury foods, for example, the popular "banana diet." One of West Germany's largest and most important international conventions was the Cologne-based General Food and Drink Fair (*Allgemeine Nahrungs- und Genussmittelausstellung*

[ANUGA]), which quickly became the world's leading food industry event. It was ambitiously envisioned not as

> a simple product fair; it is a combination of that and a massive educational display that demonstrates how products should be, how they should be produced, packaged, and displayed, which ultimately culminates in the technical advance of sales and in the general growth of productivity. Additionally, it aims to make a meaningful contribution to social peace domestically and to peaceful collaboration and growing closeness of all people on the earth.[119]

Such rhetoric supported the widespread belief that nothing represented the nation's economic miracle more effectively than well-stocked grocery-store shelves.

Overflowing abundance, however, only increased the threat of market saturation. As early as 1954, industry experts warned that the consumer food market was reaching its natural limits: "[I]n terms of food, the biological facts are always present: even at the highest level of an explosive economy, a man cannot consume beyond the limits of his personal satiety."[120] Engel's Law, defined in the middle of the nineteenth century and still one of the best established economic principles, showed that rising income results in a declining percentage of money spent on food; that is, the poor spend a higher share of their income on food than the rich.[121] During reconstruction, food purchases accounted for a little over half of the average West German's spending. This number steadily dropped as the economy grew; by 1989, food barely made up a quarter of the average German's budget.[122] Rising incomes in the FRG thus seemed to automatically mean "a falling share of the consumer dollar of the food industry."[123] The food industry realized that its only "meaningful chance for increased profit" would be if "foodstuffs are refined in a higher level than today, and in addition if we meet the growing need for appropriately pre-prepared foods."[124] Industrial processing became the necessary precondition for profit. As a necessary corollary, food industry profits became primarily achievable by increasing individual purchases in grocery stores:

> The food industry must, like every other industry, exert itself to continually create new desires to shop, it must do justice to the desire to save labor in the household, and, working with the packaging industry, it must exert itself to make shopping as easy and pleasant as possible for the housewife.[125]

West German food manufacturers thus were committed to increasing the number of processed food items available for purchase. These items, ranging from jams to soups to cookies and breads, reduced kitchen labor but, in exchange, increased the labor, as well as the cost, of shopping. The postwar food system thus relied on private food purchases to a previously unprecedented degree; shopping rapidly supplanted all other forms of food acquisition. A 1957 advertisement for cheap, highly processed Dr. Oetker's baking powder explicitly explained its value not simply in its material contribution to a particular baked good, but to its ability to insure the circulation of food and thus to the country's economic growth:

> The strength contained in this baking powder not only shapes your cake batter, but also economic progress. For example, your shopkeeper, who buys a carton with 100 packages of Dr. Oetker baking powder, will also have the following profit: 35 pounds of butter or margarine, 50 pounds of sugar, 80 pounds of flour, 35 [pounds] of raisins, 300 eggs, 50 fluid dr. of Dr. Oetker baking oil.... This lets us recognize how much Dr. Oetker products have for more than half a century helped to increase the profitability of our economy.[126]

As the industrial food economy expanded and real wages rose, food shopping was increasingly described as the German housewife's primary contribution to the national economy. As the indispensable corollary to her husband's industrial labor, women's food shopping thus played a central role in reconstruction. The importance of shopping for economic growth meant that consumers, who were generally assumed to be women, were subject to projects of optimization and rationalization similar to those imposed on the implicitly male industrial workforce. Indeed, household economists understood "proper shopping" not in terms of a specific set of products purchased, but as an ideal expression of a consumer-oriented democracy. In a 1953 consumer-education publication titled *The Power of the Housewife*, the Ministry of Nutrition reminded readers that "not only the healing of agriculture but the healing of the entire German economy depends on the housewife's ability to shop."[127] An agricultural expert explained that

> the economic power of the housewife certainly does not seem great in the individual household, yet her power is immense. It is in many ways the million-fold compounding of the smallest purchases that creates a particular branch of the economy; in countless numbers of cases [such purchases] are absolutely decisive for the prosperity not only of individual branches of the economy but of the economy on the whole.[128]

In his 1959 essay "She Buys Only the Most Expensive Foods," the West German economist Dr. Voigt argued that true "freedom of choice" in the supermarket would inevitably result in correct food purchases. He encouraged women to perceive the grocery store as the place where they could experience "one of the greatest freedoms on earth, the freedom to make your own decisions."[129] In 1966, federal nutrition minister Hermann Höcherl reminded the nation's housewives that they stood "at the steering wheel of the domestic economy," spending more than 60 billion Deutschmarks annually on food products.[130] Exercising this economic power was a foundational expression of postwar democracy—or, as economic minister Karl Schiller announced at the 1967 launch of the "Week of the Consumer and the Housewife," an expression of freedom: "the freedom of product selection, the freedom of the consumer, belongs to the core principles of our free social structure."[131]

Ironically, the close relationship between "economic freedom" and food shopping meant that women were not in fact free to do as they wanted. In this booming economy, shopping became a profound social responsibility, and many West German politicians and economists feared that women were simply not up to the task. During the early years of reconstruction, experts believed that after the distorted economy of the war and occupation years, Germany's consumers needed extensive re-education. In 1957, the DGE funded an comparative study of German and American approaches to consumer and nutritional education, which explained this specifically German problem in detail. It associated the immediate postwar moment with a demoralized consumer force:

> [I]n Germany the term "consumer" has a particular meaning ... it comes from the era of the controlled economy [i.e., rationing], when the population was divided into the categories of producer, distributor, and consumer. In this time, especially during the hunger years after the Second World War, this consumer mentality established itself in Germany. The so-called "normal consumer" was the symbol of misery of his time. He stood, humiliated, before the store counter and accepted, demoralized, what was distributed to him. He traveled night and day on cold trains for a bag of potatoes and begged farmers for a piece of bread. From this time we still associate with the term "consumer" the image of a defenseless creature who finds himself in a position of total dependency upon producers and distributors.[132]

From the perspective of economists, one of the most devastating legacies of the Third Reich was the destruction of German women's ability to shop skillfully and effectively. Economic hardship and constant state intervention meant that "the German consumer is far removed from being an active shopper with focused, goal-oriented product selection and buying." The idealized "active shopper" was depicted as being as responsible as the food industry for what was available on the market:

> One example is bread. A large number of the breads available do not meet the taste of the consumers. Nonetheless, most housewives, thanks to years of being taken care of through the bread-card, are indifferent to the quality of bread, and often seek a solution to the problem by simply trying to cover up major flaws with other side dishes, or even by ceasing to buy bread altogether in favor of other foods. Why don't they simply impose their consumer desires by expressing a clear demand for a certain product?[133]

The inadequate shopping abilities of the country's women meant that women must be taught how to shop, a notion expressed in the title of the 1962 publication *Shopping Must Be Learned*.[134] The postwar decades saw an explosion in nutritional education aimed directly at West German housewives, who became the major focus of the DGE; in addition, countless regional organizations and the mainstream press incorporated consumer education into their offerings. Beginning in the early 1950s, the federal government sponsored exhibitions and traveling shows to teach "the consumer—and especially the housewife . . . how difficult it is to earn money, but how even much more difficult it is to spend it properly."[135] Nutritionists and economists developed slogans like "Look; Choose; Buy," which was the title of a 1966 educational poster (see Figure 4.3), to encourage what they described as "rational shopping."

The most crucial shopping skill was the most basic one: determining what to purchase. Study after study revealed that women consistently selected the wrong foods at the wrong times of year and in the wrong quantities. West German consumer experts believed that women made these poor food choices because of a lack of nutritional knowledge combined with a particular susceptibility to the distractions of a vibrant consumer economy. In fact, West German consumer-education projects consistently depicted women as impossible to educate and as motivated by powerful irrational desires that worked directly against the economic agendas of postwar planners. Despite their permanent sense of frustration, however, these economists and advertising specialists continued to prioritize consumer education for women as the best, and indeed often only, way of achieving their goals.

At the same time, FRG nutritionists often ended up blaming women's poor shopping skills on the country's hard-won prosperity, which was most clearly evidenced in the overwhelming product diversity in grocery stores. As a speaker at the 1967 International Congress on Consumer Information noted, in the modern German supermarket, "the selection is so vast and at the same time so

Figure 4.3 "Look; Choose; Buy." 1966. Educational poster by H. P. Feddersen. Courtesy of Saarländisches Schulmuseum Ottweiler.

specialized that the individual consumer has no way of taking it all in . . . in this situation, the consumer is not capable of making the shopping decisions that are appropriate to her situation."[136] Study after study determined that the "majority of housewives" were "overwhelmed," as they confronted "increasing demands from her family members, an almost incomprehensible offering of foodstuffs, and advertising that is more confusing than enlightening."[137]

The recommended solution was, ironically, the industry's further expansion. According to economists, consumer-imposed pressures for rationalization would counteract the negative consequences of diversification. Improved organization and categorization of food products would grant women the necessary oversight to ensure their family's health and well-being. In fact, "rationalization" of the food supply generally meant a reduction in the diversity of actual (fresh or direct) foods available in favor of processed foods. For example, advocates of rationalization in Hamburg's farming regions, believing that "excessive variety impinges upon the ability to have an overview, as well as disturbing sales," reduced the varieties of apples available locally: "[T]wenty years ago in the old orchards by Hamburg around 400 varieties of apples were traded. Since then, we have rationalized this down to 40."[138] The consolidation of the apple market reduced crop diversity and consolidated farmers' profits, but it did not initially optimize women's shopping. As an act of further optimization, the 40 apple varietals were divided into three grades based on their major attributes, which allowed shoppers to choose the grade that best suited their needs; housewives, however, interpreted this form of rationalization as a rating system and always chose the "best" or highest-grade varieties, regardless of what they intended to do with the apples (cooked, chopped, or eaten whole). Farmers found themselves unable to sell their lower-grade varietals, and as a result, they cut the already dramatically reduced varieties of apple by another 50 percent.[139] Despite claims that it would empower the consumer while enabling more effective and efficient shopping, the standardization and rationalization of food products often ultimately reduced choice, serving industry interests rather than individual desires.

One of the most significant sticking points in West German consumer-education programs was that they mostly failed to address the issue that most concerned German housewives: affordability. Women rarely complained about lacking nutritional knowledge when confronted with the postwar explosion in processed, imported, and luxury foodstuffs, but they regularly complained about the high prices of these new products. Found in the files of various regional and national nutritional centers are consumer complaints that frequently addressed the lack of affordable staples. One housewife wrote a letter criticizing a radio program titled "Eating Cheaply and Well" that aired in West Berlin in 1951, pointing out that the proposed menu for a family of four, which was calculated for a budget of 35 Deutschmarks a week,

> included neither breakfast nor bread in that price. Can you explain to me how the wife of an unemployed man, who brings home 35 DM, should "cook cheaply and well." The things that you suggested would not even be possible for a temporary worker or employee. Your program is sheer mockery for the unemployed.[140]

An irate housewife wrote a letter to the newspaper *Der Tagesspiegel* complaining that "the press is constantly propagating the claim that frozen meat is of top quality and substantially cheaper than fresh meat," yet many shops did not even stock frozen meat; "there are many housewives who are in the same situation as I am—where is this cheap frozen beef actually available?"[141] In areas that bordered on the GDR, some housewives went so far as to "vote with their feet," deliberately prioritizing price over variety in their shopping decisions. During the 1950s, low-income West Berliners, as well as other "border-dwellers," regularly crossed into East Germany to purchase subsidized food items.[142] One West Berlin official expressed his frustration over his attempts to correct the behavior of these short-sighted West German women:

> In response to my point that [the unrestricted consumer selection of the West] is an advantage not enjoyed by the East Berlin population—in

the best case scenario they can only expand their options by purchasing expensive HO-products [HO-shops, *Handelsorganisationen*, sold particularly desirable products that did not require rationing coupons] or by shopping in West Berlin, if they grow weary of their monotonous diet—the housewives were only able to muster up the response: but the basic foodstuffs are extremely cheap.[143]

This official's refusal to recognize low price as a valid motivation for women's shopping behavior was indicative of West German experts' ideal of optimized "rational shopping," which was premised on simultaneous prosperity and self-control. In fact, housewives themselves were often blamed for the country's high prices; capitalist economists had long insisted that shopping behavior determined prices, believing that the market was shaped by, rather than dictated, consumer behavior. Thus in 1957, the FRG Ministry of Nutrition issued a scathing statement claiming to be "disappointed in the shopping habits of the housewives. On the one hand . . . they constantly complain about too-high prices, while on the other hand they render useless all official attempts to keep prices stable by insisting on buying only the most expensive products."[144]

The Hessian Department of Agriculture publicly demanded that the region's housewives "acquire better knowledge of the various products and . . . not shop carelessly." Surveys had revealed that "scarcely a housewife knows the different sorts of meat, and very few can distinguish between the many varieties of apples or the individual classifications, in order to judge their price."[145] Rather than simply demand lower prices, West German women were expected to learn to make their shopping choices by considering both longer-term and larger societal concerns rather than being guided in their choices by private and immediate desires. As Lower Saxony's minister of economics explained, "[T]he consumer should, through his selections of goods from among the many offerings, determine the nature and scope of economic development."[146] While women complained that they could not afford the foods recommended to them, household economists insisted that "proper diet is less dependent on income, and more on knowledge."[147]

In fact, many of these women's complaints were well-founded. In striking contrast to the artificially cheap food prices in the GDR, food prices in the FRG were some of the highest in Europe, with agricultural products priced on average 5 to 10 percent more than in the European Community at large and always substantially above market price.[148] Nonetheless, with the exception of the volatile atmosphere of the early 1950s, postwar economists have long noted that "food prices have never been a political issue in [West] Germany and do not constitute an important element in wage negotiations," a fact that reflects the low priority given to women's grievances.[149] It was not until the economic downturn of the 1970s that consumer protests began to publicly address prices; in 1978, for example, a scandal rocked the West German dairy industry when it was discovered that German consumers paid on average a third more than market price for their milk products. Butter, a long-cherished symbol of prosperity in Germany, was being sold at more than four times its actual cost.[150]

Such discussions were, however, the exception rather than the norm. Despite complaints, West German women internalized their responsibility as shoppers of the nation with all of the pressures and difficulties that this role entailed. Well into the 1960s, West German women continued to shop for food several times a week, more than 90 percent of them shopping during "work hours" and purchasing relatively small quantities of fresh and semi-perishable foods for that day's meals.[151] By 1971, an economist calculated that the housewives who led the country's "22.3 million households" made up the "the largest work-place and the largest consumer category of the Federal Republic."[152] This high level of economic activity depended on a rapidly expanding infrastructure of modern grocery stores. The switch to self-service supermarkets took place more rapidly and successfully in West Germany than anywhere else in Europe. "Self service" symbolized the sort of individualistic and empowered shopping that postwar economists demanded. In 1951, there were only 39 self-service stores in the entire country; within a decade, there were over 17,000; and by the middle of the 1960s, the FRG could boast more than 53,000 self-service grocery stores.[153] By 1970, West Germans purchased 32 percent of their foods in these stores, which was Europe's highest rate by a wide margin.[154] The remarkable success of the supermarket placed the FRG at the forefront of what historian Victoria de Grazia has termed the "Americanization of Europe."

The embrace of an industrial food economy, the spread of self-service stores, and the economic importance of private food consumption were not issues exclusive to the West; the GDR experienced similar trends and enjoyed a roughly analogous status within the Eastern bloc as one of the most "modernized" socialist food economies.[155] Indeed, by the end of 1961, the country had an impressive 13,000 self-service shops, a number that compares favorably to that of the much larger Federal Republic.[156] In other words, as important as canteens were for economic development and everyday life in the GDR, they never displaced or even meaningfully diminished the significance of private food consumption. Indeed, despite the socialist country's embrace of industrial production and collective consumption, private food purchases made up one of the largest portions of the average East German's budget. Indeed, food items were the only category of consumer good to enjoy constant, steady rates of growth since the country's founding in 1949. The relatively modest offerings of grocery stores during the 1950s, which distributed on average between 500 and 700 food products, had expanded by the 1980s to include almost 7000 distinct items.[157] This growth was embraced by the East German state, which recognized that consumers' food purchases injected money into the market on a daily basis, thus ensuring the flow of currency that defined a functioning economy as surely as did the industrial production of goods. A 1968 report from the GDR's Institute for Market Research noted:

> Since foods are consumed every day, and they make up more than a third of all expenses for goods, for large circles of the population they are the first criteria for evaluating quality of life. Achieving a high-quality steady [food] supply is thus not only a question of provisioning, but at the same time a political issue of the first degree.[158]

In addition to its economic and political importance, food shopping was crucial to the maintenance of the bourgeois family structure, to which the GDR proved deeply attached. A commitment to nuclear families meant that East German women continued to be responsible for familial food consumption, a responsibility that de facto required them to manage household shopping. As a result, just as in the West, shopping, like other economically important forms of labor, was continually targeted for projects of "optimization." Nonetheless, shopping proved one of the most troublesome aspects of the country's planned economy and became a critical site of political discontent and economic inadequacy. As in the West, the tension between product diversity and product prices framed frequent conflict between women consumers and the state.

Shopping was troublesome for the socialist state not only because women shopped poorly (as in the West) but also because the very act of private shopping existed in tension with the imperative that women engage in the paid workforce. Given the limited quantity of working hours, East German economic planners were well aware that women often had to sacrifice one form of labor, factory or domestic, for the other. In the GDR an overwhelming majority of women worked in the public sphere and were engaged in paid labor, making the workplace a prominent site of contact between women and the state. By 1970, three out of four East German women worked outside the home, and women made up almost half of the total workforce, giving the country the industrialized world's highest rate of female employment.[159] Because East Germany officially defined women's economic value, like that of their male counterparts, in terms of their labor productivity, grocery shopping potentially threatened their economic contributions, seeming to be the very opposite of productive work at the same time that it represented an unavoidable component of modern life.

This ideological dilemma ironically meant that shopping became one of the most labor-intensive components of daily life in the GDR, an exhausting and often unrewarding undertaking that was almost exclusively carried out by working women.¹⁶⁰ Over time the socialist state, recognizing that "a decisive place for the easing and minimizing of housework lies in the region of food shopping and supplying," developed various methods of reducing or even eliminating shopping altogether in order to allow women to use their time more productively.¹⁶¹ Unlike its equivalent in the West, modern shopping in the GDR was interpreted as meaning "less shopping" rather than "different shopping." In 1969, the women's magazine *Für Dich* (*For You*) described grocery shopping as an unpleasant chore that women would rather avoid:

> Who doesn't know the lines that form at the cashiers at the end of the week in the self-service stores? Who hasn't looked impatiently at the clock and silently canceled leisure activities because too much valuable time was spent rushing to stores and pulling out your wallet?¹⁶²

The state experimented with ways to replace traditional methods of shopping (physically visiting shops and personally selecting goods) with more streamlined methods of grocery distribution in order to save women's time and energy. For example, mail-order programs for grocery home delivery were briefly quite popular.¹⁶³ An advertisement from the late 1960s explained that such programs would allow the customer to "sit at home comfortably in her chair and choose what she wants from 450 sorts of foodstuffs and 150 household products."¹⁶⁴ Some cities promoted pre-ordering, wherein women dropped off shopping lists in the morning and picked up their goods on their way home from work. Many factories perceived shopping as a direct competitor for their workers' time, a reasonable belief as women frequently resorted to leaving work early or taking extended breaks at lunch in order to purchase groceries. As a result, some workplaces experimented with providing groceries to their employees directly by opening up small shops exclusively for employees. The East German state also embraced "self-service," which, by rationalizing and optimizing the shopping experience, would, it was assumed, allow women to work full-time. (Self-service, for example, meant staying open longer and offering an increased selection of goods, both of which were ideally supposed to streamline and simplify food shopping.) The GDR rapidly developed an array of educational programs aimed at getting working women to realize the advantages of this new shift toward self-service, with names like "Modern People Shop Modern" and "Serve Yourself."¹⁶⁵ A traveling exhibit about healthy nutrition and eating habits from the 1960s included a description of an East German grocery store. The accompanying placard insisted that the country's modern shops provided a "constant supply of fresh, high-quality foodstuffs" while simultaneously shortening shopping time, thus easing the lives of working women (see Figure 4.4).

Figure 4.4 "A specialized grocery store possesses all technical and organizational requirements in order to insure for the consumer a constant supply of fresh, high-quality foodstuffs. Self-service stores ease shopping above all for our working women." From the exhibit *Your Diet—Your Health*. Courtesy of the Deutsches Hygiene Museum.

As in the FRG, grocery stores in the GDR were enshrined in state rhetoric as proof of economic superiority. Quite differently, however, in the East, the government was convinced that price, rather than product variety or quality, was the key determinant of public satisfaction and economic stability. This focus on price was shared by the core cadre of East German politicians, many of whom had come of age during the food shortages of the Weimar Republic and believed that cheap rent and cheap food were the most effective and significant way of gaining popular support. In the words of a 1974 propaganda booklet:

> Price stability was and remains a principle of our socialist state's economic policy ... the price policy of the socialist state is determined by social considerations. This means that all vital necessities for the families of wage earners, salaried employees, and farmers must remain affordable.[166]

During the early postwar years, the government relied upon regular price reductions as a way to reward or pacify the population. For example, it dealt with the workers' uprising on June 17, 1953, by using both draconian crackdowns and proconsumer measures such as making canteen improvements and enacting widespread drops in food prices, which at the time were officially frozen. Women proved especially responsive to these strategies. One housewife noted that "the lowering of the prices was for me a great joy, when I think how we hungered in 1945 and today how we can buy so many things."[167] Five years later, the official end of rationing in 1958 was accompanied by the establishment of set prices for core commodities (e.g., rolls were 5 pfennig; a half pound of butter was 2.50 marks; a sausage was 80 pfennig), which remained constant for the duration of the state's existence.[168] A year after the construction of the Berlin Wall in 1961, in an effort to mollify an angry and anxious population the SED introduced several new and improved varieties of bread without any substantial price increases. Government propaganda always emphasized price above other criteria: "Here in the GDR we have low and stable bread prices; in contrast, the NATO-politics of West Germany lead to constant price increases ... it is clear—our bread is dramatically cheaper than the equivalent quality of bread in West Germany."[169]

East German leaders regularly rejected economists' recommendations to adjust commodity prices to better reflect their actual cost, convinced that "price increases [of basic foods] will lead to negative political consequences. In addition one must realize that class enemies could use a price increase of bread to create political discussions and arguments against our republic."[170] Such policies ignored the fact that the ways in which the population defined "basic needs" changed over time. For example, although beet sugar was quite affordable, people wanted alternative sweeteners; in 1953, a leader of the Democratic Women's League reported that "every day women come into the office and complain about honey prices."[171] These sorts of complaints contradicted the deep-seated assumption on the part of East German politicians that cheap groceries would be equated with a successful and satisfying trip to the store. In fact, price freezes of core goods led to subsidized commodities being seen as cheap rather than necessary; as a result, they were consumed in excess and wasted profligately. Since subsidized bread was famously cheaper than grain, many East Germans fed their chickens and rabbits with fresh rolls from the bakery, a profoundly expensive practice for which the state footed the bill.

The GDR's commitment to state-regulated prices was also based on the assumption that cheap goods were more likely to be purchased. However, in the East as in the West, price alone rarely determined purchasing behavior. In supermarkets, official economic priorities came into conflict with the complex habits and desires of modern consumers, who were motivated by emotional interactions with products and the shopping environment, as well as by personal and familial needs and expectations. This clash between consumer desires and needs and official interpretations and solutions meant that strategies for optimizing women's shopping experiences generally failed. For example, a 1962 report on the "realization of the policies undertaken to ease the life of the working women in the area of trade and food supply" regretted that

> working women make inadequate use of the food ordering service of the workplace grocery store, since they would rather buy basic food supplies at a store near their living area due to the often substantial distance between apartment and workplace.[172]

Women demanded more pleasant and rewarding shopping experiences, not just a reduction in the time spent shopping. Housewives' complaints about self-service shops more frequently criticized the atmosphere or cleanliness, the courtesy of the staff, and the smells and flavors of the food than the prices.

The official focus on price rather than product quality and shopping experience thus backfired in a number of ways. In the GDR, individual income was only tangentially connected to an individual's ability to consume. Because so many high-cost items were subsidized by the state, including housing, childcare, meals, and many staple products, the majority of the country's citizens had disposable income. This profoundly reduced the social value of low prices. What citizens lacked was not money but a way of spending it satisfactorily. Consumer purchases were largely determined by means of an informal economy that included systems of barter and trade, the black market, favors, bribery, and networks of personal connections (so-called Vitamin B, with "B" standing for *Beziehungen*, or "relationships").[173] An elaborately staggered system of shops further complicated the functionality of pricing structures, especially following the opening of Intershop stores in 1961, which offered high-quality and imported goods that could only be bought with West German marks. These stores were initially intended to be a way for the state to gain access to international tourists' currency, but East Germans increasingly shopped there as well. Ultimately, such alternative food markets underscored the weaknesses of the highly regulated yet dysfunctional formal economy.

Officially, state-regulated prices and the careful management of production and distribution worked in the interest of public health; experts assumed that abundant, low-priced products would ensure popular health. As Heinrich Gräfe of the Institute of Nutrition explained in 1967, "[T]hanks to the price policy of the GDR that focuses on low prices for groceries, especially basic foods, all socioeconomic groups are capable of buying the foods necessary for a healthy diet."[174] The undeniable fact that the bulk of the population did not, in fact, eat a nutritionally optimal diet belied this belief. A 1970 report on "possibilities of guiding consumer habits and establishing an appropriate diet in the population" found that "the current product selection does not ensure a reliable and stable supply of high quality nutritional foods for the healthy consumer or for the one with special dietary needs. This encourages a flawed diet, thus damaging public health."[175] Multiple studies suggested that low prices actually encouraged the consumption of unhealthy products, especially fats, sugars, alcohol, and cigarettes.[176] State control over food distribution proved similarly problematic, inspiring nutritionists to complain that distribution policies were not serving public interests. In the early 1950s, for example, the bulk of the country's blackcurrant harvest, a valued native crop that is especially high in vitamins, was being

> delivered to the alcohol industry for the production of liquor. From a nutritional perspective this is a false decision ... it is far more important to offer these [black currant] juices primarily to hospitals and sanitaria, where they can be best put to use, and then they should be evenly distributed to the entire population.[177]

Nonetheless, the sheer popularity of currant liquor made officials reluctant to re-evaluate their priorities.

The GDR continuously struggled to establish stable supply lines and create a predictable shopping experience. In the early years of reconstruction, East German working women who could not shop during working hours had difficulty acquiring even basic goods owing to inadequate store hours, limited transportation options, and irregular stocking. Though the most severe problems had been resolved by the early 1960s, inadequate and monotonous food supplies continued to be a major political problem. A 1968 report by the Institute for Market Research found that "the lack of continuity in product supply is most noticeable in the structural differences between supply and demand," noting that while the sheer quantity of goods was adequate for the population, it was distributed sporadically "in terms of time and territory." A shop's selection of goods was generally determined by geographic location; large cities, tourist destinations, and industrial regions were better supplied than smaller towns or areas with low population density. This had particular consequences for working women: "the irregularity of the offering of foodstuffs increases the time required for shopping and reduces the possibility of lowering this amount."[178]

Unpredictability and recurrent shortages produced sensations of scarcity and consumer dissatisfaction that existed alongside low food prices, high caloric intake, and well-developed collective feeding programs for adults and schoolchildren. Indeed, food supply problems in one sphere of the economy could cause devastating trickle-down effects. In the words of a 1962 report:

> When the food served in a workplace canteen does not meet expectations, this often has consequences for the dietary situation of the entire family. In such cases, workers frequently return to home cooking,

and that means often that the other marriage partner—if he or she is working—also leaves collective feeding, and also often as well the schoolchild. The consequence is a greater demand for sandwiches, which is reflected in a growing demand for sliced meats in shops."[179]

Shortages and illogical distribution proved especially galling when East Germans compared their situation with the consumer abundance of the FRG. Before the construction of the Berlin Wall in 1961, shoppers living in East Berlin and its environs could partake in the economy of the West.[180] Even after the sealing of the border, a thriving exchange of packages mailed and smuggled across the border kept Western food products flowing into the GDR, effectively maintaining the belief that extreme inadequacies in consumer goods, especially food products, were a core difference between the two German states.

Since the early 1950s, the West German government had been encouraging its populace to mail food packages across the border. These gift packages usually contained luxury items or items that Westerners imagined would seem luxurious to East Germans. As a 1954 advertisement in *Prima* magazine noted, "[W]hat you and I fill the packages and gift baskets with is not insignificant. It must be luxurious food products, butter and cheese, fish conserves, a sausage, fruit juices, a bottle of wine, valuable things for which our brothers and sisters will thank us."[181] By the 1960s, the West German National Center for All-German Aid warned against shipping widely available basic staples, noting that "unless there is a special request, you should no longer send flour, legumes, rice, sugar, tea."[182] Still in the 1980s the Federal Government was reminding the populace of

> the necessity of rational gift-giving. The simple grocery package is, in such cases, rarely still needed, since the GDR-recipient earns normal wages. Coffee, cocoa, chocolate, and chocolate products are always good since they are practically unaffordable over there. Tropical fruits always find grateful recipients. Meat and fish conserves of a high quality, of the sorts which one rarely or never finds in the GDR, are also popular.[183]

These carefully selected and, for the East German consumer, cost-free delicacies were intended to destabilize the East German market and stoke consumer dissatisfaction, and the effort was largely successful.

As they struggled unsuccessfully to improve consumer satisfaction, East German nutritionists and economists expressed particular frustration over the fact that their efforts to improve or diversify food offerings frequently backfired. They often inaccurately predicted popular desires and found that the wrong kind of product diversity could result in a financial catastrophe and even lower levels of consumer satisfaction. Shops struggled to convince shoppers to purchase new or unfamiliar products, which they frequently ignored, "especially those that are imports, due to their unfamiliar nature and usage possibilities, as well as often too-high prices."[184] Despite the public's outspoken desire for a wider range of available foodstuffs, popular tastes tended toward the familiar. Surveys exploring the low sales of high-end imports like "Soviet salmon in juice" revealed that "our working population scarcely knows this cooked high-quality fish, and prefers fish marinated in oil or a spiced sauce."[185] Often the only way to dispose of such products was to disguise them as something familiar, completely negating the value of novelty. For example, the expansion of trade relations with Iraq in the late 1950s meant the introduction of large quantities of dates to East German consumers. Contrary to expectations, there was little interest in this "exotic" product, and it accumulated, unsold, in GDR storehouses. Nutritionists were forced to develop strategies for disposing of dates by "smuggling" them into more salable products, most successfully adding them to a base for a fondant filling for chocolates.[186] This concealing of product diversity was both economically unprofitable (there were many cheaper products for filling chocolates than imported dates) and politically unproductive. Ultimately, the presence of these unwanted and unsalable products only increased impressions of inadequate supply.

Consumers' widespread discontent reflected real problems in the East German food system. During the early postwar years, food quality in shops was often lower than it was in canteens. Nutritional scientists tested the products sold in grocery stores, by butchers, and bakeries, and frequently found egregious inadequacies. A 1948 survey of 173 foodstuffs frankly reported that many products would be better fed to animals than humans, concluding that "one has the impression that their producers have absolutely no idea of the tastes and needs of the population."[187] More than a decade later, a report on the GDR food situation reported with dismay near-universally negative results. Sausage quality was "exceptionally variable due to the situation with raw supplies," butter had been "rejected by consumers due to its flavor and was often laced with abnormally high levels of bacteria," large numbers of imported Hungarian Jonathon apples had been "sprayed with dangerous arsenic pesticide, which is banned in the GDR," and recent shipments of coffee from Cuba had been "processed in inappropriate blends and [were] thus producing massive complaints from the population." The report concluded that "a core reason for quality decline and hygienic problems is the lack of appropriate, modern packing supplies. Through this the value of self-service itself is frequently put into question."[188] Unpredictable product quality and constant alternations between surplus and scarcity made East German shopping a generally unsatisfactory experience. The GDR's inability to satisfy popular appetites did not stem from the an underestimation of the economic importance of food or private consumerism but from its inability to regulate the subtleties of people's tastes.

* * *

At first glance, few European nations offer as dramatic a contrast in food systems as do East Germany and West Germany. The FRG, continental Europe's wealthiest country, had a remarkably well-developed network of supermarkets and high-end grocers. Widely admired for having achieved an "equalized middle class society" during the 1950s and 1960s, the country's prosperity, high levels of consumer spending, and low rates of class conflict made it a model for the free market generally and for postwar reconstruction specifically.[189] Under the leadership of Konrad Adenauer, West Germany embraced conservative social values, venerated stay-at-home mothers, and tried to relegate working-class activism to the socialist GDR. In contrast, the socialist East Germany had a far less enviable reputation. Extended postwar rationing and the government's close relationship with the Soviet Union encouraged impressions of an oppressive atmosphere strong on work and light on pleasure, dominated by smoking factories, long lines, and empty shops.

These East-West differences were real and often dramatic; much of the scholarship on the GDR, and on Eastern European socialism more generally, has argued that an inability to satisfy popular consumer desires was instrumental in the collapse of the Eastern bloc.[190] The situation came to a head in the GDR, where near-universal access to West German radio and television provided East Germans with virtual access to their neighbors' enviable prosperity.[191] East Germans learned to interpret consumer culture comparatively; they had more than their socialist neighbors to the East but far less than their neighbors in the West. Throughout the period of division, East Germans tended to couch critiques of their country in the language of consumption. In an interview from the early 1980s, a young East German woman explained her attitude toward her country's economy, "[A]t first glance, one could say that socialism is better than capitalism. There are no unemployed, young people are provided with apprenticeships, we have stable prices . . . but just once, I would like to enter a butcher's shop and right away get a ham or pork loin."[192]

The real inadequacies in socialist shopping culture, however, should not obscure the similarities between the two postwar German states. Whether socialist or capitalist, workers in their canteens and housewives strolling the aisles of local grocery stores were the targets of related state projects of economic optimization and political legitimation. At the same time, the niceties of personal taste meant that food exposed the limits of both socialist and capitalist governments.

The demands of reconstruction underscored food's centrality in industrial production and in private consumption, ensuring that both German states were especially invested in regulating canteens and grocery stores. In both the FRG and the GDR, food was crucial for defining gendered labor norms and determining men's and women's relationships to the economy. For workers, especially working men, the prominence of canteens in the GDR helps to explain the FRG's discomfort with its own industrial feeding programs. In contrast, in both East and West Germany, women were responsible for the shopping.[193] The relationship between food and labor, however, reached beyond meeting the caloric requirements for factory workers and calculating the optimal bread prices for a family of four. In industrial economies that are increasingly organized by efforts to monitor and optimize their populations, food in particular seems to provide direct access to women's bodies. The next chapter explores how the two German states relied on ideological constructions of "home cooking" to regulate female employment patterns and the rhythms of women's everyday lives and their family structures.

5

Kitchen Debates

The Family Meal and Female Labor in East and West Germany

The first major face-to-face debate between Soviet and American leaders in the tense atmosphere of the early Cold War took place in a kitchen. At the 1959 American National Exhibition in Moscow, Soviet premier Nikita Khrushchev and US vice president Richard Nixon spontaneously debated the advantages and disadvantages of their countries' economic and social systems against the backdrop of a dazzling "lemon yellow" kitchen exhibit built by General Electric. Nixon drew attention to the impressive array of household appliances and the modern aesthetic of the kitchen itself as representative of the freedom of choice enjoyed by American women. Khrushchev, in response, claimed that "your capitalistic attitude toward women does not occur under Communism," implying that Soviet women's value as productive workers existed outside the kitchen. When Nixon explained that these modern kitchens were intended to "make easier the lives of our housewives," Khrushchev again challenged the identification of women with kitchen work, awkwardly claiming both that the USSR provided its women with such products ("we have such things") and that Soviet women did not want them anyway.[1] The two men cordially agreed to disagree, but the international consensus was that Nixon had won the debate, largely because of the spectacular appeal of the GE kitchen exhibit.

A decade earlier, Churchill, in his famous Iron Curtain speech, had also linked the nascent Cold War with food. But Nixon and Khrushchev's sparring over women's kitchen gadgets seems far removed from Churchill's near-apocalyptic vision of global food shortages and mass starvation. By the end of the 1950s, food had become a source of pleasure and a site of mass consumption. European politicians had ceased worrying about declining crop yields or the specter of famine, and instead expressed their concerns about women's comfort and productivity in their kitchens. The contrast between those two iconic performances of the early Cold War reflects the remarkable changes that Europe underwent in the years following the war's end. These changes were especially dramatic in the cases of divided Germany. By the end of the 1950s, private purchases and energy use in the FRG had begun to approach American levels of skyrocketing consumption.[2] A decade later, in the GDR as well, kitchens reflected the country's impressive rates of industrial growth and related material improvements in quality of life. In both countries, kitchen appliances became icons of prosperity, and in both countries a woman's identity was linked to her work in the kitchen

The centrality of the kitchen in postwar German models of prosperity is testament to the particular importance of domestic food consumption during the Cold War. While the last chapter focused on the economic importance of food shopping to reconstruction, this one focuses on the ideological significance of home cooking. Of the myriad domestic responsibilities that women were expected to master, their work in the kitchen was especially significant. It was there that Germany's women most clearly revealed themselves, to use Atina Grossmann's evocative formulation, as "modernity's agents, victims, and mediators."[3] The Second World War had left in its wake fragmented families, a dramatic housing crisis, and severe food shortages. Rather than diminish the importance of family meals, these problems insured that the home-cooked family meal increased in symbolic significance. A woman's cooking represented all that postwar Germans imagined that they had lost and that they hoped to regain: familial integrity, physical and spiritual health, social stability, and material well-being.

The family meal—prepared by the mother and consumed by her husband and children—is an iconic construction of the industrial age.[4] The twentieth century ascendancy of the nuclear family in Europe accompanied new bourgeois expectations of a male breadwinner supporting his financially dependent wife and children.[5] Indeed, the viability of the nuclear family model required wives and mothers to accept responsibility for feeding their husbands and children within individual family units.[6] Both the eating and the cooking of these meals were determined by categories of familial difference and hierarchy based on age, gender, and financial roles.[7] The housewife in the kitchen became a counterpart to the husband in the workplace, an iconic figure motivated by selflessness rather than ambition, guided by instinct rather than training, and rewarded with love rather than wages.

Although this idealized model of parents and children eating with one another and no one else—separated from extended family members, servants, or workers—first became normative among the European middle classes in the nineteenth century and only became widespread in the twentieth, for the majority of Europeans the "family meal" has always been an aspiration rather than a normal or routine practice.[8] Nonetheless, despite being more fantasy than reality, women's home cooking plays an essential role in the modern industrial economy. By the 1960s, both postwar German states had achieved their respective versions of economic stability. The very real prosperity that had been produced during the first postwar decade was the result of fraught negotiations between the citizenry and the state over paid and unpaid labor. Although the West German state frequently asserted that under Communism "eating within the familial sphere has almost entirely disappeared," in fact both German states required women to accept the responsibility for feeding their families. And in both states, this was a form of labor that both coexisted and conflicted with paid labor outside of the home.[9] This unofficially obligatory work thus determined women's relationship to the domestic economy and regulated their wage labor. It also shaped one of the twentieth century's most widespread culinary innovations: the school lunch. The divided country boasted one of the world's most expansive and successful school-lunch programs (in the GDR) and included one of the few industrialized states to principally reject school lunches (the FRG). Both the proliferation of school meals and their elimination, however, can be seen as unsuccessful attempts to integrate the "family meal" into the modern industrial economy. Over and over again, home cooking was dismissed as trivial at the same time that it was obsessively regulated as a vital prerequisite for national health.

The West German Kitchen as a Modern Source of Tradition

The nineteenth century cult of domesticity that blossomed among the new bourgeoisie imagined the kitchen as the "heart of the home" and the focal point of women's collective identity. In the oft-cited German triumvirate of a woman's responsibilities—*Kinder, Kirche, Küche*—the kitchen stands alongside children and the church as a quintessentially female site. As the changing economy drew working-class women out of domestic servitude and toward other forms of wage labor, domestic cooking became for the first time the responsibility of middle- and upper-class women. Because cooking was now a nearly universal responsibility of Germany's women, modernizing their kitchens acquired particular significance. These modernizing projects, initially focusing especially on working-class women, advocated for the reform, not elimination, of women's new cooking responsibilities.[10] Progressive social critics in Weimar Germany believed that the "rationalization" of women's kitchens would "liberate" women from the home and enable their wage labor.[11] Prominent architects such as Walter Gropius, Erna Meyer, and Margarete Schuette-Lihotzky, the designer of the famous Frankfurt Kitchen, argued that kitchen layout alone determined whether a woman was "slave to her obligations or skillful mistress of them."[12]

During the Third Reich, all such radical experimentation had been eliminated in favor of a rhetorical embrace of female domesticity and women's exclusion from the public sphere. An American analysis of Germany emphasized the particularly disempowered situation of the country's housewives in the aftermath of the Third Reich; as a consequence of regressive social policies, the German woman found herself relegated yet again to *Kinder* and *Küche*, "not the mistress of her own household except in the kitchen and nursery."[13]

During the Cold War, the "modern kitchen" re-emerged as a major preoccupation of both socialist and capitalist societies, though they interpreted it quite differently. Unlike Weimar projects that had sought to experiment with and even challenge gender norms, the postwar West German kitchen was associated with the preservation of a conservative gender system and women's "traditional" role in society. In the Federal Republic, a valorization of the home kitchen was cast as a response to the disruption of "German traditions" by the many years of war and occupation. The challenges posed by inadequate food supplies, chaotic living conditions, and the severing of the traditional passing on of cookery skills from generation to generation were seen as threatening the survival of German society and culture. A cookbook from 1953 lamented that "when the times of emergency were finally over, millions of young women no longer knew the recipes that had been the pride of the household stove."[14] Surveys consistently revealed, in the words of a report from the West Berlin Committee for Nutritional Questions, that "housewives could seldom prepare meals in the manner to which they were accustomed, and a great many have forgotten how to cook."[15] The wildly popular television cook Clemens Wilmenrod dedicated his first cookbook, published in 1954, to

> the generation of women approaching thirty. Innocent, they suffered through the most horrific of youths. They spent their girlish nights not in the ballroom, but in collapsing, burning cellars . . . . They could not learn to cook during these years. Even if they had had the time, there was nothing to cook . . . . It is not surprising that they are ashamed to ask about the simplest aspects of cooking.[16]

Although populations around the world had experienced greater wartime dislocation and trauma than did Germany, intense concern over women's culinary skills was not a universal component of the postwar moment. An especially West German obsession, the conviction that the war had destroyed women's cooking abilities served as shorthand for expressing a larger distress over the value of German culture, the state of the German family, and the role of Germany's women in postwar society. Many feared that the economic pressures of reconstruction, with its new ways of organizing labor, were undermining "traditional" gender relations, particularly with respect to the housewife.

In their discussions of the postwar family, nutritionists, psychologists, and sociologists all claimed a particularly German affinity for the family meal, citing origins in a mythic past when all women had cooked three hot meals for their husbands and children every day. An ANUGA press release declared that "within just a few generations, century-long unchanging eating habits of humanity have changed entirely from the bottom up . . . . The developing process of industrialization brought with it increasingly new forms of eating that no longer take place in the home."[17] Experts emphasized the "old Germanic" roots of the word *Mahl*, or "meal," "meaning coming together. [The family meal] is where people should gather and unite, both externally and internally. The meal should be a sacred time, it should be celebrated."[18] (This attempt to claim authentic German origins for the family meal was historically inaccurate; an earlier term, *Mahal*, had originally implied the coming together of communities or large groups of people and had no connection to the nuclear-family-based dining unit envisioned by West Germans.) Popular magazines explained that cooking for the family was "a core aspect of culture in its truest sense."[19] According to a 1954 essay on the country's dietary health, a properly executed family meal

> accustoms children to traditions and orderliness, and trains them to come together at the table in a well-contained, self-controlled and civilized manner . . . the meal must be used to offer children information about the value of individual nutrients and to illuminate the linkage between biology and the mother earth, the labor of the farmer, and the performance of the mother of the family, in order to encourage them not only to give thanks for the Creation, but also for the family.[20]

Cooking was, in the words of a 1952 housekeeping guide, "the most natural expression of the highest task of the woman, motherhood and caring for the family."[21] The booming postwar genre of popular cookbooks typically assumed that a woman's home cooking guaranteed the happiness of her children and husband (see Figure 5.1). The bond between women and the kitchen framed widespread concerns over gender imbalance and social instability after the war. Women were advised to hone their kitchen skills to ensure that they acquire a husband, a particularly fraught goal given the infamous "surplus of women" after 1945. One cookbook explained that men will always "pop the question: can you cook?," and thus women who could not were responsible for their single status.[22] As the AEG electric stove ominously reminded housewives in 1963: "cooking is not only an art, it is an obligation. There is much truth in the old saying that the health, satisfaction and happiness of your loved ones are decided at the stove."[23]

Figure 5.1 Cover of *The Well-Set Table*. Petra Amadeus, *Der gedeckte Tisch: Ein Brevier für Feinschmecker*. Marbach/Neckar Süd-West Verlags- und Vertriebs GmbH, 1958. Private collection of the author.

Women's cooking was thus constructed as one of the most important sites of social regeneration for German society after the crisis of the Second World War.[24]

In 1959, the preeminent nutritional expert Dr. J. Kühnau, president of the DGE, penned a passionate defense of the home-cooked meal. The renowned nutritionist complained that the postwar decline of the family meal had "rob[bed] women of her role as leader of the nation's food consumption and production."[25] This was especially troubling given the general social instability of the current moment. In the words of a concerned familial dietician, the family meal was "the only possibility for bringing together the members of a family who are otherwise engaged in activities that pull them all apart."[26] Such rhetoric was inspired by the fantasy that the home kitchen was a storehouse of traditional values and the delicious tastes of the past. Ironically, experts made it clear that West German women required not an old-fashioned kitchen but a highly modernized kitchen in order to continue their "traditional" labor.[27]

For the average West German, the economic miracle was experienced first and most dramatically in the kitchen, where the contents of refrigerators—and the very ubiquity of refrigerators themselves, as well as of mixers, freezers, and other new kitchen technologies—distinguished postwar kitchens from their earlier incarnations. Paradoxically, this complete remaking of the kitchen was described as the only way to properly preserve or revive traditional domesticity. In other words, a return to "normality" hinged on the acquisition of products and technologies that had been either the exclusive provenance of the wealthy or that had simply not existed before 1949. In the early 1950s, the influential economist Alfred Müller-Armack recommended that the state's economic policies make the kitchen the focal point of postwar consumption because of the tremendous potential for private purchases in the realms of both cooking and eating.[28] Architects and domestic economists proclaimed that "the transformation that the kitchen has undergone during the postwar years in terms of rationality, functionality, sociological and aesthetic meaning sets this era apart from all previous phases of development."[29] Economic minister Ludwig Erhard declared 1953 "the year of the consumer"; the centerpiece of his campaign was the massive promotion of electric refrigerators. Erhard perceived the proliferation of "fridges" as an effective strategy for increasing private consumption and thus economic growth. At the time, despite widespread rhetoric normalizing these appliances, refrigerators were anything but standard. In 1950, only 4 percent of the population had one, and even after Erhard's campaign, this only increased to 10 percent. Despite these inauspicious early numbers, however, by the end of the decade, the FRG had some of the highest rates of fridge ownership in Europe, with over 40 percent of the population newly equipped.[30]

Popular culture began trying to normalize the modern kitchen long before it was actually normal. During the relatively austere 1950s, when many German housewives still lacked basic kitchen equipment or even access to electricity, cookbooks such as *Electric Cooking* coded recipes in terms of which electric household tools could be used to make them (the more the better; some recipes involved more than five separate appliances). West German cookbooks consistently encouraged women to "stroll into the modern world! Industry offers you machines, appliances, useful tools. Scientists are here to serve you with the most cutting edge research."[31] Women's journals ran regular campaigns promoting the purchase of various "labor-saving" tools, promising that it was impossible for women to fulfill their domestic obligations without them. In 1956, the first nationwide consortium dedicated to "domestic technology and kitchen design" was formed; two years later this Working Group for the Modern Kitchen (*Arbeitsgemeinschaft für die moderne Küche*) founded a professional journal, *Modern Kitchen*, which presented the kitchen as "the epitome of technical, sociological, functional, hygienic and aesthetic problems of the domestic sphere."[32]

Besides purchasing the newest technologies to ease her cooking labor, the West German housewife was expected to feed her family better and more efficiently by purchasing "convenience foods," in particular frozen, canned, and prepackaged items. By the 1960s, the West German food economy had become so industrialized that few of a housewife's cooking ingredients resembled those that had been used by her mother or grandmother. Nutritionists and home economists recommended frozen meals for picky eaters, canned produce for the freshest and healthiest fruits and vegetables, and mass-produced foodstuffs ranging from bread to soup to jams were promoted as the safest and best regulated products. The DGE established a training kitchen and advice office to teach housewives how to deal with the "spreading of prepared foods in the market," a situation that "demands from the housewife a critical engagement with the changed supply situation."[33] A 1966 *Spiegel* article enthusiastically described the "incalculable work hours that the [German deep freezing] industry saves housewives by delivering cleaned carrots, prepped red cabbage, dehydrated mashed potatoes, frozen desserts, pre-cooked Christmas duck directly to her kitchen, all cellophane-packed and only needing to be warmed." It approvingly noted dramatic increases in housewives' use of frozen foods over the past decade; almost half of the country's housewives occasionally used them, and a quarter of all West German women (up from a mere 7% a few years earlier) considered themselves "regular frozen food consumers."[34]

Thus at the same time that women's cooking was being venerated as an expression of traditional values and German cultural identity, women were continually pressured to acquire the latest kitchen products, purchase the most novel industrial food items, and to cook the trendiest recipes. This tension was not implicit but in fact framed discourse around housewives' labor. For every article or study pressuring West German women to embrace frozen, dehydrated, and prepared foodstuffs, another was published warning of the biological and cultural harms posed by these foods and insisting on the necessity of preserving "traditional" foodways. In a 1963 article evaluating the functionality of increasingly popular premade foods, titled "Seductive but Not Individual Enough: Do Prepared Meals Have a Future?," the author confidently asserted that "the experienced housewife ... quickly realizes that she cooks more economically, and above all more individually, when she cooks her own food at her stove ... what prepared meal could ever compete with an individual meal made with love, love that still today goes through the belly?"[35] Even when prepared foods were enthusiastically endorsed, experts recommended that women continue to supplement them with additional "individualizing" labor. Even simple products like canned soups required additional kitchen work to be worth serving to husbands and children; a 1960 consumer advice show warned its listeners that "the consumer should always improve a prepared soup with some fresh parsley or chives, a sausage or fresh meat, none of which substantially increases the amount of work necessary."[36] This sort of modified and scaled-down version of home cooking was necessary to preserve family and societal well-being by preventing the standardization of taste and thus preserving individuality in the face of the anonymizing tendencies of the modern world:

> Cooking out of cans, the use of prepared meals and the use of standardized flavorings lead to the de-individualization of the private kitchen ... we cannot only think of saving time for the housewife, we must also remember the worth of subjective and individual food preparation.[37]

Modernization was supposed to enable the kitchen to fulfill its ideal function of providing a respite from the harms of modernity; housewives strove to craft a optimal workspace that was simultaneously a timeless place of pleasure, leisure, and love. In contrast to the ruthless competitiveness of the industrial economy, a well-outfitted kitchen promised to eliminate "senseless steps or movements, wild chaos, and stressful nervousness," replacing them, in the words of a popular 1952 cookbook, with "quiet, order, and happiness ... a positive atmosphere in which good work in the service of the family flourishes."[38] The West German housewife cooked in order to revive her husband and children after the dehumanizing influence of wage labor and school; her kitchen provided "hours of happiness" that were "the bright spots of daily life, the core of calm around which the rest of the day rotates."[39]

The tremendous significance of this form of female labor was only underscored by its abstractness. Home cooking was a profoundly emotional rather than physical or intellectual form of work; indeed, West German economists claimed that housework, and especially kitchen work, was "more about a *being* than a *doing*."[40] It was not intended to be productive in the typical economic sense of the word, but rather in its existential purpose: "to provide a counterpart to the anonymity and animosity of the external world. Here activities cannot be measured in money. They occur not because of salary, not for changing and exchangeable strangers, but for those bound to her by fate and by trust."[41] Thus, West German social planners linked modernization and optimization not to reducing women's responsibility for her family's diet, but to preserving it by making the work itself efficient, pleasurable, and "modern." Of course, such a project entirely ignored the reality of female wage labor, which had been part of German women's lives since the nineteenth century. Despite its relative normalcy, however, female wage labor continued to be nearly exclusively portrayed as unpleasant, unnecessary, and, ultimately, destructive rather than constructive. Thus, in the FRG the goal of modernizing private kitchens was intended to support women's removal from the workforce, confirming their key societal function as emotional rather than economic.

Unlike paid labor, and unlike most other components of daily housework, cooking evoked the sensual pleasures of eating. This meant that it could be construed as an enjoyable act, as the pleasures of consumption could supplant, and even negate, the difficult labor of production. For this reason cooking seemed existentially different from "real work," an act of leisure rather than labor.[42] Claims of technological progress were crucial to this transformation. Cooking skills or formal training seemed to have become unnecessary, since with a new kitchen mixer, "the daily cooking labor can now be done with a wave of the hand."[43] Electric cooking technologies claimed to offer "fully automated food preparation," while the AEG-stove promised "new pleasures every day" by replacing cooking with button-pushing and dial-turning.[44] Even reading cookbooks was "nowadays no longer mandatory for housewives," reported *Modern Kitchen* in 1966; women were urged to dedicate themselves to their kitchens while being reminded that they needed no particular skills or notable abilities in order to do so.

This emphasis on the existential difference between wage labor and kitchen work was an implicit rationale for keeping women out of the paid workforce. The Cologne Catholic Church's warning, in 1952, that "the employment of the married woman destroys marriage and, because it is to the highest degree anti-child, destroys the people and culture"[45] reflected widely held views. Indeed, such attitudes were enshrined in West German law. Until being revoked in 1976, paragraph 1356 of the FRG Civil Code had stipulated that "women have the right to gainful employment to the extent that this is compatible with their responsibilities to marriage and the family."[46] This law was rooted in the belief that only women were capable of doing the crucial work of family cooking and that families were doomed to suffer if this cooking were to suddenly cease as women took up paid labor.

The German Nutritional Society declared that "perhaps the most important fact of modern high civilization is the employment of woman, who through paid labor is ripped from the lap of the family and thus robbed of her thousand-year-old purpose, to function as protector of her family's nutrition."[47] Experts carefully detailed the tremendous amount of domestic labor that women performed on a daily basis in order to document the impossibility of external employment. Figure 5.2 shows one such chart from a 1954 guide to modern home design, which traces the daily activities of an "average" German family. Even with a full-time housemaid (something that was far from typical in the 1950s), the mother is the busiest member of the family by a large margin, getting up first and going to bed last; in her busy day, food-related work makes up the largest portion of her labor.

West German nutritionists almost universally believed that female employment would lead to a decline in the quality of home-cooked meals. Sociologist

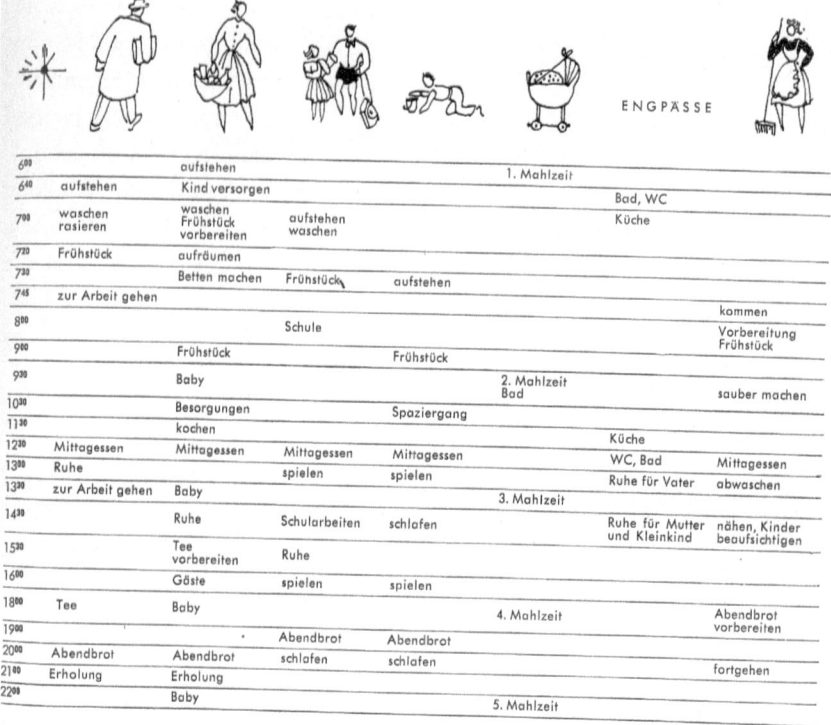

Figure 5.2 Daily schedule and activities of the housewife at home. From Erika Brödner, *Modernes Wohnen*. Riss, Munich 1954, 27. Private collection of the author.

Elisabeth Pfeil's exhaustive and influential 1961 study of female employment was quite sensitive to the fundamental problem that female work outside the home posed to the family meal:

> The mother of the family who sits at the family table and distributes food is a deeply rooted image that humanity cannot forget so easily. This is why debates over the removal of the mother from the home [through employment] cannot simply take place on the level of practical coping; instead they must engage with processes that take place in the deepest layers of the soul.[48]

A 1963 poll found that more than half the population would support a law prohibiting mothers with young children from working outside of the home.[49] Some went even further: 11 percent of women and 22 percent of men surveyed advocated the total prohibition of women's paid work in the "best interest of societal health."[50] Echoing persistent demands by male workers to protect their jobs from female competition, a 1964 survey revealed that whereas a full 30 percent of men interviewed expected from their wives "first and foremost good housekeeping and cooking skills," a mere 1 percent desired an employed wife.[51] In 1972, a West German questionnaire found that two-thirds of surveyed husbands never or rarely helped their wives with the housework.[52]

Despite such clear expressions of male discomfort, German women had long been involved in wage labor. However, it was not until the twentieth century that a majority of working women left the agricultural and domestic spheres (not coincidentally, both of these feminized workplaces are sites of food production) to take on better paid and more "modern" factory jobs and then clerical and service positions. Even during the reactionary Third Reich, the economic pressures of rearmament insured that more than half of the civilian labor force was female by 1945.[53] While the exigencies of the postwar occupation had often required women to take up paid work, the founding of the FRG in 1949 inspired a reversal of the trends of the first half of the twentieth century. The West German public sphere reflected the mounting pressure on women, especially mothers, to remove themselves from the workforce.[54] Nonetheless, almost two million women entered the workforce between 1947 and 1955. By 1961, almost half of all adult women were working for wages. Even more disturbing to many West German policymakers, a quarter of these working women had at least one small child at home.[55]

Given the widespread social condemnation and lack of state support, the many women who did work outside the home in the early FRG had a difficult time. On average, they were gone from their homes from 6 a.m. to 5 p.m., and about two-thirds of them skipped lunch in order to have time to prepare lunches for their husbands and children.[56] In the 1950s, a housewife spent about 70 hours a week performing her domestic responsibilities.[57] The average working mother, in contrast, put in an 11-hour workday and then spent up to another eight hours doing household chores, the bulk of which was food related.[58]

By the 1960s, a growing feminist movement encouraged women to express resistance to cooking, giving voice to a critique of the kitchen as an exclusively female space. For the first time, German kitchens became openly problematic. In 1962, *Der Spiegel* reported that

> the emancipation of women has created more problems than it has solved.... While 92% of German husbands perceive their domestic atmosphere, in clear self-delusion, as "happy," only 19% of their wives have the same opinion. This number strikingly correlates with the results of a survey reported by the *Bild*: 81% of wives "are sick of housework."[59]

By the end of the decade, study after study had found that the country's housewives "lack any real interest in cooking."[60] In 1973, a nationwide analysis of consumer habits found that working women usually experienced "their daily cooking as an unpleasant chore ... Due to time restrictions, they prioritize what is easy and habitual to cook, that is to say the quick preparation of a meal."[61] Despite the fact that nutritionists particularly venerated the cooking skills of educated, middle-class, stay-at-home housewives, a 1970 survey unexpectedly revealed that this demographic expressed especially strong hostility toward "daily cooking," which for them "represents a burdensome chore." One such housewife passionately explained that "the theme 'nutrition' is decidedly unpleasant. Bringing daily meals to the table, coming up with something to cook every day, is something that I find dreadful."[62]

Thus by the 1970s, popular resentment toward the "traditional" labor of the housewife seemed to pose a serious threat to societal well-being. In 1969, West Germany's minister of family affairs, Aenne Brauksiepe, had declared her ambition to "finally free the daily cooking of the stench of a burdensome domestic chore."[63] Such initiatives, partly responses to the profound upheavals of 1968, usually aimed to professionalize the country's housewives, modeling themselves on West Germany's highly standardized training programs for male workers. For example, the women's magazine *My Family and I* staged a contest called the "Cooking Diploma," which was meant "to contribute to giving a little extra recognition to the housewife's daily work." After a nationwide call for recipes, the top candidates were brought to Cologne to cook in front of a studio audience, culminating in the crowning of "Germany's No. 1 cook."[64] The contest was praised for helping to make clear "that the work of the housewife is a career like any other, a career that one must learn and in which one even takes exams."[65] More controversially, in the 1970s the conservative Christian Democratic Party supported the unsuccessful efforts of a group of German feminists, including the well-known activists Alice Schwartzer and Hannalore Mabry, to establish subsidized wages for stay-at-home housewives. Conservative politicians hoped that such a program would convince West Germany's wives of the value of this work—and discourage them from joining the paid workforce.

The East German Kitchen as Enabler of Female Wage Labor

In the socialist East, where determining what constituted "work" was a major political issue, authorities were notably ambiguous about all forms of labor carried out in the home, performed for familial rather than societal gain, and not rewarded with wages. The very attributes that gave domestic labor its particular value in the West—its isolation, gendered nature, and lack of financial recompense—marked it as grotesque in socialist logic. In the words of East Germany's first prime minister, Otto Grotewohl, "[M]an can do nothing less noble than expecting woman to be his unpaid serving girl."[66] Communism explicitly promised to bring an end to society's dependence upon the oppression and subordination of women by means of domestic labor.

Of all household chores that signaled female oppression, cooking was the most complicated to negotiate. Sweeping claims by the government that it would "liberate" women from their kitchens were more rhetorical than realistic, as East German leaders proved unexpectedly attached to women's home cooking. This feminized form of labor was distinct from, and more obviously valuable than, all other forms of domestic work. Unlike grocery shopping and cleaning, cooking was the most obviously productive domestic chore, a highly skilled form of work that was essential to the health of the population; it thus had an immediate impact on the productivity of the economy at large. Food work also consumed the largest percentage of the East German housewife's daily household responsibilities, thus compromising her ability to work outside the home. Official discourse addressed this conflict by acknowledging without resolving the inherent conflict between wage labor and domestic food preparation: that "as a working woman, she [the East German woman] cannot dedicate herself to questions of nutrition."[67]

In contrast to the West, in East Germany economic pressures demanded incorporating all adults into the workforce, a goal that encouraged the state to take an aggressive approach toward regulating domestic labor. Because of its time-consuming nature, cooking was singled out as a major obstacle preventing women from working outside the home. During the 1950s, the GDR celebrated the fact that this new socialist economy had caused woman's "previously crucial role as leader of familial food intake to continually diminish."[68] In 1952, preeminent nutritionist Arthur Scheunert explained that the "incorporation of women into the labor force" meant that family feeding habits must "undergo radical change since the work of acquiring and preparing these meals, which previously often took many hours a day, is no longer possible ... the young woman who marries is no longer able to cook and does not have the time to do so."[69] Crucially, these experts never recommended that women simply stop cooking for their families. Instead, East German authorities developed a distinct approach to the dilemma of women's role in the industrial economy, one premised on the interdependence of their paid labor and kitchen work.

East German rhetoric argued that the most basic requirement for a woman's good home cooking was her employment outside of the home. Women's "traditional" relegation to the kitchen was described as structurally linked to oppression and social and economic inequality, both issues that the GDR aimed to overcome. Rather than ending food work altogether, the hope was that once women had achieved economic equality, they would then be able to cook for their families both better and more effectively. Their cooking would thus be transformed from oppressive obligation to a fulfilling and productive form of self-expression. While the West German state believed that wage labor prevented good cooking, in the GDR women were told that proper cooking required a salaried job, which provided her with financial independence, a set of valued skills, and emotional satisfaction. Accounts of women's "traditional" prewar domesticity were reinterpreted as backward, exploitative, and lonely:

> Out of the yellowed, stained pages [of old cookbooks] suddenly emerges the unvarnished truth of the so-called good old days ... and suddenly it is anything but good, cozy, or relaxing. Not only did young women have to ... cook, fry, and bake, they also churned butter and cheese, brewed beer, sewed and bleached, made soap ... even more disturbing for us today was the humiliation and exploitation associated with kitchen work ... yes, the only good thing about these old days is that they are over![70]

While West German experts claimed that a woman's "true" self could only be realized through kitchen work, East German media emphasized the centrality of public employment and wage labor for a woman's self-realization. However, once women had achieved these landmarks, they were also expected to take up that "traditional" kitchen work as well.

As envisioned by GDR planners, the East German food system functioned as a resource and inspiration for working women who were juggling full-time employment with the need to feed their families. Unlike in the West, these jobs were cast as actually improving the caliber of women's cooking. For example, nutritionists advised women to adapt effective cooking techniques learned from their daily canteen visits; ideally "the collective feeding program will educate the domestic kitchen."[71] After all, "in the correctly organized collective feeding program, provisioning is generally better than home cooked meals in terms of healthfulness."[72] As a result, GDR nutritionists claimed that "collective feeding establishments must become a model for practical, healthy, economical and tasty eating. Thus they will become a positive influence on domestic cooking and the daily diet, and contribute to the health and productivity of the population."[73]

Factory newspapers published canteen recipes for their female readers, helpfully scaling them down from four hundred servings to four; workplace lectures taught women the basics of modern cooking and food hygiene, and educational posters were displayed at various factories explaining core nutritional principles: "it is not the big piece of fatty meat, but a sensible, variety-filled combination of all available foods that is the centerpiece of our daily nutrition."[74] Because men, women, and children were expected to eat in school or factory canteens, "family feeding only remains responsible for the breakfast and evening meal."[75] This meant though that private cooking continued to be mandated; in addition to their obligation to work outside the home, East German women were told that it was their home-cooked meals "upon which productivity and pleasure in work depend."[76] Participation in the workforce reduced the amount of time that a woman spent cooking and improved both her quality of life and her cooking. Canteens not only fed female workers; they also subtly taught them how be better cooks. Higher wages were equated with increased nutritional knowledge and better food choices. Increased opportunities for peer socialization made women happier and thus more effective at creating the necessary positive and warm atmosphere at the dining room table. Rather than eliminate it, East German socialism transformed kitchen labor from a form of capitalist exploitation into an empowering form of feminine self-expression.

Proper cooking in the GDR thus did not rely upon restoring the lost skills of well-loved grandmothers, nor did it require the wide array of technological appliances that was normalized in the West. Instead, socialist cooking was described as "scientific" or "rational" cooking. This was, in the words of an extensive 1953 report, "a flexible, scientifically based conception of kitchen work ... which requires a critical and creative mindset."[77] Instead of emotions and fond memories, there was a general emphasis on the scientific aspects of home cooking:

> Have you ever thought about the enormous scientific work—the research, pondering, calculations, tests and not least of all the incredibly precise handiwork—necessary to send a manned spaceship around earth or into the atmosphere? Now you are probably asking: what does this have to with the publication of a modern cookbook, written in accord with the newest discoveries of nutritional science? ... I can answer quite simply—a great deal! For in cooking ... there is just as much research, considerations, calculations, and tests.[78]

Even during the serious material restrictions of the occupation years, socialist publications embraced this model of aggressive modernization when it came to private food preparation. A 1948 Soviet zone publication on the current food situation defined the kitchen as a place where "science and technology are anchored in the kingdom of the woman."[79] The well-known nutritionist and cookbook author Elisabeth Wieloch explained, in her 1964 edition of *Healthy through Vegetables*, that modernization had "expanded the demands and tasks assigned to women," requiring "a break with the eating habits of yesterday. What an individual eats, and what a woman cooks, can no longer be random, ruled by superstition and ignorance. Solid knowledge is the base of our new style of eating."[80]

The East German state developed multiple venues for offering the necessary (re-)education. Like the DGE in the West, East Germany's central nutritional research institute, the Central Institute for Nutrition (Zentralinstitut für Ernährung or ZfE), regularly published pamphlets, posters, and cookbooks aimed at teaching women modern cooking techniques. The Dresden Hygiene Museum, an internationally renowned center of health education, focused particular attention on dietary questions, releasing short films, touring exhibits, and other multimedia displays to teach GDR citizens, especially women, how to cook better. Cookbooks and nutritional education programs emphasized such new and "modern" cooking techniques as steaming instead of boiling foods; not soaking cut vegetables; and eating more frequent, smaller meals. Tellingly, most East German cookbooks were written by university-trained nutritionists and professional chefs, often working in collectives made up of various nutritional experts; in contrast, in the West "housewives" or the occasional celebrity wrote them, generally passing on long-cherished family recipes or telling personal stories, rather than relying on professional culinary training or nutritional expertise.

This East German "scientization" of cooking implied a de-gendering of kitchen work, which was seen as a positive byproduct of culinary modernization. Men as well as women authored GDR cookbooks, and state rhetoric self-consciously described the gender-neutral kitchen as the new norm. Indeed, the official East German goal of redistributing kitchen labor across genders and generations had little counterpart in the FRG. Rhetoric, however, had little to do with reality. East German nutritionists and household economists had long recognized that men's reluctance to take on cooking responsibilities was one of the major factors limiting women's social equality. Leading GDR nutritionist Wilhelm Ziegelmayer warned in 1947, "clearly, the revolution of the kitchen is difficult to pull off. One comes into conflict not with the resistance of the housewife as cook, but with the lack of desire on the part of the man to go without what he has been accustomed to, and to adjust himself to a new diet."[81]

Over the course of the postwar years, the East German state steadily expanded home economics programs for boys as well as girls, "since future husbands, far more so than earlier, will need to help their wives with shopping and preparing meals."[86] A 1960 report on nutritional education in the school system argued that

> it should be obvious, without further explanation, that [male] students ... should be made capable of preparing simple meals (goulash and potato salad) on their own, so that, in the case of familial or personal emergencies (for example sickness of the mother or

later the wife) they are capable of ... independently making meals for themselves or their family for a set amount of time.[87]

Cookbooks made a point of using either "gender-neutral" language or of explicitly addressing both men and women as their target audiences. According to a 1967 East German culinary guide, successful socialist cooking meant that "all members of the family are equally responsible for the aspects of the diet that remain within the household and, within reasonable limits, all of them can take over aspects of its preparation: women and men, adults and often as well children."[82] After all, "responsibility for the diet is no longer only that of the woman, but is generally that of the family, the workplace, and the society. This development is crucially driven by the fact that every single member of society has a stake in resolving the food problem in one way or another."[83] In practice, this meant encouraging a fairer distribution of domestic labor among family members. New kitchen techniques and technologies promised to reduce a woman's labor not only by taking over some of her traditional tasks, but by simplifying them enough to allow "every family member and every guest [to] easily play cook, and at the same time entertain himself mightily, and observe how his senses and those of everyone else are aroused by their work." Women were advised to boil their potatoes in their skins, for example, not only because of the added nutritional value but because it meant that the labor of peeling would be done by whoever ate that potato.[84] "All who eat the meal must also play a role in creating it," an obligation that demanded that women now delegate and carefully supervise cooking tasks.[85]

Such educational gestures proved to have little impact on women's actual housework obligations. Women's magazines repeatedly carried out surveys to track men's participation in household labor; these usually rationalized the striking lack of improvement instead of documenting a "revolution in the kitchen." As a result, women began increasingly to voice their dissatisfaction with the so-called double burden, complaints that were simultaneously recognized and dismissed by the state. Acknowledging that women's unpaid labor at home limited their professional advancement and work productivity, the SED announced, at its eighth National Congress held in 1971, that "without underestimating the help given by men in the household, it remains a fact that the main burden is borne by women."[88] Adult men, rather than children or the elderly, remained the country's largest untapped source of kitchen labor. Despite a five-year plan initiated in 1966 to reduce women's domestic labor, a report on the food economy found that the average woman performed at least three times more food-related work a week than did the average man.[89] The report found that "a whole series of regularly occurring household chores remain for psychological and traditional reasons the responsibility of women," and noted "in the realm of food provisioning and preparation there is substantial room for reducing and easing housework."[90] Yet alongside their sincere desire to see women join the workforce, the primarily male socialist planners of the GDR continued to perceive cooking as a definitionally female activity.

In January 1970, the East German women's magazine *Für Dich* initiated one of the most successful columns in its history: "Some Men Like to Cook." The column ran for a full year and received frequent letters and contributions from its declared target audience: East German men. Such was its success that in March the title of the column was changed to "Many Men Like to Cook." The column was marketed as a way for men to exchange information with other men about their cooking experiences; the demographics of the magazine's readership, as well as frequent jokes and asides to the "real" family cooks (i.e., women), made it clear that the column was actually intended as entertainment for female readers. The main purpose was to both exoticize and denigrate men's cooking. The column was thin on recipes and cooking techniques, focusing instead on anecdotes about the wacky results when men cooked, generally highlighting their incompetence in the kitchen.

This seemed the general consensus rather than an exception to the rule. Two decades after the establishment of "really existing socialism," popular journals acknowledged that, when it came to cooking, "a recipe for re-educating men does not exist," recommending instead that each woman learn "what strategy works best for her" in order to trick her husband into taking over the occasional breakfast prep or the post-dinner washing up.[91] Even East Germans who explicitly strove for gender equality conceptualized the woman as the ultimate kitchen authority: "of course the housewife has the last word—and ultimately the primary responsibility—in tasting and flavoring the dishes."[92] Male cooking was always framed as atypical, complementary rather than primary.

The ineffectiveness of the "re-education" of East German men reflected the limitations of the larger project of modernizing the GDR food system. It was clear that physical conditions and the material environment influenced the quality of meals and women's experience of cooking as much as education about gender equality. The "revolution in the kitchen" required not only new ways of thinking, but an actual new physical space that would enable the socialist approach to cooking. In the East, unlike the West, the kitchen was not enshrined as the emotional center of the home or a domestic showpiece, but conceptualized as a space where labor could be performed efficiently and effectively, making it possible for women (and occasionally men) to quickly leave it for more productive work elsewhere.

East German architects eschewed what they described as a "traditional" kitchen, generally imagined as either a large eat-in room that was an airy "prison of the middle class" or a dingy, dark hovel where proletariat women labored over coal stoves. Their ideal solution, based on the modernist architectural experiments of the interwar years, was the so-called P2 model kitchen, a prefabricated kitchen design that was incorporated in various forms into the country's vast housing projects. With barely enough room for a single person to work, this tiny but modern kitchen was, like the Frankfurt kitchen that had inspired it, intended to be a "functional room that eased kitchen work—for the well-being and emancipation of the housewife."[93] The East German embrace of modern kitchen technologies, prefabricated buildings, and processed foodstuffs was therefore in some ways analogous to those processes in the West. However, the goal was to decrease a woman's cooking labor so she could enter the workforce, not so she could spend more time with her family, as in the FRG. Since the "fulfillment of the five-year-plan is the responsibility not only of all workers, but also of all housewives," a guide to the IKA Mini-Kitchen, an early model of kitchen mixer, warned that "we cannot underestimate the amount of hard labor that is bound up with this responsibility [of cooking], especially when that woman is employed and therefore must accomplish her domestic tasks in her spare time." These appliances were created to resolve this pressure: "electric domestic tools are here to ease women's burden."[94]

Despite being a crucial part of the official embrace of modernization, new kitchen appliances remained unattainable for most East German women. No domestic space as clearly exposed the country's relative poverty and underdeveloped consumer landscape as clearly as did these kitchens, especially in contrast to the remarkably well-equipped kitchens of the FRG. By the late 1950s, East German private consumption levels were just two-thirds those of the FRG, and it was not until 1970 that more than half of East German households finally owned a refrigerator.[95] This meant that socialism constructed an alternative definition of the "modern kitchen" that attempted to divorce modernity from intensive consumption. Products were frequently advertised as modern labor-savers even when they were hand-powered instead of electric. Postwar cookbooks, such as *Healthy Kitchen* from 1960, taught readers ostensibly modern techniques as a way of substituting for truly modern products that were unavailable to the average consumer. The savvy housewife learned how to keep foods fresh even without an electric refrigerator by storing food in damp linen sacks or by crafting a "butter-freshener" from a clay flower pot.[96]

Similar difficulties surrounded processed foods, which were a major focus of East German nutritional research and the subject of much rhetorical celebration. Hoping to decrease food costs and reduce imports, the state supported the development of a diverse range of artificial and processed foods, from canned soup and dehydrated vegetables to chocolate substitutes and "industrially produced baking mixes and flours."[97] These food products were marketed to the East German public as a way to cut down working women's kitchen labor. In 1959, the Free German Labor Union addressed the food industry on behalf of women workers, stating that "the production of half-finished and prepared dishes like broiled meats, prepared salads, peeled potatoes, washed vegetables, aspic, must be supported."[98] Nutritionists imagined the creation of "an entire row of products which help the housewife to prepare tasty and healthy meals with little time and energy,"[99] in particular asserting the advantages of "pre-prepared foods (frozen and canned), pre-cleaned vegetables, peeled potatoes, salads, etc."[100] A 1966 study on "time spent in meal preparation in the household and possibilities for its reduction" recommended the industrial preparation of commonly prepared recipes which had been found to be especially time-consuming: roasts, roulades, celery and bean salad, and most fish dishes.[101] In 1961, one of the GDR's largest producers of frozen and canned produce, VEB Leipziger Feinkost, submitted a request for new, higher quality equipment in order to meet "the pressing need to produce nutritionally high value conserves," a steadily growing demand "since the working woman lacks the necessary time to clean raw fruits and vegetables."[102]

Creating and marketing new food products, however, required a greater economic investment and more advanced technologies than the East German state was willing to provide. Inadequate industrial infrastructure limited the production of processed commodities. Lack of sufficient domestic, commercial, and industrial freezer space created great difficulties for the distribution of frozen foods, which are generally considered one of the most important advances in the postwar food industry. These difficulties, for example, created the infamous "fish-stick mountain" of 1971, when almost 40 tons of fish sticks rotted in GDR storehouses because grocery stores refused to stock them due to their lack of freezers.[103] Whether because these foods were produced in too-limited quantities or because the individual housewife lacked the products necessary to consume them (fridges, freezers, or specific kitchen gadgets), working women rarely had access to the products that had ostensibly been developed specifically for them. At best, instead of reducing women's kitchen labor, East German processed foods and kitchen machines simply changed the kind of work that was required; at worst unpredictable supplies and poorly made and poorly packaged products actually increased the demands of women's food work.

Thus despite this wide array of strategies to reduce women's cooking, a 1968 survey found that the typical employed East German woman spent an average of three hours a day on food-related activities. The study concluded that "in this way, their [workforce] productivity is limited and the ability to win over more unemployed women [to join the workforce] is reduced."[104] In 1986, almost two decades later, despite impressive expansion of state support for working mothers, a survey found that two-thirds of all women reported that kitchen work was the most time-consuming of their domestic responsibilities—and that it was their sole responsibility.[105] Despite the East German state's commitment to women's participation in the labor market, it proved incapable of imagining a family that did not rely on women's unpaid kitchen work.

Feeding Children in Public: School Lunches and the Family Meal

Although East German planners never abandoned their goal of modernizing home spaces and food technologies, the only truly effective strategy for reducing female kitchen labor proved to be feeding family members outside the home. Because women's kitchen labor was both culturally and economically bound up with children's health in particular, state-provided school lunches remade women's societal roles in ways that new kitchens, modern foodstuffs, and a rhetorical embrace of gender equality could not. The success of East Germany's school-lunch program, however, was both hard-won and incomplete. It took postwar nutritionists and economists more than two decades to convince East German women to relinquish their responsibility for their children's diets.

Prior to the founding of the GDR, school lunches had not been popular in Germany. Many European countries had established large, centralized meal programs for urban children by the turn of the twentieth century, but in Germany early public-feeding programs remained decentralized and highly regional. Where they did exist, they were generally understood as antipoverty programs and thus organized by charities, churches, or individual philanthropists. Most Germans had first become familiar with school lunches at the end of the First World War, when American Quakers provided free meals to hungry German children. As a result, these meals came to be associated with crisis, military defeat, and international relief. This pattern seemed to repeat itself in 1945, when German children again became the beneficiaries of international food aid in the form of hot school lunches.

During the Hunger Years, school meals were one of the most popular and politicized programs of the Allied occupation forces, who for the first time in Germany's history expanded the scope of school lunch programs to reach a substantial percentage of the juvenile population. Despite structural similarities across the zones, the different occupation powers understood the purpose and goal of school lunch programs quite differently. Whereas the American zone, with the support of Herbert Hoover, embraced a strategy of providing high-quality meals to the neediest children, the Soviets strove to make meals universally available as a way of stabilizing public health. In the American-dominated Western zones, school-lunch programs were short-lived, because their continued association with poverty, collectivity, and foreign aid made them anathema in the newly developing free market.[106] One of the most dramatic effects of the 1948 currency reform was the rapid drop in participation in school-meal programs, as these lunches became too expensive for parents who were scrambling to feed themselves and their children, resulting in a temporary worsening of children's overall health.[107] Nonetheless, the West German state consistently criticized school meals as evidence of material poverty and social and familial crisis. Ignoring widespread requests that the provision of subsidized meals for children be continued, in 1950 the FRG voted to stop providing hot school meals and to replace them with subsidized milk distribution, a policy that remained standard in Germany even after reunification in 1990 and still continues today.

Cast not as an antipoverty policy but as a core tenet of modern society, key to public health and worker productivity, the school meal was central to East German self-conceptualization throughout the country's four decades of existence. Their conspicuous presence, however, belies just how complicated it was to normalize and popularize school meals among working mothers. The first official School Lunch Bill of the GDR, the 1950 *Anordnung*, mandated that schools provide a complete hot meal to children, replacing the previously standard, relatively meager cold lunch of rolls and meat, jam, or cheese. The SED anticipated that there would be tremendous popular support for the bill, which was expected to reduce housework and thus enable women to work outside the home, while at the same time improving the diets of schoolchildren.

East German parents, and especially mothers, unexpectedly rejected this new policy, claiming that it was both unnecessary and unwanted. Although they accepted the provision of cold snacks and milk, mothers were opposed to the warm meals, which consisted of a grain, a vegetable, and, occasionally, meat, seeing these more substantial meals as an encroachment on their rights as parents and a threat to the well-being of their children. Parents' organizations and women's groups petitioned local and national educational boards to receive exemptions from this statewide policy. Local newspapers throughout the country published numerous complaints that these school meals would render mothers' cooking unwanted or redundant:

> Experience has shown that children were either so full from this meal that, when they arrived home in the afternoon, they did not want the hot meal their mothers had provided for them, or that there were mothers who from laziness did not prepare a warm meal for her children because she believed that they had received enough to eat in school.[108]

East German mothers rejected the official claim that labor in the workforce should replace labor at home. Instead, an investigative report from 1951 found that "parents absolutely want their children to partake of their warm lunch in their home, a meal which, as a result of the improvements in the food situation, is more individual, better, and tastier, and which allows [parental] control over the diet of children."[109]

Even as mothers increasingly took up full-time work outside the home, they found ways to provide home-cooked meals for their children, either by giving them lunches to take to school, preparing a precooked meal the child could heat up at home, or leaving work at the child's lunchtime to cook. Many families shifted the primary meal of the day to dinner, so that women could cook full meals for their children after work. No one could force children to eat the school meals, nor were parents easily convinced of the benefits of a communal hot school meal. This resistance proved surprisingly robust. Neither improvements in the country's economic development nor in the general health of the population in the 1950s resulted in an increased acceptance of hot school lunches. Nutritionists and educational specialists watched in frustration as, despite aggressive state-funded propaganda campaigns, "every year the number of participants sank. The growing prosperity of our workers, the continually improving food provisioning, all allowed many parents to forego the additional meal for their children at school."[110]

Throughout the 1950s and 1960s, participation rates in school-lunch programs consistently lagged far behind rates of female employment. A 1957 survey of 11 large East German cities revealed the disappointing fact that, although 41 percent of children had mothers who were employed full-time, only 30 percent participated in school-meal programs.[111] In an attempt to attract more students into school cafeterias, in 1958, the year that marked the end of rationing, the SED passed Ruling No. 3, guaranteeing a free lunch to all children of working or needy parents.[112] Recognizing that "the weary working mother has scarcely the time and energy for lengthy food preparation, to clean and cook vegetables, to steam potatoes etc., in order to offer her entire family a filling and from day to day varied meal," the GDR declared, using familiar rhetoric, its commitment to "free[ing] working mothers from having to cook in the evening, especially since both mothers and fathers usually receive an adequate warm lunch at their workplace canteens."[113] In 1965, an internal report on national nutritional campaigns emphasized that school lunches "reduce for women (and, in those families where equality reigns, also for men) physical and time expenditure that is tied to the supplying of the self and the family, allow for equality in the workplace and give women the opportunity for further qualifications outside of the workplace."[114]

However, the report did not admit that these opportunities were not immediately embraced by East German women. As in the West, women attempted to both work outside the home and feed their children. Mothers had to be continually reminded that they profited from school meals and that it was "the school meal program that first made it possible for many mothers to pursue their careers in peace."[115]

This tension between the East German state and the people it was attempting to "liberate" was only gradually and partially resolved. After 1971, under the new leadership of Erich Honecker, the SED initiated a series of reforms intended to reduce the "double burden" and improve working women's quality of life. Above all else, this meant transforming the school-meal program into a popular replacement for the home kitchen. By increasing funding for infrastructure and thus increasing meal accessibility in poorly served rural areas, and by improving the quality of the school lunches across the board, the GDR finally began to achieve impressive participation growth. As the East German economy grew, so too did participation in collective meals, which were increasingly interpreted as a sign of a healthy economy and an accepted element of modern family structure. Unlike the contentious workplace canteen, which never was fully accepted by the adult population, the school-lunch program was on its way to becoming one of the state's flagship social programs.

In 1974, a propaganda booklet written for international audiences explained that the country boasted such high rates of employment among married women because East German women "consider it more interesting and more satisfying to create something of their own than to remain confined to the kitchen."[116] Mothers were warned against obsessively spending too much time and energy on mothering their children. Poor childhood nutrition, especially obesity, was attributed to women being too fixated on feeding their children; a 1972 nutritional education film depicted a mother force-feeding cake to her weeping son while assuring viewers rhetorically that "naturally you don't act like this woman—you are not throwing your child out of an airplane."[117]

By the 1980s, more than 85 percent of East German school children were eating at least one hot meal a day at school, and mothers who cooked the midday meal for their children were anomalies. Largely thanks to the program, children's health steadily improved. Moreover, this aspect of socialist food policy shaped East German women's attitude to their careers and their families. By the 1980s, 60 percent of the GDR's women claimed that their careers and their families were of equal significance, an idea scarcely conceivable in the FRG.

Despite these real achievements, school lunches did not sever the ties binding East German women to their kitchens. Women were both formally and informally involved in the school-meal program to an especially high degree, which was actively supported by the same government that asserted that school meals should reduce, not expand, mothers' cooking responsibilities. During the 1950s, the vast majority of school canteens were staffed by housewives without formal training, which was encouraged by a state hard-pressed for labor. A 1960 study of the hygienic standards of school cafeterias in the district of Potsdam interviewed a school director who reported that "we have almost exclusively volunteer mothers for the kitchen staff"; unfortunately, their lack of training meant that the nutritionally balanced recipes provided by the state were "rarely used; often they are entirely unknown or are stuffed away in the desk of the school secretary."[119] Nonetheless, assuming that mothers innately understood children's eating needs in key ways, nutritionists recommended that the local school board "contact at least one mother knowledgeable about cooking in every district, who will supervise the preparation of the school meals in the canteen kitchens, and who will follow through on problems."[118] This was standard practice until the 1970s; an Institute for Food Research memo recommended that schools, "in order to overcome possible labor shortages, win over temporarily unemployed mothers to work as assistants in the preparation [of school lunches], as they happily perform this daily labor as a societal obligation."[120] It was taken as self-evident that the best solution for poorly prepared and flavorless meals was to incorporate mothers, who would ensure that "the preparation of meals takes place with enthusiasm and love."[121]

By the 1970s, most school cafeterias were finally staffed by trained and paid full-time workers. However, the labor of these women (and they were mostly women) continued to be framed by a maternalist language that distinguished school meals from the masculine and rationalized workplace canteen. State propaganda insisted that children's meals be cooked by women, transforming school lunches into collectivized versions of "family meals" (see Figure 5.3). Discussions of workplace canteens generally emphasized the training and scientific knowledge of male cooks, whereas reporting on school cafeterias focused on emotional values rather than the professional expertise of the staff. The *Ostsee-Zeitung* reported in October 1981 on a school where "five women cook with love and flavor their dishes with heart." These chefs "don't only fill the stomachs of the students; they also fill their hearts, for they are mothering them."[122] School cafeteria cooks regularly emphasized that good cooking, like good mothering, "requires more work, but we don't avoid that. We cook with love."[123] In fact, GDR officials attributed growing participation rates to the fact that most school cafeterias were run as "women's collectives," transforming public facilities into familial communities in which members "have an open ear for family problems, and the willingness to help each other out."[124]

Despite the nearly total elimination of home-cooked lunches in the GDR, home cooking continued to be a highly valued—and highly gendered— component of everyday life. In 1989, "despite the development of the service sector and the technological equipping of housewives," and especially despite one of the world's most extensive school meal programs, East German women continued to spend two to three hours a day on housework, while the majority

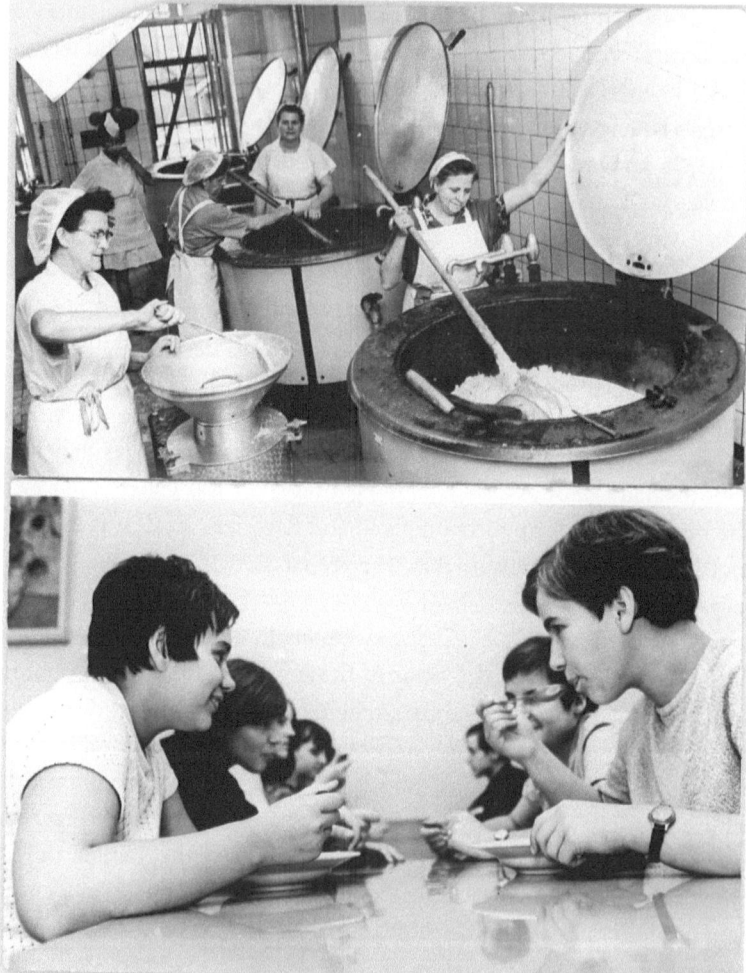

Figure 5.3 "Leipzig factory providing school meals. The female workers of a Leipzig factory canteen are cooking lunch for students of the 9th and 10th classes . . . This praiseworthy initiative ensures that students receive an appropriate lunch." 1969. BArch Bild 183-H0918-0009-001 / Raphael.

of men spent less than one.[125] This seeming paradox is explained by the country's novel approach to school lunches, in which they were cast as an essential component of a modern economy and a crucial support for female employment—even as they confirmed the importance of maternal cooking. Prepared by women and constructed as a core component of socialist mothering, school lunches encapsulated the state's struggle to resolve the troubled relationship between women and paid labor.

In contrast, schoolchildren in West Germany ate lunches at home that were cooked by their mothers, who came to accept this chore as an standard component of daily life. This expectation shaped school structure as well as women's daily workloads; West German schools were based on a half-day model that released children in the early afternoon, at which point they were expected to return home to eat their hot lunches.

A 1962 study showed that 80 percent of all West German mothers, whether or not they were employed, prepared home-cooked hot lunches for their children, and a full 40 percent prepared both hot lunches and hot dinners every day.[126] Despite the widespread protests of the cancellation of the school-meal program in 1950 and recurrent debates over childhood nutrition and mothers' inadequate cooking skills during the postwar decades, West German nutritionists claimed that because of low levels of female employment and the fact that "German parents want to have their children at home for their meals for educational reasons and to strengthen family life," the school meal could never be part of the country's social policy.[127] In a 1961 *Der Spiegel* article, an FRG pediatrician asked rhetorically whether "reheating food, quick snacks (bread and butter to go) or institutional cooking can replace the hot lunch prepared by the mother and longed for at the end of the school day? After all, those intimate kitchen table-conversations with mother . . . provide incomparable opportunities to the child."[128]

Even as school meals became normalized throughout both Eastern and Western Europe and across the industrialized world, West Germany continued to distinguish itself through its continued opposition to school lunch programs.[129] At an international conference on school programs in 1976, the West German speakers were the only participants to identify the hot school meal as a threat to childhood health, claiming (contrary to research findings in most other European countries) that "according to our studies, children who receive a warm school lunch are on average less well fed than those who eat a warm lunch at home."[130] School meals were conceptualized as being incompatible with the free market and consumer capitalism, which prioritized individualism and "free choice"; in contrast, school meals gave children "absolutely no opportunity to express individual wishes by the distribution of the individual dishes."[131] West German pediatrician Dr. G. Gutezeit, in an essay on the "impact of school meals on the parental home," claimed that mothers' hot home-cooked lunches represented "a last piece of autonomy that must be defended, something that above all mothers feel in regard to their children and state institutions."[132]

Despite the opinions of these experts, surveys and studies in the FRG revealed extensive popular support for school-provided meals, especially among mothers. A national survey of West German housewives from the mid-1960s revealed that 77 percent favored state-sponsored school breakfasts, "regardless of income and regional traditions."[133] (Because of the short duration of the West German school day, there was particular interest in providing a full breakfast rather than lunch.) As part of a larger critique of the country's school system, the government's opposition to school meals came under attack; leading postwar sociologist Helge Pross pointed out in 1975 that "regardless of whether the mother prepares a modest snack or a full warm meal, in any case she is forced into the kitchen because of the half-day school system. Because Germany has no full-day schools, mothers must spend the afternoon cooking; that is how the country can afford to remain with half-day schools."[134]

This push for school meals was linked to the rise of second-wave feminism in the 1970s, which in West Germany focused special attention on women's double burden, and particularly the burden of kitchen labor. The 1977 Women's Summer University, which convened in West Berlin, was dedicated to debates over women's housework. Participants issued a series of demands to liberate women from their exclusive responsibility for cooking and cleaning for their families; only when society at large takes on these tasks, they claimed, can "cooking no longer be daily necessity but desire."[135] Beyond the critiques of what Alice Schwartzer referred to as the "slave-character of housework," the unhappiness of the West German housewife became a widely referenced trope in mainstream culture.[136] In 1977, for example, the German actress Johanna von Koczian had a hit pop song called "A Little Housework," in which she complained about her domestic responsibilities: "the little bit of household takes care of itself, says my husband . . . how a woman can even complain is incomprehensible . . . the little bit of cooking is really not so bad, says my husband."

Nonetheless, state educational institutions in West Germany continued to resist implementing lunch programs. In 1976, the West Berlin newspaper *Tagesspiegel* reported that in response to pressure from parents, more than a dozen middle schools had opened cafeterias but that "they are only allowed to offer cold dishes, sausages, sweets, and alcohol-free drinks. Warm meals, with the exception of sausages, are excluded so that as much as possible competition to a nutritionally balanced lunch meal is not offered."[137] In addition to providing their husbands with a hot meal at the end of the work day—replacing the customary light evening repast (*Abendbrot*) with a meat-based full meal—mothers continued to be responsible for preparing hot lunches for their children. In fact, as Dr. Pross had noted, the postwar West German school schedule was premised on unemployed or underemployed mothers being available to cook and care for their children during the work week.[138] Through the 1970s and 1980s, the majority of women, over 90 percent in some areas, continued to prepare warm lunches for their children.[139] Although the preparation of a hot dinner steadily declined over the postwar decades, replaced by restaurants and lighter meal options, hot home-cooked lunches continued to be standard fare for the FRG's school children.

West Germany conceptualized its reliance on home-cooked lunches as definitional to its identity—and to its difference from the GDR. As a 1986 booklet by the West German Friedrich Ebert Stiftung called *Everyday Life in the GDR* explained:

> Something that is totally different from the Federal Republic is what in the GDR is called public feeding ... because in the GDR most women work, but also because children in preschool and school eat a majority of their meals in public canteens ... in the GDR people cook much less in households than we do.[140]

Such assertions of difference belie the fact that the socialist GDR shared with the capitalist FRG the internalization and normalization of women's responsibility for their families' diets, as well as the fact that this responsibility ensured that food acquisition, preparation, and clean-up were the largest component of women's daily housework. There were, of course, important national differences in the kind and quantity of this food labor. In the East, by the 1980s lunches were almost never eaten at home and were eaten separately by children and parents, and dinners were frequently of the cold variety (*Abendbrot*) rather than hot. In contrast, in the West the majority of women continued to prepare hot lunches for their children and themselves during the week while their husbands ate at restaurants and canteens. Dinner became the primary meal of the day because it was the only meal that both parents ate together. These differences, more than the GDR's minimally higher level of male participation in the kitchen, were the main reasons that East German women spent substantially less time actually cooking than West German women. On the other hand, despite East Germany's embrace of modern cooking techniques and West Germany's celebration of "old-fashioned" culinary wisdom, East German women continued to can, pickle, and jelly fruits and vegetables at much higher rates than in the West, where store-purchased items quickly substituted for home-made ones.

East German policies did little to ease women's double burden. The sheer volume of products, recipes, and kitchen equipment being produced and marketed reveals the extent to which the socialist state naturalized female domestic labor. This paradox was sometimes acknowledged, only to be rationalized away. A 1957 article on "the role of state feeding programs in the development of socialism," while discussing the embrace of new kitchen technologies for the housewife and collective meal programs, pointed out that "at first glance it might seem as if these are two mutually exclusive tendencies, as an increased production of products for the private kitchen encourages [kitchen work] and complicates the development of collective meal programs." While the author claimed that the two programs should be seen as supporting each other in the goal of "freeing working women from the time-consuming labor of the kitchen," their coexistence made equally clear the fact that the one would never actually replace the other.[141] Certainly, East Germany's greatest success in this regard was its school-lunch program. Nearly universal and heavily subsidized school meals did encourage women to join the workforce. This freedom, however, was not equivalent to the much-vaunted "liberation from the kitchen" that socialist theorists had claimed to embrace. On the contrary women's cooking continued to be perceived as playing an essential role in maintaining children's health and societal well-being.

East German women were outspoken in their protests against this double burden; however, they also adopted various strategies to balance these responsibilities, usually at the expense of their careers. These strategies included working shorter days or taking part-time employment, choosing workplaces close to their homes, and forgoing career advancement by not pursuing certifications and external training opportunities.[142] Women in the GDR consistently earned less than their male counterparts, received fewer promotions, and occupied lower-status positions in most fields. Ironically, women's exceptionally high employment rates actually discouraged meaningful reform; women's willingness to take on underpaid and relatively undesirable labor removed the pressure on the government to rationalize wage scales and optimize productivity, and thus indirectly strengthened sexist organizational structures in the workplace.[143]

* * *

The postwar "revolution in the kitchen" ultimately failed to revolutionize women's domestic labor. Despite a rhetorical commitment to easing women's burdens, various attempts to redistribute domestic kitchen labor, and education programs aimed at teaching new and more efficient food-processing strategies, women continued to do almost all the cooking in the GDR. The increased availability of kitchen appliances and processed foodstuffs also did little to reduce this labor. The only policy that meaningfully reduced women's domestic workload was the expansion of school lunches and workplace canteens. East German women had initially resisted but eventually came to demand state-provided hot meals for their children and, to a lesser degree, for themselves and their husbands. Yet a continued insistence on the importance of "home cooking" meant that the private kitchen did not wither away, nor did the assumption that women would cook for their families. This trend was even more striking in the FRG, where economic modernization and the expansion of household technologies and culinary innovations were not hampered by the restrictions of a planned economy. At the same time that a remarkable amount of West Germany's postwar capital was poured into modernizing the country's kitchens, the majority of women's daily housework continued to be preparing meals for their children and husbands.

In divided Germany, neither the socialist nor the capitalist state proved capable of imagining a society in which cooking was not done by women or meal consumption was separated from the nuclear family. As a result, policies directed at women were shaped by the paradoxical ambition to modernize the kitchen while maintaining women's "traditional" role as feeder of her family. Certainly, these struggles over private kitchen labor seem far removed from the crippling fears of hunger that had dominated the first half of the century. Their prominence in economic and public-health discourses, however, as well as in popular culture, reveals the high stakes of the fantasy of the family meal. By mandating women's double burden, this fantasy effectively guarantees the industrial state a permanent source of unpaid domestic labor, which in turn relegates women to lower-paid and lower-status employment.

Requiring that women cook for their families neither safeguards individual health nor ensures social stability. By the 1970s, as the relatively austere years of reconstruction receded in memory, a new and unexpected health threat emerged. Nutritionists on both sides of the Iron Curtain were disturbed to see that, despite widespread prosperity and regardless of where adults and children ate their daily meals, their populations seemed to be becoming obese. The resultant language of chaos and crisis that shaped nutritional discourse during the last two decades of Germany's division in fact harkened back to the tensions of the early years of the Cold War. In the end, obesity proved to be as disturbing, and ultimately as intractable, a threat as hunger.

6

Fighting Fat

Obesity and the Healthy Body in the Late Cold War

In 1968, the international best-seller *The Population Bomb* warned that the world was rapidly reaching its saturation point. The author, the American biologist Paul Ehrlich, predicted that the global food supply would soon be incapable of meeting demand. He opened the book with the dramatic declaration that "the battle to feed all of humanity is over. In the 1970s hundreds of millions of people will starve to death in spite of any crash programs embarked upon now."[1] Seeming to confirm such dire predictions, in 1972 economists and agronomists began announcing a "global food crisis," the first such catastrophe since the famines and shortages that had followed the Second World War. Food prices rose precipitously in the United States, and famine threatened much of Asia and Africa.[2] That same year, West and East Germany both released major epidemiological studies confirming that their populations were suffering from a so-called obesity epidemic, as levels of fatness for the first time represented a significant threat to public health.[3]

To many observers, it was clear that these two trends were linked; activists and environmentalists pointed to overconsumption in the West as a crucial factor contributing to looming shortages of vital resources elsewhere.[4] The late 1960s and early 1970s had been times of social conflict and instability across much of the world. In West Germany, generational tensions inspired student protests and a shift in government. In 1969, the Social Democrat Willi Brandt became chancellor, marking the end of the conservative Christian Democratic coalitions that had dominated West German politics since the country's formation in 1949. One of Brandt's major goals was the normalization of relations with the GDR. In the GDR, Erich Honecker replaced Walter Ulbricht as head of the country's Central Committee in 1971, representing the only transfer of power in the country's 40-year life span. Honecker, like Brandt, ushered in a more pragmatic political era, declaring that socialism was compatible with a modern consumer culture and increased private spending. East Germans, he promised, would finally be able to consume the "finer things" that their relatives in the West had long enjoyed.

In both German states, doctors had documented steady growth in the number of overweight citizens since 1949. (In East and West Germany, "overweight" was defined as weighing 20 percent more than the recommended "normal weight" (*Normalgewicht*) for his or her height). Just a few years after images of haggard women and skeletal children had broadcast Germany's suffering around the world, the population had re-acquired its reputation as a nation of stoutness. In this weight gain, Germans were following a trajectory seen throughout most of the industrialized world. Changes in the quality and quantity of foods being consumed, differences in eating and working patterns, as well as an aesthetic shift that elevated the slender body to both ideal and norm, meant that industrialized societies were increasingly plump societies. Indeed, the fatter the population became, the more society valorized slimness, which seemed to represent "the body of beauty, of productivity, and of superiority."[5] This tension between the desire to be slim and the reality of widespread overweight is so ubiquitous that it has become paradigmatic of the modern condition.

Although experts have established a clear link between "modern lifestyles" and high levels of overweight [*Übergewicht*], the reasons that modern lifestyles are so fat-inducing are vague. The United States has generally been the case study for the relationship between modernization and obesity. Some of the most frequently cited explanations are government subsidies that support cheap, high-calorie foods and discourage the consumption of healthier ones; an unregulated advertising industry; the disappearance of home-cooked meals; the ubiquity of cars, televisions, and sedentary occupations; and the dramatic decline in physical activity since the Second World War. In divided Germany, nutritionists had distinct and sometimes contradictory ways of explaining their population's respective increases in overweight. As they struggled to treat citizens' weight problems in the 1970s and 1980s, both socialist and capitalist doctors attempted to identify why and how industrial modernity was making their citizens fat. The weight-loss strategies that were developed, ranging from trendy diets to reduced-calorie foods to behavior modification techniques, reveal surprising commonalities between the FRG and the GDR—and they were also similarly ineffective in both states. Thus, the case studies of East and West Germany shed new light on the emergence of obesity as a political problem, challenging normalized America-centric models and suggesting new ways of conceptualizing the relationship between modern states and fatness.

Economic Reconstruction and the Rise of Obesity

In West Germany, doctors began warning about the health risks of being overweight even before the Allied occupation had ended. They often described the currency reform of 1948 as the symbolic beginning of German fatness. Within months of the FRG's founding in 1949, nutritionists began warning that "since the general changes in the diet [caused by the currency reform], in a surprisingly short time the observations of obesity are multiplying, wherein doubtless an excess of food ... plays a decisive role."[6] In 1950, the annual health report for the city of Aachen noted that "one must, with a portion of the population, already again speak of physical limitations due to serious fat acquisition."[7] A cartoon from the same year shows plump Germans splashing happily on the beach as they enjoy their new leisure time, blithely unaware of how much space they are taking up, thanks to the gustatory pleasures of their booming postwar economy (see Figure 6.1).

As soon as they had made it through the Hunger Years, West Germans began celebrating the large-scale consumption of food in public eating contests, popular songs, and social gatherings. In June 1950, the women's magazine *Für Sie* ran its first cover story dedicated to weight loss, titled "How Do I Lose 18 pounds?"[8] A dieting manual warned that "along with whipped cream and ham sandwiches, chocolate, and smoked eel, concerns about ones' figure have re-emerged."[9] By 1957, the food industry was nostalgically describing the postwar *Fresswelle*—or wave of gorging—as the corporeal expression of the famed West German "economic miracle":

Figure 6.1 "Since the currency reform, it's been impossible to get through here." From *Constanze: die Zeitschrift für die Frau und für Jedermann* 12 (1950).

When economic restrictions were lifted in our land, the hungry population threw itself first of all on foodstuffs that had been denied them for so long. The need to eat to satiety overshadowed at first all other wishes, although they had also been ignored just as long. The food industry was in a favorable situation; things were purchased without critical evaluation and in large quantities as long as they were products that had disappeared from the consumers' gaze for long enough.[10]

Such enthusiastic eating reshaped postwar bodies. A nutritionist in 1956 wrote that "since here in the Federal Republic all groceries are again available in abundance, the number of overweight people has been growing on a regrettable scale."[11] In 1946, the German medical profession had estimated that a mere 2 percent of the population was overweight (prewar rates were estimated at around 12%).[12] Within a few years, however, these rates had risen dramatically. By the beginning of the 1960s, over a third of the adult population was considered medically overweight.[13] More than anything else, this dramatic change in German bodies—from the scrawny and miserable forms of the Hunger Years to the plump consumers of the postwar *Fresswelle*—marked a break with the troublesome past and the beginning of a new, fatter Germany.

Germans had long had an international reputation for being "heavy." In the nineteenth century, Bismarck's massive body was thought to represent the generous appetites of his citizens. Germans' allegedly larger frames were often contrasted to the purportedly petite bodies of the French, so that the two powerhouses of Europe symbolized opposing models of corporeality. During the first half of the twentieth century, American and European depictions of German men generally portrayed them as plump, subsisting on a diet of sausage and beer; when it came to women, they were also thought to place "greater value . . . upon the robust, solid form than on passing styles or slimness."[14] During the occupation, Allied doctors had claimed that German reports of underweight were misleading because they were based on comparisons with what the population thought of as their "normal weight," which was, according to American doctors, actually "overweight."

The particular form of postwar fatness helped to define the FRG as a land of unprecedented consumer abundance. The population's rapid accumulation of excess fat was popularly celebrated as the well-earned "fulfilling of the food deficits accumulated during the scarcity years."[16] It was based on an implicit calculation linking past hunger to present fatness—the fatter the body became after 1949, the skinnier it must have been before. Thus, West Germans' fatness seemed to confirm their earlier collective suffering and, by extension, their political innocence. In the 1950s, a former German POW developed a commercial weight-loss product that was inspired by his experience of hunger during the Second World War. While imprisoned, the trained baker had gathered wild herbs to use as a hunger suppressant to help him cope with daily rations of "only a slice of white bread and a plate of watery soup." A few years after his release, the financially strapped young man suddenly had an epiphany: "what had suppressed hunger in times of need . . . should also be effective at allowing a voluntary fasting without the sensation of hunger." In 1955, he introduced chocolate-coated Voluma-Sticks, based on his original herbal concoction, to the West German public with the slogan "breakfast in a matchbox."[17] Such commercialization of German hunger reveals how fatness represented both a radical break with the past and a return to a much-longed-for "normalcy."

On the one hand, nutritionists blamed Germany's past hunger for its current fatness: "there is no doubt that the false eating habits following the economic crises and wars of the last decades are responsible for the development of flawed popular diet."[18] On the other hand, the link between West Germany's economic miracle and its citizens' growing girth implied a causal relationship between the free market and excessive food consumption, as embodied in the oversized form of the economic minister, Ludwig Erhard.

The excessive consumption of food, along with associated health harms, was initially conceptualized as a primarily male problem. By the end of the 1950s, the FRG had diagnosed itself as being in the midst of an "epidemic" that was attacking the men who were responsible for the country's economic miracle. Doctors often described the postwar explosion in overweight, diet, and stress-related heart problems among West Germany's elite men, dubbed "Manager's Disease" [*Managerkrankheit*], as a long-term consequence of *Hungerkrankheit*, a reaction to the extreme "stresses and suffering" of the war and postwar years.[19]

At the same time, because it was reputedly caused by the modern, sedentary, high-stress lifestyle of West Germany's middle class, Manager's Disease also reflected the country's prosperity and implicitly challenged the values of postwar German society: if economic growth was killing the country's men, was it sustainable or even productive? In 1951, *Der Spiegel* had reported that West Germany's "educated elite are being worked to death . . . 50% more leading business men die than the statistical average."[20] By the 1960s, medical discourse had became entirely preoccupied with this condition, and the nutritionist H. Holtmeier warned that

> while we have been successful in overcoming the dangerous epidemics of past centuries, now the best and most productive generations of our *Volk* are dying of heart disease, the consequence of high blood pressure and false diet. Currently only 36% of the male population reach the statistically average retirement age, while 64% retire early due to premature inability to work.[21]

In 1965, the country's first cookbook targeting "overweight businessmen" was published. *Are You Eating Right, Mr. Manager?* encouraged its middle-class male readers to lose weight, since "your firm has the right to demand a productive employee, your family needs a dependable provider."[22] Importantly, this particular kind of fatness was not a result of excessive consumption, but of a commitment to economic productivity. Stress and physical inactivity—the inevitable byproducts of the sort of managerial labor demanded by the postwar consumer economy—was making them fat. Thus these unhealthy men seemed both the heroes and the victims of the economic system that they were creating.

During the 1950s and 1960s, the problems thought to cause Manager's Disease had been primarily white-collar problems and thus unconnected to factory workers and other wage laborers. These blue-collar workers were rarely described as fat and their health per se was not a particular political concern. Instead, nutritionists worried about the diets of working-class men only insofar as they hoped to control and optimize their productivity. The size of their bodies was less significant than the value of their labor. Experts acknowledged that "of course the early death of a common worker or housewife is much less noticed and not much discussed in the public sphere," while the sickness of a "manager" caused tremendous concern about the health of the nation as a whole.[23] This meant that this first wave of postwar fatness reflected a distinct sympathy with its middle-management sufferers, who were afflicted with a sickness perceived as being largely out of their control.

The FRG's remarkable economic growth confronted its first major challenge in the early 1970s, when the 1973 oil crisis and subsequent recession, which included the first global food crisis since the Second World War, ushered in a series of economic downturns, stagflation, depression, and increasing social tensions across much of the world.[24] Suddenly, West Germany's prosperity seemed less stable and its profits more precarious; as a result, the working class also became more potentially threatening. The industrial slowdown inspired an official end to guest worker (*Gastarbeiter*) recruitment, which meant that Germans themselves were increasingly expected to take on the undesirable sorts of labor previously reserved for foreign temporary workers; at the same time, the gradual shift to a post-Fordist, service-oriented economy meant that labor itself was being redefined. An irreversible decline in traditional blue-collar jobs accompanied the rise of positions in the information technologies and other desk-bound positions; the growth in computing and robotics meant the dramatic reduction of manual labor.

Alongside these social and economic changes, the 1970s also witnessed the emergence of the so-called obesity epidemic as the paradigmatic "disease of civilization" (*Zivilizationskrankheit*). This was also the first time that unhealthy overweight was associated with the working class and, especially, women. New medical consensus held that fatness was "largely dependent on social class . . . overweight in lower classes is much more widespread than in higher ones."[25] The irrelevance of bodily strength or physical fitness to postindustrial productivity was a major factor in rising obesity rates; a sales clerk, secretary, or office worker, unlike a miner, carpenter, or factory worker, could perform his or her work regardless of weight. This meant that the economic threat posed by obesity could not simply be cast in terms of productivity decline. Whereas environmental and social pressures had been blamed for the fatness of Germany's managerial classes, working-class people were blamed for their unhealthy lifestyles and poor choices, victims of their inadequately developed senses of taste. Working men, according to a 1983 report, revealed "certain conservative eating habits that tend toward the consumption of known and familiar foods."[26] They had bad taste not only in food but also in women; "women of the lower classes" were found to be even more overweight than their husbands, which was largely attributed to the fact that "the men of these classes have retained in their hearts a Rubin-esque beauty ideal: they prefer to see the mother of their children a little plump."[27]

In 1975, *Der Spiegel* released its very first issue dedicated to obesity. Entitled "The Battle for the Pounds," the lead article announced dramatically that "47 million Germans have accumulated too much fat."[28] It was the first of many issues that would address the "obesity crisis." Nutritionists and economists regularly did cost-benefit analyses of working-class fatness. When wealthy managers got sick, economists worried about the money that would be lost if they died; the concerns expressed over more humble workers were about the cost of keeping them alive. FRG experts noted with horror the growing medical costs associated with obesity, which increased from 446 million Deutschmarks a year in the mid-1950s to approximately 3.7 billion in 1972.[29] In 1979, a quarter of the male workforce was reported to have taken early retirement for health reasons, and fully half of the country's deaths were attributed to diet-related heart problems.[30]

The obesity epidemic required a recalculation of the relationship between individuality and food consumption. Instead of celebrating private eating as a positive expression of economic progress, the new medical consensus was that "modern society" was the primary cause of Germans' fatness. In what in many ways echoed earlier fears that modernity was destroying the family meal, West German nutritionists believed that the population had been healthier during a vaguely defined preindustrial era when society, diets, and bodies had existed in a sort of natural harmony. In 1979, Hans-Jürgen Teuteberg, the country's leading historian of popular eating habits, published an influential study whose very title challenged the consumption-oriented ethos of the economic miracle. *Improper Eating in Prosperity* described "industrial society" as the "internal and external social root of Germans' poor diet," claiming that "the mass phenomenon of obesity" had consequences that "are in essence just as dangerous as the undernourishment of earlier centuries or in today's third world countries."[31] In 1979 the Federal Court of Justice officially recognized obesity as a disease, requiring health-insurance companies to cover the costs of treatment.[32] By the mid-1980s, some estimates claimed that "sicknesses caused by diet, that is to say sicknesses caused by false eating habits (too much meat, sugar, salt) as well as in particular the consumption of industrially processed foodstuffs" were costing West German taxpayers 40 billion Deutschmarks a year.[33]

In the GDR, the emergence of widespread overweight was also intertwined with the shape of the postwar economy. As in the West, as early as 1952 East German magazines were offering recipes and weight-loss advice, generally targeting women, whose "sincere pleasure in eating combined with a lack of [nutritional] knowledge" was preventing them from eating properly.[34] Initially, the increase in the incidence of overweight remained relatively modest. Because of extended rationing, food consumption did not increase as dramatically or as early as it did in the FRG. Nonetheless, despite recurrent shortages of particular foods and relative austerity in terms of the variety of available groceries, caloric intake was quite high. In fact, shortages in staple products—especially butter and meat—often revealed excessive consumption rather than inadequate supply. East Germans established a pattern of high food consumption early on that continued for the duration of the Cold War.

The rise in the number of overweight East Germans challenged West German assumptions that the GDR was a space of permanent hunger and food absence. While excessive food purchases in the FRG represented prosperity and self-indulgence, in the GDR they were held up as evidence of an underdeveloped economy and individual deprivation. A 1961 *Spiegel* article explained that "the catastrophic lack of industrial products in middle Germany [i.e., the GDR] leads to an artificial crisis in food supply, because GDR citizens ... invest in their daily food consumption the money that they ... would rather spend on washing machines, textiles, cars and televisions."[35]

That which West Germans saw as pathological was a source of mingled pleasure and frustration. In 1959, GDR nutritionists warned that the country was "perhaps ten years behind the USA and five years behind the Federal Republic of Germany" in rates of overweight.[36] This reflected a distinct sort of pride in having achieved impressively Western levels of food consumption. By the 1960s, East Germany had developed its first major weight-loss treatment program in response to the growing numbers of patients seeking help. (Previously, severely overweight individuals had been checked into a clinic or hospital for very expensive individualized treatment.) This program, which treated 337 patients in 1961, emphasized teaching new eating strategies. Despite its moderate success—more than half of the patients lost more than 5 percent of their total body weight—the program was not extended, because the obesity problem was still not deemed pressing enough to warrant the associated costs.

Until the 1970s, obesity remained a marginal concern to the East German state, only one of many health problems in a population that was thought to still be in the process of learning how to eat in a healthful and modern way.[37] Nutritional education emphasized gaining general nutritional knowledge rather than formal dieting; through the 1950s and 1960s, tips for gaining weight were as common as those for weight loss. Indeed, the problem of underweight, which was associated with poverty and physical weakness, seemed much more threatening. Doctors routinely expressed concern about adults and especially children who were too skinny rather than too fat, and there was a nationwide network of summer camps designed to help fatten up underweight children and young adults. Nutritionists generally advised moderation, not slimness, as the ideal. Indeed, an "obsession" with weight loss was often disparaged as typical of capitalist rather than socialist societies, representing the oppression of women, as well as a sort of general societal superficiality. Certainly, East German popular culture normalized a wider array of body sizes than did its West German equivalent, and extreme dieting was much less common. The popular entertainer Helga Hahnemann even dedicated a 1983 hit song to her doomed struggle to lose weight: "What haven't I tried, I tortured myself with diets, I counted every bite, I wanted to be delicate and slim. Cakes were taboo, I ate only plain quark, and despite it all still stayed big," only to conclude that "fat people are fun and not really so dumb, thin people are always nervous and stressed . . . I am fat and will stay fat!"[38]

Such differences notwithstanding, during the 1970s, the GDR's medical establishment also insisted that obesity had become a major health crisis. A national study of obesity published in 1970 estimated that a third of the adult population was seriously overweight and noted that obesity's "spread in the GDR (as in all developed countries) has taken on epidemic character, and everything points to the fact that it will continue to grow in scope and severity."[39] Unlike in the FRG, socialists often described widespread fatness as proof of the country's economic and social success. German socialists, looking back on a century shaped by the misery of inadequate food supplies, saw their greatest victory in having abolished hunger, which they claimed was literally impossible under socialism.[40] A 1973 speech on "nutrition in a socialist society" noted with pride that "in contrast to earlier times and past social orders, every citizen of our republic has enough to eat; everyone is free of the misery of watching his or her children go hungry while others waste food."[44] A GDR canteen chef interviewed in 1989 framed her decades of kitchen work in terms of historical progress:

> Often I must think about how things were 30 years ago [in factory canteens] . . . most workers brought their sandwiches from home. The

thought of schnitzel or fried potatoes was absurd! Only bread and cold cuts, which were often so modest. Three options for lunch? That was not even imaginable.[45]

Although the health risks of obesity were recognized, the growing size of the population's stomachs also seemed an embodiment of material success: "The fact that our socialist state, with its hardworking population, has led us out of the chaos and misery of the total collapse [of 1945], that large segments of the population can afford to treat themselves . . . is the best proof of our successful labor."[43] One of the first national studies of overweight claimed that "the high standard of living in the GDR" was responsible for the "incredible spread of obesity."[41] The head of the national Committee for Health Education declared in 1986 that

> our current health problems are the problems of a rich society; from the outset we should see this, and for all complaints about the widespread overweight and the growing abuse of natural stimulants [i.e., coffee and sugar] we should not forget that, after all, we wanted this high quality of life and we fought hard for it.[42]

Even as they attempted to lower individual caloric intake, nutritionists struggled with near-ubiquitous definitions of prosperity as "connected to a high consumption of meat, butter, sweets made from refined flour, etc."[46]

As a result, the GDR was much less consistent than the FRG in rejecting fatness. East Germany's commitment to modernization meant that the health problems associated with being overweight could not be solved with a return to older lifestyles (family meals) and foodways (less meat, simple cooking). Instead, continued modernization was seen as the solution to the problem. The past was associated with hunger and misery, which meant that the socialist future was de facto healthy; in this intrinsically optimistic ideology, the goal was simply to speed up the process of getting to that future optimal state of being. Although West German experts predicted a steady worsening of public health, a 1988 report on healthy eating habits in the GDR by the Organization of Dietetic Food Products confirmed the country's "political commitment to the maintenance of health, productivity, and pleasure in life," and predicted that "the transition to the 1990s will include placing even higher expectations for a healthy life style, especially in terms of a healthy diet, on the population."[47] Indeed, East German nutritionists explicitly criticized the FRG's condemnation of modernity. At the official opening of a new "National Workgroup for Healthy Living and Health Education" in 1968, the opening speech noted disparagingly that the West blamed its current health crises on "a certain hecticness, the hunt for profit, the instability, the emerging luxury market, the absence of movement, the increased psychic tension, the increased pollution of air and water, the chemicalization of life, atomic energy for peaceful purposes, etc." In contrast to these "diseases of civilization," as they were termed, the speaker claimed that in the East,

> technology is not blamed; instead it is and will remain what it has always been: a servant and helper of humanity. Man remains master of the machine. For humanity, civilization-diseases are not simply fate, they are negative consequences of a not yet consciously supported and inadequate adaptation to these quickly changing environmental conditions.[48]

The strong association of socialist progress with abundant food consumption problematized any advocacy of self-restraint or moderation. An undated proposal for developing national nutritional-advice centers reminded East German medical experts not to pursue their healthy ends too zealously and instead to adopt a more moderate tone when addressing the public: "[W]e all want to enjoy eating and drinking: everyone should have access to sausage, schnitzel, roast goose, whipping cream. After all, we can all afford it financially—but one should always ask oneself whether this does the body, and health, a good turn."[49] The particular foods invoked in this passage are significant; while West Germany associated prosperity and pleasure with the consumption of exotic and imported foods, the GDR emphasized the delights of domestically produced stables such as meat products and dairy. By the 1970s, however, these simple foodstuffs were being consumed in record quantities. The fact that the GDR had the highest per capita rate of butter consumption in the world by 1978 was a source of pride for government officials, at the same time that it was increasingly anathema to nutritionists.[50] This contradiction resulted in awkward constructions, as in the pamphlet *Your Diet, Your Health*, which claimed that "we are proud that in our state workers eat butter. But one must say to them that the exclusive consumption of butter can lead to health problems."[51] Head of state Honecker described his personal diet as a sort of model of socialist eating, combining an ascetic denial of exotic foodstuffs with abundant consumption of simple (and distinctly unhealthy) canteen foods:

> [E]very morning I ate one or two rolls with only butter and honey; for lunchtime I was in the Central Committee [canteen]; there I had either sausage with mashed potatoes, macaroni with bacon or goulash, and in the evenings I ate a little something at home, watched some TV and went to sleep . . . Thus I never lost my connection to the *Volk*.[52]

Such culinary rhetoric conflicted with the nutritional goals of a society struggling to lose weight. Some nutritionists argued that there was a paradox inherent in efforts to continually improve the quality of foodstuffs, as this ultimately encouraged its consumption, and "from a physiological perspective, a reduction and not an increase in food consumption is to be aimed for."[53] The idea that the government should encourage people to eat less not only ran against the association of prosperity with abundance; it also threatened an already tenuous GDR consumer equilibrium wherein expenditures on foodstuffs provided a crucial outlet for excess money. As early as 1963, general secretary Ulbricht had warned of this imbalanced consumer behavior in a high-profile speech before the SED, in which he noted, "[I]t is a serious problem that the population of the GDR currently spends substantially more money for food and drink than for industrial products. The percentage of our spending that is on food is 55%, that of industrial products 45%. In West Germany and other industrial countries, this ratio is reversed."[54]

A decade later, the extensive report "The Nutritional Situation in the GDR" still found that "the population increasingly has quantities of money that up to now could not be satisfied with the offerings of industrial products, so they use it in growing quantities for higher cost foods and drinks."[55] This problem was not easily remedied; the East German state consistently proved more capable of producing foodstuffs than other consumer goods.

High levels of food consumption pleased economists but concerned nutritionists, who began calculating the costs, instead of profit margins, of the population's excessive eating. A 1971 report found that "overweight and its consequences cost our republic approximately more than 600 million marks, of which about 400 million are due to loss of productivity."[56] A year later, experts estimated the "consequences of a false diet" at about 1.5 billion marks a year, making up more than 10 percent of the country's total health costs.[57] Between 1972 and 1989, the number of registered diabetics in the GDR almost doubled, from 340,000 to 650,000.[58] Doctors were especially alarmed by a stagnation in average life expectancy, which they blamed primarily on diet-related problems.[59] Nutritionists attacked economic policies of the 1980s that were aimed at increasing profits and decreasing costs, claiming that these policies "support[ed] the sale of products that are diametrically opposed to the principles of a healthy diet," such as candy and processed foods, all of which had especially high profit margins.[60] In 1985, an analysis of popular dietary trends determined that "in the GDR the nutritional situation is above all shaped by overeating and the resultant overweight of about 30 percent of the population."[61] A study completed just months before the fall of the Berlin Wall shockingly claimed that more than three out of four deaths in the GDR "are caused by sicknesses in which a false diet played an especially important role."[62]

Learning to Lose Weight

Despite their different explanations for the postwar causes of obesity, East and West Germany shared similar interpretations of the condition's scope, harm, and treatment. As a result, they developed surprisingly similar, and similarly ineffective, strategies for reducing calorie consumption and achieving popular weight loss. By the 1970s, both states agreed that weight loss was necessary for economic as well as societal health, and they had developed varied methods of educating their respective populations on how to lose weight and stay slim. Their weight-loss strategies also had the same primary target audiences: women—not because they were more overweight than men but because they regulated private food consumption—and workplace canteens, the primary collective feeding venue for adults, especially adult men.

In West Germany, the need to promote weight loss rapidly evolved into an extensive nutritional-education system that aimed to improve housewives' food purchases and preparation. These programs were almost entirely unsuccessful. In the mid-seventies, a report commissioned by the Federal Center for Health Education (*Bundeszentrale für gesundheitliche Aufklärung* [BZgA]) noted that "despite years of nutritional education, the dietary situation of the population of the FRG has not improved" and that it was in fact steadily worsening.[63] When the Ministry of Youth, Families, and Health commissioned a report in 1973 on consumer attitudes toward healthy eating, they were initially encouraged to find that "at least verbally housewives place a great value on healthy nutrition"; most women self-reported that "health concerns" were their primary consideration when designing family meals. However, "the actual behavior of housewives in their meal planning contradicts these answers. Only 17 percent of housewives actually act in a healthy way, and deep psychological examinations revealed that taste [rather than health] dominates their decisions."[64]

Although there consistently proved to be little correlation between knowing the nutritional value of foods and eating healthfully, nutritionists continued to emphasize educating consumers as the key weapon in the fight against overweight.[65] This emphasis confirmed women's responsibility for both causing and curing obesity. In fact, repeated studies had found that "the husband is the major obstacle to changing eating habits [because] he wants his wife to give to him the same dishes that he loved to get from his mother"[66]; nonetheless, West German policymakers insisted that "the focus [of nutritional education] will continue to be on women. They must finally learn exactly how to provide their husbands with good snacks, and on the other hand they must pay more attention to their own diet."[67] The existence of obesity thus revealed profound inadequacies in women's skills as shoppers and as cooks.

Because home-cooked meals were so central to West German models of family health and good mothering, fatness began to be viewed as a sign of familial dysfunction. Studies suggested that working-class mothers in the FRG were "more bound to a traditional housewife role," less open to modern nutritional information, and themselves fat—all factors thought to contribute to childhood overweight.[68] Nutritionists found less educated parents especially difficult to work with as they were "relatively infrequently willing to see their own excessive eating as responsible for the [children's] overweight."[69] But rather than develop better outreach for working-class families, West German nutritionists chose to focus instead on pregnant women "of the well-educated middle class."[70] It was while working with these educated stay-at-home mothers that nutritionists developed a new model of family-focused nutritional education, which aimed for an "increase in planned and focused shopping (for example through shopping lists) and the institutionalization of family meals" as effective methods of weight loss.[71] In other words, the adoption and propagation of middle-class lifestyle norms was marketed as a solution to excess weight gain among the working class.

These programs had little measurable impact; indeed, the new threat of childhood obesity emerged at the same time these education programs were being propagated.[72] In 1977, *Der Spiegel* ran the dramatic cover story "Fat Children: Too Much of Everything," which reported that up to a quarter of the nation's children were overweight, and that one in eight was clinically obese.[73] Two years later, *Die Zeit* reported that "half of all Germans under the age of 35 and every tenth child in this land is, according to the experts, too fat."[74] The author blamed smothering maternal overfeeding for destroying children's ability to "distinguish between hunger feelings and emotional tensions. This missing ability to discriminate is the reason that many obese people respond to psychological grief and stress with eating."[75] Nutritionists increasingly turned to psychology to understand the country's fatness, claiming that obesity's "originary cause, as with other addictions, largely lies in the recesses of a good or less good childhood."[76]

Predictably, West German doctors argued that a "return" to traditional structures of domesticity—maternal cooking, female unemployment, eating family meals at home—was the best strategy for fighting overweight. This meant that mothers were the "single greatest variable determining childhood obesity."[77] Despite studies that revealed that unemployed housewives were generally heavier than their employed counterparts, the nutritional establishment promoted the idea that "the wide-spread employment of both parents often works against healthy eating habits."[78] The DGE published dramatic "true stories of families with eating problems," which highlighted maternal absence as the reason for children's poor diet. A typical story explained how "latch-key children become fat." It told the story of the brothers Rölf and Christian, who whiled away their afternoons eating French fries with mayonnaise. After all, "why should they rush home, no one is waiting there. Mom only gets home at 4:30 and father's workday goes until 6 p.m."[79]

Although most programs aiming to improve children' diets targeted mothers, West Germany did develop nutritional education programs directly addressing children and youth. Most were failures, such as the federally funded contest centered on the fictitious characters of Zym, a fluffy white giant who "stood for a proper diet," and his nemesis "Dr. Fu with his agents from the Institute for False Nutrition."[80] The ineffectiveness of this expensive nationwide project meant that "nutritionists and advisers are now asking themselves if it makes sense to educate children about proper diet with the help of these kinds of figures."[81] Similarly unsuccessful was a program aimed at teenagers; the "beat-folklore-quiz" paired nutritional lectures with rock and roll music: "Unfortunately these interesting lectures were in part drowned out by the loud beat-rhythms," and it quickly became clear that most of the participants "had come to this event more for entertainment than from the desire for [nutritional] information."[82]

The ineffectiveness of these sorts of educational programs inspired new ways of approaching the problem of obesity; nutritionists began emphasizing how psychology and individual "behavior" rather than education determined food choices. Dieticians for the first time began thinking about socialization skills and interpersonal interactions. The director of the nationwide weight-loss campaign "Diet and Movement" even asserted that "the help of a so-called 'behavior guide'—a la Knigge—would be useful in achieving the change" necessary for true success.[85] This idea encouraged nutritionists to adapt the American trend of behavior-modification therapy. Behavior-modification therapy had been developed in the 1960s to treat addiction; the 1972 international best-seller *Slim Chance in a Fat World* heralded its acceptance as a method for battling overweight, first in the United States and then around the world. The idea was that "eating behavior can be controlled as readily as any other behavior—e.g. driving on the right side of the road, writing on an even line, or completing a work assignment."[86] Or, as an unpublished 1979 paper on nutritional education explained: "behavior that results in the increase of risk factors is generally learned false behavior. Learned false behavior can in principle be modified."[87]

With attention-grabbing headlines, such as "spectacular weight-loss records" and "weighty success with the club of slimness-awareness," articles in regional and national newspapers across the country promoted behavior-modification programs as surefire ways to lose weight and keep it off.[88] A 1974 article from the *Kölner Stadt-Anzeiger* announced that "no less than 45% of German citizens ... think that they are too fat and would like to lose weight. Now a new and very promising path can be offered to them." Unlike prior dieting regimes that "only in the rarest cases had long-term success," these programs promised to permanently change the "abnormal eating habits" of overweight people.[89] The largest behavior-modification program, "Lose Weight Rationally," ran in multiple cities simultaneously in the late 1970s and early 1980s. It aimed not only to achieve short-term weight loss, but to permanently change "the behaviors that are typical of a false diet," resulting in "a change in the entire dietary behavior."[90] Participants were encouraged to put their "eating habits under the magnifying glass" by filling out forms after each meal with headings such as "My Observations While Eating" and the "Protocol of Daily Food Intake."[91] Some versions worked with a reward system, assigning point values to specific weight-loss targets and awarding prizes for high total scores.[92] Others were punitive, requiring participants to make a deposit of 120 Deutschmarks at the beginning of the program; the money was paid back on a weekly basis if participants properly carried out the program but nonrefundable otherwise.[93] Despite impressive numbers of participants and this wide array of strategies, success again proved elusive. Although 81 percent of participants did initially lose weight, and 71 percent thought of the program as a "success," almost none of the participants maintained their new eating habits.[94] Most regained all the weight they had lost within five weeks of the conclusion of the program. Further follow-up studies revealed, surprisingly, that the "most consistent positive result of the program is not weight loss, but reduction in the consumption of alcohol and over-the-counter medications."[95]

Behavior modification proved especially ineffective for housewives with children, the primary target audience of West German dieticians. Program leaders explained this failure by claiming that these women began from a "more problematic starting point (more prior attempts to lose weight, more problems with one's own willpower, more problems with feelings of hunger etc.)."[96] Feedback from the participants, however, suggested that the programs had not addressed the specific reasons for individual overweight. For example, one working woman with four children, who had not lost weight in the program, explained in the final survey that she was "under constant stress, partially due to problems with my children or anger caused by the office, and, to put it bluntly, I stuff everything in my mouth!" Although she completed all the segments of the program faithfully, her lack of success caused her to reject the general use-value of behavior modification; instead she believed that she needed "psychological treatment that also addresses my emotional problems."[97]

In the end, behavior-modification programs never replaced traditional dieting as the primary strategy for slimming in West Germany. By the mid-seventies, a growing percentage of the population self-identified as overweight, and an even higher number of people were on, or planned to go on, some sort of diet. These diets took varied forms, and included several notable experiments with large-scale or collective dieting. In 1975, West Germany's public broadcast service aired a radio program on weight loss that inspired a record 120,000 listeners to mail in requests for the associated DGE-issued diet plan.[83] A year later, a televised "diet reality show" aired as part of the regular health series *Gesundheitsmagazin Praxis*. The program, which included interviews and discussions of such topics as portion control, shopping, meal frequency, and snacking and offered viewers a direct phone line to a professional nutritionist, received 32,000 applications for 300 available spots.[84]

Such programs, however, were the exception rather than the rule, as most West German diets remained individual, private, and voluntary. Such diets relied on low-calorie recipes (women's magazines published literally thousands of weight-loss recipes during the 1970s and 1980s), thus underscoring the link between women's cooking and overweight. The self-declared "simple" 1972 Brigitte-Diet, for example, promised to make "getting slim and staying slim easier" by offering women 70 recipes of 400, 200, or 100 calories each, from which a woman could assemble her 1,000 calorie daily food intake.[98] A year later, a revised version offered 105 meals and a total daily intake of 1,200 calories.[99] These diets were so popular that a network of diet clubs developed to provide group support to individual dieters. By 1980, there were over a hundred such clubs reaching across Germany, Switzerland, Austria, and Holland.[100] Other diets emphasized restricting the kinds of food consumed rather than total calorie intake. *Für Sie* developed a rotation diet in which the dieter consumed only one kind of food (i.e., eggs, fish, or apples) each day for two weeks.[101] For women who were not sure which diet to choose, or who needed to prepare various diets to meet the different tastes of her family, *Für Sie*, in 1978, offered a medley of seven different diets that could be mixed and matched, all providing 800 calories a day.[102] By the mid-1980s, experts estimated that there were "approximately 40 different slimming diets and fasts currently being promoted. Even the pure 'zero diet' [total fasting] is still popular, although it is well known that it can lead to circulatory problems, arthritis, and bladder stones."[103]

While such fad diets had traditionally appealed to younger and childless women, in keeping with the larger patterns of the anti-obesity discourse, they now increasingly targeted middle-aged married women, who were expected not only to cook for their families but also to enforce their necessary weight-loss regimes. Indeed, most of these diets were predicated on the assumption that women had total control over their families' food consumption. Dieticians thus recommended that women "establish their [new] eating behavior as a familial behavior, [so that] influence can be exerted on other overweight family members."[104] The DGE was especially interested in publishing stories about families who had lost weight together. In their 1983 publication celebrating 30 years of "keeping an eye on the dinner plates of the population," the organization told the story of "Maria Wagner, housewife and mother," who "through nutritional advising from the DGE not only lost weight, but also learned to feed [her] entire family healthier." Her family's success confirmed that "nutritional problems can only be avoided by those who are responsible for food and drink and who stand at the stove: housewives and mothers."[105]

East Germany's budget-conscious emphasis on preventative or prophylactic approaches to public health meant that nutritional education was also the favored strategy for fighting obesity; and as in the West, these programs were generally unsuccessful at reducing overweight. By the mid-1960s, East German nutritionists began calling for "intensively pursued nutritional propaganda" as an "effective method of increasing work productivity, achieving a reduction in sickness, and maintaining the health of retirees."[106] However, funding for this effort remained limited; monies were more likely to go into the food-processing industry and the development of new kitchen technologies than to the far less exciting area of nutritional education.[107] Nonetheless, it seemed clear that the East German public lacked a firm grasp of basic dietary principles. Surveys revealed a varied but generally quite disappointing level of knowledge about what constituted a "healthy diet." A 1970 survey found that, while 80 percent of consumers knew that high consumption of fruits and vegetables was part of a healthy diet, "only 40% favor a low-fat diet and only 30% think eating smaller portions is necessary."[108]

The emergence of the obesity epidemic in the 1970s finally convinced the state to increase funding for nutritional education. Beginning in 1973, nationally funded "healthy-eating weeks" were scheduled across several densely populated districts, accompanied by "46 exhibitions of healthy eating, thirteen press conferences, five canteen-competitions," and various local events.[109] That same year, the GDR's press agency began to publish "numerous articles, interviews and answers to various aspects of ministry decisions, including the improvement of school meals, workers' canteens, and the work of the Trademark Association for Dietetic Products [*Warenzeichenverband diätetische Erzeugnisse.*]" It also sponsored televised and press educational shows to improve nutritional knowledge. The popular TV programs *Visite* and *Umschau*, as well as Radio DDR, ran daily or weekly "diet-tips" and nutrition segments, and the magazine *Freie Welt* published an 12-part series on healthy eating called "Learning How to Eat."[110] In 1978, the country's first paperback weight-loss guide, *Weight-Loss Cooking Made Easy*, was published "to enable overweight people, or those with a tendency toward overweight, to prepare a focused reduction-diet through easy to apply recommendations." This book was a sign of a larger shift away from offering technical nutritional advice and toward giving readers practical daily weight-loss strategies. For example, the publisher's evaluation of this weight-loss guide highlighted the fact that the author did not provide "extensive discussion of nutritional science," marking a departure from previous "scientific-educational" publications in this field.¹¹¹ Between 1971 and 1980, national scientific and nutritional organizations had organized "more than 1500 popular scientific lectures, published more than 1,400 general interest publications, produced more than 300 radio and TV programs, as well as published popular science films and countless books, monographs and brochures on the theme of a healthy diet."¹¹²

Even more than in the West, the rise in obesity was matched by an explosion of weight-loss and nutritional education programs that ran in print media, radio, and television. The scale of these programs was impressive—the 1987 radio series "Slim for Vacation" reportedly drew around 60,000 listeners,¹¹⁷ and inspired "many female and male listeners" to request the diet brochure that was "made available by Radio DDR to accompany this treatment."¹¹⁸ The Hygiene Museum, Central Institute for Nutrition, and other state health institutions produced numerous short films, radio programs, and publications promoting weight loss.

These varied greatly in message and content; some continued simply to convey basic nutritional information, especially about calories. Because many experts believed that obesity's social acceptability was part of the problem, other films and programs demonized overweight by linking it with capitalist oppression. The script for an early educational film on healthy eating, for example, opened with a shot of an obese man driving a car; in rapid succession came images of "children playing in miserable dark courtyards, a chain smoker with a double cognac, sitting in a smoke-filled room, already looking sickly . . . fighting scenes in Algeria, an overfull appointment calendar on a writing desk, [and] fat women eating whipped cream."¹¹⁹ An educational poster produced by the Dresden Hygiene Museum (see Figure 6.2) depicted a self-absorbed man eating alone at a restaurant to warn of the dangers of overeating. His location and the bottle of wine on the table suggest that this sort of gluttonous, asocial eating is associated with bourgeois rather than working-class eating habits. Advanced capitalism (marked by managerial rather than "productive" labor), addictive behavior, and excessive consumption all were made analogous to obesity.

Committed to the dissemination of information as a way of influencing behavior, East German nutritionists consistently discouraged dieting, insisting that the "only effective approach [to obesity] is prevention!"¹¹³ For socialist nutritionists, the so-called trend, or fad, diets represented the pitfalls of capitalism. As part of a larger, profit-driven food industry, these diets preyed on individual insecurities, winning adherents based on aesthetic rather than health considerations. In the late 1970s, when the Atkin's Diet was rapidly spreading throughout the United States and Western Europe, its recommendations for high-fat, low-carbohydrate eating were cited as an example of the "flooding of the public sphere with false and one-sided nutritional information" that was typical of "capitalist conditions."¹¹⁴ In 1977, doctors published the results of a long-term study on 71 men

Figure 6.2 "Overweight. Excessive Eating Leads to Overweight." Courtesy of Deutsches Hygiene-Museum.

and women suffering from moderate to severe levels of overweight; each participant was assigned one of three different dieting regimes: the so-called zero diet, a 300-calorie-a-day liquid diet based on juice mixed with protein powder, and a 600-calorie diet and a 1,200-calorie diet both based on a varied food intake. The study found that losing weight by dieting was possible if it was done in a completely regulated environment, but that fewer calories or an unmonitored nutritional intake resulted in serious health harms, including inadequate protein levels and urinary problems, which threatened to cancel out the benefits of the actual weight loss.[115] Such research confirmed East German nutritionists' inclination to avoid promoting specific diets; instead, they recommended diverse and abundant intake of low-calorie foods. This approach did not necessarily correlate with the desires of GDR citizens however, who insisted on emulating the fad diets that were so widespread across the border despite the official recommendations. In 1975, one citizen wrote, in response to the article "Point-Diet Is a High Risk Diet," that the "point diet" had actually helped him lose weight, whereas "the diet that you recommend—abundant fruit and vegetables, whole grain products, fish, low-fat dairy and meats—I tried earlier without success."[116]

As much as officials disliked the constantly changing landscape of trendy weight-loss regimes, socialist medicine's support of prophylactic education encouraged group weight loss projects. Dieting groups were based on the notion that weight loss would be more pleasurable and effective when done with others. Programs such as the Berlin-based "Participate—Become Slim" relied on participants to self-monitor their eating habits (in this case following a set 1,200-calorie-a-day diet). Group meetings were held to record results, learn nutritional facts, and engage in exercise.[120] The program was open to both men and women; as in the West, women were the primary targets, but here because they were themselves overweight, not because of the fatness of their families. Here, women's employment was never cited as a causal factor of childhood or female overweight; instead, programs targeting women assumed that they worked full-time. In fact, many weight-loss programs were sponsored by factories and other workplaces; for example, the electronics manufacturer Kombinat VEB Narva Rosa Luxemburg offered a weight-loss course for "women who work on the conveyer belt or in the office."[121]

Similarly emphasizing social relations, East German cartoons, films, and comic books for children often suggested that good eating habits were best learned by socializing with adults and especially with other children.[122] The Hygiene Museum in Dresden published a children's book titled *How the Stick-Boy Conquered the Kobold Huckedack*. The story taught that the only way for the "stick-boy" to achieve his optimal weight was to learn "a couple of excellent recipes" that he cooked for himself and his friends.[123] In typical GDR rhetoric, the story emphasized that children are responsible for their own diet, at the same time teaching that their personal decisions had implications for the entire social group. Such messages are particularly striking when compared to analogous West German texts, such as the DGE-produced story *Lothar Is Too Fat*. Aimed at mothers rather than children, it tells the tragic tale of Lothar, who was "often teased by his classmates because he is so fat . . . from pure self-loathing Lothar eats ever more and more, especially sweets."[124] Lothar is too fat because his mother's job in a shop prevents her from cooking, leaving him to subsist on his favorite food: French fries. Although both stories portray weight management as key to gaining peer acceptance, *Lothar Is Too Fat* makes mothers responsible for their children's obesity and pathologizes the child who designs his own diet. This is in sharp contrast to the GDR, where children were depicted as "naturally" knowing what and how much to eat. Nutritionists pushed for an improved nutritional curriculum in school so that children could better feed themselves—"we should strive to achieve that all high school graduates have an adequate knowledge of a healthy diet and that they are able to put this knowledge in a responsible way into practice."[128] In the 1980s, as East German nutritionists began to see childhood obesity as a distinct health concern, they again implied that less parental control, not more, would achieve better results. The remarkable growth in school-meal participation during this time, growing from 50 percent in 1971 to 75 percent in 1980, was attributed to meeting "the general goal of communicating to the widest possible circles of the population the basic principles of a healthy diet as a core component of a healthy lifestyle, and how to put this into praxis through daily nutrition."[125] The problem of overweight only underscored, in the eyes of nutritionists, the need for school lunches, which were needed precisely because mothers were assumed to be incapable of healthfully feeding their children. Even the GDR's extensive nutritional-education programs were "not enough to break the habits of eating as mother did and her mother before her. This is why the meals provided in nurseries and schools are so important."[126] Teachers complained about "parents' attitudes toward healthy eating. Not infrequently cakes, sweets, or pure white-flour products are given to the children"[127] instead of the recommended rye bread. When mothers in the GDR were blamed for their children's dietary ill health, the solution was to have them prepare fewer meals for their children, not to get them to cook more or differently.

The relationship between collective eating programs and the rise of obesity was much debated in both East and West Germany, and both states responded to the health crisis by modifying their feeding programs to maximize health and minimize weight gain. Strategic differences in their approaches reflect their different ideological understandings of the importance of collective meals and of the meaning and consequences of fatness. Nutritionists in the GDR conceptualized collective meals as a key method for improving public health, both by preparing healthful meals and by improving the quality of home cooking: "The public feeding system must feed its participants tastily and rationally with minimum expense, and thus offer a model for how what is best for health, tastiness, and wallet can be made in the domestic sphere from the available foodstuffs."[129] Rather than being intrinsically unhealthy, professionally planned collective meals were expected to have an "educative impact on food consumption in the private household, and [to work] against excessive calorie consumption."[130] In the late 1960s, the East German Ministry of Health noted that "generous support of collective feeding programs would be far and away the quickest way to an immediate improvement in popular health and in addition would have substantial pedagogical impact on the eating habits of the entire population."[131]

The country's growing rates of overweight were interpreted as evidence of serious problems in East Germany's collective feeding programs.[132] In 1968 the Health Ministry sponsored the formation of a research group to explore "problems in the research of healthy diet of the population especially in terms of public eating establishments."[133] Nutritionists believed that "improper usage of collective feeding" was one of the main causal factors for the "steadily increasing number of citizens who require a diet (currently 20% of the total population)."[134] In addressing this unfortunate trend, canteens themselves were expected to facilitate popular weight loss. By the 1970s, caloric reduction was the primary nutritional goal for canteens cooks; achieving it required modifying many traditional recipes (e.g., casseroles, sausages), as well as introducing new, "healthier" ones (fresh salads and steamed vegetables). In 1975, the British *Morning Star* reported admiringly on the positive impact of the GDR's canteens on public health. The canteens' centralized semi-computerized recipe collection, described as "staggeringly simple—despite the complexity of its details," included 1,350 regional dishes; each entry included the

> recipe, quantities needed for various groups, from infants to heavy workers, caloric content, minerals, vitamins, and cost per head . . . so the school, kindergarten, old folks home, clinic or whatever fills in a simple form and the computer prints out every suitable menu for the age, type of consumer, season, and so on.

These "carefully balanced meals" promised to provide a defense "against the main enemy—fat—while ensuring a more healthy diet in other ways."[135] Canteen and restaurant menus were also required to include nutritional data on all menus, a policy that received positive coverage even in the usually skeptical West German press.[137] As impressive as such policies were, however, they were rarely followed in practice, as these "tips for those who eat in the canteen," from 1987, make clear: "if the caloric value of the dishes, in accordance with legal requirements, is communicated, choose dishes that are around 500 calories. . . . With casseroles request a small portion and do not take any sides (sausage, bread, or roll)."[138] Even though East German law mandated that all workers be provided a "nutritious warm meal in accordance with basic nutritional guidelines," most of the country's canteens rarely or never offered low-calorie or "dietetic" meals.[136] Most distressing of all, research found that official policies and carefully calculated recipes had little direct bearing on the meals provided in canteens. Canteens and cafeterias tended to serve food that satisfied worker desires rather than nutritional guidelines. Studies consistently revealed that, for the canteen patron, the nutritional quality of the food was of secondary concern; on the contrary, East German citizens were "increasingly placing demands on the culinary and aesthetic side of food offerings, since these aspects are most immediately apparent to the consumer."[139] Canteen cooks felt pressured to prioritize the novelty and appearance of the dish rather than health.

In the West, the rise in obesity was interpreted as proof that canteens were unhealthy and overused. Working men continued to be encouraged to eat home-made lunches; nevertheless, West German nutritionists felt compelled to reform the canteens rather than advocate for their elimination. The 1976 National Nutritional Report, authored by the DGE, estimated that six million people regularly ate at canteens, and that the average person consumed 13.8

meals a month in the workplace.[140] These meals, experts assumed, "play no small role in the fact that the daily caloric intake of the German citizen is on average 20 percent over his need, and the fact that more than half of the population is suffering from overweight."[141] In attempting to understand why canteens had such negative health consequences nutritionists were, however, surprised to find that ignorant or poorly trained staff were rarely the problem. A nationwide survey from the early 1970s found that, although canteen meals were often designed to have nutritional content superior to that of the average home-cooked meal, the patrons themselves were the primary "limiting factor." A series of interviews with cooks from dozens of large canteens found that they were all actively working to reduce the fat and calorie content of their meals, but that "these efforts are often quasi-sabotaged by the canteen eaters, who expand limited portions by extra helpings, or who, when they have the choice, reject healthy food for a hearty meal." Bosses and factory owners often encouraged cooks to serve foods that made workers happy rather than healthy, proving "more interested in questions of price and complaints about flavor than in health values."[142] As in the GDR, canteens menus were consumer-driven, as workers demanded meals centered around meat and other high-fat foods.

Having found that "the canteen eater is the greatest opponent of healthy eating," nutritionists determined that the best way to reduce adult overweight was by reforming popular tastebuds.[143] In 1977 the BZgA organized the first canteen-led weight-loss program "Fit not Fat" (*Fitt statt fett*). The program, initiated by minister of health Antje Huber, brought together "business leaders, factory boards, and cooks in a united front in the battle against stomach fat and love handles."[144] The program was heavily advertised in the FRG media, and the over-the-top national press party included a "group exercise competition for desk workers," after which all the attendees received a (distressingly high-calorie) gingerbread tennis racket with a marzipan tennis ball as a parting gift.[145] There were even plans to release an album of songs composed for the program, including such potential hits as "If I Only Were the Moon (I Wax and Wane)" and "I Remain True to My Size."[146]

Despite this impressive governmental investment, "interest remained substantially below what was anticipated."[147] Having invited 20,000 companies to participate, planners anticipated that a minimum of 5,000 would sign up; instead, only 679 ordered the fairly pricey educational materials, and only 19 percent of those requested more than the initial introductory package.[148] There were complaints over the costs—factory owners had wrongly assumed that educational materials would be offered free of charge—and many questioned the effectiveness of state-organized interventions in personal health. Follow-up interviews revealed that the most popular items were not the calorie charts or recipe collections, but "bumper stickers for cars," suggesting that even simple appeals to walk or bike to work had been unsuccessful. The program's newsletter, *Profi-Tips*, was not only unpopular among workers but rife with factual errors; the expert advisers were horrified by content that made them "to put it mildly, laugh out loud," including tips like "you can every now and then treat yourself in the evening to a steak or eggs; the minimal fat content will do no harm."[149] Despite these structural weaknesses, the West German nutritionists who were directing the program blamed its failure on the "psychological barriers" to "rational communication" among the "less educated classes, who, experience has shown, typically are rarely engaged by intellectually demanding and complex information."[150] This demonization of working-class bodies and minds was commonplace in West German anti-obesity discourse. For example, invoking new fears of the unemployed that accompanied the economic struggles of the 1970s, a health-insurance company produced a poster reminding workers that "a full plate was not a full-time job" (see Figure 6.3). It is clear from the man's body and clothes, as well as his choices of food and drink, that he is a worker. Such working men were generally perceived as incapable of appropriately regulating their own diets.

Obesity as a Crisis of Consumer Culture

In both German states, the persistent lack of success in changing eating habits required policymakers to come up with innovative approaches to weight loss. Under socialism and capitalism, doctors expressed their frustration that "in our diet, in contrast to the generally rational behavior in daily life, be it in the workplace, social activities or in the family, emotional impulses control the situation even to the point of irrationality."[151] Alongside their unsuccessful educational and medical efforts, nutritionists eventually turned to the marketplace to resolve this crisis. The twentieth-century conception of obesity as a disease was premised on the standardized figure of a modern consumer confronting an industrialized marketplace. As a result, in the East as well as the West, fatness revealed a crisis in consumer habits. This meant that the solution was to be found not in a rejection of consumer culture but in its further expansion. Specifically, weight loss would have to be achieved not by eating or purchasing less food but more.

Despite East Germany's notorious struggles with maintaining supplies of consumer goods, socialist nutritionists asserted that "above all . . . the continued development of new products" was the only way to achieve a "reduction in high-calorie overeating and its consequences."[152] Products surprisingly emerged as more important for weight loss than nutritional knowledge; in 1971 weight loss doctors pointed out that "despite all sorts of health educational policies and

Figure 6.3 "A full plate is not a full-time job." Signatur 8A.5.14 (R). Courtesy of Deutsches Hygiene Museum, Dauerleihgabe der Novartis Behring. Photo by David Brandt.

all medical recommendations, an inadequate supply of dietetic products is the reason that dietetic regimes are not followed by patients."[153] A major goal in the country's battle against obesity was increasing the quality and quantity of low-calorie and dietetic foodstuffs. What generally distinguished the GDR from capitalist food systems was its centralized or planned structure—which, theoretically, meant that professional nutritionists could determine which foodstuffs the public had access to. Regulating the food products available to consumers should have ensured that nutritionists could directly influence what people ate; if healthy foods were available, then healthy foods would be consumed.

East German nutritionists had long mocked West Germany for its overflowing shelves of "countless reduced calorie products with the aim of company profit [all of which] have led to a confusion and destabilization of the consumer."[154] Now these same nutritionists were arguing that a radical expansion in precisely those "reduced calorie" products was the solution to the country's obesity. By the 1970s, the East German government was echoing West German claims that citizens' health depended on good shopping practices: "the consumer decides for a proper or false diet with his purchases and preparation of foods according to his individual dietary habits."[155] This new emphasis on marketing specific products and shopping strategies as the keys to healthier eating prompted one visitor of the Hygiene Museum's exhibit *Your Diet, Your Health* to complain that the exhibit "seemed more like a mini-convention of the food industry than an educational program."[156]

East German medical experts determined that improved product selection would be central to their anti-obesity efforts, and they exerted pressure on the food industry to expand such offerings. In 1974, East German factories were producing 74 diabetic and "special diet" foods, 23 reduced-calorie items, and 35 healthy children's food products.[157] Ten years later, the number of products had grown to more than 200 dietetic, diabetic, and reduced-calorie foods.[158] The Trademark Association for Dietetic Products received increased funding to regulate this growing market, which it channeled into monitoring and expanding the ON (*optimierte Nahrung,* or "optimized food") stamping program, which designated the products that met a high standard of quality and consistency in a variety of criteria, including reduced calories, high fiber, low fat, reduced sugar, or safe for diabetics. Stamped products were color-coded; a green dot, for example, meant reduced-calorie. Figure 6.4, from a guide to dietetic food products, shows the variants of ON labels being produced in the late 1970s; by the mid-1980s, 140 products were receiving the stamp, and the number continued to grow until 1990.[159]

This explosion in popular weight-loss products was part of Honecker's much vaunted consumer turn. The new GDR general secretary, recognizing that the country's restricted consumer culture was a source of tremendous dissatisfaction, proclaimed his commitment to improving the production of everyday consumer goods instead of the traditional focus on heavy industry. Yet financial considerations always determined the details of such economic decisions. In the case of dietetic products, economists sought to marry cost reduction to popular

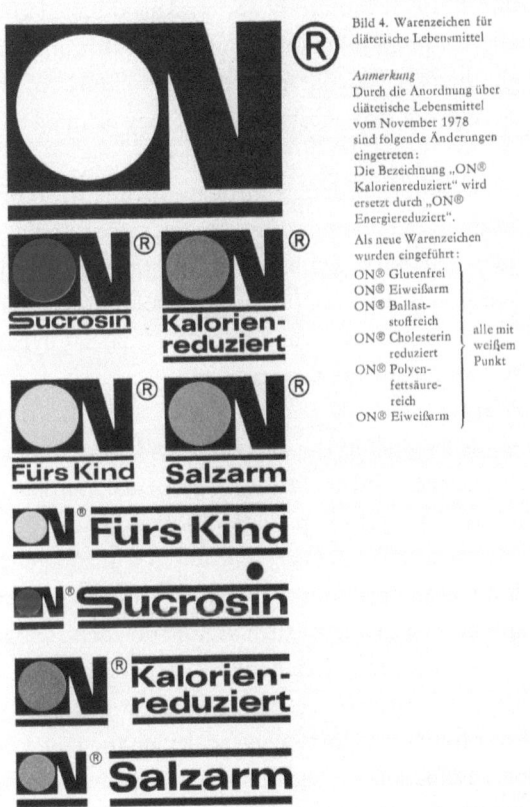

Figure 6.4 Product labels for ON dietetic foods. From *Lebensmittel für die gesunde Ernährung*. Leipzig: Fachbuchverlag, 1978, 83. Private collection of the author.

weight loss. In 1982, at the Tenth Party Congress of the SED, a new Consumer Goods Program announced that "in the realm of the food industry, product development concentrates on the reduction of imports through the increased use of domestic products, the improvement of the nutritional qualities of products, and the expansion of the offerings for specific consumer groups."[160] This meant that products based on any new recipes had to at least "break even in cost" and be "economically practical" in order to be approved for production, regardless of their health benefits.[161]

According to economic analysts, the production costs of new weight-loss recipes could be reduced in several ways. The most common was reducing the use of imported ingredients, but labor and packaging costs could also be reduced. For example, in August 1971, the candy and packaged baked goods industry committed to a multiyear program of improving the "nutritional-physiological" makeup of their products to encourage weight-loss; most of the proposed changes also decreased production costs. By 1975, they planned to

> produce more voluminous products through the mixing in of air into sweets; increase the water content of sweets; increase the milk protein content in candies and packaged baked goods; reduce the calories in candy and baked goods by substituting high calorie ingredients with low calorie substances and fillers; and to reduce calories in candy and baked goods by using artificial sweeteners.[162]

They also recommended reducing the size of individual bonbons; since consumers are generally accustomed to "eating a particular number of bonbons [at each sitting], in this way a caloric reduction of the diet can be achieved."[163] Generally, the East German food industry saw the new mandate to reduce the calorie content of food as an opportunity to exploit "already known and available replacement ingredients and fillers," such as milk powders, margarine, water, and starches.[164] Other substitutions included replacing lemon juice with regionally produced rhubarb, and switching domestic fruits for imported nuts[165]; low-sugar fruit fillings promised to cut costs while achieving the target of 12 percent to 13 percent calorie reduction.[166] "Healthier" sausages were developed that replaced up to 2 percent of meat content with supplements including milk powder, starches, protein powder, and egg powder, saving, in 1985 alone, 3,000 tons of meat.[167] Nutritionists focused special attention on the production of bread, a staple of the East German diet, calling for an increase in so-called special or health breads, which were made from whole grains and fortified with protein powders or vitamins; because these breads were both tastier and more filling than standard white-flour loaves, it was hoped that they would reduce the amount of bread eaten as well as enabling consumers to minimize necessary toppings, especially cheese and cold cuts. To this end, four new recipes—Trend Bread, Drift Bread, Buttermilk Bread, and Weekend Bread—were developed in 1972 alone.[168]

Despite these surges in product development, the real availability of these new dietetic foods remained problematic. The country was plagued by recurrent shortages in precisely the foods that nutritionists most wanted the population to consume. This was especially true of ON and reduced-calorie foods. Despite impressive increases in the numbers of ON foodstuffs developed and approved over the 1970s and 1980s, actual production was sporadic and unpredictable. A 1987 study found inadequate supplies of low-gluten and protein-supplemented foods, and "despite there being seventy recipes for diabetic baked goods, including ten new, high quality recipes," almost none of these were regularly available to consumers.¹⁶⁹ The most popular new dietetic recipes, such as the sought-after *Hallesches Vollkornbrot* and *Mecklenberger Landbrot*, required advanced baking technology or particular ingredients (respectively, a grain-based syrup and puffed rye), which meant that many smaller bakeries or local factories were incapable of producing them.¹⁷⁴ Random samplings at supermarkets found that the general labeling of "healthy" foods was so inadequate that they could not be "clearly distinguished from the normal product supply," and attempts to create special dietetic shops, sections, or aisles were unsuccessful.¹⁷⁰ Similarly, the unreliable consumer landscape encouraged economic pragmatism rather than healthfulness. For example, most artificial sweeteners—seen by nutritionists as a key component of weight-loss products—were not produced in the GDR, making it very difficult for the average citizen to substitute them for domestically produced beet sugar.¹⁷¹

Distribution, too, was a major problem, causing both regional shortages and surpluses. In fact, uneven distribution was dictated by the state; for example, in the face of limited supplies of certain healthy dairy products, a 1970 memo ordered the prioritizing of East Berlin and Leipzig, "because both regions are under strong observation from the West and every form of dissatisfaction here thus has automatic political consequences."¹⁷² Rural areas and smaller towns were seen as having limited political significance and thus less deserving of weight-loss "supplemental" foodstuffs.¹⁷³ This was especially counterproductive since rural areas generally had higher levels of overweight than the urban centers.

Perhaps the most persistent shortages were chronic inadequacies in the GDR's supply of fresh fruits and some vegetables. Although the population was actually consuming more fruits and vegetables per capita than the FRG by the 1970s, most of it was preserved, pickled, or canned—something that was incompatible with the international trend toward fresh and especially imported tropical fruits. Although bananas and oranges might not have been absolutely necessary for a healthy diet, replacing meats and fats with such produce was a popular weight-reduction initiative that proved embarrassingly difficult to achieve in the GDR. One of the country's earliest experiments with a weight-loss program had been unsuccessful because "except for conserves, there were almost no fruits or vegetables; even cabbage and sauerkraut were infrequent."¹⁷⁵ Even in the major agricultural areas, there were recurrent supply and distribution problems; in the late 1970s, the farming region Werder Havel had "scarcely any fruit available to buy, even asparagus [a regional specialty] was unavailable to the general populace."¹⁷⁶ In some areas, regional governments were reduced to asking local populations to bring their privately grown fruits and vegetables to local processing plants to stock shop shelves.¹⁷⁷

Supply-related pressures affected the GDR's food economy at all levels of consumption, distribution, and production—and rarely in ways that accorded with nutritional recommendations. Frequently, an East German food company would decide to modify a product or a restaurant would change a recipe at the expense of popular health. Profit rarely aligned with caloric reductions.[178] Even the highly regulated ON labeling system was subject to constant abuse by a food industry pressured by the bottom line. In a typical example, nutritionist Dr. Grütte insisted that the ON label should "not [be] an option for sweets, as sweets are from a nutritional perspective always disadvantageous."[179] Despite this nutritionally sound argument, economic ambitions for increased sales led to the approval of a new "calorie reduced" label, to be used "for those products which have had some reduction in calories, but have not met the requirements for a 'reduced calorie foodstuff.'"[180] The label was specifically intended for filled chocolates and other candies, which generated some of the highest profits in the East German food industry. Openly dismissing experts' concerns that "nutritionally un-useful products will advertise for an increased consumption through this specified label," the food industry successfully defended such nonsensical and ultimately counterproductive measures.[181] Both the socialist "planned economy" and capitalist "advertising" thus participated in the reinvention of unhealthy foodstuffs as pseudo-healthy "calorie-reduced" ones.

While recognizing the nutritional challenges caused by the frequent shortages and unreliable supplies, nutritionists found that the country's overweight was primarily caused by the excessive consumption of unhealthy foodstuffs, just as had been the case in the FRG. This realization caused the venerated frozen prices of the GDR's staple foods to come under fire from health experts as well as economists by the end of the 1970s. The very existence of obesity implied that one of the core components of the GDR's socialist economy—its aggressive policy of food subventions—harmed the health of the population. It had long been acknowledged that food subsidies meant that "certain products are so strongly protected by the state that they are not used rationally, but are treated in a wasteful manner or used in the wrong way."[182] Debates over obesity suggested that abundant cheap food was destroying the health of East German citizens as well as harming the economy.

Nutritionists called for a massive reformulation of the country's pricing system; it was hoped that this would both change the kinds of foods that people purchased and, controversially, reduce the total quantity of food consumed. A 1970 report on "steering consumer habits and securing a healthy diet for the population" noted that "the price of foodstuffs functions inadequately as a stimulant for proper diet and in part supports tendencies toward a false diet," noting for example that fattier cuts of meat were usually cheaper than leaner cuts.[183] Similarly, most of the "special breads" made of higher-quality whole-grain flours were more expensive than subsidized white- and mixed-flour breads, and thus were produced in lower quantities.[184] The new mantra became 'health should determine price.' A 1972 report recommended with respect to dairy products "where lower-fat [production] is actually cheaper, price things accurately. With products where low-fat [production] is more expensive, don't price accurately. With foods that we do not want people to eat, do not aim for increasing profits."[185] In an controversial expression of his profound frustration, in 1970 the director of the ZfE, Helmut Haenel, made the distinctly unsocialist proposal to institute a "fat tax" because "all appeals and propaganda have been unsuccessful," and "colleagues with overweight continue to be a burden to health services and medical professionals in addition to being unproductive."[186] (The proposal found little domestic support and was widely covered by West German media, which portrayed it as a "Nazi-style" intervention in the private sphere.)[187] For the most part, however, all recommendations to make eating more expensive remained theoretical. Politicians were convinced that any increase in the prices of high-calorie staples like meat or butter would threaten social stability. Political and economic considerations continued to determine what foods were produced, when they were available, and how much they cost.

The economic downturn of the 1980s aggravated these problems, and resulted in declining consumer selection in the GDR during its final decade of existence. While the reforms of the 1970s had brought about some improvements in the consumer economy, the recession and the debt crises of the following decade, which resulted in price increases, reduced state spending, and labor unrest in the West spelled catastrophe for the fiscally precarious GDR. Even products that had previously been widely available suddenly disappeared from the shelves.[188] A 1983 study on the food-supply situation noted that "the variety of options for the consumer has worsened and in 1982 the range of assortments in the shopping centers only reached 50% of the goal established in 1974."[189] A damning internal report noted that "the spectrum of foodstuffs in 1982 is only half of that in 1974 . . . a few years ago, it was assumed that every citizen of our republic could feed himself healthfully from the grocery selection; this is today only true in a limited way."[190] These problems further meant that "many consumers are increasingly skeptical about new products, and many products are actually being produced in decreasing quality."[191] In the end, despite almost two decades of concentrated weight-loss product development, a 1988 analysis by the Trademark Association for Dietetic Products found that "the structure of grocery supplies in the GDR has the following crucial flaws: the percentage of fatty pork, butter fat, eggs, sweets, and sugar and alcohol-rich drinks in the average diet is too high . . . the percentage of plant oils, fruit, vegetables, grains, and fish is too low."[192]

East German citizens expressed frustration over the state's inability to provide them with healthy foods. In a 1988 study, overweight diabetic patients reported that poor taste, low quality, and limited selection were major reasons that they did not stick to their diets; more than 60 percent believed that "a larger selection of diabetic foodstuffs will positively impact overweight and metabolism."[193] One diabetic wrote a letter addressing the "particular flavorlessness" of diet-sausages, complaining bitterly that "the fact that there are herbs and spices with which tasty dietetic sausage can be produced clearly would create too much effort for the production factories and make too little profit."[194] Experts warned that "without a transformation of grocery and menu offerings, which essentially correlates to contemporary consumer wishes," GDR citizens would continue to eat too much fat, sugar, and salt indefinitely.[195] Embarrassingly, the staff nutritionist at a nutritional education presentation in Senftenberg found out that "many visitors confirmed that our grocery stores did not offer the presented healthy food items like Rheinisch black bread, oat bran, and the [whole-grain] products of VEB Albert Kunz."[196] In 1975, the overweight professional chef Claus Kulka blamed the failure of his diet directly on the country's supply issues—not the lack of particular foods but his inability to find a detailed calorie chart. Kulka asked rhetorically, "[W]hat use for us is it when healthy lifestyles are advocated by our media, but the required simple, basic products that are cheap to produce cannot be found anywhere?"[197] The Institute for Market Research polled consumers about grocery supplies; between 1974 and 1980, the number of respondents who reported always having access to the healthy "specialty breads" shrank from 35.6 percent to 30.7 percent, and the number who "practically never" had them rose from 22.8 percent to 24 percent.[198] Even the availability of fresh produce declined; whereas at the beginning of the 1970s half the country's working population ate fresh fruit or vegetables with their evening meal, this number had dropped to less than 35 percent by the end of the 1980s.[199]

In addition to these structural problems, the popular media continued to promote eating habits that directly contradicted current health recommendations. The popular magazine *Guter Rat*, for example, in 1976 defended its reliance on high-calorie recipes by claiming that

> for years our readers have enjoyed the little special occasion, at which they occasionally present their guests with something special on the table. From this perspective we see absolutely no contradiction in the fact that we exceed the caloric limits and yet also speak of a healthy diet.[200]

Indeed, nutritionists constantly expressed their frustration with their lackluster support from the popular press:

> Occasionally we find support in the press, but often they make things especially difficult for us. There were great difficulties with getting an article promoting whole grain noodles published in the newspaper. They said, 'with whole grain noodles we are taking a step backwards,' or 'this means that lean years are coming our way.' At this point a colleague spontaneously took a pot of whole grain noodles to the press and thus finally convinced the editorial board [to publish the article.][201]

The local press frequently published advertisements for new products that were only thinly disguised as articles, in order to help "steer" the populations' purchasing patterns. Unfortunately for efforts to support weight loss, this strategy was often used to encourage the purchase of surplus items. By the 1970s dairy fat had become one of the country's most abundant and undesirable surplus commodities, because it was extracted to produce the reduced-fat versions most people drank. The need to use up this excess fat inspired a dairy in Brandenburg to produce a new, extra-high-fat milk with a 3.2 percent fat content. (Up to this point, standard milk in the GDR was sold at 3% fat.) Local newspapers published announcements for the new product using statements provided by the dairy industry which proclaimed that

> milk is healthy, for its fat is easily digestible and thus especially good for the body; milk refreshes, for it rapidly builds up the strength that has been exhausted through hard physical or mental energy; and it keeps you slim. Thus, you should use the opportunity to drink fattier milk and instead limit your consumption of the difficult-to-digest fats in butter and margarine.[202]

In response, several nutritionists wrote angry letters to the Ministry of Health, reporting that "mystical and misleading advertisements are being produced for the new fattier milk products that are in contradiction to general nutritional knowledge and are certain to create false ideas in our population."[203] Dr. Haenel, in a letter to the Brandenburg newspaper *Brandenburgische Neueste Nachrichten*, debunked the claims word by word:

> [T]hat milk keeps you feeling fresh is an assertion that cannot be proven and certainly one that cannot be generalized . . . the question of slimness is a question of caloric balance, not a question of individual food products. Who eats too much, regardless of whether the calories come from milk, pork, eggs, cake, or other foodstuffs, and who has a tendency to accumulate fat, will become fat: he who eats less, even if he does not drink milk, is or will become slim . . . thus, a food that . . . increases fat consumption is from a nutritional perspective not to be specially recommended.[204]

Haenel's rejoinder appeared alongside promotional releases for the new milk, but the higher-fat milk continued to be praised and widely distributed.

Interestingly, far from being particular to the GDR's food economy, the problem of excess milk fat was endemic in postwar Europe. The West German dairy industry, too, had long promoted the consumption of high-fat dairy products in order to dispose of this excess, against the interests of public health. In 1968, Hermann Höcherl, the West German minister of food and agriculture, began calling for children to "only drink full-fat milk," which recently had also been increased from 3 percent to 3.5 percent fat. Higher-fat milk was promoted in order to combat the "constantly growing milk flood and butter mountain in Europe's economic community"—despite the fact that nutritionists agreed that "in view of the current nutritional situation . . . a milk with not-too-high fat levels should be recommended."[205] A decade later, with the obesity crisis in full swing, the new, and distinctly overweight, agricultural minister Joseph Ertl continued to support flooding the West German market with high-fat dairy to shrink the country's "butter mountain." As a critical article in the trade journal *Handelsblatt* noted, the minister opposed official programs advocating weight-loss because of the potential economic consequences of fostering "discrimination against the golden yellow, creamy spreadable fat," fearing that "Germans will start to spread their breakfast rolls only with lettuce leaves, and European butter stores will become immeasurably large."[206]

As in the East, West German nutritionists blamed the country's weight problem on supply issues. But in this wealthy capitalist economy, limited selection—the bane of the GDR—was not the issue. In the "consumer wonderland" of the FRG, it was precisely the wide array of constantly available food products, both diet and standard, that was identified as the problem. Because overweight was associated with both overconsumption and consumption of the wrong products, it challenged the embrace of consumerism that was at the heart of the country's postwar identity. The West German government's reluctance to interfere in the consumer economy by regulating advertising came head-to-head with the economic harms associated with obesity.

Advertising, normally cast as a positive market force benefiting both the public and the economy, came under criticism from dietary experts and angry consumers who felt that the drive for profit was outweighing concern for general health and well-being. Since the boom days of postwar reconstruction, there had been complaints about unethical or misleading claims made by the West German food industry. Many of these products used pseudo-scientific evidence to make health claims related to weight loss. For example, the American Kraft Cheese Company authored an article on popular health that was published in

Der Spiegel, in 1953. "A Primary Problem of Our Age: Scientists and Doctors Give Advice" acknowledged that improper diet was West Germany's leading health problem, yet boldly claimed that "well-known nutritionists highlight in particular the essential natural power of milk and milk products. Among milk products, Velveeta cheese made by Kraft has an especially important position. Famous researchers . . . note in their research the special advantages of Velveeta cheese for dietetic eating."[207]

A few years later, an article on chocolate published by the food industry's main journal countered the "frequently held opinion that chocolate is especially threatening to slimness, and that as a result the natural desire for beloved chocolate products should be repressed." In fact, the text continued, "new studies recommend that people who tend toward overweight consume several pieces of chocolate before large meals" in order to reduce their hunger at mealtime, thus supporting weight loss.[208]

Reflecting its commitment to unfettered consumption, the West German food industry trained children to see advertisements as a source of accurate and unbiased knowledge. A nutritional curriculum for middle-school children reminded its young target audience that "were it not for advertising, the consumer would not know what new products there are on the market; additionally, the typical consumer today gets most of his knowledge about new foodstuffs and their make-up as well as their meaning for health overwhelmingly from advertising."[209] Representatives of the food industry argued that the general public, "especially housewives," was more than capable of evaluating contradictory claims and health information.[210]

West German nutritionists were far less optimistic about the press's role in supporting public health. A 1967 publication on home economics and nutrition complained that "the press and advertisements could potentially be capable of changing the dietary habits of consumers, but they do little in this direction because they instead orient themselves to the masses."[211] Home economists had long worried that the country's housewives were incapable of successfully negotiating the country's food system; augmenting this general problem, the food industry's misleading claims, they believed, would produce a sort of "burn-out" effect, ultimately causing shoppers to entirely disregard health considerations when making their purchases.

The obesity crisis of the 1970s only increased the variety of food products available, presenting the West German housewife with a staggering array of ever-changing options. For the first time, along with considerations of cost and taste, calorie content became a primary evaluative category for food purchases. If East German women could not find many reduced-calorie foods on the shelves, West German housewives had dozens to choose from, all making competing and often wildly inaccurate claims about their efficacy. As a result, dieting in the FRG was remarkably complicated and required great flexibility on the part of the shopper; not only did specific weight-loss products need to be selected, but each one required a different method of implementation. Some diet foods required extreme shifts in eating habits, like a new variety of low-calorie cracker, which recommended replacing the main meal of the day with three cracker-based snacks, with a resultant drop in caloric intake from 800 to a mere 111 calories.[212] Other weight-loss products claimed weight-loss could be achieved without changing individual eating habits. The diet soda Fanta promised women that they could "let yourself enjoy getting slim" by simply replacing their normal sugary soda with this new calorie-free version.[213] Dr. Kousa's prepackaged diet meals promised dieting women that finally "losing weight can be easy."[214] Consumers were allowed to eat as much as they wanted, as long as they relied exclusively on Dr. Kousa's products. Taking an entirely different tack, the *You Are Allowed* brand of margarine and jams admonished consumers that "you are allowed . . . to eat within limits. Let's not kid ourselves, eating will never make you slimmer."[215] The world of weight-loss products was so complex that women's magazines began running regular columns to familiarize their readers with "new products on the diet market, and inform you about important discoveries in the nutritional world."[216]

Among the most popular weight-loss products developed by the booming postwar German chemical industry were the new artificial sweeteners and diet pills. The West German medical establishment had been prescribing weight-loss drugs for decades; a 1954 study on obesity, for example, recommended amphetamines as a standard treatment, finding that obese women taking these pills not only lost on average .6 kilos a week, but that they "felt very good for the duration of the program, and took the pills enthusiastically."[217] The large-scale rise in overweight led to a parallel rise in pill consumption; television, radio, and print media was saturated with advertisements for weight-loss drugs such as Recatol, which advertised itself as "one weight-loss program that will take away many pounds, but not a gram of pleasure."[218] Even more widespread was the use of artificial sweeteners, dozens of which emerged on the market throughout the 1960s and 1970s. Sugar substitutes, such as Sionen, promised to "help you to stay slim or become slim—as long as you also generally pay attention to calories, and have patience."[219]

Such products inspired fear, hope, and confusion among consumers, who were advised to take advantage of them even as they were being warned that they could cause cancer, hypertension, or birth defects. Cyclamate, an artificial sweetener that had been banned in the United States but remained legal in the FRG, was one of many such products, becoming a major source of consumer anxiety during the late 1960s and early 1970s. An overweight 62-year-old who, "under advice of a doctor, went on a diet that required using the [cyclamate-based] sweeteners of the firm Kauvit in Munich for sweetening my foods and drinks," described his "great fear that . . . I have cancer symptoms in me . . . I can't sleep from fear."[220] An angry 87-year-old retiree, after reading about potential health risks, wrote to the manufacturer of the artificial sweetener Assugrin requesting reimbursement for the 1,000 packets that he had purchased, as well as advice about safely destroying the product.[221] A Dr. Wolfgang Liese complained in a letter to minister of health Käte Strobel that "wide segments of the population, especially diabetics and the overweight, are concerned and have been placed in unnecessary fear by undisciplined and contradictory press statements" about artificial sweeteners, but the problem proved impossible to regulate.[222] By the 1980s, both politicians and consumers were openly criticizing the fact that the West German food industry spent over 1 billion Deutschmarks yearly "to increase their profits often with misleading advertising and without considering consumers and their health"—a daunting sum when compared with the 10 million Deutschmarks budgeted for the country's nutritional education programs.[223] Unsurprisingly, all efforts to educate consumers proved almost entirely ineffective, and West Germany made few inroads in the struggle against obesity.

This failure to improve the nation's eating habits was not simply a medical problem; it seemed to challenge the vitality of West German society at large. A West German nutritionist, in 1973, warned that "from the perspective of health, the food situation of the population in the FRG is today as bad as it was in 1948, only with reversed symptoms and the difference that a lot of money is being spent for a diet that makes you sick."[224] Redeploying the language of German victimization that had been developed during the Hunger Years, nutritionist Herbert Krauss warned that Germany's growing fatness was as great a tragedy as the starvation of concentration camp inmates: "the results of a flawed diet for a person who, in contrast to a concentration camp inmate, never experiences hunger, are less dramatic, yet one cannot say, in the face of the suffering of such a falsely nourished person, that they are less miserable."[225] Similarly, a report from 1966 claimed that "in no previous era has life expectancy in Germany . . . been so profoundly threatened by diet-caused sicknesses, which today in West Germany are the leading cause of deaths."[226] If their colleagues decades earlier had worried that inadequate food supplies and malnutrition threatened the very existence of the German *Volk*, nutritionists in the late Cold War warned that "our diet has become a ticking bomb," placing the health and well-being not only of individuals but of West German society at large at risk.[227] Too much of a good thing proved as bad, and perhaps even worse, than too little.

* * *

Sociologist Pierre Bourdieu influentially argued that "tastes in food also depend on the idea each class has of the body and of the effects of food on the body, that is, on its strength, health and beauty."[228] The proliferation of obesity across class lines—as a body that seems to defy the values of "strength, health and beauty"—reveals that popular tastes can also destabilize and confound the industrial state. Obesity challenged core economic and political values of both German states, confirming the larger claim that individual food consumption poses a profound challenge to modern governmentality.[229] The modern state relies upon the industrialized food system to control the bodies of its citizens; fatness, in contrast, represents the primacy of individual desires over such biopolitical ambitions. These too-big bodies expose peoples' inherently flawed tastes, in turn locating them outside the regulatory bounds of the state. In this reading, a person's weight can inscribe new boundaries between state and individual, public and private.

Indeed, in both German states, fatness destabilized economic systems and cultural norms. Faced with the intractability of individual tastes, West German nutritionists felt compelled to advocate governmental intervention into private consumer habits. According to postwar capitalist ideology, a healthy market was free and self-regulating, just as individuals were assumed to be free to regulate their economic and biological input and output. In 1981, the agricultural minister Joseph Ertl asserted that

> in our free market economy, what the consumer chooses for his food remains up to him ... in our society no one can and no one wants to forcibly prescribe to the consumer how he is supposed to eat ... final responsibility remains with each individual to maintain his own health through a rational diet.[230]

Despite such convictions, however, the ideology of personal freedom met its limits in the postwar obesity epidemic. Nutritionists began to perceive the free market as a major health threat. West German food scholar Hans-Jürgen Teuteberg declared, in 1979, in what almost sounds like East German rhetoric, that

> whoever, in an egoistic and shortsighted way, asserts that "my beer-belly belongs to me" and believes that his personal freedoms are endangered by a state-sponsored snooping around in his dietary habits, is clearly ignoring the fact that the collective poor behavior of large sections of the population compromises the freedom and the wallet of others, who must pay for the enormous health harms.[231]

Body weight was not a personal decision, but an obligation. West Germany's largest health insurance company, the AOK, produced a series of posters depicting (slim) celebrities who declared that "only elephants can weigh what they want—not me!"[232] In the face of widespread health problems, an individual's weight was to be determined by the medical profession, or, increasingly, the height-weight tables of insurance companies. Overweight became an active harm to society, and as such was a choice that individuals should not be allowed to make.

In analogous ways, the failure of East Germany's weight-loss strategies prompted nutritionists to reconceptualize the relationship between the socialist economy and the population's eating habits. The obesity crisis challenged a central assumption of GDR socialism: that the establishment of a modern, industrialized food economy would automatically improve the health of the populace. By the 1980s, faced with scores of overweight citizens, the state espoused a seemingly Western rhetoric by empowering consumers to be responsible for themselves and to make "correct choices." Frustrated nutritionists began discouraging food-based social gatherings and encouraging "self-absorption" and a focus on external appearance; they attempted to exploit personal insecurities and the desire to be attractive to change how people ate, especially women and teenagers. But advice to reduce overall food consumption clashed with the economic interests of the food industry, as well as with the state's political commitment to subsidizing high-calorie staples like butter and pork.

Both state socialism and consumer capitalism waged the "battle against the bulge" in vain. East and West German nutritionists described obesity, which they blamed on diets that were "too fatty, too salty, and too sweet," as one of the most serious health challenges facing their respective governments. Experts in both states emphasized the high medical costs associated with obesity and blamed poor parenting skills, especially on the part of mothers, for producing overweight children. Thus, despite important differences—the West German belief that the solution lay in the private home and family, and the East German assertion that collective eating programs could best remedy the problem—the two states similarly failed to regulate and optimize their citizens' bodies.

Nonetheless, body size became central to the political imagination of both Cold War states. From the earliest days of division, West Germans consistently imagined East Germans as fatter (representing their proletarian lack of cultural capital) and hungrier (representing their poverty) then they were. The FRG's media eagerly reported on food shortages and consumer crises across the border; such information, along with the steady shipment of *Westpäckchen* (West packages) to the East, encouraged the idea that citizens of the GDR barely had enough to eat. At the same time, by the 1960s, the FRG had begun regularly relaying tales of widespread overweight among East Germans—which was interpreted as a sign of a pathological economic system. In 1965, *Der Spiegel* bitingly noted that "the GDR—as always ten years behind progress—has finally reached the stage of the 'eating wave.' Walter Ulbricht's cherished dream of reaching global superiority has finally been realized—at least on the scale."[233] A decade later, when West Germany was in the midst of its own obesity epidemic, *Die Zeit* announced that in the GDR "obesity has gradually acquired an epidemic character," graphically describing "84,000 tons of excess fat" that was "wobbl[ing] around the GDR." The report diagnosed this overweight as existentially different from the Western variant, which was blamed on excessive consumer choice. In the East, fatness was a cipher of displaced desires. "Food seems to make up for difficulties, stresses, and disappointments. It is often a substitute for pleasures that one can no longer enjoy."[234]

East Germans were quick to point out the paradoxes in these assumptions. As early as 1960, in the touring exhibit *Your Nutrition, Your Health*, the question was bitingly asked, "Don't you think that it is odd that the Western press lies about one famine or another [in the GDR] while our doctors are using all of their powers of convincing to get us to not overfeed ourselves?"[235] At the same time, socialist propaganda also suggested that West German fatness was different, and far worse, than their own domestic variant. Across the border, the bellies of wealthy bankers were swollen from the consumption of lobster, champagne, and imported delicacies, treats that had been acquired through the sweat of an underpaid and underfed working class. This rhetoric, however, had little purchase among East German citizens, who were themselves convinced of the desirability of the West's consumer paradise. As a result, it was Western fantasies of the simultaneously starving and fat East German that shaped Germany's reunification in 1990. This, in turn, reveals the importance of bodies in the modern political imaginary.

Epilogue

Yes, We Have No Bananas: Negotiating Past and Future in Reunified Germany

In the days and weeks that followed the fall of the Berlin Wall on November 9, 1989, throngs of East Germans rushed over the newly permeable border. Giddy men, women, and children filled the towns and cities that lay west of the Wall. West Berlin in particular was overwhelmed; roads were impassable, shops sold out of most of their stock, and normal life briefly ground to a halt. The Federal Republic's satiric magazine *Titanic* dedicated its November issue to the historic moment, with a cover image depicting the smiling *Zonen-Gabi*, or "Gabi from the Eastern zone" (see Figure 7.1). Dressed in an ill-fitting jean jacket a decade out of fashion, her curly red hair shorn in an unfashionably boyish cut, Gabi's goofy grin shone out of her freckled face. In her left hand, she clutched an enormous cucumber, its green skin carefully pulled down to resemble a half-peeled banana. The headline was Gabi's proud exclamation "my first banana." The image was a tremendous success, reproduced as both a postcard and full-sized poster, and it still graces the walls of many student apartments in unified Germany.

More than anything, it was Gabi's peeled cucumber that made her a star. One of the few fresh vegetables consistently available in the GDR, the cucumber was a staple of diets in both halves of Germany, where the plant flourished in the Central European climate. The heart of the joke is Gabi's almost virginal lack of knowledge of the exotic, imported banana. She looks like she is about to devour the whole cucumber without realizing that this is the same watery fruit she has been consuming in salads and sandwiches her entire life. Yet, ironically, it was for this that Gabi was assumed to have torn down the Wall in the first place—to finally gain access to those long-desired bananas.

Bananas had long been an obsession for both East and West Germans, who early on had recognized them as an important symbol of postwar prosperity and luxury consumption. In 1954, Konrad Adenauer had, despite intense protests by

Figure 7.1 "Gaby from the Eastern Zone (17) in Paradise (the FRG): 'My First Banana.'" Cover image, *Titanic* 11 (November 1989).

France, successfully negotiated the FRG's right to import bananas tax free, making them one of West Germany's cheapest fruits.[1] Indeed, Adenauer had been so committed to cheap bananas that in 1957 he threatened to boycott the new European Community (EC) were his country not granted this unique privilege.[2] As early as 1953, West German cookbooks contained chapters titled "What Do I Do with All These Bananas?"[3] In 1961, the country produced its first cookbook dedicated exclusively to banana recipes.[4] More so than in any other European country, in West Germany bananas were integrated into daily eating habits, as housewives were taught to bake, broil, fry, and mash them and serve them with sweet desserts as well as savory roasts, in drinks and as confections. By 1989, West Germany's yearly banana consumption had risen to 800,000 tons, making it Europe's biggest banana importer, putting it behind only the United States in per capita consumption.[5]

In contrast, East Germany had little access to cheap bananas. The GDR's primary source of tropical fruits, Cuba, was not a major banana producer, and supplies from Africa and Asia were unreliable and often prohibitively expensive. In the early 1960s, the Ministry of Trade managed to negotiate a massive banana exchange with Vietnam, but the imported bananas were dried because of limited refrigerated shipping capacity; sales of the dried fruits were catastrophic. Pleas from the food industry to the minister of economy to reduce or cancel these banana imports were rejected "in the interests of political trade relations."[6] Attempts to market them as bread-spreads, ingredients for baked goods, and as candy flavoring were unsuccessful; one of the country's largest producers of candies and baked goods regretfully reported "a distinct aversion on the side of the consumer for products with [dried] bananas in them."[7] This unfortunate episode was the country's first and last experience with an overabundance of the tropical fruit. Even during the peak of the GDR's consumer economy, fresh bananas were usually available only during the winter holidays and then in limited quantities. However, almost all East Germans occasionally ate bananas, and certainly no one was entirely unfamiliar with them.

The 1989 *Titanic* cover was only the most famous of a veritable flood of cartoons and satiric images memorializing the Fall of the Wall that focused on bananas. The yellow fruits were regularly depicted as the object of all-consuming desire on the part of East Germans. A light-hearted 1998 discussion of the socialist food economy narrated the fictitious story of Elfriede S as a metaphor for the vanished state:

> As she turns around the corner where the baked goods are, a scream slips from Elfriede S that shakes the whole store. Shopping list, basket, and Elfriede S fall to the ground. Valuable seconds are lost. Elfriede S staggers up. She lets the shopping list be and stuffs, with great presence of mind, a bag of bananas in her basket. At the cashier she gets five twenty-cent pieces with which she storms the nearest telephone to alert her relatives.[8]

Indeed, bananas seemed ubiquitous during the drama of unification. In Berlin, groups of West German retirees gathered at the Brandenburg Gate in the days following the Fall of the Wall to greet East German newcomers with free bananas. Pictures of frantic grocers trying to protect mounds of bananas from long-deprived Easterners projected a mixture of humor and very real fear. Cartoons, jokes, and anecdotes depicted the Fall of the Wall as a sort of modified food riot, wherein ravenous East Germans stormed the West in their overwhelming desire for luxury foodstuffs.[9]

This was, of course, not the politicized hunger that had inspired the bread riots of the First World War or the pathos-ridden suffering of the occupation years but a sort of postmodern hunger for the delicacies of the global marketplace. In a 2009 article titled "How the GDR Became a Banana Republic," *Die Zeit* reported that after the Fall of the Wall, "[banana] prices exploded, as did their consumption."[10] Although consumption levels quickly stabilized, there is no doubt that reunification radically increased East Germans' banana eating. This seemed to come at a price for West Germans. After German unification, in the face of the new post–Cold War global economy, the EC decided to end the country's historically special treatment. In 1991, former West German newspapers reported with horror that "Brussels is determined to drastically raise the banana price"; for the first time since the end of the Second World War, Germany's banana prices increased to match levels in the rest of Western Europe.[11] Although it was not true that East German appetites were responsible for bananas' increased cost, the coincidence of reunification and the establishment of a standardized EU banana import tax seemed to symbolize the fact that, from a West German perspective, absorbing the former GDR was both costly and unpalatable.[12] No longer were bananas cheaper than home-grown produce, cheap enough to be given away to poor friends and hungry relatives as a sign of collective prosperity.

Despite West Germans' shock at their rising banana prices, it was East German rather than West German diets that were expected to be radically remade in the wake of reunification. Because a dysfunctional food system had become an especially important symbol of socialism's flaws, Westerners assumed that food consumption would be the first and most valued site of East German "catching up" to the West. At a meeting in March 1990, the head of Berlin's food industry predicted that an uncontrolled "fetishization of Western brand products on the part of the East German consumer" would doom all remaining GDR food-producing companies.[13] A 1997 study of the eating habits of former East Germans described, in language evocative of the West's postwar *Fresswelle*, a population that had been "living with and used to the typical shortcomings and supply deficits of planned eastern food markets" and was suddenly faced with "the overwhelming and stable variety of western food supplies within weeks." It warned the consequence would be a period of "turbulences and extremes in consumer behavior through curiosity and catching up on new foods."[14] Nutritionists anticipated a "strong catch-up phase towards Western food consumption patterns," predicting dramatic increases in the purchasing of fresh fruit, convenience foods, breakfast cereals, and dairy products.[15]

East German eating habits did change after reunification but not as much as had been expected. East Germans shifted their purchasing power away from formerly subsidized staples—bread, potatoes, alcohol, and meats—and towards tropical fruits and other luxury foodstuffs.[16] Some of the greatest changes in everyday diet were the result of the closure of workplace canteens and school cafeterias after 1990. Impressive growth in fresh fruit purchases did not entirely substitute for the almost complete collapse of the GDR's extensive private gardening communities, which had previously supplied a large percentage of the country's produce needs.[17]

In the immediate aftermath of reunification, East German desires were focused on foods that were conceptualized as "Western," ranging from exotic imports to West German versions of pan-German staples like sausages or pickles. Many food companies saw former Easterners as a significant untapped market. Some attempted to exploit these appetites, as with the notoriously flavorless supersized white rolls, marketed as "Western"; they were made extra large with "an extra shot of baking powder" rather than actually being composed of more bread dough.[18] Generally, producers assumed both extreme hunger and an extreme naïveté among former GDR citizens; promotional material for the novelty frozen dessert "Whirla-Whip," which was being marketed at the first *Grüne Woche* exhibition since the opening of the border, enthusiastically addressed this new child-like consumer audience: "Whirla-Whip offers 1000 varieties of frozen yogurt on two square meters ... simply every imaginable flavor made exactly according to customer wishes ... for visitors from the GDR or East Berlin, Whirla-Whip offers its product free or for a special price."[19]

However, despite seductive prices, East Germans found often these new "Western" foods less palatable than anticipated, a realization that often correlated with a general disenchantment with reunification. In an interview several years after reunification, an East German woman remembered that "in the first month after the fall of the Wall, I gained 25 pounds! I had to try out every chocolate bar—Toblerone, Rittersport. And the nice large rolls! But then we saw that they were only made out of air and we wanted our *Ossi* rolls back."[20] In 1993, *Der Spiegel* reported that East German bakeries had recently been gripped by "intensive *Ostalgie* [nostalgia for the Socialist East] ... to the happiness of their customers they are again baking small, firm rolls 'like before' and 'according to the old GDR recipe.'"[21] Within just a few years, former East Germans began to seek out the foods and products they had consumed under socialism, proudly asserting a distinct history and cultural identity and embracing their particular tastes.[22] A 1993 survey found that 82 percent of East Germans preferred "native" food products to those produced in the West.[23]

This rekindling of interest in East German foods seemed to many Westerners counterintuitive, if not absurd. The GDR's food culture had been the aspect of everyday life that most graphically represented the miseries of the collapsed country. Yet, this surprising development has stood the test of time. Over the past two decades and contrary to expectations, the East German food landscape has become the focal point of distinctly positive memories and acts of re-creation on both sides of the former border. German and non-German cultural commentators frequently voice their surprise at the pervasive sense of loss many former East Germans express.[24] While many scholars have explored the fantastical type of nostalgia common to many post-socialist societies, few have paid attention to food's prominence in this nostalgia—a form of pseudo-memory defined by literary theorist Svetlana Boym as the longing for a home that no longer exists or that never existed.[25]

Since 1989, a genre of nostalgia cookbooks has developed in Germany. Many of these books address audiences of Westerners assumed to be unfamiliar with the GDR's culinary culture; for example, the *GDR Baking Book* includes, alongside carefully selected recipes, a list of socialist "tips and tricks"—recipes for substitutions for expensive or rare ingredients including almonds, raisins, marzipan, and heavy cream—that are intended to add a touch of authenticity to the book, which otherwise reads like a standard German cookbook.[26] It also includes lengthy introductions to several food products that have survived reunification, including bonbons like Hallorenkugel, Kathi brand cake mixes, and Filinchin crackers. These products are recommended as giving the consumer a distinct "taste of the East." Other cookbooks aimed at an East German audience expressed their longing for "our cuisine" and "our country." Rather than teach "foreigners" new ways of cooking, these books assert that "for forty years not only did we live differently than in the West, but we also cooked and ate differently—and that should not simply be forgotten."[27] Relying on insider references and humorous anecdotes, they claim to preserve "GDR cuisine" as a valued aspect of daily life, something that "neither reunification nor the new possibilities and influences of the past years [after 1989] have erased."[28] Like a photo album or scrapbook, these cookbooks invite their readers to "prepare these recipes and luxuriate in memories."[29]

Food's importance for remembering the past and imagining the future at least partially explains why some East German foods continue to be produced in reunified Germany.[30] Ironically, their presence in a shop has become a sign of a "Western," consumer-oriented and highly diversified selection of wares. Interestingly, former West Germans have been particularly avid consumers of East German nostalgia products, purchasing reissued East German foodstuffs and dining in "typically" East German novelty restaurants. Musician Kai Niemann's hit song "In the East" (*Im Osten*), which insists that "the butter here tastes more like butter / And the sparkling wine also more like wine / actually almost everything is a little better than in the West," was popular on both sides of the former border. The film *Good Bye Lenin*, replete with frequent references to East German foods like sausages and Spreewald pickles, sold out in movie houses across the country. One of the most popular *Ostalgie* products was a 1996 card game called Taste the East (*Kost the Ost*), whose cards have detailed descriptions of dozens of East German food products; over ten thousand games were sold in the first week of production.[31]

The consumption of such products is better understood as the pursuit of fantasies rather than memories. For former East Germans, the total disappearance of the GDR's food system—from actual food products to physical sites of eating to patterns of socialization and food acquisition—makes truly re-creating East German food an impossibility. For West German cooks, consuming "East German" dishes primarily confirms particular conceptions of the former East. The GDR, the last in a long line of vanished twentieth-century German states, thus continues to be the object of projected fears and desires. The importance of food in such memory projects reflects the ways in which former East and West Germans struggle to come to terms with their divided past and shared present.

As the ostensible winner of the Cold War, the prosperity of the Federal Republic seems to confirm Western superiority and imply the growing irrelevance of the GDR. But the rhetoric that frames *Ostalgie* complicates narratives of victory and defeat. Fantasies of East Germans during the *Wende* (the Turn), as the process of reunification is known in Germany, were expressed in a culinary vocabulary that had a longer history, invoking themes that pervaded Germany's twentieth century—fears of hunger, expressions of gendered and racial identities, and shifting geopolitical ambitions. These themes have continued to shape the twenty-five years since the end of the Cold War, suggesting that postindustrial economies continue to rely on the food system as a crucial source of their power. Through this food system, biopolitics shapes ordinary peoples' lives not only through governmental policies but also through economic activities, daily rituals, and family relations.

The Bittersweet Tastes of Past, Present, and Future

During the Cold War, East Germany became a cipher of hunger. In the FRG itself, the small socialist country evoked the suffering of fellow Germans under a communist dictatorship. While the East had been imagined in both Weimar and Nazi Germany as an Edenic space of plentitude and regeneration that would resolve current hungers, this new "East" of the GDR was depicted as a landscape of abiding hunger that above all highlighted the abundance of the West. West German descriptions of life in the GDR relied on tropes of hunger and deprivation that were established during the postwar Hunger Years: this was a land defined by poorly stocked stores, empty shelves, shoddily produced foodstuffs, and flavorless and obligatory canteen meals. Echoing wartime convictions that the Soviets aimed to starve the German people, the West German agricultural expert Frieda Wunderlich claimed as late as 1958 that the goal of the Soviet Union was "above all the ruin of East German agriculture."[32] More generally, like generations of Americans and Europeans before them, many West Germans believed that a socialist government inherently resulted in mass hunger. *Der Spiegel* regularly reported throughout the 1950s and 1960s that "hunger, the vulture that circles over the socialist reconstruction, is hovering over the German Soviet zone."[33] Until the construction of the Berlin Wall in 1961, the FRG's most important agricultural convention, the *Grüne Woche*, offered free products to all East German visitors, who were assumed to suffer from food shortages. Beginning in the late 1950s, the West Berlin government began stockpiling groceries in city storehouses because advisers were predicting severe food shortages in the wake of an anticipated reunification; decades before Gabi was depicted devouring her "banana," West German economists imagined hordes of half-starved East Germans gobbling up their supplies of sugar, butter, and meat.[34]

The GDR's association with hunger meant that, in the West German imagination, the country became a constant reminder of a painful past. Western visitors described trips across the border as encounters with a sort of suffering, scarcity, and deprivation that was historically, if not personally, West Germans' own. *Der Spiegel* explained in 1990 that the West German tourist traveling to the East "quickly sees that he is on a journey in a foreign land, the land of his own past."[35] And, when they reflected on their past, West Germans were overwhelmed by memories of hunger.

Indeed, their own past hunger not only confirmed but actually maintained the reality of East German hunger, as the FRG's steady shipment of "food aid" packages across the border confirmed. In 1954, the West German journal *Prima* mused that

> food packages seem to be a permanent aspect of our age. Before the currency reform, many lives depended on them. That's how it was with us. Then came the great [currency] reform, and suddenly we were no longer dependent on the food packages. *We* were not. But on the other side of the oft-cited curtain not much has changed, and so we now send packages across it.[36]

Even as the GDR struggled with its growing obesity epidemic in the 1970s and 80s, these packages continued to flow.[37] Inspired by the tremendous success of the airlift, such explicitly political usage of food aid had been especially common during the early years of the Cold War. In 1953, in the immediate aftermath of the June 17 uprising, the United States had initiated a controversial Food Relief Program intended to destabilize the socialist government. The program called for the distribution of packages containing luxury food items, including sweets, meats, fats, and processed foods, to every GDR citizen; all that was needed to claim a food package was an East German identification card. By the time the program was dismantled in October 1953, more than five million boxes had been distributed, reaching a remarkable one-third of the GDR's population.[38] Such transnational projects to feed hungry Germans proved a constant through both world wars and Cold War, revealing the interconnectedness of the industrial food system and the multiple forms of modern warfare.

Notably, the disappearance of East Germany in 1990 did not make the category of German hunger irrelevant. Instead, it allowed this hunger to emerge in new forms, losing its Cold War association with communism and instead returning to its earlier incarnation as a form of apolitical human suffering that demanded moral recognition. Since 1990 cultural critics have noted that one of the most striking aspects of German national identity has been an intense interest in the county's historic suffering—specifically, the suffering of non-Jewish Germans during and immediately after the Second World War. A resurgence of interest in the Hunger Years has inspired reissues of wartime and postwar "poverty cookbooks," as well as various television films and docudramas with titles like "The Hunger Winter: Surviving in Bombed Out Germany."[39] As had been the case during the actual occupation, this rediscovery of German suffering has inspired comparisons with the Holocaust. Unlike during the Hunger Years, when analogies between disparate categories of starved bodies inspired assertions of the human "right to food," these newer comparisons assert the collective right to embrace a narrative of both national pride and national victimhood.

In fact, the reunification of Germany in 1990 evoked earlier projects of nation-making in many ways. As had been the case after both world wars, the Cold War ended with the creation of a new German state. As had always been the case, creating new Germans was a political and economic project that focused special attention on food consumption as a way of performing citizenship. The ultimate triumph of the West over the East meant that shopping became valorized as the political-economic act that could successfully unite a long-divided populace. As historian Rainer Gries evocatively put it, "the epiphany of the West German system revealed itself at specific significant locations, above all at shops and supermarkets."[40] In other words, the centrality of shopping to West German identity meant that East Germans would have to be taught how to consume in a "Western style" as part of their initiation into the post–Cold War world.[41]

In anticipation of Easterners' inadequate shopping skills, the Ministry of Food, Agriculture, and Forestry sponsored a nutritional-education outreach program in 1991. The program retrofitted several large busses as mobile educational facilities and distributed one to each former East German province. In the program's first year, these buses were visited by over 200,000 former East Germans of all ages, genders, and occupations.[42] However this educational program, like its Cold War predecessors, proved incapable of meaningfully altering people's shopping techniques. Instead, it merely pathologized the East German consumer (much as earlier programs had pathologized housewives), implying that one of the GDR's greatest harms were the creation of inadequate shopping skills among its citizens. The shifting politics of food in Germany thus offers a window onto the close connection between citizenship and consumption, historicizing what US historian Lizabeth Cohen has termed the construct of the "citizen-consumer."[43] *Modern Hungers* has argued that, in capitalist as well as socialist economies, citizens' food consumption is always perceived as inadequate, yet it is also intrinsically resistant to optimization.

After reunification, East Germans' poor shopping skills were assumed to make them especially prone to obesity. However, obesity proved a pan-German problem. As early as 1992, nutritionists reported that "similar tendencies toward an unhealthy diet as well as an increase in diet-related illnesses have been noted in both sections of Germany."[44] Despite sweeping political and social changes in the wake of the *Wende*, contemporary German obesity rhetoric has remained strikingly similar to that of the Cold War. Medical professionals continue to interpret fatness as a result of an inadequate or unhealthy consumer marketplace, women's inadequate cooking skills, and unhealthy workplace canteens. In 2001, Renate Künast, Germany's minister of consumer protection, blamed the fact that "in the last 15 years, the number of overweight children and youth has more than doubled" on the massive expansion of foods and snacks marketed to children.[45] In 2013, *Der Spiegel* reported that more than a third of the German workforce lacked access to healthy food at their workplace, finding that half of all working men ate only snacks and sweets during the day, followed by an enormous dinner at home. A concerned insurance spokesperson reminded the country's employers that "worker health is decisive in determining company success in the form of increased motivation and better work results."[46] Unified Germany, the "fattest country" in continental Europe, has toyed with the idea of taxing high-calorie foodstuffs and has instituted various nutritional education programs in schools and workplaces while trying to determine why it is that people insist on purchasing high-calorie and unhealthy foods. Unsurprisingly, despite all such interventions, the numbers on the nation's scales keep rising.

Reunification has meant the loss of an "other" Germany upon which flawed food consumption and production could be projected. With the disappearance of this disordered East German body, ethnicity and race have become more prominent in contemporary discussions of the obesity crisis and the "healthy German body." Nutritionists increasingly blame the country's growing immigrant population, especially Turks, for the country's high levels of overweight. These discussions echoed the racialized language of obesity that has long been widespread in the United States and several other European nations, where ethnic minorities are frequently held responsible for the problem of fatness. Such language ignores the actual history of so-called obesity epidemics; for example, a comparison of East and West German struggles with obesity reveals the ubiquity of the problem independent of population demographics, thus suggesting its deeper biopolitical implications. Obese bodies, much like raced bodies, demand resolution by the state at the same time that they are inherently unresolvable. They are, as Kathleen LeBesco has claimed, "revolting bodies" in the fullest and most troubling sense of the word.[47]

During division, it was not race but gender that became central to the two German states' imaginings of the self and of the other; as a result, since reunification, gender constructions have continued to reinforce and reify the persistent "wall in the mind" [*Mauer im Kopf*]. Gender shaped the two countries' respective food systems, as patterns of female shopping and cooking shaped distinctive cultures of employment and family structures. In the FRG, nearly universal female employment in the GDR became a widely invoked symbol of the country's brutality. A 1952 brochure put out by the Ministry of All-German Questions titled "Work, Work, Work! The 'new rights' of the woman in the Soviet zone," explained that East German women "realized with horror that the value of an individual is exclusively based on his or her productivity as a worker," something that was intrinsically at odds with women's most important work: "the maintenance of family bonds."[48] Here, of course, no work was more important than the voluntary labor of home cooking. According to West German rhetoric, when a woman was forced

> out of the protective four walls of her home ... marriage and family will fall apart under this pressure. The husband will have to take care of himself, home offers him little more than a place to sleep at night, factory canteens are responsible for feeding him ... all personal values will disappear.[49]

Thus a distorted gender system was inseparable from a dysfunctional food culture. On the other hand, the actual quality of East German women's labor was rarely directly discussed; instead, critiques of the GDR tended to emphasize women's experiences as consumers. A West German article about women's lives in the GDR from the mid-1960s described a typical woman's day not in terms of wage labor but consumer labor. Her time was "spent in shopping, or rather 'organizing' and cooking. And when her husband comes home from work in the evening and sits down at the table that has been set more with imagination than with good things, his wife is exhausted from all the trivial errands."[50]

Different expectations of women's wage labor posed a major challenge to the process of the *Wende*; East German women's inability to find employment in unified Germany is the main reason why they were often described as the "losers" of reunification.[51] In 1990, when fewer than half (47%) of all married women with young children in the FRG worked, 94% of East German mothers did.[52] This was to change radically within months of reunification, as East German businesses shut down, were bought out, or were entirely restaffed; women remained the first fired and the least desirable workers for West German employers. East German women were not only accustomed to working; they wanted to work. During the early 1990s, surveys consistently revealed that, despite abysmal employment rates, women from the former GDR wanted to work full-time as well as have children; 89% described the ideal marriage as one with equal employment and familial involvement for both parents.[53] In contrast, a 1996 survey of former West German women found that only 8% wanted to work full-time and have children.[54]

Beyond determining women's expectations of employment, West Germany's gendered food culture shaped broader social policies in the reunified country. Among the first victims of unification were East Germany's mass-feeding programs, especially school lunch programs. Initially, East German nutritionists tried to cast reunification as a positive impetus for canteen reform, calling for "new ideas, creativity and the courage to take a risk . . . in order to entirely change the profile of collective meals in terms of quality, variability, diversity and attractiveness of the offerings." They warned of the importance of preserving the GDR's "multidimensional network of 75,000 establishments of collective meals . . . that currently provide over 11 million citizens with meals."[55] Such early ambitions, however, collapsed under the weight of economic pressures and the enduring West German aversion toward collective meals, especially for children. As the East German educational system was brought into line with that of West Germany, school cafeterias were immediately threatened. As early as 1991, a study found that in the territory of the former GDR "many people (more than 70%) have radically changed their diet . . . Instead of using workplace canteens or school meals as was typical in the East, today lunch is most frequently eaten at home."[56] Unspoken in such reports are the massive implications for women's wage and domestic labor.

The rapid dismantling of the East German school-meal program was one of the most reported-on and most distressing consequences of the *Wende*. Newspapers from the former GDR reported widespread concern over the negative effect of these closures on both childhood health and women's economic independence.[57] Complaints over the fate of East German children's meals were so ubiquitous that they inspired a lengthy article in the *Frankfurter Allgemeine Zeitung*, "As if School Meals Were the Most Important Thing,"[58] in which the author Kurt Reumann complained that East Germans only cared about childcare and school meals, rather than "bigger" political and economic concerns.[59] This book has argued that the significance of school lunches for mothers in the GDR was neither surprising nor foolish. Familial feeding patterns have profoundly shaped women's domestic lives and working habits throughout the century and across different regimes, in West Germany as much as in East Germany.

In 2009—twenty years after Germany's reunification—only 44 percent of mothers with young children were active in the workforce, meaning that "Germany still lags behind the rest of Europe" in terms of gender equity.[60] This low rate is in significant part due to limited state support for full-day schools and daycare centers. Although surveys reveal that more than half of the country's parents want full-day schools with a lunch program, West German nutritionists still associate such schools with dysfunctional families, problem students, and inadequate mothering; the vast majority of German schools end midday, and do not offer a lunch.[61] In 2010 the *New York Times* reported on this conservative holdover, noting that "ten years into the twenty-first century, most schools in Germany still end at lunchtime," a policy that "has powerfully sustained the housewife/mother image of German lore," and that results in remarkably low rates of female employment after childbirth.[62] Despite a rhetorical acceptance of female employment, the new German state has been reluctant to abandon the ideal of the mother at home cooking for her children and husband. In 2012, echoing early West German postwar discourse, *Die Zeit* wondered whether a modern German woman should be forced to work, or if she was "allowed to be a [full-time] housewife." The article waxed nostalgic for the pleasures of a bygone age when "the middle class housewife was in charge. The center of her life was the kitchen, where she dedicated herself to the preparation of meals with a commitment that today, in the age of the frozen pizza, is unimaginable."[63] Such fantasies of "mother's cooking" as authentic, premodern, or traditional belie the fact that home cooking has always been central to the way in which modern industrial economies regulate female wage and domestic labor.

Over the course of the twentieth century, the questions of what, how, and why Germans ate were decisive for personal well-being and happiness, for national economic and social development, for individual and community health, and for the emergence of specific patterns of food production and consumption. Food thus shaped the German citizenry's respective imaginings of the self and the other, as well as their everyday activities, their social networks, and their political ambitions. The collapse of the GDR has not resolved an overwhelming discomfort with women's role in the industrial economy, nor has it settled the dilemma of the too-fat German. Perhaps more surprisingly, the new nation's considerable wealth has not rendered hunger irrelevant as a category of considerable political power—and here, yet again, race has become especially relevant. The history of modern Germany makes abundantly clear that, even as states change their forms in profound and often profoundly violent ways, they continue to rely on the industrial food system for methods of managing populations, shaping peoples' bodies, and structuring their daily lives.

NOTES

Introduction

1. "Deutsche führen Liga der Dicke an," *Berliner Zeitung*, April 20, 2007.
2. "Regierung setzt Deutsche auf Diät," *Berliner Zeitung*, May 10, 2007.
3. Quote taken from http://old.isanh.com/slimming/index.php, accessed on September 5, 2016.
4. Hübner, *Konsens, Konflikt und Kompromiss*, 134.
5. Connelly, *Fatal Misconception*, 28; Davis, *Late Victorian Holocausts*.
6. Davis, *Late Victorian Holocausts*.
7. Nally, "Biopolitics of Food Provisioning," 49.
8. For scholarship on the German nutritional sciences during the Third Reich, see Thoms, "Einbruch, Aufbruch, Durchbruch"; Heim, *Plant Breeding and Agrarian Research*.
9. Treitel, "Max Rubner," 11. More generally, Bunton and Petersen, *Foucault, Health and Medicine*.
10. Coveney, *Food, Morals and Meaning*, 22.
11. For a powerful recent discussion of modern state formation during this era, see Maier, *Leviathan 2.0*.
12. Foucault, *Security Territory Population*, 1.
13. According to Foucault, in modern structures of governmentality,

    there will no longer be this phenomenon of scarcity, of massive, individual and collective hunger that advances absolutely and in step and without discontinuity . . . there will no longer be any scarcity in general, on condition that for a whole series of people, in a whole series of markets, there was some scarcity, some dearness, some difficulty in buying wheat, and consequently some hunger, and it may well be that some people die of hunger after all . . . thus the scarcity-event is split. The scarcity-scourge disappears, but scarcity that causes the death of individuals not only does not disappear, it must not disappear. (Foucault, *Security Territory Population*, 41–42)

    Anna Selmeczi has expanded Foucault's argument to argue that modern governmentality intrinsically incorporates the abandonment of sections of the population by accepting the existence of famines among certain peoples but not others. Selmeczi, ". . . we are being left to burn," in Kiersey and Stokes, *Foucault and International Relations*, 175.
14. Foucault, *Birth of Biopolitics*, 13.
15. For a recent analysis of this phenomenon, see Patel, *Stuffed and Starved*.
16. Watts, "Heart of Darkness," 25.
17. Forster, "World War I," 51.
18. Collingham, *Taste of War*, 12.
19. Lévi-Strauss, *Raw and the Cooked*; Douglas, *Purity and Danger*.

20. It remains unusual for German history books to explore both the world wars and the Cold War. A recent and outstanding exception is Monica Black's *Death in Berlin*.
21. See Davis, *Late Victorian Holocausts*; Vernon, *Hunger*.
22. Because of the centrality of the British Blockade to the German experience of World War I, there are several excellent studies of Germany's food system during the war. See Offer, *First World War*; Davis, *Home Fires Burning*. Recent works on the Third Reich have drawn attention to the centrality of food concerns during the Nazi invasion of the East and the Holocaust. Snyder, *Black Earth*; Tooze, *Wages of Destruction*; Gerlach, *Krieg, Ernährung, Völkermord*. The largest body of scholarship on the politics of food has concentrated on the Allied occupation from 1945 to 1949. See Steege, *Black Market*; Grossmann, *Jews, Germans, and Allies*.
23. Ferguson, "Culinary Nationalism."
24. Salaman, *History and Social Influence of the Potato*; Soluri, *Banana Cultures*.
25. There have been some recent studies of German foodways. See Heinzelmann, *Beyond Bratwurst*; Bach, *Kitchen, Food, and Cooking*.
26. On the emerging prominence of "food history" in historical scholarship, see Freedman, Chaplin, and Albala, *Food in Time and Place*. Also see Claflin and Scholliers, *Writing Food History*.
27. Braudel, *Civilization and Capitalism*.
28. The classic study remains Mintz, *Sweetness and Power*.
29. Marx, *German Ideology*, 47.
30. The exception is the substantial attention that has been paid to famines under communist rule, especially in China and the USSR. See Middell and Wemheuer, *Hunger, Nutrition and Rationing*.
31. Bohstedt, *Politics of Provisions*.
32. Vernon, *Hunger*, 5.
33. Vrints, "Beyond Victimization, 102. See also Davis, *Home Fires Burning*.
34. Rothenberg, *Art of Warfare*, 130.
35. Food and War, December 5, 1940, National Committee on Food for the Small Democracies Records, box 138, Hoover Institution Archives.
36. For an important discussion of the relationship between racism and the starving body in Nazi concentration camps, see Agamben, *Remnants of Auschwitz*.
37. Edkins, *Whose Hunger*, 83.
38. Foucault, *Birth of Biopolitics*, 328.
39. For just a few among numerous titles, see Brownell and Horgen, *Food Fight*; Gilman, *Fat*.
40. Edith Sheffer's monograph is a model of this sort of approach. Sheffer, *Burned Bridge*.

Chapter 1

1. Hoover, "Weapon of Food," 197.
2. Wagemann, *Die Nahrungswirtschaft des Auslandes*, 53.
3. Nützenadel, "World without Famine," 15.
4. Koistinen, *Mobilizing for Modern War*, 1.
5. Geyer, "Teuerungsprotest und Teuerungsunruhen," 324.
6. Münzenberg, *Über Grösse, Ursache und Bekämpfung der Hungersnot*, 21.
7. Jourdain, "Air Raid Reprisals," 551.
8. Hull, *Scrap of Paper*, 176.
9. Jourdain, "Air Raid Reprisals," 550.
10. Van der Kloot, "Ernest Starling's Analysis," 190–191.
11. Kramer, *Dynamic of Destruction*, 154.
12. "How Germany's Food Problem Was Met," *New York Times*, April 16, 1916.
13. Quoted in von François, *Deutschlands Hungersnot*, 45.
14. Herwig, "Total Rhetoric, Limited War," 195.
15. Quoted in Verhey, *Spirit of 1914*, 194.
16. Monger, *Patriotism and Propaganda*, 21.
17. Veit, *Modern Food, Moral Food*, 61.
18. Smith, *Food in Wartime*.

19. Tooze, *Deluge*, 74.
20. Jones, "Nitrogen: Its Fixation," 428.
21. Melillo, "First Green Revolution."
22. Charles, *Master Mind*, 175.
23. Jones, "Nitrogen: Its Fixation," 419.
24. Pranke, "Cyanamid Industry," 80. When Haber was awarded the 1918 Nobel Prize for ammonia production, there was great protest as many claimed that his invention had prolonged the war and thus increased the resultant suffering and death. In its award speech, however, the prize committee described his discovery not as a military but an agricultural innovation, "an exceedingly important means of advancing agriculture and the welfare of mankind." Quoted in Brown, *A Most Damnable Invention*, 231.
25. "Chemistry and the War," *Outlook* 117 (October 3, 1917).
26. Beveridge, *Blockade and the Civilian Population*, 9–10.
27. Teuteberg, "Food Provisioning on the German Home Front," 60.
28. "Britain to Control Fats: New Branch of the Munitions Ministry Is Established," *New York Times*, March 10, 1917.
29. See Russell, *War and Nature*, 2001. This relationship continued over the twentieth century, from German chemist Gerhard Schrader's accidental discovery of nerve gas in 1936 while working on developing insecticides to the United States' use of DDT in the Vietnam War.
30. Lummel, "Food Provisioning," 18.
31. See Davis, *Home Fires Burning*.
32. "Crops May Decide Fate of Germany," *New York Times*, August 13, 1916.
33. "Crops May Decide Fate of Germany," *New York Times*, August 13, 1916.
34. Veit, *Modern Food, Moral Food*, 57.
35. Chickering, *Imperial Germany*, 42.
36. Burchardt, "Die Auswirkungen der Kriegswirtschaft," 72.
37. Bessel, *Germany after the First World War*, 35; Chickering, *Imperial Germany*, 41; Teuteberg, "Food Provisioning on the German Home Front," 60.
38. Bessel, *Germany after the First World War*, 35.
39. Burchardt, "Die Auswirkungen der Kriegswirtschaft," 68.
40. Kramer, *Dynamic of Destruction*, 153.
41. Lummel, "Food Provisioning," 20. The German army's policy of aggressive requisitions and food seizures in the lands that it occupied further augmented soldiers' diets.
42. Feldman, *Great Disorder*, 58; Moeller, "Dimensions of Social Conflict."
43. Van der Kloot, "Ernest Starling's Analysis," 190–191.
44. Der Kriegsernährungsamt, *Die Kriegsernährungswirtschaft 1917*, 75.
45. Quoted in Reagin, *Sweeping the German Nation*, 78.
46. Quoted in "How Germany's Food Problem Was Met," *New York Times*, April 16, 1916.
47. "Germany Unlikely to Increase Crops; Food Situation May Not Become Any Worse but Scarcely Can Improve," *New York Times*, February 17, 1917.
48. Wagemann, *Die Nahrungswirtschaft*, 1.
49. "We Have Enough Food," *New York Times*, January 28, 1917.
50. An sämtliche Zeitungen, Zeitschriften und Korrespondenzen, March 22, 1917, BArch R3601/513.
51. An sämtliche Zeitungen, Zeitschriften und Korrespondenzen, March 22, 1917, BArch R3601/513.
52. "Germany Unlikely to Increase Crops; Food Situation May Not Become Any Worse but Scarcely Can Improve," *New York Times*, February 17, 1917.
53. "Crops May Decide Fate," *New York Times*, August 13, 1916.
54. Bruntz, *Allied Propaganda*, 111.
55. Bruntz, *Allied Propaganda*, 45.
56. Hueppe, *Unser täglich Brot*, 133.
57. Liulevicius, *War Land on the Eastern Front*, 204.
58. Der "Brotfrieden" mit der Ukraine, March 15, 1918, BArch R3601/475.
59. Die Ukraine als Getreideausfuhrland, February 9, 1918, BArch R3601/475.

60. Wirtschaftsvernunft und Wirtschaftsmoral: ein Kapital zur Ernährungspolitik, March 31, 1918, BArch R3601/475.
61. Surface and Bland, *American Food*, 193.
62. Quoted in Howard, "Social and Political Consequences," 183.
63. An Herr Reichskanzler, November 27, 1922, BArch R43 I/1261.
64. Berliner Medizinische Gesellschaft, *Starving of Germany*, 7.
65. Unsere Ernährung. Selbsterhaltung oder Untergang? January 25, 1919, BArch R3601/485.
66. Feldman, *Great Disorder*, 103.
67. Recent scholarship has begun to dispute the idea that the blockade was the primary cause of Germany's food problems. Many factors contributed to these shortages, including Germany's severing of trade relations with nations that had previously supplied it with foodstuffs (especially significant in the case of Russia) and the shortsightedness of its wartime food policies, which prioritized military needs over civilian ones. The British had long claimed that Germany's food crisis was due not to actual shortages but to the poorly organized and inequitable distribution of food. See Starling, *Report on Food Conditions*, 4. Such revisionist accounts also generally provide less extreme statistics for the harms the shortages caused. One such economic estimate claimed that "the war at its worst caused the loss of not much more than a decade of public health progress." See Offer, *First World War*, 38.
68. This number is extremely difficult to determine because it relies on judgment calls regarding "normal" vs. "extra" deaths.
69. Hull, *Scrap of Paper*, 168.
70. Roerkohl, *Hungerblockade und Heimatfront*, 309.
71. Heyll, "Der Kampf ums Eiweissminimum," 2771.
72. Black, *Death in Berlin*, 22.
73. Quoted in Miller, Potthoff, and Matthias, *Die Regierung der Volksbeauftragten*, 205.
74. Horne and Kramer, *German Atrocities*.
75. Hull, *Absolute Destruction*, 230.
76. Watenpaugh, *Bread from Stones*.
77. Bane and Lutz, *Blockade of Germany*, 691.
78. Bane and Lutz, *Blockade of Germany*. 739.
79. Hoover, *Food in War*, 11.
80. David Wilhelm, "Feeding a Starving World," *The Independent*, February 8, 1919.
81. Bane and Lutz, *Blockade of Germany*, 16.
82. "The March of Events," *World's Work*, January 1919.
83. Koistinen, *Mobilizing for Modern War*, 263.
84. Veit, *Modern Food, Moral Food*, 6.
85. United States Congress, *Foodstuffs and Supplies for Europe*, 4.
86. Bane and Lutz, *Blockade of Germany*, 416.
87. Bane and Lutz, *Blockade of Germany*, 16.
88. "The March of Events," *World's Work*, January 1919.
89. "The March of Events," *World's Work*, January 1919.
90. Bane and Lutz, *Blockade of Germany*, 638–639.
91. United States Congress, *Foodstuffs and Supplies*, 12.
92. United States Congress, *Foodstuffs and Supplies*, 5.
93. Bane and Lutz, *Blockade of Germany*, 798.
94. Bane and Lutz, *Blockade of Germany*, 676.
95. Allen, "Sharing Scarcity," 381.
96. United States Congress, *Foodstuffs and Supplies*, 12.
97. Conditions in Germany, July 3, 1920, Friends' War Victims' Relief Committee Records, box 2, Hoover Institution Archives.
98. Report, February 27, 1920, Friends' War Victims' Relief Committee Records, box 2, Hoover Institution Archives.
99. Report, February 27, 1920, Friends' War Victims' Relief Committee Records, box 2, Hoover Institution Archives.
100. The Degradation of the Germans, 1919, Friends' War Victims' Relief Committee Records, box 2, Hoover Institution Archives.

101. Conditions in Germany, July 3, 1920, Friends' War Victims' Relief Committee Records, box 2, Hoover Institution Archives.
102. Starving the German Nation, May 12, 1920, Friends' War Victims' Relief Committee Records, box 2, Hoover Institution Archives.
103. Bane and Lutz, *Blockade of Germany*, 673.
104. Starving the German Nation, May 12, 1920, Friends' War Victims' Relief Committee Records, box 2, Hoover Institution Archives.
105. Starling, *Report on Food Conditions*, 10.
106. Goldring, *What the Army Thinks of the Blockade*, n.p.
107. Brailsford, *Across the Blockade*, 122.
108. Germany was followed by Poland and Czechoslovakia, which received around 270,000 and 230,000 respectively. Bane and Lutz, *Organization of American Relief*, 606.
109. Bane and Lutz, *Organization of American Relief*, 650.
110. Arnold-Forster, *Blockade*, 31.
111. Between 1923 and 1924 American philanthropists formed the American Committee for the Relief of German Children. The committee raised more than four million dollars in private donations to continue these feeding programs, which at their peak reached over a million German children. See Curti, *American Philanthropy Abroad*, 277. Unlike the ARA, the Children's Fund was a purely voluntary private charity. Although many of its supplies were donated directly by the Congress, the organization lacked an official charter or any formal affiliation with the US government. In addition to supporting these organizations, German Americans sent an estimated $120,000,000 in private aid to German citizens between 1919 and 1921. Strickland, "American Aid to Germany," 257.
112. Rodgers, "Herbert Hoover and American Relief," 32.
113. Bane and Lutz, *Blockade of Germany*, 691.
114. Surface and Bland, *American Food*, 198.
115. Surface and Bland, *American Food*, 84.
116. Carruth, "War Rations and the Food Politics," 776.
117. Cullather, *Hungry World*, 22.
118. Schumann, *Political Violence in the Weimar Republic*.
119. Bessel, *Germany after the First World War*, 19, 213.
120. Feldman, *Great Disorder*, 101.
121. Bessel, *Germany after the First World War*, 196.
122. Torp, *Konsum und Politik in der Weimarer Republik*, 66–67.
123. "Crops May Decide Fate," *New York Times*, August 13, 1916.
124. Drahn und Leonhard, *Unterirdische Literatur*, 54.
125. Lüdtke, "Hunger in der Großen Depression," 169.
126. Drahn und Leonhard, *Unterirdische Literatur*, 80.
127. Drahn und Leonhard, *Unterirdische Literatur*, 62.
128. Lüdtke, "Hunger in der Großen Depression," 171.
129. "Hilft den Hamburger Hafenarbeiter," 1923, German Subject Collection, box 20, Hoover Institution Archives.
130. "Hunger," German Subject Collection, box 18, Hoover Institution Archives.
131. Wurm, Mann, and Barthel, *Hunger in Deutschland*, 29.
132. Auf das Schreiben, June 18, 1921, BArch R43I/1270.
133. Rubmann, *Hunger!*, 36.
134. Many wartime food riots actually confirmed and strengthened the political status quo. As women gathered to denounce profiteering or demand a lowering of bread prices, they called on the Imperial government to resume its traditional political responsibilities instead of demanding a change in government. Davis, *Home Fires Burning*.
135. Schumann, *Political Violence in the Weimar Republic*, 14.
136. Lefevre, "Lebensmittelunruhen in Berlin," 359.
137. Feldman, "Kriegswirtschaft und Zwangswirtschaft."
138. Schumacher, *Land und Politik*, 61–62.
139. Die Fehler unserer Kriegsernährung, February 19, 1918, BArch R3601/475.
140. von François, *Deutschlands Hungersnot*, 4.

141. von François, *Deutschlands Hungersnot*, 5.
142. Der Pogrom am deutschen und am russischen Volke, German Subject Collection, box 44, Hoover Institution Archives.
143. Quoted in Feldman, *Great Disorder*, 779.
144. Kruse and Hintze, *Sparsame Ernährung*, n.p.
145. Horne and Kramer, *German Atrocities*, 373–374.
146. Hull, *Scrap of Paper*, 5.
147. Richter, *Family Life in Germany*, 13.
148. See, for example, Schall, *Relief for the Distressed and Starving*; League of Nations, "Economic Depression and Public Health"; League of Nations, "Most Suitable Methods."
149. Unsere Ernährung. Selbsterhaltung oder Untergang? BArch R3601/485. See also Schaeffer, *War against Women and Children*.
150. Rübner, *Hauptbericht der freien wissenschaftlichen Kommission*, 17.
151. Rübner, *Hauptbericht der freien wissenschaftlichen Kommission*, 16.
152. Hull, *Scrap of Paper*, 241.
153. Ehrenberg, *Volksernährung und Christentum*, 5.
154. An Staatssekretäriat Pünder, January 15, 1932, BArch R431/2427.
155. Menne and FitzGerald, *Armistice and Germany's Food*, 96.
156. Menne and FitzGerald, *Armistice and Germany's Food*, 5.

Chapter 2

1. League of Nations, "Economic Depression and Public Health," 425.
2. Dornheim, "Rasse, Raum und Autarkie."
3. Miller, "Pre-War Nazi Agrarian Policy," 176.
4. Miller, "Pre-War Nazi Agrarian Policy," 176.
5. Nathan and Fried, *Nazi Economic System*, 89.
6. Clauß, *Der Kampf ums Brot*, 37–38.
7. Offer, "Blockade of Germany," 183.
8. Simmons, "Starvation Science."
9. Veit, *Modern Food, Moral Food*, 102.
10. von Wendt, *Kost und Kultur*, 7. As leaders in these sciences, Germans felt the loss of their colonies after World War I especially sharply. Nonetheless, despite having lost their direct access to colonial bodies, nutritionists continued their research into the racial underpinnings of diet, analyzing the diet of peoples in areas as far flung as the mountains of Tibet and Pakistan in order to discover optimal recipes for Aryan and non-Aryan bodies alike. See Bircher, *Hunsa: Das Volk*.
11. Simmons, "Rasse und Ernährung," 158.
12. Über den Ernährungszustand der deutschen Kinder, August 19, 1921, BArch R43 I/1259.
13. Fischer and Heimann, *Deutsche Kinderfibel*, 139.
14. Doris Kirkpatrick, "Role of Woman in Germany; She Works Because She Must and She Fears That Another War Will Take Her Sons," *New York Times*, September 26, 1937.
15. Shub, *Starvation over Europe*, 9.
16. Goldberg, "Racial States," 245.
17. Hitler, "Das Winterhilfswerk ist für uns Nationalsozialisten," 716–717.
18. See *Eintopf-Gerichte*; Horn, *Der Eintopf—Das deutsche Spargericht*; Weichardt, *101 Eintopf-Gerichte*; Lutz, *Eintopf-Gerichte von Julie Lutz*; Richert, *Bereite dein Eintopf-Gericht*; Schubuth, *Schmackhafter Eintopf, frohe Esser*.
19. Werdelmann, *Der Marschbefehl des Gaues Kurmark*, 31.
20. Köstlin, "Der Eintopf der Deutschen," 223.
21. Winckel, "Zukunftsprobleme der deutschen Volksernährung," 57.
22. Werdelmann, *Der Marschbefehl des Gaues Kurmark*, 15.
23. Quoted in Zolling, *Zwischen Integration und Segregation*, 170–171.
24. Clauß, *Der Kampf ums Brot*, 11.
25. Hertwig, *Richtige Ernährung*, 2.
26. Nelson, *ABC des langen Lebens*, 13.

27. Rösch, *Hausfrauen, jetzt verwendet*, 5.
28. Die deutsche Arbeitsfront, *Gemeinschaftsverpflegung in Lager*, 106.
29. Reagin, "Marktordnung and Autarkic Housekeeping," 19.
30. Reichsausschuß für Volkswirtschaftliche Aufklärung, *Ernährungspolitik und Schule*, 5.
31. "Unnötige Angstkäufe," 169.
32. "Unsere Ernährungslage," 8.
33. Dittmar, *Deutschland erweitert seinen Nahrungsraum*, 5.
34. Haas, *Veränderungen in der deutschen Volksernährung*, 53.
35. Clauß, *Der Kampf ums Brot*, 26.
36. Darré, *Der Schweinemord*.
37. Meyer, "Drei Jahre Forschungsdienst," 1.
38. Betr: die Weltmission der Kartoffel in Mitteleuropa und Afrika, December 11, 1917, BArch R3601/470.
39. Glatzel, *Nahrung und Ernährung*, 253.
40. Nothnagel, *Harmonische Ernährung*, 5.
41. Betr: Bezeichnung des prittlbacher Gewürzes mit Pfeffergeschmack, August 30, 1944, BArch NS3/1431.
42. Max Winckel, "Hunger und Politik." *Zeitschrift für Volksernährung* 10 (May 20, 1937).
43. Betr: Vitaminierung von Mehl, July 4, 1951, DIFE Nr. 246.
44. Daun, *Geschäfte mit dem Hunger*, 6.
45. Daun, *Geschäfte mit dem Hunger*, 154.
46. Reichsausschuß für Volkswirtschaftliche Aufklärung, *Ernährungspolitik und Schule*, 29
47. Quoted in Gies, "Aufgaben und Probleme der nationalsozialistischen Ernährungswirtschaft," 481.
48. Daun, *Geschäfte mit dem Hunger*, 5–6.
49. Reichsausschuß für Volkswirtschaftliche Aufklärung, *Ernährungspolitik und Schule*, 8.
50. Gerhardt, *Nazi Hunger Politics*, 52.
51. Meyer, *Bodenordnung als volkspolitische Aufgabe*, 11.
52. Quoted in Corni and Gies, *Blut und Boden*, 170.
53. Zischka, *Brot für Zwei Milliarden Menschen*, 6–7.
54. Reichsausschuß für Volkswirtschaftliche Aufklärung, *Ernährungspolitik und Schule*, 7.
55. Betr. Festgerichte, November 19, 1935, Stadtarchiv Düsseldorf RW 47/129.
56. Neumann, "Nutritional Physiology in the 'Third Reich,'" 50.
57. Miller, "Pre-War Nazi Agrarian Policy," 181.
58. Betr: Institut für Vitamin- und Ernährungsforschung, August 25, 1939, DIFE Nr. 199.
59. Total government spending between 1936 and 1943 was distributed as follows: humanities, 11,810,924 RM; natural sciences and technology, 15,016,642 RM; and biology and agricultural sciences, 17,423,868.377 RM. Flachowsky, *Von der Notgemeinschaft zum Reichsforschungsrat*, 378–379.
60. Thoms, "Innovative Power of War," 257.
61. "German Dieticians See Hope in Yeast: Chemists Attack Food Problem by Stretching Efficiency of Vegetable Albumen, Sawdust as Fodder Base," *New York Times*, March 27, 1938.
62. Gerson, "Feeding the German Army," 1471.
63. C. Lester Walker, "Secrets by the Thousands," *Harpers*, October 1946.
64. Black, "Food: War and Postwar," 3.
65. Betr: Koniferennadeln als Vitaminträger für Kriegsgefangenen im Heimatkriegsgebiet, February 18, 1943, BArch R3601/2366.
66. Jacobeit and Kopke, *Die biologisch-dynamische Wirtschaftsweise im KZ*, 120.
67. Hitler, *Mein Kampf*, 3.
68. Hertwig, *Richtige Ernährung*, 26.
69. Winckel, "Hunger und Politik."
70. Quoted in Corni and Gies, *Blut und Boden*, 451.
71. Wölfer, *Der deutsche Mensch in der Landwirtschaft*, 175–176.
72. Kraft, *Wahrheiten über das Brot*, 2.
73. Melzer, *Vollwerternährung*, 183.
74. Nicosia, "Jewish Farmers in Hitler's Germany," 375.

75. Blackbourn, *Conquest of Nature*, 243.
76. Heim, *Plant Breeding and Agrarian Research*, 19.
77. Smith, *German Land Hunger*, 249.
78. "Der Ostraum—die Kornkammer Europas," *Gemeinschaftsverpflegung mit Volksernährung* 5 (December 1942).
79. Sicherung der Zukunft, 1942, BArch NS26/2123.
80. Winckel, "Zukunftsprobleme der deutschen Volksernährung," 58.
81. Aly, *Hitler's Beneficiaries*, 104–106.
82. Erhöhung der Brot- und Fleischrationen, September 14, 1942, BArch R 43 II/614.
83. Kay, "Germany's Staatssekretäre," 685.
84. Klemann and Kudryashov, *Occupied Economies*, 253.
85. Klemann and Kudryashoz, *Occupied Economies*, 105.
86. Burchardt, "Die Auswirkungen der Kriegswirtschaft," 94.
87. Klemann and Kudryashoz, *Occupied Economies*.
88. For example, less than 10% of the more than nine million tons of grain seized from the Soviet Union ended up in Germany. Voglis, "Surviving Hunger," 19.
89. Europe at the Mercy of Germany for Food, November 10, 1942, National Committee on Food for the Small Democracies Records, box 148, Hoover Institution Archives.
90. Müller, "Stalingrad," 132.
91. Kunz, "Das Beispiel Charkow."
92. Quoted in Kühne, *Belonging and Genocide*, 106.
93. Müller, "Stalingrad," 138.
94. Psychological Warfare Division, January 7, 1945, Daniel Lerner Collection, box 2, Hoover Institution Archives.
95. Betr: Mitführung von Nahrungsmitteln in das Reichsgebiet, July 4, 1944, Siemens-Archiv 11098.1.
96. Betr: Ernährungslage, August 24, 1944, DIFE Nr. 234.
97. Protokoll, August 3, 1944, Daniel Lerner Collection, box 6, Hoover Institution Archives.
98. Wehrmacht, August 1, 1944, Daniel Lerner Collection, box 6, Hoover Institution Archives.
99. The Wehrmacht didn't know: Concentration Camp Atrocities, February 21, 1945, Daniel Lerner Collection, box 3, Hoover Institution Archives.
100. Germany's Food Situation Stable, September 22, 1944, Daniel Lerner Collection, box 7, Hoover Institution Archives.
101. "Hinter glänzender Fassade: Hunger!," 74.
102. "Deutschland gab Europa," 341.
103. "Vorboten der Lebensmittelrationierung," 80.
104. "Hinter glänzender Fassade: Hunger!," 74.
105. Die Parole des Feldmarschalls für die Erzeugungsschlacht 1940, February 16, 1940, BArch R 43 II/613.
106. "Die Frage nach den Vorräten," 181.
107. "Deutschland gab Europa," 341.
108. "Drüben und hüben," 216. This is simply false; Greece suffered from a horrific famine because of the Nazi occupation policy. Hionidou, *Famine and Death*, 261.
109. "Deutschland gab Europa," 341.
110. "Hinter glänzender Fassade: Hunger!," 74. See also "Hungersnot: Wie Gewöhnlich," 50.
111. Germany's Food Situation Stable, September 22, 1944, Daniel Lerner Collection, box 7, Hoover Institution Archives.
112. Fishburn, "Won't Starve until Fall," 38.
113. Goldberg, "Racial States," 246.
114. Betr: Lebensmittelversorgung von Juden, November 2, 1942, Siemens-Archiv 11098.2.
115. Spiekermann, "Vollkornbrot in Deutschland," 42–43.
116. Betr: Lebensmittelversorgung von Juden, November 2, 1942, Siemens-Archiv 11098.2.
117. Rundspruch Nr. I/449, December 12, 1940, Landesarchiv Berlin, B Rep 010-20/1677.
118. Rundspruch Nr. I/463, December 21, 1940, Landesarchiv Berlin, B Rep 010-20/1677.
119. Betr: Lebensmittelversorgung von Juden, November 2, 1942, Siemens-Archiv 11098.2.

120. Betr: Lebensmittelversorgung der Juden im Arbeitseinsatz, February 18, 1943, BArch R3601/2366.
121. Gellately, *Gestapo and German Society*, 136.
122. Betrifft: Abgabe von Gartenbauerzeugnissen vom Handel an den Verbraucher, August 16, 1941, Stadtarchiv Köln, Kölner Preisbehoerde 530/175.
123. Preisbehörde, August 11, 1941, Stadtarchiv Köln, Kölner Preisbehoerde 530/175.
124. Betrifft: Abgabe von Gartenbauerzeugnissen vom Handel an den Verbraucher, August 16, 1941, Stadtarchiv Köln, Kölner Preisbehoerde 530/175.
125. Langer, "Die Front gegen den Hunger," 268.
126. For example, "Vom Borschtsch und Schtschi," 5.
127. Verbrauch von Nahrungsmitteln durch jüdische Bevölkerung und Häftlinge, November 9, 1988, DIFE Nr. 226.
128. Verbrauch von Nahrungsmitteln durch jüdische Bevölkerung und Häftlinge, November 9, 1988, DIFE Nr. 226.
129. Tooze, *Wages of Destruction*, 366.
130. German Position on Food Held Good, January 18, 1943, National Committee on Food for the Small Democracies Records, box 148, Hoover Institution Archives.
131. Betr: Lebensmittelversorgung der Juden, June 1, 1942, BArch R 43 II/614.
132. Betr: Lebensmittelversorgung der Juden, June 1, 1942, BArch R 43 II/614.
133. Bonwetsch, "Sowjetische Zwangsarbeiter," 532.
134. Quoted in Obens, *Wir hatten viel Hunger*, 77.
135. See BArch R3101/14475.
136. Branntweinzuteilung an Ausländer, January 5, 1945, Siemens-Archiv 11097.1.
137. Quoted in Schäfer, *Zwangsarbeiter und NS Rassenpolitik*, 102.
138. Ernährungs- und Beschaffungslage, July 1, 1942, DIFE Nr. 225.
139. An alle Lagerkommandanten, October 23, 1943, DIFE Nr. 225.
140. Quoted in Heim, *Plant Breeding and Agrarian Research*, 74.
141. Biraud, "Health in Europe," 634.
142. Extracts from Letters from Foreign Workers, June 13, 1945, Daniel Lerner Collection, box 9, Hoover Institution Archives.
143. Betr: Lebensmittelzuteilungen an ausländische Zivilarbeiter, April 17, 1943, BArch R3601/2366.
144. Betr: AZ-Wochenkarten, November 23, 1942, Siemen-Archiv 11097.1.
145. Ernährungs- und Beschaffungslage, July 1, 1942, DIFE Nr. 225.
146. Erster Bericht über den Ernährungsgrossversuch an ausländischen Arbeitskräften, September 1, 1944, DIFE Nr. 225.
147. See Siemens-Archiv 11097.1.
148. Betrifft: Erfahrung mit Ausländern, April 9, 1943, Siemens-Archiv 19022.
149. Verpflegung der Ostarbeiter, June 1944, BArch R55/23538.
150. Gerlach, *Krieg, Ernährung, Völkermord*.
151. Quoted in Schäfer, *Zwangsarbeiter und NS Rassenpolitik*, 43.
152. These stereotypes continued after war's end, when the Russians' ostensibly minimal nutritional requirements made them models for Germans facing their own food crisis. For example, a 1948 cookbook offering tips for the "fight against starvation" looked to "Russian folk cuisine" as a model; the author notes that Russians, who purportedly subsisted exclusively on "porridge, bread, vegetables and sunflower seeds," not only survived, but the "bulk of the population is in this way healthy, has excellent teeth, is productive and biologically superior to our city population and regrettably also our rural population." Saller, *Kampf dem Hunger*, 16–17.
153. Quoted in Corni and Gies, *Blut und Boden*, 534.
154. Betrifft: Verpflegung sowjetischer Kriegsgefangener im Heimatkriegsgebiet, December 23, 1941, Werner Klatt Collection, folder 23, Hoover Institution Archives.
155. Quoted in Bach and Leyendecker, *Ich habe geweint*, 94.
156. Quoted in Bach and Leyendecker, *Ich habe geweint*, 94.
157. Spindler and Horbelt, *Tante Linas Kriegskochbuch*, 124.
158. Quoted in Blackbourn, *Conquest of Nature*, 292.

159. Snyder, *Bloodlands*, xiv.
160. According to an American agricultural expert writing in the midst of postwar reconstruction, "German agricultural production in the Second World War did not exhibit signs of serious disruption until 1944." Raup, "Postwar Recovery," 2.
161. Higgins, "Germany's Bid for Agricultural Self Sufficiency," 456.
162. Klemann and Kudryashoz, *Occupied Economies*, 256.
163. Baten, *Autarchy, Market Disintegration*, 6.
164. Wulff, *Arbeitslosigkeit und Arbeitsbeschaffungsmassnahmen*, 159–160.
165. Höfler-Waag, *Die Arbeits- und Leistungsmedizin*, 70.
166. Kluge, "Kriegs- und Mangelernährung," 68.
167. Baten, *Autarchy, Market Disintegration*, 22.

Chapter 3

1. Knight and Rotha, *World of Plenty*, n.p.
2. Schultz, *Food for the World*, 334.
3. Schultz, *Food for the World*, viii.
4. Sayre, "Rebuilding a War-Torn World," 89.
5. United Nations Conference on Food and Agriculture, *United Nations Conference*, 480.
6. United Nations Conference on Food and Agriculture, *United Nations Conference*, 523.
7. United States Department of Agriculture, *Food for Freedom*, 3.
8. Hoover, *We'll Have to Feed the World Again*, 5.
9. Hoover, *Can Europe's Children*, 4.
10. Beaumont, "Starving for Democracy," 57.
11. Hoover, *Can Europe's Children*, 5.
12. University of Cambridge, *Studies of Undernutrition*, 44.
13. Mollison, "Observations of Cases of Starvation, 5.
14. Kavanaugh, *ORT, the Second World War*, 61.
15. Hottinger, *Hungerkrankheit, Hungerödem, Hungertuberkulose*, 32.
16. Quoted in Steinert, *Nach Holocaust und Zwangsarbeit*, 61.
17. Brink, *Ikonen der Vernichtung*; Knoch, *Die Tat als Bild*.
18. Knoch, *Die Tat als Bild*, 142.
19. Helweg-Larsen, *Famine Disease in German Concentration Camps*, 13.
20. Webster, "From Nazi Legacy to Cold War," 95.
21. Lipscomb, "Medical Aspects of Belsen," 313.
22. Murray, "Recovery from Starvation," 507.
23. Hottinger, *Hungerkrankheit, Hungerödem, Hungertuberkulose*, 234.
24. Mollison, "Observations of Cases of Starvation," 5.
25. For example, African Americans, many of whom had served in the US army in the war against Nazi Germany, used imagery of the Holocaust as a symbol of racial persecution in their own struggle for civil rights; the executive secretary of the NAACP Walter White, for example, complained that "negro veterans … have been done to death or mutilated with savagery equaled only at Buchenwald." Anderson, *Eyes off the Prize*, 63.
26. Paul Betts has noted that postwar socialists openly rejected this "anti-historical" model of a universal set of human rights and instead advocated rights that were socially and politically specific—"social" rights rather than "human" rights. Betts, "Socialism, Social Rights and Human Rights," 408.
27. Helweg-Larsen, *Famine Disease*, 17.
28. Wildenthal, *Language of Human Rights*, 521.
29. Mazower, "Strange Triumph of Human Rights."
30. Bourne, *Starvation in Europe*, 123.
31. Quoted in Steinert, *Nach Holocaust und Zwangsarbeit*, 18.
32. Hirschmann, *Embers Still Burn*, 99.
33. David Walker, "66 Fat SS Girls Face Lean Time until Trial Day," *Daily Mirror*, May 26, 1945.

34. Right-wing British revisionist historian and Holocaust denier David Irving dedicated an entire book to the plan, claiming that "the Morgenthau plan would have meant the death of about ten million Germans due to starvation and disease during the first two years after the end of the war, in addition to the one million who died in the air raids and the three million who died while being expelled from the Eastern regions." Irving, *Der Morgenthau-Plan*, 7.
35. Kimball, *Swords or Ploughshares?*, 25–26.
36. "Potsdam Agreement Protocol of the Proceedings, August 1, 1945," http://www.nato.int/ebookshop/video/declassified/doc_files/Potsdam%20Agreement.pdf, accessed on December 2, 2016.
37. See "German PoW Ration Cut—'Civvy' Food Call by M.P.," *Daily Mirror*, April 24, 1945.
38. Radio Report to the American People on the Potsdam Conference (August 9, 1945), by Harry S. Truman, http://millercenter.org/president/truman/speeches/speech-3821, accessed on December 3, 2016
39. "Food Stocks Gone, M'narney Reports: Tells Hoover Supply Will Not Sustain Life," *New York Times*, April 14, 1946.
40. Zweiniger-Bargielowska, *Austerity in Britain*; Bentley, *Eating for Victory*.
41. Warum keine Milchzulagen?, November 17, 1947, Landesarchiv Berlin B Rep 012/9.
42. Auszug aus der Besprechung, September 19, 1945, Landesarchiv Berlin B Rep 209/1551.
43. Auszug aus der Besprechung, September 19, 1945, Landesarchiv Berlin B Rep 209/1551.
44. This "incidental" group made up anywhere between 20% and 40% of the population of the Soviet zone.
45. Harsch, *Revenge of the Domestic*.
46. Gries, *Die Rationen-Gesellschaft*, 96.
47. Wer hat Anspruch auf Zusatzverpflegung?, December 9, 1948, BArch DR2/296.
48. University of Cambridge, *Studies of Undernutrition*, 6.
49. Economic Sub-Commission, Eisen-Giesserei, June 9, 1947, Siemens-Archiv 7542.
50. Quoted in Tieke, *Nach der Stunde Null*, 177.
51. Hungerdemonstrationen im Westen, April 3, 1947, BArch DL1/175.
52. In turn, the Soviets dismissed such accusations as "all lies [and] entirely inaccurate." Presseinformation der deutschen Verwaltung für Handel und Versorgung, February 22, 1947, BArch DL1/123.
53. OMGUS, *German Understanding*, 1.
54. OMGUS, *German Understanding*, 3.
55. OMGUS, *German Understanding*, 5.
56. Orlopp, *Im Kampf gegen den Hunger*, 3.
57. Rothenberger, *Die Hungerjahre nach dem Zweiten Weltkrieg*, 64.
58. Strotdrees, *Höfe, Bauern, Hungerjahre*, 210.
59. Ausschnitte aus einem Informationsbericht des Kreisnachrichtenamtes, May 27, 1946, Sächsisches Staatsarchiv Dresden 11393/211.
60. Gesundheitsgefährdender Überstand in der Ernährungswirtschaft, July 31, 1946, Sächsisches Staatsarchiv Dresden 11391/1758.
61. Pressespiegel Sowjetische Zone, August 5, 1946, BArch DL1/123.
62. Betr: Butter aus der Provinz Sachsen, March 27, 1946, Sächsisches Staatsarchiv Dresden 11393/221.
63. Betr: Gemüsehandlung Vinken, July 30, 1947, Stadtarchiv Köln 530/336.
64. Blick in den Westen, 1947, Landesarchiv Berlin C Rep 120/3239.
65. An das Haupternährungsamt Berlin, October 26, 1947, Landesarchiv Berlin B Rep 012/131.
66. "Hunger-Jubiläum. Es fing so harmlos an," *Der Spiegel* 13 (1947).
67. Grossmann, "Grams, Calories, and Food," 116.
68. Ausschnitte aus einem Informationsbericht des Kreisnachrichtenamtes, May 20, 1946, Sächsisches Staatsarchiv Dresden 11393/211.
69. Letter from Hugo v. Girgensohn, January 31, 1948, United States President's Famine Emergency Committee Records, box 12, Hoover Institution Archives.
70. Letter from Klara Karpf, May 1947, United States President's Famine Emergency Committee Records, box 12, Hoover Institution Archives.

71. Die Brücke der Menschlichkeit: ausländische Liebesgabensendungen für US-Zone, July 15, 1946, BArch R86/3585.
72. Trittel, *Hunger und Politik*, 74.
73. Ferdinand Bertram, "Über Ernährungsschäden vom Standpunkt der zentralen Regulationen Teil II," *Deutsche medizinische Wochenschrift* 5, no. 8 (1948).
74. Quoted in Trittel, *Hunger und Politik*, 110.
75. Die Überwindung des Hungers, August 19, 1949, BArch Z/6/I/239.
76. To the Justice Officer Traunstein, November 4, 1945, Germany (Territory under Allied occupation, 1945-1955: U.S. Zone) Office of Military Government for Bavaria. Kreis Traunstein Records, box 4, Hoover Institution Archives.
77. Quoted in Schulze, *Unruhige Zeiten*, 297.
78. The postwar international food crisis was fodder for anti-Semitism around the world. The Swiss writer Borge Jensen wrote a booklet entitled *World Food Shortage: A Communist-Zionist Plot*. The book linked Communism and Judaism by claiming that "permanent famine and food-rationing were two of the outstanding features of the immense areas controlled directly by the Jewish bureaucracy of Moscow, and, ultimately, by the Jewish international banking houses of Wall and Pine Street, New York." Jensen, *World-Food-Shortage*, 6. For similar arguments from within occupied Germany, see Warum das Volk hungert! Die Lüge von der Welternährungskrise, November 13, 1946, BArch R86/3585.
79. "Bavarian Resists Allies Food Plan," April 3, 1947, United States President's Famine Emergency Committee Records, box 7, Hoover Institution Archives.
80. Steinert, *Nach Holocaust und Zwangsarbeit*, 190.
81. Grossmann, *Jews, Germans, and Allies*, 164.
82. In 1946, the 266,000 DPs in the British zone received the same standard rations as German civilians. The primary difference was that DP workers received more generous supplemental rations. Former camp inmates and victims of Nazi persecution received an extra 400 calories a day. In the American zone, DPs living in internment camps received food that was from American stocks and therefore of a higher quality than that of the other occupying powers. This food made up between 2,000 to 2,400 calories a day; those who could prove their "persecuted" status were given an additional daily supplement. US-British Bipartite Food and Agriculture Panel, *Food and Agriculture*, 62. In the Soviet zone, "Victims of Fascism" were allotted more generous rations than ordinary civilians received, but the food was from standard German supplies. See Landesarchiv Berlin B Rep 209/1551.
83. Grossmann, *Jews, Germans, and Allies*, 112.
84. Zweig, "Feeding the Camps," 840.
85. Quoted in Schulze, *Unruhige Zeiten*, 121.
86. Quoted in Schulze, *Unruhige Zeiten*, 287.
87. Denkschrift für die deutsche Wirtschaftskommission, May 15, 1948, Sächsisches Staatsarchiv Dresden 11393/321.
88. Resolution der deutschen Ärzte zur deutschen Ernährungslage, June 15, 1947, Landesarchiv Berlin B Rep 012/131.
89. Quoted in Trittel, *Hunger und Politik*, 156.
90. Denkschrift für die deutsche Wirtschaftskommission, May 15, 1948, Sächsisches Staatsarchiv Dresden 11393/321.
91. Gillmann, "Beitrag zum Problem der Unterernährung," 192.
92. An die Wirtschaftskommission, February 26, 1950, BArch DQ1/1386.
93. Resolution der deutschen Ärzte zur deutschen Ernährungslage, June 15, 1947, Landesarchiv Berlin B Rep 012/131.
94. Resolution der deutschen Ärzte zur deutschen Ernährungslage, June 15, 1947, Landesarchiv Berlin B Rep 012/131.
95. Schulten, *Die Hungerkrankheit*, 43.
96. Quoted in Erker, *Ernährungskrise und Nachkriegsgesellschaft*, 178.
97. Brandt, *Germany: Key to Peace*, 90-91.
98. Grenzstadt Elend in Görlitz, August 6, 1945, Sächsisches Staatsarchiv Dresden 11391/1758.
99. Quoted in Rothenberger, *Die Hungerjahre*, 196.

100. "Brief," *Der Spiegel* 22 (1947).
101. Obenaus, "Hunger und Überleben," 365.
102. Price and Schorske, *Problem of Germany*, xi.
103. Stolper, *German Realities*, 256.
104. For more on Gollancz's impact on British policy in occupied Germany, see Farquharson, "Emotional but Influential."
105. Böhringer, *Zur Versorgungslage des europäischen Kontinents*, 46–47.
106. Böhringer, *Zur Versorgungslage des europäischen Kontinents*, 71.
107. Langer, *Famine in Germany*, 9.
108. Langer, *Famine in Germany*, 10.
109. Quoted in Bentley, *Eating for Victory*, 150.
110. Quoted in Frank, "New Morality," 243.
111. Macdonald, *Shall Europe Starve?*, 10.
112. Macdonald, *Shall Europe Starve?*, 8.
113. Hazel Hazlitt, "Germany in the World Economy," *New York Times*, November 19, 1945.
114. Gollancz, *Leaving Them to Their Fate*, 17.
115. Quoted in Biess, *Homecomings*, 52.
116. "Sie kehren zurück," *Für Dich*, November (1949).
117. "So ist es in Rüdersdorf, so war es in den Konzentrationslagern," *Für Dich* 37 (October 1950).
118. *Grundfragen unserer Ernährungswirtschaft*, 6.
119. Ziegelmayer, *Neue Nahrungsquellen*, 10.
120. *Unsere Ernährung*, 3.
121. Gold, *Wartime Economic Planning*, 463.
122. Quoted in Gold, *Wartime Economic Planning*, 464–465.
123. Hoffmann, "Introduction: Genealogies of Human Rights," 16.
124. Behind the World News, March 29, 1947, United States President's Famine Emergency Committee Records, box 7, Hoover Institution Archives.
125. Clay, *Decision in Germany*, 267.
126. Baur, "From Victim to Partner," 116; Rothenberger, *Die Hungerjahre*, 112.
127. Joice, *CRALOG*, 5.
128. "Food Stocks Gone, M'narney Reports: Tells Hoover Supply Will Not Sustain Life," *New York Times*, April 14, 1946.
129. US-British Bipartite Food and Agriculture Panel, introduction to *Food and Agriculture*, n.p.
130. Hoover, *No Reconstruction without Food*, 10.
131. Joice, *CRALOG*, 8.
132. Um die Ernährung, March 2,1947, United States President's Famine Emergency Committee Records, box 16, Hoover Institution Archives.
133. Letter from Peter Gast, September 5, 1947, United States President's Famine Emergency Committee Records, box 12, Hoover Institution Archives.
134. Betr: Bitte um Fürsprache zur Abänderung einer militärischen Vorschrift zur Linderung der Wohnraumnot in Deutschland, March 13,1947, United States President's Famine Emergency Committee Records, box 12, Hoover Institution Archives.
135. Letter from Rosa Strobl, March 15, 1947, United States President's Famine Emergency Committee Records, box 16, Hoover Institution Archives.
136. While Berliners did experience severe limitations of their normal foodstuffs during the blockade, the delivery of American supplies ironically gave them a far higher caloric intake than that of the general population of occupied Germany.
137. Parrish, *Berlin in the Balance*, 494–495.
138. Jedes Kind weiss, daß der 'Telegraf' lügt, March 10, 1949, Landesarchiv Berlin B Rep 010-02/686.
139. Jedes Kind weiss, daß der "Telegraf" lügt, March 10, 1949, Landesarchiv Berlin B Rep 010-02/686.
140. Sie wollen nun wieder zurück! Gespräche mit Westberlinern, die im Ostsektor kauften—Kartoffeln und Kohle als "Gründe," April 3, 1949. Landesarchiv Berlin B Rep 010-02/688.
141. Der Ostköder zieht nicht, November 15, 1948, Landesarchiv Berlin B Rep 010-02/686.
142. Davison, "Political Significance of Recognition," 328.

143. Steege, *Black Market*, 215–216.
144. Blockadeaufhebung—ein Erfolg weiblicher Opferbereitschaft, May 12, 1949, Landesarchiv Berlin B Rep 002/25925.
145. Blockadeaufhebung—ein Erfolg weiblicher Opferbereitschaft, May 12, 1949, Landesarchiv Berlin B Rep 002/25925.
146. Blockadeaufhebung—ein Erfolg weiblicher Opferbereitschaft, May 12, 1949, Landesarchiv Berlin B Rep 002/25925.
147. Fliegende Festungen über Berlin,1947, Berlin C Rep 120/3239.
148. Wortlaut der Erklärung, May 1949, Landesarchiv Berlin B Rep 002/25925.
149. "Soviet May Help Europe with Food," *New York Times*, July 5, 1947.
150. *Special Study of Operation "Vittles"*, 12.
151. Arendt, "Aftermath of Nazi Rule," 343.
152. Moeller, *Protecting Motherhood*, 12.
153. *Special Study of Operation "Vittles"*, 11.
154. Friedmann, "Political Economy of Food," 261.
155. Ruttan, *Why Food Aid?*, 9.
156. United States Agency for International Development, *Celebrating Food for Peace*.
157. Bundy, "Food for Peace Program," n.p.
158. Friedmann, "Political Economy of Food," 248.
159. Jachertz and Nützenadel, "Coping with Hunger," 100.
160. Watts, "Heart of Darkness," 26.
161. The famous line ("Erst kommt das Fressen, dann kommt die Moral") has been variously translated and interpreted. See, for example, Arendt, *Origins of Totalitarianism*, 355.

Chapter 4

1. Schildt and Sywottek, "'Reconstruction' and 'Modernization,'" 437.
2. Wiesen, "Overcoming Nazism."
3. Quoted in Trittel, *Hunger und Politik*, 8.
4. "Excerpts from Robertson's Address to the German Parliament in the Ruhr Area," *New York Times*, April 8, 1948.
5. Kraut, "Ernährungsphysiologie als Grundlage," 77.
6. Peppler and Cremer, "Fragen der modernen Gemeinschaftsverpflegung," 313.
7. Nahrung für die Scholle, June 27, 1947, United States President's Famine Emergency Committee Records, box 16, Hoover Institution Archives.
8. Tanner, *Fabrikmahlzeit*, 68.
9. Nitti, "Food and Labour-Power of Nations," 61.
10. "Human Body and Food: Law Governing Its Consumption and Utilization Shown by the Respiration Calorimeter Experiments," *New York Times*, March 23, 1899.
11. Tanner, *Fabrikmahlzeit*, 30.
12. Maier, "Between Taylorism and Technocracy," 31.
13. Tanner, *Fabrikmahlzeit*, 95.
14. Deutsch, *Building a Housewife's Paradise*, 192.
15. Carter, *How German is She?*, 7.
16. Thoms, "Industrial Canteens in Germany," 351–372.
17. Roerkohl, *Hungerblockade und Heimatfront*, 233.
18. Curtis-Bennett, *Food of the People*, 269.
19. Die deutsche Arbeitsfront, April 17, 1942, BArch R 43 II/614.
20. W. Werner, *"Bleib Übrig!,"* 126; Spiekermann, "Pfade in die Zukunft?," 32.
21. Questioned by the American forces in 1947, Kraut declared under oath that the primary goal of his wartime research had been "improving the diet" of foreign workers. The nutritionist implausibly claimed that he "always visited the [concentration] camp kitchens and sampled the camp food. Everywhere that I went I always found proof of the sincere desire to feed all foreign workers, including prisoners of war, as much as possible," Eidesstattliche Erklärung, May 17, 1947, DIFE 225 Nr. 294.

22. Klee, *Deutsche Medizin*, 187. In 1963, Schenck was made Reparation-Expert for Starvation-Damages in the West German League of Homecomers, which advocated on behalf of German POWs being held in the Soviet Union.
23. Historian Andreas Dornheim has noted that agricultural policy and agricultural sciences are the areas of the West German state apparatus that had the highest rates of personnel continuity with the Third Reich yet are the least researched. Dornheim, "Rasse, Raum und Autarkie."
24. Wildt, "Changes in Consumption as Social Practice," 303.
25. Decke and Pilz, *Gastronomische Versorgung im Betrieb*, 9.
26. "Aus dem Wirken eines Multimillinärs, 7.
27. Zur Diskussion über das warme Essen im Betrieb, April 18, 1952, BArch DE1/27413.
28. "So sollte eine Werkküche," 19.
29. Not every worker in the Soviet zone actually had access to these meals. The original bill provided for a hot meal only for full-time workers in factories in high-priority fields, primarily industrial production and transportation. Hübner, *Konsens, Konflikt und Kompromiss*, 22.
30. Betr: Kontrolle der Werkverpflegung, February 18, 1949, BArch DY34/20203.
31. Betr: Werkküchenkontrolle des Buntmetallwerkes Hettstadt, February 10, 1949, BArch DY34/20203.
32. Küchenkontrolle in der Eisen- und Stahlgießerei Meier und Weichelt, January 25, 1949, BArch DY34/20203.
33. Wer hat Anspruch auf Zusatzverpflegung?, December 9, 1948, BArch DR2/296.
34. Wer hat Anspruch auf Zusatzverpflegung?, December 9, 1948, BArch DR2/296.
35. Betr: Werkküchenkontrolle des Buntmetallwerkes Hettstadt, February 10, 1949, BArch DY34/20203.
36. An Füllsack, November 15, 1947, Landesarchiv Berlin B Rep 010-02/536.
37. Bericht über den am 1.4.1950 durchgeführten Erfahrungsaustausch von 30 Küchenchefs zwecks Verbesserung des Werkküchenessens, April 11, 1950, SAPMO-BArch DY34/24042.
38. Vorläufige Richtlinie zur Überführung von Werkküchen und Werkkantinen aus der Bewirtschaftung durch die Betriebe in Werkrestaurants in der Bewirtschaftung durch den volkseigenen Handel, April 28, 1959, BArch DL1/3839.
39. In 1969, the institute was formally incorporated into the national Academy of Sciences and renamed the Central Institute of Nutrition of the Academy of Science of the German Democratic Republic.
40. Zietze, *Gelenkte Ernährung*.
41. Steiner, *Plans That Failed*, 43, 84.
42. Landsman, *Dictatorship and Demand*, 147.
43. Steiner, *Plans That Failed*, 109.
44. Steiner, *Plans That Failed*, 59.
45. Bericht über die Verordnung betr: Verbeserung des Werkküchenessens von 9.4.1953 und die Tätigkeit der Werkküche im Kunstseidenwerk Friedrich Engels, Premnitz, May 7, 1953, BArch DY34/27795.
46. Bericht über die Tagung des ZV der IG Chemie zur Verbesserung des Werkküchenessens am 17.6.1953, June 19, 1953, BArch DY34/27848.
47. Denkschrift über die Schaffung einer zentralen Lehrküche, June 23, 1953, BArch DC6/89.
48. "Werkküche ständig um Qualität bemüht," *Neues Deutschland*, March 24, 1977.
49. "Kantine Geschlossen," *Der Tribüne*, January 25, 1964.
50. Referat für die Konferenz zur besseren Versorgung der Werktätigen in den Betrieben am 6.3.1961, March 2, 1961, BArch DY34/20033.
51. Referat für die Konferenz zur besseren Versorgung der Werktätigen in den Betrieben am 6.3.1961, March 2, 1961, BArch DY34/20033.
52. Betr: Verbesserung des Werkküchenessens und der Schulspeisung, April 25, 1952, BArch DE1/27413.
53. Bericht über die Verordnung betr: Verbesserung des Werkküchenessens, May 7, 1953, BArch DY34/27795.
54. Haenel, Zobel, and Möhr, "Probleme der gesellschaftlichen Speisenwirtschaft."
55. Zobel, "Ernährungswissenschaftlich und technologisch begründete Prognose," 1.

56. Bericht über den Stand der Gemeinschaftsverpflegung in den Betrieben, November 9, 1961, BArch DY34/24570.
57. Zur Diskussion über das warme Essen im Betrieb, April 18, 1952, BArch DE1/27413.
58. Bericht über die Tagung des ZV der IG Chemie zur Verbesserung des Werkküchenessens am 17.6.1953, June 19, 1953, BArch DY34/27848.
59. Was muß vom Werkessen verlangt werden?, DIFE 260 Nr. 138.
60. Vorläufige Richtlinie zur Überführung von Werkküchen und Werkkantinen aus der Bewirtschaftung durch die Betriebe in Werkrestaurants in der Bewirtschaftung durch den volkseigenen Handel, April 28, 1959, BArch DL1/3839.
61. Wege zur Erreichung der Rentabilität der Werkküchen und zur Verbeserung der Qualität des Werkküchenessens, 1951, BArch DY34/8506.
62. Zur Diskussion über das warme Essen im Betrieb, April 18, 1952, BArch DE1/27413.
63. "Gemeinschaftsverpflegung im Betrieb," 2.
64. Möhr, *Zur Ernähungssituation in der DDR*, 13.
65. Gräfe, *Vollwertige Gemeinschaftsverpflegung*, 29.
66. Vorläufige Richtlinie zur Überführung von Werkküchen und Werkkantinen aus der Bewirtschaftung durch die Betriebe in Werkrestaurants in der Bewirtschaftung durch den volkseigenen Handel, April 28, 1959, BArch DL1/3839; Wnuck, "Gemeinschaftsverpflegung muß vollwertig sein," 327; Probleme bei der Realisierung ernährungs- und kochwissenschaftlicher Forderungen in der Praxis der Arbeiterversorgung und Schulspeisung, 1971, DIFE 420 Nr. 17.
67. Haenel, Zobel, and Möhr, "Probleme der gesellschaftlichen Speisenwirtschaft," 35.
68. Zobel, *Zur Gemeinschaftsverpflegung Werktätiger*.
69. Information über die Ergebnisse durchgeführter Untersuchungen zur Hygiene der Gemeinschaftsverpflegung in den Territorien und Betrieben der DDR, May 29, 1986, BArch DQ1/11988.
70. Information über die Ergebnisse durchgeführter Untersuchungen zur Hygiene der Gemeinschaftsverpflegung in den Territorien und Betrieben der DDR, May 29, 1986, BArch DQ1/11988.
71. Quoted in Scarpellini, *Material Nation*, 126–127.
72. Foucault, *Birth of Biopolitics*, 84.
73. Schildt and Sywottek, "'Reconstruction' and 'Modernization,'" 419.
74. Betr: Zuschuss zur Gemeinschaftsverpflegung, April 5, 1954, BArch B106/59463.
75. Hajek, "Für und wider den großen Topf," 1.
76. Kühnau, "Die Frau als Hüterin," 6–7.
77. Die Betriebs-Kantine, May 29, 1969, Siemens-Archiv Li 158.
78. In fact, by the 1960s, restaurants were feeding more workers than canteens were. Gedrich and Albrecht, *Datenrecherche der Entwicklung der Haushaltsausgaben*.
79. Florian, "Gemeinschaftsverpflegung," 1885.
80. Cremer, *Gemeinschaftsverpflegung*, 2.
81. "Das war Massenverpflegung," 18–20.
82. Quoted in Horbelt and Spindler, *Tante Linas Nachkriegsküche*, 317.
83. Betr: Zuschuss zur Gemeinschaftsverpflegung, April 5, 1954, BArch B106/59463.
84. Schnabel, "Die Gemeinschaftsverpflegung für den Betrieb," 41.
85. "Gemeinschaftsverpflegung—Nicht Massenfütterung," 4.
86. Die Betriebs-Kantine, May 29, 1969, Siemens-Archiv Li 158.
87. Thoms, "Industrial Canteens in Germany."
88. Maier, "Between Taylorism and Technocracy," 29.
89. Die Betriebs-Kantine, May 29, 1969, Siemens-Archiv Li 158.
90. Besuch in unsere Werksküchen, May 1954, Siemens-Archiv Li 158.
91. "Gemeinschaftsverpflegung—Nicht Massenfütterung," 4.
92. Ein Gang durch die Berliner Siemens Kasinos, July 1954, Siemens-Archiv Li 158.
93. Die Millionen Schlüsselkinder der Bundesdeutschen, 1966, BArch B116/30525.
94. Cremer, *Gemeinschaftsverpflegung*, 141.
95. Bilz, "Gemeinschaftsverpflegung und Nahrungswahl," 170.
96. Florian, "Gemeinschaftsverpflegung," 1885.

97. Jubilaumsansprache für Herrn Goldbach, February 27, 1955, Siemens-Archiv Li 158; Niederschrift über die Tagung der Kasinoleiter, January 15, 1962, Siemens-Archiv Lm 131.
98. Entwurf: Kantinenessen und Gemeinschaftsverpflegung. Weiteres Ergebnis der Einkommens- und Verbrauchsstichprobe 1962/63, 1966, BArch B116/24256.
99. Klosterkötter, "Hygenische und sozialhygienische Gesichtspunkte," 783.
100. Cremer, *Gemeinschaftsverpflegung*, 248.
101. "Gemeinschaftsverpflegung: Nicht Massenfütterung," 4.
102. "Viele Köche verderben (nicht) den Brei Ä 5.
103. Effizienzkontrolle der Massnahmen der Bundeszentrale für Gesundheitliche Aufklärung, 1978, BArch B310/865.
104. Grenzwerte bei der Planung von Gemeinschaftsverpflegungseinrichtungen und technische Auswirkungen für die Teilnehmer des Internationalen GV-Kongresses, 1981, BArch B116/68110.
105. DGE, *Ernährungsbericht 1988*, 238.
106. Betr: Verbraucherfragen, January 29, 1957, Landesarchiv Berlin B Rep 010-02/314.
107. Quoted in Grünbacher, *Making of German Democracy*, 83.
108. Klatt, "Food and Farming in Germany," 58.
109. Andersen, *Der Traum vom guten Leben*, 12.
110. Logemann, *Trams or Tailfins*, 41.
111. Wildt, "Changes in Consumption," 307.
112. Wolfgang Krüger, "Erhards Wunderkur hilft doch. Der Mechanismus der Märkte gibt breiten Raum für freie Entscheidungen der Menschen," *Die Zeit*, October 13, 1955.
113. Prinz, *Der Sozialstaat hinter dem Haus*, 335.
114. Raup, "Postwar Recovery of Western German Agriculture," 1.
115. Schmidt, "Postwar Developments in West German Agriculture," 153.
116. Fine, *World of Consumption*, 163.
117. Sonnemann, "Was darf die Ernährungsindustrie," 40.
118. Wildt, *Am Beginn der "Konsumgesellschaft"*, 78.
119. Agrardienst, October 4, 1955, BArch B116/1597.
120. Bei der Eröffnung der ANUGA, October 1, 1955, BArch B116/1597.
121. Holcomb, Park, and Capps, "Revisiting Engel's Law," 1.
122. Weggemann, "Entwicklung des Ernährungsverhalten," 22.
123. Byrne and Capps, "Does Engel's Law Extend," 31.
124. Bei der Eröffnung der ANUGA, October 1, 1955, BArch B116/1597.
125. Bei der Eröffnung der ANUGA, October 1, 1955, BArch B116/1597.
126. Advertisement, *Die Ernährungswirtschaft*, 44.
127. Haskerl, "Verbraucherausschußarbeit im Dienste der Hausfrau," 20.
128. Sich, "Die Macht der Hausfrau," 3.
129. Voigt, "Sie kauft nur das Teuerste," 6.
130. Die Küche als Bühne in Ernährungspolitik, October 26, 1966, BArch B116/24256.
131. Ansprache des Bundeswirtschaftsministers Prof. Dr. Karl Schiller bei der Eröffnung der Woche des Verbrauchers und der Hausfrau, November 6, 1967, BArch B102/256608.
132. *Mehr Käuferbewusstsein*, 12.
133. *Mehr Käuferbewusstsein*, 15.
134. Haselmayr, *Einkaufen will gelernt sein*.
135. Alle sollen besser leben Rationalisierungs-Ausstellung, June 1953, BArch B116/1610.
136. Verbraucherberatung in Berlin, 1967, BArch B116/24256.
137. Schneider, *Die Ernährung in ihrer Bedeutung*, 19.
138. Volkswirtschaft vom Kochtopf aus gesehen, February 2, 1963, Landesarchiv Berlin B Rep 010-02/752.
139. Volkswirtschaft vom Kochtopf aus gesehen, February 2, 1963, Landesarchiv Berlin B Rep 010-02/752.
140. An das BKE, October 9, 1951, BArchB012/131.
141. Als Abonenntin ihres Blattes, August 19, 1958, Landesarchiv Berlin B Rep 010-02/314.
142. Patrick Major argues that West German purchasing of cheap foodstuffs in the East contributed to the GDR's food shortages in the late 1950s. Major, *Behind the Berlin Wall*, 49.

143. Beifolgenden Brief der Vorsitzenden des Demokratischen Frauenbundes Berlin, July 2, 1957, Landesarchiv Berlin B Rep 010-02/314.
144. Unvernuft der Käufer ist Hauptgrund für hohe Preise, February 22, 1957, Landesarchiv Berlin B Rep 010-02/327.
145. Landwirtschaft fordert bessere Warenkenntnis der Hausfrauen, January 15, 1954, BArch B012/132.
146. Verbraucher: Politische Korrespondenz, July 10, 1973, Landesarchiv Berlin, B Rep 010/1467.
147. "Viele Hausfrauen ernähren sich falsch," 143.
148. Hendriks, "Politics of Food," 37.
149. Hendriks, "Politics of Food," 42.
150. The difference in price was DM 824.33 vs 205.69 per 100 kg. "Obendrauf noch ein Trinkgeld.' Spiegel- Report über Bauernlobby und Agrarzuschüsse," *Der Spiegel* 50 (1978).
151. Stübler, "Entwicklungstendenzen der Ernährung," 66.
152. Cover image, *Rationelle Hauswirtschaft*.
153. Wildt, "Changes in Consumption," 310.
154. This was less than the American rate of 70%, but more than twice as much as the next highest nation of France—where only 14% of daily foodstuffs was purchased at supermarkets. By 1971, West Germany had 2,000 giant supermarkets; France, 1833; Italy, 538; and Belgium, 400. De Grazia, *Irresistible Empire*, 403.
155. Pence and Betts, *Socialist Modern*.
156. Landsman, *Dictatorship and Demand*, 188.
157. Weggemann, "Entwicklung des Ernährungsverhaltens," 35.
158. Die künftige Entwicklung der Verbrauchererwartungen an das Sortiment, die Bearbeitung, die Qualität und die Verpackung der Nahrungsmittel, January 1, 1968, BArch DL102/189.
159. Harsch, *Revenge of the Domestic*, 303.
160. Pence, "'You as a Woman Will Understand,'" 251.
161. Komplexes Programm: Erleichterung und Verringerung der Hausarbeit, June 30, 1966, Stadtarchiv Leipzig 20237/31647.
162. "Bestellt und ins Haus Gebracht, oder keine Minute mehr für den Einkauf als notwendig," *Für Dich* 33 (August 1969).
163. Kaminsky, *Wohlstand, Schönheit, Glück*, 43.
164. "Bestellt und ins Haus Gebracht, oder keine Minute mehr für den Einkauf als notwendig," *Für Dich* 33 (August 1969).
165. Kaminsky, *Wohlstand, Schönheit, Glück*, 51.
166. Hell, *How Do People Live in the GDR*, 53.
167. Schevardo, *Vom Wert des Notwendigen*, 290–291.
168. Kaminsky, *Wohlstand, Schönheit, Glück*, 49.
169. Verkäuferinnen fragen—wir antworten, February 12, 1962, BArch DY30/IV2/6.10/17.
170. Betr: Einführung einer neuen Brotsorte, January 26, 1962, BArch DY30/IV2/6.10/17.
171. An Bundesvorstand DFD, June 1953, BArch DC6/46.
172. Bericht über die Verwirklichung der Massnahmen zur Erleichterung des Lebens der werktätigen Frauen auf dem Gebiet des Handels und der Versorgung, June 30, 1966, Stadtarchiv Leipzig 20237/31099.
173. Schneider, *Familie und private Lebensführung*, 250.
174. Gräfe, *Richtige Ernährung, gesunde Menschen*, 12.
175. Möglichkeiten zur Steuerung der Verbrauchsgewohnheiten und Durchsetzung einer zweckmässigen Ernährung der Bevölkerung im Prognosezeitraum, February 10, 1970, BArch DL102/9.
176. Die künftige Entwicklung der Verbrauchererwartungen an das Sortiment, die Bearbeitung, die Qualität und die Verpackung der Nahrungsmittel, January 1, 1968, BArch DL102/189.
177. Vorschlag Nr. 5: Säfte und andere Erzeugnisse aus hochwertigen vitaminreichen Früchten, March 30, 1953, DIFE Nr. 222.
178. Die künftige Entwicklung der Verbrauchererwartungen an das Sortiment, die Bearbeitung, die Qualität und die Verpackung der Nahrungsmittel, January 1, 1968, BArch DL102/189.
179. Fischer, "Einige Probleme der Entwicklung," 34.

180. An Elli Schmidt, May 18, 1953, BArch DC6/3.
181. Prima: Abschrift, February 18, 1954, BArch B116/8075.
182. Quoted in Härtel, "Ostdeusche Bestimmungen," 48.
183. Friedrich-Ebert-Stiftung, *Der Alltag in der DDR*, 61.
184. Betr: Preisherabsetzung für schwer absetzbare und verderbgefährdete Waren, August 3, 1953, BArch DC6/46.
185. Betr: Preisherabsetzung für schwer absetzbare und verderbgefährdete Waren, August 3, 1953, BArch DC6/46.
186. Betr: Dattelimporte, May 27, 1961, BArch DY30/148.
187. Jahresbericht 1948, January 1949, DIFE Nr. 104.
188. An Haenel, October 8, 1961, DIFE Nr. 424.
189. The West German sociologist Helmut Schelsky coined this phrase in his controversial thesis on the FRG's economic miracle. Schelsky, *Wandlungen der deutschen Familie*.
190. Landsman, *Dictatorship and Demand*; Crew, *Consuming Germany in the Cold War*; Bren and Neuburger, *Communism Unwrapped*.
191. Gumbert, *Envisioning Socialism*.
192. Madarasz, *Working in East Germany*, 169.
193. Neve, *Sold! Advertising and the Bourgeois Female Consumer*, 41.

Chapter 5

1. "Nixon and Khrushchev Argue in Public as U.S. Exhibit Opens," *New York Times*, July 25, 1959.
2. Gerber, *Küche, Kühlschrank, Kilowatt*, 134.
3. Grossmann, *Reforming Sex*, 5.
4. Elias, *Civilizing Process*; Ariès, *Centuries of Childhood*; Kertzer and Barbagli, *History of the European Family*.
5. Stone, *Family, Sex and Marriage*.
6. Charles, "Food and Family Ideology," 100.
7. Zaretsky, *Capitalism, the Family and Personal Life*, 24.
8. In England, birthplace of the industrial revolution, even well into the twentieth century families consumed few meals as a nuclear family unit. Sarah Olive, "Myth of Togetherness around the Table," *Times Higher Education* (online edition), May 25, 2007, https://www.timeshighereducation.com/features/the-myth-of-togetherness-around-the-table/209127.article, accessed December 3, 2016. In the United States, the model of the nuclear family was not standard until the end of the Second World War. Moreover, since peaking in the 1950s, the number of people living in a "traditional" nuclear family has been steadily dropping. May, *Homeward Bound*.
9. Kühnau, "Die Frau als Hüterin," 6–7.
10. Nolan, *Visions of Modernity*, 212.
11. The most famous of these projects was Schütte-Lihotsky's design for the Frankfurt Kitchen, a revolutionary attempt to rationalize kitchen labor by consolidating space and optimizing building materials to save both time and money and increase women's productivity and pleasure in kitchen work.
12. Quoted in Kuhn, *Wohnkultur und kommunale Wohnungspolitik*, 145.
13. Schaffner, *Father Land*, 34.
14. Aureden, *Was Männern so Gut Schmeckt*, 40.
15. Niederschrift über die 18. Arbeitsbesprechung des Berliner Komitees für Ernährungsfragen, April 24, 1950, Landesarchiv Berlin B Rep 012/131.
16. Wilmenrod, *Es liegt Mir auf der Zunge*, 14–15.
17. Die Zukunft bringt grosse Aufgaben: Bedeutung der Verpflegung ausser Haus steigt weiter, February 24, 1977, BArch B116/68110.
18. Saul, "Die Ernährung im Dienst," 130.
19. Prima: Abschrift, February 18, 1954, BArch B116/8075.
20. Saul, "Die Ernährung im Dienst," 130.
21. Haskarl and Clauss, *Die Macht der Hausfrau*, 34.

22. Haselmayr, *Einkaufen will gelernt sein*, 8.
23. Meyer-Haagen, *Das elektrische Kochen*, 14.
24. Betts, "Manners, Morality, and Civilization."
25. Kühnau, "Die Frau als Hüterin," 9.
26. Saul, "Die Ernährung im Dienst," 130.
27. In 1982 the sociologist Charles Thrall noted the "conservative use of household technology," finding that these ostensibly liberating products "rationalize the specialized position of the woman as the family's household worker." Thrall, "Conservative Use," 186.
28. Gerber, *Küche, Kühlschrank, Kilowatt*, 95.
29. Sell, "Die Arbeitsgemeinschaft," 11.
30. Gerber, *Küche, Kühlschrank, Kilowatt*, 99.
31. Scharfenberg, *Kochbuch für die Hausfrau*, 5.
32. Sell, "Die Arbeitsgemeinschaft," 12.
33. Verbraucherinformation über Ernährungsgüter, 1967, BArch B116/24256.
34. "Grete im Wunderland," *Der Spiegel* 52 (1966).
35. Verlockend, aber nicht individuell genug: haben Fertiggerichte eine Zukunft?, October 9, 1963, Landesarchiv Berlin B Rep 010-02/328.
36. Fünf Millionen Teller Suppe monatlich: beträchtliche Zunahme des Verbrauchs von kochfertigen Suppen, January 20, 1960, Landesarchiv Berlin B Rep 010-02/328.
37. Schneider, *Die Ernährung in ihrer Bedeutung*, 18.
38. Bürgel, *Kochen Braten Backen*, 14.
39. Haase-Nothnagel, *Harmonische Ernährung*, 44.
40. Pfeil, *Die Berufstätigkeit von Müttern*, 215.
41. Pfeil, *Die Berufstätigkeit von Müttern*, 216.
42. See Orland, *Wäsche Waschen*, for a history of household technology over the twentieth century.
43. Quoted in Wildt, *Am Beginn der "Konsumgesellschaft"*, 149.
44. Meyer-Haagen, *Das elektrische Kochen*, 14.
45. Ruhl, *Verordnete Unterordnung*, 177.
46. Schissler, "Social Democratic Gender Policies," 515.
47. Kühnau, "Ernährungsphysiologische Gesichtspunkte," 2.
48. Pfeil, *Die Berufstätigkeit von Müttern*, 39.
49. Schissler, "Social Democratic Gender Policies," 518.
50. Junker, *Die Lage der Mütter*, 164.
51. Quoted in Grünbacher, *Making of German Democracy*, 243.
52. Schwartzer, *Lohn, Liebe*, 16.
53. Mouton, *From Nurturing the Nation*, 15.
54. Cornelissen, "Traditionelle Rollenmuster," 53.
55. Moeller, *Protecting Motherhood*, 150.
56. Lunch preparation alone could be tremendously labor intensive; one "child-rich" mother had to spread 68 slices of bread for her family's sandwiches every day. Pfeil, *Die Berufstätigkeit von Müttern*, 304.
57. Wildt, *Am Beginn der "Konsumgesellschaft"*, 128–130.
58. Pfeil, *Die Berufstätigkeit von Müttern*, 302.
59. "Galeere des Glücks," *Der Spiegel* 27 (1962).
60. Vortrags- und Diskussions-Nachmittag des Berliner Komitees für Ernährungsfragen, July 1, 1953, Landesarchiv Berlin, B Rep 012/132.
61. Einstellung und Verhalten der Verbraucher zur gesunden Ernährung, September 1973, BArch B310/45.
62. Informationsverhalten, Einstellungen und Motivationen zum Thema Ernährung, 1979, BArch B310/703.
63. Nachfolgend die Lesezuschrift von Frau Minister Brauksiepe, March 25, 1969, BArch B189/3003.
64. An das BM für Familie und Jugend, March 18, 1969, BArch B189/3003.
65. Nachfolgend die Lesezuschrift von Frau Minister Brauksiepe, March 25, 1969, BArch B189/3003.
66. Schubert, *Die Frau in der DDR*, 51.

67. Wieloch, *Gesund durch Gemüse*, 12–13.
68. Gräfe, *Richtige Ernährung*, 120.
69. Scheunert, *Ernährungsprobleme der Gegenwart*, 18.
70. Drummer and Muskewitz, *Kochkunst aus dem Fernsehstudio*, 144–145.
71. Haenel, Zobel, and Möhr, "Probleme der gesellschaftlichen Speisenwirtschaft," 35.
72. Semmler, *Gesunde Ernährung*, n.p.
73. Möhr, *Zur Ernährungssituation in der DDR*, 28.
74. Haenel, Zobel, and Möhr, "Probleme der gesellschaftlichen Speisenwirtschaft," 35.
75. Scheunert, *Ernährungsprobleme der Gegenwart*, 19.
76. "Bei knapper Zeit mit Liebe kochen," *Frau von Heute* 14 (April 4, 1952).
77. Denkschrift über die Schaffung einer zentralen Lehrküche, June 23, 1953, BArch DC6/89.
78. Drummer and Muskewitz, *Kochkunst aus dem Fernsehstudio*, 5.
79. Winckel, *Nahrung und Zubereitung*, 24.
80. Wieloch, *Gesund durch Gemüse*, 12–13.
81. Ziegelmayer, *Neue Nahrungsquellen*, 17–18.
82. Gräfe, *Richtige Ernährung*, 120.
83. Die Entwicklung des Bedarfs in ausgewählten Bereichen der Gemeinschaftsverpflegung, December 31, 1971, BArch DL102/595.
84. Winnington, *Rationelles Kochen, gesunde Ernährung*, 18.
85. *Gesunde Küche leicht gemacht*, 32.
86. Letter from Prof. Dr. Dobberstein to Dr. Täufel, February 10, 1961, DIFE Nr. 423.
87. Gründsätze für die Vertretung von Ernährungsfragen im Schulwesen, December 1960, BArch DR2/4112.
88. Einhorn, "Socialist Emancipation," 293.
89. Die künftige Entwicklung der Verbrauchererwartungen an das Sortiment, die Bearbeitung, die Qualität und die Verpackung der Nahrungsmittel, January 1968, BArch DL102/189.
90. Komplexes Programm: Erleichterung und Verringerung der Hausarbeit, June 30, 1966, Stadtarchiv Leipzig 20237/31647.
91. "Muß die Hauswaage schief hängen?," *Für Dich* 50 (February 1969).
92. *Gesunde Küche leicht gemacht*, 32.
93. Müller, *Leben in der Platte*, 69.
94. Elektrowärme Sörnewitz, *Praktische Winke für die IKA Kleinküche*, 2.
95. Steiner, *Plans That Failed*, 84, 130.
96. Krauß, *Gesunde Küche*, see the images between pages 160 and 161.
97. Enderlein and Lange, *Das Backbuch*, 2.
98. Kaminsky, *Wohlstand, Schönheit, Glück*, 78.
99. *Gesunde Küche leicht gemacht*, 3
100. Komplexes Programm: Erleichterung und Verringerung der Hausarbeit, June 30, 1966, Stadtarchiv Leipzig 20237/31647.
101. Der Zeitaufwand bei der Speisenzubereitung im Haushalt und Möglichkeiten seiner Reduzierung, October 15, 1966, BArch DL 102/187.
102. Betr: Verarbeitungsmethoden für Obst- und Gemüse-Sterilkonserven, January 17, 1961, DIFE Nr. 187.
103. Ciesla and Poutrus, "Food Supply in a Planned Economy," 155.
104. Die künftige Entwicklung der Verbrauchererwartungen an das Sortiment, die Bearbeitung, die Qualität und die Verpackung der Nahrungsmittel, January 1968, BArch DL102/189.
105. Matheja-Thaeker, *Alternative Emanzipationsvorstellungen*, 215.
106. Weinreb, "Hot Lunches in the Cold War."
107. Thurnwald, *Gegenwartsprobleme Berliner Familien*, 48.
108. Schulspeisung—warm oder kalt?, March 6, 1950, BArch DR 2/2422.
109. Betr: Schulspeisung, June 21, 1951, BArch DR 2/725.
110. Neuregelung der Schulspeisung erfüllt viele Wünsche, January 1956, BArch DR 2/4449.
111. Boenheimm "Wird die Schulspeisung," 1459.
112. Marcusson, *Das Wachstum von Kindern*, 129.
113. Der derzeitige Stand der Schulkinderspeisung in der DDR und Vorschläge zu ihrer weiteren Verbesserung, 1958, BArch DR 2/1967.

114. Die Aufgaben der Ernährungspropaganda in der DDR, December 15, 1965, DIFE Nr. 212.
115. Rolf Henschel, "... Nun Lasst es euch Schmecken," *Für Dich* 6 (1968).
116. Hell, *How Do People Live in the GDR*, 45.
117. Arbeitstitel Ernährung, August 31, 1961, BArch DQ 1/1972.
118. Unsere Kinder sollen gut und kräftig essen!, January 25, 1956, BArch DR 2/4449.
119. Erfahrungsbericht über die Schulspeisung vom Standpunkt eines Bezirks-Hygiene-Instituts, 1961, DIFE Nr. 423.
120. Denkschrift: Ernährungsfragen im Schulwesen der Deutschen Demokratischen Republik, January 25, 1961, DIFE Nr. 187.
121. Protokoll über die Sitzung am 15.3.1951, March 16, 1951, BArch DR 2/725.
122. "Straße der Besten: Fünf Frauen kochen mit Liebe und würzen mit Herz," *Ostsee-Zeitung*, October 12, 1981.
123. "Das größte Lob," *National-Zeitung*, October 13, 1984.
124. "Gute Zensuren für gute Gerichte," *National Zeitung*, October 12, 1982.
125. Gysi, *Familienleben in der DDR*, 157.
126. *Die Frau und ihre Küche*, 57.
127. Kraut and Wirths, *Mehr Wissen um Ernährung*, 104.
128. "Wenn die Eltern nicht zu Hause sind," *Die Zeit* 19 (May 1961).
129. Monika Mattes has traced the history of the half-day school in the FRG, noting the continued adherence to this model even at times of strong popular desire for full-day schools, most notably during the atmosphere of educational reform in the 1970s. Mattes, *Das Projekt Ganztagsschule*, 133.
130. Droese, Stolley, van Oost, and Kersting, "Erhebungen zur Ernährung," 149.
131. Droese, Stolley, van Oost, and Kersting, "Erhebungen zur Ernährung," 159.
132. Gutezeit, "Rückwirkungen der Schulverpflegung," 192.
133. Die Ergebnisse der Schulbrotteste in der Bundesrepublik Deutschland, May 22, 1966, BArch B 116/30525.
134. Quoted in Wierlacher, *Vom Essen in der deutschen Literatur*, 23.
135. "Kann Hausarbeit verweigert werden?," 139.
136. Schwartzer, *Lohn, Liebe*, 11.
137. "Schüler machen sehr unterschiedlich vom Schul-Mittagsessen gebrauch," *Tagesspiegel*, April 11, 1976.
138. By the mid-seventies, educational experts estimated that a total of 183 whole-day schools were providing full midday meals to their students, feeding about 100,000 West German children. Werner, "Schulverpflegung in der Bundesrepublik Deutschland," 136.
139. Droese, "Erste Erfahrungen über das Mittagessen in Ganztagsschulen."
140. Friedrich-Ebert-Stiftung, *Der Alltag in der DDR*, 12.
141. Körner, "Die Rolle der staatlichen Gaststätten," 3.
142. Gysi and Meyer, "Leitbild: berufstätige Mutter," 159.
143. Hübner, "Arbeiterklasse als Inszenierung," 210.

Chapter 6

1. Ehrlich, *Population Bomb*, xi.
2. Friedmann, "Political Economy of Food."
3. For an excellent study of obesity in East and West Germany that takes a very different approach from my own, see Thoms, "Separated, but Sharing a Health Problem."
4. Robertson, *Malthusian Moment*, 11.
5. Elliott, "Big Persons, Small Voices," 140.
6. Voit, "Leitsymptom: Fettsucht,"1106.
7. Quoted in Ruhl, *Frauen in der Nachkriegszeit*, 114.
8. "Für Sie 30 Jahre," *Für Sie* 21 (1978).
9. Quoted in Grünbacher, *Making of German Democracy*, 230.
10. Georg Bergler, "Absatzproblem der Ernährungsindustrie," *Die Ernährungswirtschaft* 2 (1957).
11. Bansi, "Die Fettsucht, ein Problem der Fehlernährung," 151.

12. Tropp, *Ernähren Sie sich richtig*, 7.
13. Günther, "Sozialmedizinische Bedeutung der Fettsucht," 386.
14. Schaffner, *Father Land*, 40.
15. Ellerbrock, *"Healing Democracy"*, 309.
16. Quoted in Ruhl, *Frauen in der Nachkriegszeit*, 114.
17. "Stäbchen gegen den Hunger," *Der Spiegel* 3 (1955).
18. Holtmeier, "Ernährungsprobleme der Gegenwart," 310.
19. Kury, *Der überforderte Mensch*, 130.
20. Ein Hauptproblem in unserer Zeit, July 15, 1953, BArch B142/1550.
21. Holtmeier, "Ernährungsprobleme der Gegenwart," 310.
22. Tropp, *Ernähren Sie sich richtig*, cover jacket.
23. Managerkrankheit und Pseudo-Erholung, November 21, 1953, BArch B142/1550.
24. Gerlach, "Die Welternährungskrise 1972-1975," 546.
25. Übergewicht als Risikofaktor, 1972, BArch B310/704.
26. Psychologische Grundlagen des Ernährungsverhaltens und Möglichkeiten seiner Beeinflussung, December 20, 1983, DIFE Nr. 91.
27. Annelies Furtmayr-Schuh, "Zu wenig Eisen, zu wenig Vitamine: Neue Formen der Mangelernährung nehmen zu," *Die Zeit*, October 10, 1980.
28. "Ernährung: Den Dicken fehlt ein Faktor," *Der Spiegel* 39 (1975).
29. Neuloh and Teuteberg, *Ernährungsfehlverhalten im Wohlstand*, 37.
30. Neuloh and Teuteberg, *Ernährungsfehlverhalten im Wohlstand*, 37; Arbeitsgemeinschaft der Verbraucherverbände, *Iß modern, iß gesund!*, 3.
31. Neuloh and Teuteberg, *Ernährungsfehlverhalten im Wohlstand*, 21, 37.
32. "Null-Diät zum Null-Tarif," *Die Zeit*, January 9, 1981.
33. Berufung eines Ernährungsrates, December 20, 1985, BArch B196/96696.
34. "Achten Sie auf Ihre schlanke Linie?," *Die Frau von Heute* 43 (October 1952).
35. "Lemmers Konserven," *Der Spiegel* 29 (1961).
36. Kerr-Boyle, "Orders of Eating and Eating Disorders," 71.
37. Poliklinische Entfettungskuren mit Appetitzügler, Kostumstellung, und Tri-Jod-Thyronin, February 15, 1961, BArch DF4/63280.
38. Helga Hahnemann, "Dicke Da," 1983.
39. Müller, "Zur Verbreitung der Fettsucht," 1001.
40. Ahrends, *Gesicherte Ernährung, ein Wert des Sozialismus*.
41. Müller, "Zur Verbreitung der Fettsucht," 1001.
42. Voß, "Wie erreichen wir den Bürger?," 64.
43. Ein heisses Eisen? Ernährungsberatung, 1959, DIFE Nr. 104.
44. Die Ernährung in der sozialistischen Gesellschaft, September 25, 1973, DIFE Nr. 228.
45. "Was die Leute so mögen," *Für Dich* 32 (July 1989).
46. Ein heisses Eisen? Ernährungsberatung, 1959, DIFE Nr. 104.
47. Rahmenprogramm zur weiteren Durchsetzung einer gesundheitsorientierten Ernährung in der DDR, September 1988, DIFE Nr. 195.
48. Kommitee für gesunde Lebensführung und Gesundheitserziehung in der DDR, 1968, BArch DQ 113/8.
49. Ein heisses Eisen? Ernährungsberatung, 1959, DIFE Nr. 104.
50. OECD Committee for Agriculture, *Prospects for Agricultural Production*, 111.
51. Deine Ernährung, deine Gesundheit, 1960, Sächsisches Staatsarchiv Dresden WA-F 1160 Nr. 163.4 Bd. 1.
52. Quoted in Merkel, *Wunderwirtschaft*, 314.
53. Entwicklung neuer und gesundheitsfördernder Ernährung, April 1980, BArch DQ 1/11988.
54. Sozialistische Einheitspartei Deutschlands, *Protokoll der Verhandlungen des VI Parteitages*, 153.
55. Die Ernährungssituation in der DDR, 1972, BArch DG 5/823.
56. Mecklinger, "Aspekte der Prophylaxe und Therapie," 53.
57. Die Ernährungssituation in der DDR, 1972, BArch DG 5/823.
58. Fehlverhalten bei Patienten mit Diabetes Mellitus, June 12, 1989, BArch DQ 119/1375.
59. Rahmenprogramm zur weiteren Durchsetzung einer gesundheitsorientierten Ernährung in der DDR, September 1988, DIFE Nr. 195.

60. Information über die Ernährungssituation in der Deutschen Demokratischen Republik, September 6, 1985, BArch DC 20/23106.
61. Erfordernisse und Möglichkeiten der Gestaltung einer gesundheitsfördernen Ernährung, August 1985, BArch DQ 1/24622.
62. Rahmenprogramm zur weiteren Durchsetzung einer gesundheitsorientierten Ernährung in der DDR, September 1988, DIFE Nr. 195.
63. Briefing zur Kampagne "Ernährung und Bewegung," May 30, 1974, BArch B310/38.
64. Einstellung und Verhalten der Verbraucher zur gesunden Ernährung, September 1973, BArch B310/45.
65. Effizienzkontrolle der Massnahmen der Bundeszentrale für gesundheitliche Aufklärung, 1979, BArch B310/865.
66. "Verbraucher-Gewohnheiten wandelbar," 18; Steller, *Zwischenmahlzeiten ausser Haus*, 44.
68. Übergewicht im Kindesalter und Erziehungsverhalten der Mutter, 1982, BArch B310/717.
69. Die Rolle des Sports und der Ernährung bei einer wirksamen Gesundheitserziehung von übergewichtigen Kindern, March 23, 1990, BArch DQ1 19/222.
70. Zum Thema Aufklärung zu gesundheitsgerechtem Ernährungsverhalten, May 17, 1979, BArch B310/300.
71. Übergewicht als Risikofaktor, 1972, BArch B310/704.
72. Despite the media's emphasis on overweight children, during these decades more mothers requested advice for underweight children than for too-plump ones. See, for example, letters collected in BArch B310/45.
73. "Dicke Kinder: Von allem zuviel," *Der Spiegel* 52 (1977).
74. Stefan Gergely, "Panne im Hungerzentrum. Ist die Fettsucht eine Störung des biochemischen Regelsystems?," *Die Zeit*, May 4, 1979.
75. Stefan Gergely, "Panne im Hungerzentrum. Ist die Fettsucht eine Störung des biochemischen Regelsystems?," *Die Zeit*, May 4, 1979.
76. Elena Schöfer, "Kochen mit dem Therapeuten," *Die Zeit*, May 4, 1979.
77. Übergewicht im Kindesalter und Erziehungsverhalten der Mutter, 1982, BArch B310/717.
78. Gesundheitserziehung und Schule: Curriculum "Ernährung und Gesundheit," 1976, BArch B310/504.
79. Essgeschichten. Ernährungsschwierigkeiten, was dahintersteckt und was man tun kann, November 7, 1979, BArch B310/274.
80. Pietsch, "Möglichkeiten und Erfahrungen der Ernährungsberatung," 105.
81. Pietsch, "Möglichkeiten und Erfahrungen der Ernährungsberatung," 106.
82. Pietsch, "Möglichkeiten und Erfahrungen der Ernährungsberatung," 108.
83. "Ernährung: den Dicken fehlt ein Faktor," 129.
84. Die Wirksamkeit der ZDF Senderreihe gegen das Übergewicht, 1977, BArch B310/828.
85. Änderungsvorschläge, 1974, BArch B310/328.
86. Stuart and Davis, *Slim Chance in a Fat World*, 204.
87. Überlegungen zu Aufklärungsmassnahmen über die richtige Ernährung, March 9, 1979, BArch B310/300.
88. See articles collected in BArch B189/9042.
89. Neue Methode entwickelt: so können Dicke dünner werden, November 7, 1974, BArch B310/328.
90. Wirksamkeitskontrolle des BZgA Kurses "Abnehmen aber mit Vernunft," June 1982, BArch B310/915.
91. Abnehmen aber mit Vernunft, BArch B310/274.
92. Abnehmen aber mit Vernunft, BArch B310/274.
93. Verhaltenstherapie des Übergewichts, 1975, BArch B310/706.
94. Wirksamkeitskontrolle des BZgA Kurses "Abnehmen aber mit Vernunft," June 1982, BArch B310/915.
95. Wirksamkeitskontrolle des BZgA Kurses "Abnehmen aber mit Vernunft," July 1983, BArch B310/926.
96. Wirksamkeitskontrolle des BZgA Kurses "Abnehmen aber mit Vernunft." Zusammenfassung der Ergebnisse, 1982, BArch B310/912.

97. Wirksamkeitskontrolle des BZgA Kurses "Abnehmen aber mit Vernunft," June 1983, BArch B310/923.
98. "Schlank werden kein Problem," *Brigitte* 1 (1973).
99. "Abnehmen mit Spass," *Für Sie* 6 (1974).
100. The magazine offered all registered groups a monthly newsletter and questionnaire, enabling members to be entered in Brigitte's central weight-loss database.
101. "Super Diät. 10 Pfund leichter in 14 Tagen," *Für Sie* 19 (1984).
102. "Neue Wochenend-Blitz-Diäten: Weg mit dem Urlaubsspeck," *Für Sie* 17 (1978).
103. "Schrei aus der Tiefe des Bauches," *Der Spiegel* 15 (1985).
104. Wirksamkeitskontrolle des BZgA Kurses "Abnehmen aber mit Vernunft." Zusammenfassung der Ergebnisse, 1982, BArch B310/912.
105. "Wenn Ihnen gesundes Essen und Trinken in den letzten 30 Jahren immer bewußter wurde," Deutsche Gesellschaft für Ernährung, 1983, n.p. Pamphlet accessed in the DGE library, Bonn.
106. Die Aufgaben der Ernährungspropaganda in der DDR, December 15, 1965, DIFE Nr. 212.
107. Möglichkeiten zur Steuerung der Verbrauchsgewohnheiten, February 10, 1970, BArch DL102/9.
108. Möglichkeiten zur Steuerung der Verbrauchsgewohnheiten, February 10, 1970, BArch DL102/9.
109. Festlegungsprotokoll der Beratung der AG Gesunde Ernährung, June 21, 1974, BArch DF5/1638.
110. Massnahmen der Öffentlichkeitsarbeit, November 9, 1973, BArch DC9/698.
111. Angaben für Titelannahmeverfahren, March 13, 1978, BArch DQ1/24501.
112. Ketz, "Der Beitrag der Gesellschaft für Ernährung," 926.
113. Müller, "Nationale und internationale Ernährungsprobleme," 48.
114. Die Teilnahme an Symposium "Nutritional, Psychological and Social Aspects of Obesity," September 30, 1976, DIFE Nr. 384.
115. Kucher, "Fettsucht: bei ambulanter Therapie," 1589.
116. Leserzuschrift, May 17, 1975, DIFE Nr. 233.
117. Kerr-Boyle, "Orders of Eating," 126.
118. Ketz and Eichhorn, *Schlank aber wie?*, jacket flap.
119. Szenarium: Gesunde Ernährung: ein Teil des gesunden Lebens, March 6, 1961, BArch DQ1/1972.
120. Kerr-Boyle, "Orders of Eating," 131.
121. "Guter Rat: Schlank werden und schlank bleiben," *Für Dich* 19 (1979).
122. The DHMD also produced several short films for youth consumption: *Fat Children* (1975), *Weight* (1973), and *Schlaraffenland* (1980). Dresden Hygiene Museum, Dhm-2003-727.
123. Hambach, *Wie das Strichmännlein den Kobold Huckedack besiegte*, 1965.
124. Gesundheitserziehung und Schule: Curriculum "Ernährung und Gesundheit," 1976, BArch B310/504. Because Lothar's mother works outside the home, she had no time to prepare breakfast, forcing Lothar to purchase cake, soda, or a "double order of fries" from the local bakery every day.
125. Ketz, "Der Beitrag der Gesellschaft für Ernährung," 924.
126. *Morning Star* Reports Healthy Card-Index Meals, January 7, 1975, DIFE Nr. 233.
127. Die Rolle des Sports und der Ernährung bei einer wirksamen Gesundheitserziehung von übergewichtigen Kindern, March 23, 1990, BArch DQ119/222.
128. Information über die Ernährungssituation in der Deutschen Demokratischen Republik, September 6, 1985, BArch DC 20/23106.
129. Zur Entwicklung der Volksernährung, October 27, 1969, DIFE Nr. 228.
130. Die Entwicklung des Bedarfs in ausgewählten Bereichen der Gemeinschaftsverpflegung, December 31, 1971, BArch DL 102/595.
131. Entwurf: Gesellschaftliche Speisenwirtschaft, March 6, 1969, BArch DQ1/2098.
132. Zur Erarbeitung von Empfehlungen zur grundlegenden Verbesserung der Situation auf dem Gebiet der gesunden Ernährung, November 14, 1968, BArch DA 1/7929.
133. Zur Erarbeitung von Empfehlungen zur grundlegenden Verbesserung der Situation auf dem Gebiet der gesunden Ernährung, November 14, 1968, BArch DA 1/7929.

134. Die Ernährungssituation in der DDR, 1972, BArch DG 5/823.
135. *Morning Star* Reports Healthy Card-Index Meals, January 7, 1975, DIFE Nr. 233.
136. Entwicklungskonzeptionen zur Versorgung der Bevölkerung mit diätetischen Lebensmitteln bis 1990, June 1984, BArch DF5/1588.
137. DDR-Gaststätten sollen mehr gesundheitsfördernde Speisen anbieten, July 13, 1973, BArch B116/68110.
138. Ketz and Eichhorn, *Schlank aber wie*, 19.
139. Die Entwicklung des Bedarfs in ausgewählten Bereichen der Gemeinschaftsverpflegung, December 31, 1971, BArch DL 102/595.
140. Ernährungsbericht, 1976, BArch B189/9076.
141. Ertl reagiert sauer auf Antje Hubers "Fitt statt Fett" Aktion, July 25, 1977, BArch B116/68110.
142. Erweiterter Konzeptionstest für eine Kampagne Gemeinschaftsverpflegung, November 1976, BArch B310/712.
143. Erweiterter Konzeptionstest für eine Kampagne Gemeinschaftsverpflegung, November 1976, BArch B310/712.
144. Ertl reagiert sauer auf Antje Hubers "Fitt statt Fett" Aktion, July 25, 1977, BArch B116/68110.
145. Presse-Informations-Gespräch, November 20, 1975, BArch B310/330.
146. An Antje Huber, August 2, 1977, BArch B310/274.
147. Erfolgskontrolle der "Fit statt Fett Aktion," 1978, BArch B310/832.
148. Erfolgskontrolle der "Fit statt Fett Aktion," 1978, BArch B310/832.
149. An Herr MR Dr. Krusen BMJFG, September 19, 1977, BArch B310/331.
150. Konzeptionelle Überlegungen und Lösungsansatz für die Kampagne "Ernährung und Bewegung," November 15, 1974, BArch B310/37.
151. Kommt jetzt das süße Leben?, March 19, 1974, DIFE Nr. 233.
152. Wange, "Die Anforderungen der gesunden Ernährung," 59.
153. Mecklinger, "Aspekte der Prophylaxe," 52.
154. Die Teilnahme an Symposium "Nutritional, Psychological and Social Aspects of Obesity," September 30, 1976, DIFE Nr. 384.
155. Letter from Dr. Otto Spengler to Rolf Kaulfersch, February 27, 1975, BArch DQ 1/10550.
156. Deine Ernährung, deine Gesundheit, 1960, Sächsisches Staatsarchiv Dresden WA-F 1160 Nr. 163.4 Bd. 1.
157. Bericht über den Stand der Qualität neuer und weiterentwickekter Erzeugnisse für die rationelle Ernährung, BArch DF5/1638.
158. Entwicklungskonzeptionen zur Versorgung der Bevölkerung mit diätetischen Lebensmitteln bis 1990, June 1984, BArch DF5/1588.
159. Entwicklungskonzeptionen zur Versorgung der Bevölkerung mit diätetischen Lebensmitteln bis 1990, June 1984, BArch DF5/1588.
160. Konsumgüterprogram zu Ehren des X. Parteitages, July 21, 1982, BArch DF5/1730.
161. Mundliche Information zur Mitwirkung an der Sortimentskonzeption, June 8, 1983, BArch DQ1/11518.
162. Programm zur ernährungsphysiologischen Verbesserung von Erzeugnissen der Süss- und Dauerbackwarenindustrie, August 15, 1971, BArch DG5/1911.
163. Programm zur ernährungsphysiologischen Verbesserung von Erzeugnissen der Süss- und Dauerbackwarenindustrie, August 15, 1971, BArch DG5/1911.
164. Beschluss über die Ausarbeitung und Durchsetzung von Massnahmen der gesunden Ernährung, BArch DG5/823.
165. Zu Ergebnisse und Problemen bei der effektiven Nutzung der zur Verfügung stehenden Rohstoffe für die Nahrungsguterproduktion, September 6, 1985, BArch DC20/23106; and Konsumgüterprogramm zu Ehren des X. Parteitages, July 21, 1982, BArch DF5/1730.
166. Beschluss über die Ausarbeitung und Durchsetzung von Massnahmen der gesunden Ernährung, BArch DG5/823.
167. Zu Ergebnisse und Problemen bei der effektiven Nutzung der zur Verfügung stehenden Rohstoffe für die Nahrungsguterproduktion, September 6, 1985, BArch DC20/23106.

168. Beschluss über die Ausarbeitung und Durchsetzung von Massnahmen der gesunden Ernährung, BArch DG5/823.
169. Entwicklungskonzeptionen zur Versorgung der Bevölkerung mit diätetischen Lebensmitteln bis 1990, June 1984, BArch DF5/1588.
170. Information über die Ernährungssituation in der Deutschen Demokratischen Republik, September 6, 1985, BArch DC20/23106.
171. Arbeitsgruppe für Organisation und Inspektion, September 6, 1985, BArch DC20/23106.
172. Versuch zur Behebung des Engpasses in der Lebensmittelversorgung durch Prioritätslisten, February 25, 1970, BArch B206/1748.
173. Beratung des Fachausschusses "Qualität," April 9, 1981, BArch DF5/1638.
174. Betr: Konsumgüterproduktion zum X. Parteitag der SED, April 23, 1980, BArch DF5/1730; and Betr: Berichterstattung zum Stand und zu Problemen bei der Realisierung des Konsumgüterprogrammes, September 16, 1980, BArch DF5/1730.
175. Poliklinische Entfettungskuren mit Appetitzügler, Kostumstellung, und Tri-Jod-Thyronin, February 15, 1961, BArch DF4/63280. In addition, the initial plan to distribute thyroid medication as an additional weight-loss support could not be carried out since such pills had been unavailable in the GDR for years.
176. Versorgungslage im Raum Werder Havel, [late 1970s], BArch B206/1746.
177. See notes in B206/1748.
178. Bericht über den Stand der Qualität neuer und weiterentwickekter Erzeugnisse für die rationelle Ernährung, BArch DF5/1638.
179. Protokoll über die Beratung der AG Gesunde Ernährung, March 23, 1973, BArch DF5/1638.
180. Abgabe einer Kalorienverminderung in der Kennzeichnung, April 13, 1973, BArch DF5/1638.
181. Abgabe einer Kalorienverminderung in der Kennzeichnung, April 13, 1973, BArch DF5/1638.
182. Mundliche Information zur Mitwirkung an der Sortimentskonzeption, June 8, 1983, BArch DQ1/11518.
183. Möglichkeiten zur Steuerung der Verbrauchsgewohnheiten, February 10, 1970, BArch DL102/9.
184. For example, a whole-grain wheat bread contained 6% more wheat bran and cost 30 cents more than the standard wheat loaf. "Protokoll der Beratung des Fachausschusses Qualität," October 30, 1980, BArch DF5/1638.
185. Die Ernährungssituation in der DDR, 1972, BArch DG5/823.
186. Helmut Haenel, "Die Besteuerung der Korpulenz," *Deutsches Allgmeines Sonntagsblatt* 48 (1970).
187. Gabriel Laub, "Steuer pro Kilo Lebendgewicht," *Die Zeit*, November 13, 1970.
188. Ten Dyke, "Tulips in December," 259.
189. Das gegenwärtige Ernährungsniveau und die Versorgungssituation, February 10, 1983, BArch DF5/1587.
190. Mundliche Information zur Mitwirkung an der Sortimentskonzeption, June 8, 1983, BArch DQ1/11518.
191. Mundliche Information zur Mitwirkung an der Sortimentskonzeption, June 8, 1983, BArch DQ1/11518.
192. Rahmenprogramm zur weiteren Durchsetzung einer gesundheitsorientierten Ernährung in der DDR, September 1988, DIFE Nr. 195.
193. Fehlverhalten bei Patienten mit Diabetes Mellitus, June 12, 1989, BArch DQ119/1375.
194. Betr: Diabetiker, January 28, 1975, BArch DQ1/10550.
195. Rahmenprogramm zur weiteren Durchsetzung einer gesundheitsorientierten Ernährung in der DDR, September 1988, DIFE Nr. 195.
196. Deine Ernährung, deine Gesundheit, 1960, Sächsisches Staatsarchiv Dresden WA-F 1160 Nr. 163.4 Bd. 4.
197. Letter from Claus Kulka to Redaktion, June 4, 1975, BArch DQ1/10550.
198. Spezifische Verbrauchsprobleme auf dem Gebiet der Ernährung, 1981, BArch DL102/1454.

199. Spezifische Verbrauchsprobleme auf dem Gebiet der Ernährung, 1981, BArch DL102/1454.
200. "Brief," 1.
201. FDGB, Gewerkschaften und Gemeinschaftsverpflegung, 29.
202. Ab 1 Juli wird neue fettreiche Milch im Handel angeboten, July 13/14, 1974, DIFE Nr. 465.
203. An Thymien, September 18, 1974, DIFE Nr. 465.
204. An Redaktion der BN, July 17, 1974, DIFE Nr. 465.
205. "Butter im Trog," *Der Spiegel* 31 (1968).
206. Ertl reagiert sauer auf Antje Hubers "Fitt statt Fett" Aktion, July 25, 1977, BArch B116/68110.
207. Ein Hauptproblem in unserer Zeit, July 15, 1953, BArch B142/1550.
208. "Kakao, Schokolade, Pralinen," 155.
209. Gesundheitserziehung und Schule: Curriculum "Ernährung und Gesundheit," 1976, BArch B310/504.
210. Betr: irreführende Werbung für Lebensmittel, December 18, 1953, BArch B142/1550.
211. "Verbraucher-Gewohnheiten wandelbar," 19; Gesundheitserziehung und Schule: Curriculum "Ernährung und Gesundheit," 1976, BArch B310/504.
212. "Schlank mit *Für Sie*," *Für Sie* 7 (1974).
213. Advertisement, *Brigitte* 10 (1980): 255.
214. Advertisement, *Für Sie* 6 (1974): 126.
215. Advertisement, *Brigitte* 10 (1980): 213.
216. "Schlank mit *Für Sie*," *Für Sie* 7 (1974).
217. Rostalski, "Fortschritte in der Behandlung," 1111.
218. Advertisement, *Brigitte* 10 (1980).
219. Advertisement, *Für Sie* 2 (1974): 71.
220. Letter from Magda Hubert to Dr. Strobel, October 26, 1969, BArch B189/1175.
221. Letter from Friedich Rupp to Strobel, October 24, 1969, BArch B189/1175.
222. Letter from Wolfgang Liese to Minister Strobel, November 2, 1969, BArch B189/1175.
223. Berufung eines Ernährungsrates, December 20, 1985, BArch B196/96696.
224. Lippki, Lode, and Teut, *Essen in der Arbeitswelt*, 37.
225. Krauß, *Gesunde Küche*, 12.
226. Zur Änderung der Ernährungsgewohnheiten in Deutschland, August 1966, BArch B116/24260.
227. Ess-kapaden Schaden: vernünftig Essen hält in Form, March 21, 74, BArch B310/52.
228. Bourdieu, *Distinction*, 190.
229. Wright and Harwood, *Biopolitics and the 'Obesity Epidemic'*.
230. Rede zur Eröffnung des internationalen Kongresses für Gemeinschaftsverpflegung, September 10, 1981, BArch B116/68110.
231. Neuloh and Teuteberg, *Ernährungsfehlverhalten im Wohlstand*, 12.
232. See posters in Deutsches Hygiene Museum Dresden, Dhm-2003-727.
233. "Süß und fett," *Der Spiegel* 35 (1965).
234. "Gegen die Fettsucht der Genossen," *Die Zeit*, March 5, 1976.
235. Deine Ernährung, deine Gesundheit, 1960, Sächsisches Staatsarchiv Dresden WA-F 1160 Nr. 163.4 Bd. 2.

Epilogue

1. Cadot and Webber, "Banana Splits and Slipping over Banana Skins."
2. 66. Sitzung am 12. März 1957 Deutsch-französische Verhandlungen über den Bananenzoll im gemeinsamen Außenzolltarif des Gemeinsamen Marktes, Kabinettsprotokolle der Bundesregierung, http://www.bundesarchiv.de/cocoon/barch/k1/x/x1956e/kap1_2/kap2_29/para3_6.html, accessed on December 3, 2016.
3. Aureden, *Was Männern so gut schmeckt*.
4. Adam, *Bananen-Schlemmereien*.
5. Brunner and Pfeifer, *Zum Beispiel Bananen*, 73.

6. Betr: Getrocknete Bananen, December 11, 1962, BArch DE4/14571.
7. Betr: Getrocknete Bananen, December 11, 1962, BArch DE4/14571.
8. Stregel and Tweder, *Deutsche kulinarische Republik*, 45.
9. Seeßlen, "Die Banane."
10. "Wie die DDR zur Bananenrepublik wurde," *Die Welt*, November 9, 2009.
11. Seeßlen, "Die Banane," 55.
12. A 1991 cartoon depicted a West German man slipping on a banana peel and screaming as he fell, "Damned reunification." *Eulenspiegel*, May 1991. Leftist critics of the newly unified and powerful Germany began calling it a "banana republic.'" Seeßlen, "Die Banane," 58.
13. Auf der gemeinsamen Pressekonferenz der Gewerkschaften HNG, HBV, NGG, March 29, 1990, BArch DC20/6796.
14. Winkler, Brasche, and Heinrich, "Trends in Food Intake in Adults," 283–284.
15. Mensink and Beitz, "Food and Nutrient Intake," 1008.
16. Donat, "Die Entwicklung des Ernährungsverhaltens," 16.
17. Prinz, *Der Sozialstaat hinter dem Haus*, 319.
18. "Wehre dich täglich," *Der Spiegel* 52 (1993).
19. Messeangebot der internationalen Grünen Woche Berlin 1990, January 24, 1990, BArch DF5/1588.
20. Berdahl, "(N)Ostalgie for the Present," 201.
21. "Wehre dich täglich," *Der Spiegel* 52 (1993).
22. Gries, "Geschmack der Heimat," 1058.
23. "Wehre dich täglich," *Der Spiegel* 52 (1993).
24. Jarausch, "Beyond the National Narrative," 336.
25. Boym, *Future of Nostalgia*. Studies of memory and material culture have usually focused on such icons of socialist dysfunction as drab housing projects or the Trabi car. For an important exception, see Caldwell, Dunn, and Nestle, *Food and Everyday Life*.
26. Otzen and Otzen, *DDR-Backbuch*, 23
27. Scheffler, *Alles Soljanka oder wie?*, 2.
28. Scheffler, *Alles Soljanka oder wie?*, 6.
29. Scheffler, *Alles Soljanka oder wie?*, 9.
30. Merkel, "Changing Meanings in East German Consumer Culture," 264.
31. Berdahl, "(N)Ostalgie for the Present," 197.
32. Wunderlich, *Farmer and Farm Labor*, 50.
33. "Schweinemord," *Der Spiegel* 2 (1953).
34. Betr: Arbeitsgruppe "Lebensmittelindustrie," June 21, 1956, Landesarchiv Berlin B Rep 010 02/316.
35. "Die ungleichen Deutschen: Es ist ein anderes Leben," *Der Spiegel* 39 (1990).
36. Prima: Abschrift, December 4, 1953, BArch B116/8075.
37. In addition to generosity toward their "hungry bothers," West Germans led international donation lists for African famine victims, again owing to their own memories of hunger. In 1969, agricultural economist Theodor Dams explained that food aid "acquires in the Federal Republic of Germany an additional accent, thanks to the memories of the American food donations to the hungry population in the time after the Second World War." Dams, *Nahrungsmittelhilfe*, 6.
38. Ingimundarson, "Eisenhower Administration, the Adenauer Government." For the East German government's response, see Umsonst ist am Teuersten, 1953, Landesarchiv Berlin B Rep 002/1770.
39. Niven, *Germans as Victims*; Cooke and Silberman, *Screening War*.
40. Gries, "Geschmack der Heimat," 1043.
41. Berdahl, *On the Social Life of Postsocialism*, 34.
42. Unexpectedly, these educational units found the most resonance not among their target audience of middle-class housewives but among the newly unemployed, who were hoping for tips on shopping and food preparation in the face of reduced incomes and rising grocery bills. Krause, "Mobile Beratung und Information über Ernährung," 255.
43. Cohen, *Consumer's Republic*; Strasser, McGovern, and Judt, *Getting and Spending*.

44. Friebe and Möhr, "Ausgewählten Ergebnisse zu Einstellungen," 3.
45. "Die dicken Kinder von Deutschland," *Spiegel Online* (July 2002), accessed December 3, 2016, http://www.spiegel.de/politik/deutschland/fehl-ernaehrung-die-dicken-kinder-von-deutschland-a-206135.html.
46. "Gesunde Ernährung im Job fällt vielen schwer," *Spiegel Online* (2013), accessed December 3, 2016, http://www.spiegel.de/gesundheit/ernaehrung/fast-jedem-dritten-faellt-eine-gesunde-ernaehrung-am-arbeitsplatz-schwer-a-889907.html.
47. LeBesco, *Revolting Bodies*; Guthman, *Weighing In*.
48. Arbeiten, Arbeiten, Arbeiten! Die "neuen Rechte" der Frau in der Sowjetzone, 1950, BArch DQ1/1396.
49. Arbeiten, Arbeiten, Arbeiten! Die "neuen Rechte" der Frau in der Sowjetzone, 1950, BArch DQ1/1396.
50. Loehlin, *From Rugs to Riches*, 44.
51. Young, *Triumph of the Fatherland*.
52. Kolinsky, *Women in 20th century Germany*, 111.
53. Ferree, "Rise and Fall of 'Mommy Politics,'" 105.
54. Pfau-Effinger, "Der soziologische Mythos von der Hausfrauenehe," 177.
55. Entscheidungsvorlage für die Herausgabe der neuen Zeitschrift "Gemeinschaftsverpflegung," January 24, 1990, BArch DC9/9348.
56. Essverhalten und Essstörungen in Ostdeutschland, 1991, BArch B310/722.
57. Throughout 1990 and 1991, East German newspapers ran frequent articles bemoaning the dismantling of school lunches. See, for example, Gabriele Oertel, "Geschmacklose Kost aus den Rathäusern," *Neues Deutschland*, December 14, 1990; Gabriele Oertel, "Na dann, Mahlzeit!," *Neues Deutschland*, January 31, 1991; Heide Schlebeck, "Doch nur ein Windei zum Frühstück," *Berliner Zeitung*, September 21, 1990.
58. Kurt Reumann, "Als sei Schulspeisung das Wichtigste: was Schüler und Eltern in der DDR gegenwärtig am meisten bewegt," *Frankfurter Allgemeine Zeitung*, March 13, 1990.
59. Reumann condemned East German parents' "hysteria," and suggested that worried mothers "stay at home so that they themselves could be responsible for their own children's upbringing." Reumann, "Als sei Schulspeisung das Wichtigste."
60. Bredtmann, Kluve, and Schaffner, "Women's Fertility and Employment Decisions."
61. "Hier ist immer was los," *Der Spiegel* 3 (2002).
62. Katrin Bennhold, "In Germany, a Tradition Falls, and Women Rise," *New York Times*, January 17, 2010.
63. Sabine Rückert, "Darf man Hausfrau sein?," *Die Zeit*, October 31, 2012.

BIBLIOGRAPHY

Archival Sources

Bundesarchiv, Berlin-Lichterfelde (BArch)

DA 1	Volkskammer der DDR
DC 20	Ministerrat der DDR
DC 6	Staatliche Kommission für Handel und Versorgung beim Ministerrat.
DC 9	Presseamt beim Vorsitzenden des Ministerrates der DDR
DE 1	Staatliche Plankommission (1949–1961 [1963])
DE 4	Volkswirtschaftsrat der DDR (1961–1965)
DF 4	Ministerium für Wissenschaft und Technik
DF 5	Amt für Standardisierung, Messwesen und Warenprüfung (ASMW)
DG 5	Ministerium für Bezirksgeleitete Industrie und Lebensmittelindustrie
DL 102	Institut für Marktforschung
DL 1	Ministerium für Handel und Versorgung
DQ 1	Ministerium für Gesundheitswesen
DQ 113	Nationales Komitee für Gesundheitserziehung der DDR
DQ 119	Fachschule für Gesundheits- und Sozialwesen "Prof. Dr. K. Gelbke"
DR 2	Ministerium für Volksbildung
DY 30	Parteitage und Parteikonferenzen der SED
NS 26	Hauptarchiv der NSDAP
NS 3	SS-Wirtschafts-Verwaltungshauptamt
R 55	Reichsministerium für Volksaufklärung und Propaganda
R 86	Reichsgesundheitsamt
R 3601	Reichsministerium für Ernährung und Landwirtschaft
R 43I	Reichskanzlei

Stiftung Archiv der Parteien und Massenorganizationen der DDR im Bundesarchiv (BArch–SAPMO)

DY 30 /IV 2/6.10	Abt. Handel, Versorgung und Aussenhandel
DY 34	Freier deutscher Gewerkschaftsbund

Bundesarchiv, Koblenz (BArch)

B 102	Bundesministerium für Wirtschaft
B 106	Bundesministerium des Innern

B 116	Bundesministerium für Ernährung, Landwirtschaft und Forsten
B 142	Bundesministerium für das Gesundheitswesen
B 189	Bundesministerium für Familie, Senioren, Frauen und Jugend
B 196	Bundesministerium für Forschung und Technologie
B 206	Bundesnachrichtendienst
B 310	Bundeszentrale für gesundheitliche Aufklärung
Z/6/I/239	Verwaltung für Ernährung, Landwirtschaft und Forsten des Vereinigten Wirtschaftsgebietes—Büro d. Dir. Schlange-Schöningen

Hoover Institution Archives, Stanford University, California

Daniel Lerner Collection
Friends' War Victims' Relief Committee Records
German Subject Collection
Germany (Territory under Allied occupation, 1945–1955: US Zone) Office of Military Government for Bavaria. Kreis Traunstein Records
National Committee on Food for the Small Democracies Records
United States President's Famine Emergency Committee Records
Werner Klatt Collection

Deutsches Institut für Ernährungsforschung (DIfE)

91, 104, 187, 195, 199, 212, 222, 225, 226, 228, 233, 234, 260, 384, 420, 423, 424, 465

Landesarchiv Berlin

B Rep 010-02	Senatsverwaltung für Wirtschaft und Ernährung
B Rep 012	Senatsverwaltung für Gesundheit
B Rep 002	Der regierende Bürgermeister von Berlin/Senatskanzlei
B Rep 209	Bezirksverwaltung Wilmersdorf
B Rep 010	Senatsverwaltung für Wirtschaft
C Rep 120	Magistrat von Berlin, Abteilung Volksbildung
C Rep 113	Magistrat von Berlin, Abteilung Handel und Versorgung

Sächsisches Hauptstaatsarchiv Dresden

11391	Ministerium für Arbeit und Sozialfürsorge
11393	Ministerium für Handel und Versorgung
WA-F 1160	Deutsches Hygiene-Museum Dresden: Wanderausstellungen

Siemens AG Corporate Archive

11097.1, 11098.1, 11098.2, 19022, 7542, Li 158, Lm 131

Stadtarchiv Düsseldorf

RW 0047	Kreisernährungsamt Düsseldorf-Mettmann

Historisches Archiv der Stadt Köln

530/175	Kölner Preisbehörde
1824	Deutsches Gesundheits-Museum

Stadtarchiv Leipzig

20237	Bezirkstag und Rat des Bezirkes Leipzig
21112	Verlag für die Frau

Bibliography

Newspapers and Periodicals

NEWSPAPERS

Berliner Zeitung, Der Tribüne, Deutsches Allgemeines Sonntagsblatt, Die Zeit, Frankfurter Allgemeine Zeitung, National-Zeitung, Neues Deutschland, New York Times, Ostsee-Zeitung, Tagesspiegel, Daily Mirror, The Independent

JOURNALS

Ärztliche Wochenschrift, Brigitte, British Medical Journal, Das deutsche Gesundheitswesen, Das Großküchen-Magazin, Der Spiegel, Deutsche medizinische Wochenschrift, Die Agnes Karl-Schwester, Der Krankenpfleger, Die Ernährung, Die Ernährungsdienst, Die Ernährungsindustrie, Die medizinische Welt, Die moderne Küche, Die neuzeitliche Gaststätte, Die Welt, Ernährungsforschung, Ernährung und Verpflegung, Frau von Heute, Für Dich, Für Sie, Gastronomie, Gemeinschaftsverpflegung mit Volksernährung, Harpers, Hauswirtschaft und Volksernährung: Fachzeitschrift für rationelle Haushaltsführung, Kochpraxis und Gemeinschaftsverpflegung, Medizinische Welt, Mitteilungen des Instituts für Bedarfsforschung, Münchener medizinische Wochenschrift, Rationelle Hauswirtschaft: Fachblatt für die hauswirtschaftliche Führungskräfte, The Outlook, The Lancet, The World's Work, Times Higher Education, Verbraucherdienst, Volksernährung und Kochwissenschaft, Zeitschrift für Allgemeimmedizin, der Landarzt, Zeitschrift für Gemeinschaftsverpflegung, Zeitschrift für Volksernährung, Zeitung für die gesamten Hygiene und ihre Grenzgebiete

Books and Theses

A Special Study of Operation "Vittles." New York: Conover-Mast Publications, 1949.
Adam, Hans Karl. *Bananen-Schlemmereien: ein mannigfaltiges Rezeptbuch.* Munich: Heimeran, 1961.
Agamben, Giorgio. *Remnants of Auschwitz: The Witness and the Archive.* New York: Zone Books, 2000.
Ahrends, Klaus. *Gesicherte Ernährung, ein Wert des Sozialismus.* Berlin: Dietz, 1987.
Allen, Keith. "Sharing Scarcity: Bread Rationing and the First World War in Berlin, 1914–1923." *Journal of Social History* 32, no. 2 (1998): 371–393.
Aly, Götz. *Hitler's Beneficiaries: Plunder, Racial War, and the Nazi Welfare State.* New York: Metropolitan, 2007.
Andersen, Arne. *Der Traum vom guten Leben: Alltags- und Konsumgeschichte vom Wirtschaftswunder bis Heute.* Frankfurt: Campus, 1997.
Anderson, Carol. *Eyes off the Prize: The United Nations and the African American Struggle for Human Rights, 1944–1955.* Cambridge: Cambridge University Press, 2003.
Arbeitsgemeinschaft der Verbraucherverbände, ed., *Iß modern, iß gesund! Kleine Ernährungslehre für Jedermann. Ein Beitrag zur Erhaltung und Verbesserung der Volksgesundheit.* Bonn: Arbeitsgemeinschaft d. Verbraucherverbände, 1969.
Arendt, Hannah. "The Aftermath of Nazi Rule: Report from Germany." *Commentary* 10 (1950): 342–353.
Arendt, Hannah. *The Origins of Totalitarianism.* New York: Harcourt, 1968.
Ariès, Philippe. *Centuries of Childhood: A Social History of Family Life.* New York: Vintage, 1965.
Arnold-Forster, William. *The Blockade 1914–1919: Before the Armistice and After.* Oxford: Clarendon, 1939.
Aureden, Lilo. *Was Männern so gut schmeckt: Eine kulinarische Weltreise in 580 Rezepten.* Munich: Deutscher Taschenbuch-Verlag, 1953.
"Aus dem Wirken eines Multimillionärs: der Lieblings-Gastronom Adenauers." *Die neuzeitliche Gaststätte* 3 (1956): 7.
Autorenkollektiv. "Kann Hausarbeit verweigert werden?" In *Frauen als bezahlte und unbezahlte Arbeitskräfte: Beiträge zur 2. Berliner Sommeruniversität für Frauen, Oktober 1977,* edited by Berliner Sommeruniversität für Frauen, 151–158. Berlin: Frauenbuchvertrieb, 1978.
Bach, Dieter, and Jochen Leyendecker. *Ich habe geweint vor Hunger: deutsche und russische Gefangene in Lagern des zweiten Weltkriegs.* Wuppertal, Germany: P. Hammer, 1993.

Bane, Suda Lorena, and Ralph Haswell Lutz. *The Blockade of Germany after the Armistice, 1918–1919; Selected Documents of the Supreme Economic Council, Superior Blockade Council, American Relief Administration, and Other Wartime Organizations.* Stanford, CA: Stanford University Press, 1942.

Bane, Suda Lorena, and Ralph Haswell Lutz, *Organization of American Relief in Europe, 1918–1919.* Stanford, CA: Stanford University Press, 1943.

Bansi, H. W. "Die Fettsucht, ein Problem der Fehlernährung." In *Probleme der vollwertigen Ernährung in Haushalts- und Großverpflegung*, edited by Deutsche Gesellschaft für Ernährung, 151. Frankfurt: Umschau-Verlag, 1956.

Baten, Jörg. "Autarchy, Market Disintegration, and Health: The Mortality and Nutritional Crisis in Nazi Germany, 1933–1937." Munich: Center for Economic Studies and IFO Institute for Economic Research, 2002.

Baur, Philipp. "From Victim to Partner: CARE and the Portrayal of Postwar Germany." In *Die amerikanische Reeducation-Politik nach 1945: interdisziplinäre Perspektiven auf 'America's Germany'*, edited by Katharina Gerund and Heike Paul, 115–140. Bielefeld: Transcript, 2015.

Beaumont, Joan. "Starving for Democracy: Britain's Blockade of and Relief for Occupied Europe, 1939–1945." *War and Society* 8, no. 2 (1990): 57–82.

Belinda, Davis. *Home Fires Burning: Food, Politics, and Everyday Life in World War I Berlin.* Chapel Hill: University of North Carolina Press, 2000.

Bentley, Amy. *Eating for Victory: Food Rationing and the Politics of Domesticity.* Urbana: University of Illinois Press, 1998.

Berdahl, Daphne. "(N)Ostalgie for the Present: Memory, Longing, and East German Things." *Ethnos* 64, no. 2 (1999): 192–211.

Berdahl, Daphne. *On the Social Life of Postsocialism: Memory, Consumption, Germany.* Bloomington: Indiana University Press, 2010.

Berliner medizinische Gesellschaft, ed. *The Starving of Germany: Papers Read at Extraordinary Meeting of United Medical Societies Held at Headquarters of Berlin Medical Society, Berlin, December 18th, 1918.* Berlin, 1919.

Bessel, Richard. *Germany after the First World War.* Oxford: Clarendon, 1993.

Betts, Paul. "Manners, Morality, and Civilization: Reflections on Postwar German Etiquette Books." In *Histories of the Aftermath: The Legacies of the Second World War in Europe*, edited by Frank Biess and Robert G. Moeller, 196–214. New York: Berghahn, 2010.

Betts, Paul. "Socialism, Social Rights and Human Rights: The Case of East Germany." *Humanity: An International Journal of Human Rights, Humanitarianism, and Development* 3, no. 3 (2012): 407–426.

Beveridge, William. *Blockade and the Civilian Population.* Oxford: Clarendon, 1939.

Biess, Frank. *Homecomings: Returning POWs and the Legacies of Defeat in Postwar Germany.* Princeton, NJ: Princeton University Press, 2006.

Bilz, Rudolf. "Gemeinschaftsverpflegung und Nahrungswahl in psychologischer Sicht." In *Vollwertige Ernährung und Gemeinschaftsverpflegung*, 145–181, edited by J. C. Somogyi and H. Kapp. Basel: Karger, 1961.

Biraud, Y. M. "Health in Europe." *Quarterly Bulletin of the Health Organisation* 10, no. 4 (1943/44): 557–699.

Bircher, Ralph. *Hunsa: Das Volk, das keine Krankheit kennt.* Bern: Hans Huber, 1942.

Black, John. "Food: War and Postwar." *Annals of the American Academy of Political and Social Science* 225 (1943): i–vii.

Black, Monica. *Death in Berlin: From Weimar to Divided Germany.* Cambridge: Cambridge University Press, 2000.

Blackbourn, David. *The Conquest of Nature: Water, Landscape, and the Making of Modern Germany.* New York: W. W. Norton, 2007.

Boenheimm, M. and I. Leetzi. "Wird die Schulspeisung ihrer Aufgabe gerecht?" *Das deutsche Gesundheitswesen* 13, no. 45 (1958): 1459–1464.

Böhringer, Robert. *Zur Versorgungslage des europäischen Kontinents im Herbst 1945.* Zürich: Rascher, 1945.
Bohstedt, John. *The Politics of Provisions: Food Riots, Moral Economy, and Market Transition in England, c. 1500–1850.* London: Routledge, 2010.
Bonwetsch, Bernd. "Sowjetische Zwangsarbeiter vor und nach 1945: ein doppelter Leidensweg." *Jahrbücher für Geschichte Osteuropas* 41 (1993): 532–546.
Bourdieu, Pierre. *Distinction: A Social Critique of the Judgement of Taste.* Cambridge, MA: Harvard University Press, 1984.
Bourne, G. H. *Starvation in Europe.* London: G. Allen & Unwin, 1943.
Boym, Svetlana. *The Future of Nostalgia.* New York: Basic Books, 2001.
Brailsford, Henry Noel. *Across the Blockade: A Record of Travels in Enemy Europe.* New York: Harcourt, Brace and Howe, 1919.
Brandt, Karl. *Germany: Key to Peace in Europe.* Claremont, CA: Claremont College, 1949.
Braudel, Fernand. *Civilization and Capitalism, 15th-18th Century.* Vol. 1: *The Structures of Everyday Life, the Limits of the Possible.* New York: Harper and Row, 1982.
Bredtmann, Julia, Jochen Kluve, and Sandra Schaffner. "Women's Fertility and Employment Decisions under Two Political Systems: Comparing East and West Germany before Reunification." Ruhr Economic Paper No. 149, November 2009. Accessed online at http://ssrn.com/abstract=1505346 on October 24, 2016.
Bren, Paulina, and Mary Neuburger, eds. *Communism Unwrapped: Consumption in Cold War Eastern Europe.* New York: Oxford University Press, 2012.
Brink, Cornelia. *Ikonen der Vernichtung: öffentlicher Gebrauch von Fotografien aus nationalsozialistischen Konzentrationslagern nach 1945.* Berlin: Akademie, 1998.
Brown, Stephen. *A Most Damnable Invention: Dynamite, Nitrates, and the Making of the Modern World.* New York: St. Martins Press, 2005.
Brownell, Kelly, and Katherine Horgen. *Food Fight: The Inside Story of the Food Industry, America's Obesity Crisis, and What We Can Do about It.* Chicago: Contemporary, 2004.
Brunner, Ursula, and Rudi Pfeifer. *Zum Beispiel Bananen.* Göttingen: Lamuv-Verlag, 1993.
Bruntz, George. *Allied Propaganda and the Collapse of the German Empire in 1918.* Stanford, CA: Stanford University Press, 1938.
Bundy, McGeorge. "The Food for Peace Program as Viewed from an Interest of US National Security." In *Food for Peace: Proceedings of the National Conference, American Food for Peace Council*, n.p. Washington, DC: US Department of State, 1964.
Bunton, Robin, and Alan Petersen, eds. *Foucault, Health and Medicine.* New York: Routledge, 2013.
Burchardt, Lochar. "Die Auswirkungen der Kriegswirtschaft auf die deutsche Zivilbevölkerung im Ersten und im Zweiten Weltkrieg." *Militärgeschichtliche Zeitschrift* 15 (1974): 65–98.
Bürgel, Lucie. *Kochen, Braten, Backen mühelos in der modernen Gasküche.* Berlin-Halensee: Linde, 1952.
Byrne, Patrick, and Oral Capps. "Does Engel's Law Extend to Food Away from Home?" *Journal of Food Distribution Research* 27, no. 2 (1996): 22–32.
Cadot, Olivier, and Douglas Webber, "Banana Splits and Slipping over Banana Skins: The European and Transatlantic Politics of Bananas." Robert Schuman Center for Advanced Studies Working Papers 2001/03, European University Institute, Florence, Italy, 2001. Accessed online at http://hdl.handle.net/1814/1712 on December 7, 2016.
Caldwell, Melissa, Elizabeth Dunn, and Marion Nestle, eds. *Food and Everyday Life in the Postsocialist World.* Bloomington: Indiana University Press, 2009.
Carruth, Allison. "War Rations and the Food Politics of Late Modernism." *Modernism/Modernity* 16, no. 4 (2010): 767–795.
Carter, Erica. *How German Is She? Postwar West German Reconstruction and the Consuming Woman.* Ann Arbor: University of Michigan Press, 1997.
Charles, Daniel. *Master Mind: The Rise and Fall of Fritz Haber, the Nobel Laureate Who Launched the Age of Chemical Warfare.* New York: Ecco, 2005.

Charles, Nickie. "Food and Family Ideology." In *The Politics of Domestic Consumption: Critical Readings*, edited by Stevi Jackson and Shaun Moores, 100–115. London; New York: Prentice Hall, 1995.

Chickering, Roger. *Imperial Germany and the Great War 1914–1918*. Cambridge: Cambridge University Press, 2004.

Chickering, Roger. "World War I and the Theory of Total War. Reflections on the British and German Cases." In *Great War, Total War: Combat and Mobilization on the Western Front, 1914–1918*, edited by Roger Chickering and Stig Forster, 35–53. Cambridge: Cambridge University Press, 2000.

Ciesla, Burghard, and Patrice Poutrus. "Food Supply in a Planned Economy." In *Dictatorship as Experience: Towards a Socio-Cultural History of the GDR*, edited by Konrad Jarausch, 143–162. New York: Berghahn, 1999.

Claflin, Kyri, and Peter Scholliers, eds. *Writing Food History: A Global Perspective*. London: Bloomsbury, 2012.

Clauß, Wolfgang. *Der Kampf ums Brot*. Berlin: Reichsnährstand Verlag, 1938.

Clay, Lucius. *Decision in Germany*. Garden City, NY: Doubleday, 1950.

Cohen, Lizabeth. *A Consumer's Republic: The Politics of Mass Consumption in Postwar America*. New York: Random House, 2003.

Collingham, Lizzie. *The Taste of War: World War II and the Battle for Food*. New York: Penguin, 2011.

Connelly, Matthew. *Fatal Misconception: The Struggle to Control World Population*. Cambridge, MA: Harvard University Press, 2008.

Cooke, Paul, and Marc Silberman, eds. *Screening War: Perspectives on German Suffering*. Rochester, NY: Camden, 2010.

Cornelissen, Waltraud. "Traditionelle Rollenmuster: Frauen- und Männerbilder in den westdeutchen Medien." In *Frauen in Deutschland, 1945–1992*, edited by Gisela Helwig and Hildegard Maria Nickel, 53–70. Bonn: Bundeszentrale für Politische Bildung, 1993.

Corni, Gustavo, and Horst Gies. *Blut und Boden: Rassenideologie und Agrarpolitik im Staat Hitlers*. Idstein: Schulz-Kirchner, 1994.

Coveney, John. *Food, Morals and Meaning: The Pleasure and Anxiety of Eating*. New York: Routledge, 2006.

Cremer, Hans-Dietrich. *Gemeinschaftsverpflegung*. Darmstadt: D. Steinkopff, 1962.

Crew, David, ed. *Consuming Germany in the Cold War*. Oxford: Berg, 2003.

Cullather, Nick. *The Hungry World: America's Cold War Battle against Poverty in Asia*. Cambridge, MA: Harvard University Press, 2010.

Curti, Merle. *American Philanthropy Abroad: A History*. New Brunswick, NJ: Rutgers University Press, 1963.

Curtis-Bennett, Noel. *The Food of the People: Being the History of Industrial Feeding*. London: Faber and Faber, 1949.

Dams, Theodor. *Nahrungsmittelhilfe; Ein Beitrag zur Beseitigung des Hungers in der Welt?* Aachen: Misereor-Aktuel, 1969.

Darré, Walther. *Der Schweinemord*. Munich: Verlag der NSDAP, 1937.

"Das war Massenverpflegung im Jahre 1932: Ein schon längst vergessenes Kapital." *Kochpraxis und Gemeinschaftsverpflegung* (April 1961): 18–20.

Daun, Gustav Erich. *Geschäfte mit dem Hunger*. Goslar: Blut und Boden, 1939.

Davis, Mike. *Late Victorian Holocausts: El Niño Famines and the Making of the Third World*. London: Verso, 2001.

Davison, W. Phillips. "Political Significance of Recognition via Mass Media: An Illustration from the Berlin Blockade." *Public Opinion Quarterly* 20 (Spring 1956): 327–333.

Decke, Heini, and Herbert Pilz. *Gastronomische Versorgung im Betrieb*. Berlin: Verlag die Wirtschaft, 1965.

Der Kriegsernährungsamt, ed. *Die Kriegsernährungswirtschaft 1917*. Leipzig: Druck der Spamerschen, 1917.

Deutsch, Tracey. *Building a Housewife's Paradise: Gender, Politics, and American Grocery Stores in the Twentieth Century*. Chapel Hill: University of North Carolina, 2010.

Deutsche Gesellschaft für Ernährung, ed. *Ernährungsbericht 1988*. Bonn: DGE, 1988.

"Deutschland gab Europa mehr zu essen. UNRRA bedeutet Hungersnot." *Gemeinschaftsverpflegung mit Volksernährung* 20 (October 1944): 341.

Die deutsche Arbeitsfront, ed. *Gemeinschaftsverpflegung in Lager und Werksküchen*. Berlin: Verlag der deutschen Arbeitsfront, 1940.

"Die Frage nach den Vorräten—deutsche Erfahrungen—gegenerische Fehlspekulationen." *Gemeinschaftsverpflegung mit Volksernährung* 8 (April 1943): 181.

Die Frau und ihre Küche. Munich: Kindler, 1962.

Dittmar, Hans. *Deutschland erweitert seinen Nahrungsraum durch Landeskulturmaßnahmen*. Berlin: Deutsche Informationsstelle, 1941.

Donat, Peter. "Die Entwicklung des Ernährungsverhaltens der DDR-Bevölkerung vor und nach der Währungsreform." In *Ernährung in Deutschland nach der Wende: Veränderungen in Haushalt, Beruf und Gemeinschaftsverpflegung*, edited by Thomas Kutsch and Sigrid Weggemann, 1–20. Witterschlick: M. Wehle, 1996.

Dornheim, Andreas. "Rasse, Raum und Autarkie. Sachverständigengutachten zur Rolle des Reichsministeriums für Ernährung und Landwirtschaft in der NS-Zeit." Bundesministerium für Ernährung, Landwirtschaft und Verbraucherschutz, 2011. Accessed online on December 7, 2016. http://www.bmel.de/SharedDocs/Downloads/Ministerium/RolleReichsministeriumNSZeit.pdf?__blob=publicationFile.

Douglas, Mary. *Purity and Danger: An Analysis of the Concepts of Pollution and Taboo*. London: Ark, 1984.

Drahn, Ernst, and Susanne Leonhard. *Unterirdische Literatur im revolutionären Deutschland während des Weltkrieges*. Berlin: Gesellschaft und Erziehung, 1920.

Droese, W. "Erste Erfahrungen über das Mittagessen in Ganztagsschulen. Zugleich ein Beitrag zur Gemeinschaftsverpflegung von Kindern. *Deutsche medizinische Wochenschrift* 98, no. 34 (1973): 1563–1567.

Droese, W., H. Stolley, G. van Oost, and M. Kersting. "Erhebungen zur Ernährung bei Schulverpflegung in der Bundesrepublik Deutschland." In *Internationale Arbeitstagung Schulverpflegung*, edited by Günter Schlierf, 149–162. Frankfurt: DGE, 1976.

"Drüben und hüben. Anglo-amerikanische und deutsche Nahrungsversorgung." *Gemeinschaftsverpflegung mit Volksernährung* 16 (August 1944): 216.

Drummer, Kurt, and Käthe Muskewitz. *Kochkunst aus dem Fernsehstudio: Rezepte—praktische Winke—literarische Anmerkungen*. Leipzig: Fachbuchverlag, 1968.

Edkins, Jenny. *Whose Hunger? Concepts of Famine, Practices of Aid*. Minneapolis: University of Minnesota Press, 2000.

Ehrenberg, Paul. *Volksernährung und Christentum*. Berlin: Wichern-Verlag, 1920.

Ehrlich, Paul. *The Population Bomb*. New York: Ballantine, 1968.

Einhorn, Barbara. "Socialist Emancipation: The Women's Movement in the German Democratic Republic." In *Promissory Notes: Women in the Transition to Socialism*, edited by Sonia Kruks, Rayna Rapp, and Marilyn Young, 282–305. New York: Monthly Review Press, 1989.

Eintopf-Gerichte: 70 Vorschläge und Rezepte für gute Eintopf-Gerichte von 10 bis 50 Pfennig mit genauer Preis-Angabe. Berlin: Ullstein, 1933.

Elektrowärme Sörnewitz, ed. *Praktische Winke für die IKA Kleinküche*. Sörnewitz: Eigenverlag, 1950.

Elias, Norbert. *The Civilizing Process*. Oxford: Blackwell, 1994.

Ellerbrock, Dagmar. *"Healing Democracy": Demokratie als Heilmittel: Gesundheit, Krankheit und Politik in der amerikanischen Besatzungszone 1945–1949*. Bonn: Dietz, 2004.

Elliott, Charlene. "Big Persons, Small Voices: On Governance, Obesity, and the Narrative of the Failed Citizen." *Journal of Canadian Studies* 41, no. 3 (2007): 134–149.

Enderlein, Hanna, and Uta Lange. *Das Backbuch*. Leipzig: Verlag für die Frau, 1967.

Erker, Paul. *Ernährungskrise und Nachkriegsgesellschaft: Bauern und Arbeiterschaft in Bayern 1943–1953*. Stuttgart: Klett-Cotta, 1990.

Farquharson, John. "'Emotional but Influential': Victor Gollancz, Richard Stokes and the British Zone of Germany, 1945–9." *Journal of Contemporary History* 22, no. 3 (July 1987): 501–519.

Feldman, Gerald. *The Great Disorder: Politics, Economics, and Society in the German Inflation, 1914–1924.* New York: Oxford University Press, 1997.

Feldman, Gerald. "Kriegswirtschaft und Zwangswirtschaft: die Diskreditierung des Sozialismus in Deutschland während des Ersten Weltkrieges." In *Der Erste Weltkrieg. Wirkung, Wahrnehmung, Analyse*, edited by Wolfgang Michalka, 456–484. Munich: Piper, 1994.

Ferguson, Priscilla. "Culinary Nationalism." *Gastronomica* 10, no. 1 (2010): 102–109.

Fine, Ben. *The World of Consumption: The Material and Cultural Revisited.* London: Routledge, 2002.

Fischer, Herbert. "Einige Probleme der Entwicklung der Einrichtungen der Gemeinschaftsverpflegung." *Mitteilungen des Instituts für Bedarfsforschung* 1 (1962): 34.

Fischer, Ruth, and Franz Heimann. *Deutsche Kinderfibel.* Berlin: Rowohlt, 1933.

Fishburn, Howard. "Won't Starve until Fall." *Science News-Letter* 43, no. 3 (January 16, 1943): 38–39.

Flachowsky, Soren. *Von der Notgemeinschaft zum Reichsforschungsrat: Wissenschaftspolitik im Kontext von Autarkie, Aufrustung und Krieg.* Stuttgart: Steiner, 2008.

Florian, H. J. "Gemeinschaftsverpflegung: Angewandte Präventivmedizin." *Münchener medizinische Wochenschrift* 110, no. 34 (1968): 1884–1893.

Foucault, Michel. *The Birth of Biopolitics: Lectures at the College de France, 1978–79.* New York: Palgrave Macmillan, 2008.

Foucault, Michel. *Security, Territory, Population.* Basingstoke, UK: Palgrave Macmillan, 2007.

Frank, Matthew. "The New Morality: Victor Gollancz, 'Save Europe Now' and the German Refugee Crisis, 1945–46." *Twentieth Century British History* 17, no. 2 (2006): 230–256.

Freedman, Paul, Joyce Chaplin, and Ken Albala, eds. *Food in Time and Place: The American Historical Association Companion to Food History.* Berkeley: University of California Press, 2014.

Freier Deutscher Gewerkschaftsbund, ed. *Gewerkschaften und Gemeinschaftsverpflegung.* Berlin: Tribüne, 1958.

Friebe, C., and M. Möhr. "Ausgewählten Ergebnisse zu Einstellungen im Ernährungsverhalten in der ehemaligen DDR." *Zeitschrift für Ernährungswissenschaft* 31, no. 2 (1992): 2–18.

Friedmann, Harriet. "The Political Economy of Food: The Rise and Fall of the Postwar International Food Order." *American Journal of Sociology* 88 (1982): 248–286.

Friedrich Ebert Stiftung, ed. *Der Alltag in der DDR.* Bonn: Verlag Neue Gesellschaft, 1986.

"Gemeinschaftsverpflegung im Betrieb. Interview mit Gerhart Stropp, Direktor der zentralen Forschungs- und Informationsstelle, Arbeiterversorgung bei der Hauptdirektion Wismut Handel, Karl- Marx-Stadt." *Gastronomie* 1, no. 3 (1970): 1–2.

"Gemeinschaftsverpflegung—nicht Massenfütterung." *Kochpraxis und Gemeinschaftsverpflegung* 12 (1954): 4–5.

Gedrich, K., and M. Albrecht, *Datenrecherche der Entwicklung der Haushaltsausgaben für Ernährung in der zweiten Hälfte des 20. Jahrhunderts.* Materialenband Nr. 3. Freising-Weihenstephan, 2003.

Gellately, Robert. *Gestapo and German Society: Enforcing Racial Policy.* Oxford: Oxford University Press, 1991.

Gerber, Sophie. *Küche, Kühlschrank, Kilowatt: zur Geschichte des privaten Energiekonsums in Deutschland, 1945–1990.* Bielefeld: Transcript, 2015.

Gerhardt, Gesine. *Nazi Hunger Politics: A History of Food in the Third Reich.* Lanham, MD: Rowman & Littlefield, 2015.

Gerlach, Christian. "Die Welternährungskrise 1972–1975." *Geschichte und Gesellschaft* 31, no. 4 (2005): 546–585.

Gerlach, Christian. *Krieg, Ernährung, Völkermord. Deutsche Vernichtungspolitik im Zweiten Weltkrieg.* Zürich: Pendo-Verlag, 2001.

Gerson, M. "Feeding the German Army." *New York State Journal of Medicine* 41, no. 13 (1941): 1471–1476.

Geyer, Martin. "Teuerungsprotest und Teuerungsunruhen 1914–1923. Selbsthilfegesellschaft und Geldentwertung." In *Der Kampf um das tägliche Brot: Nahrungsmangel, Versorgungspolitik und Protest, 1770–1990*, edited by Manfred Gailus and Heinrich Volkmann, 319–345. Opladen: Westdeutscher, 1994.

Gies, Horst. "Aufgaben und Probleme der nationalsozialistischen Ernährungswirtschaft 1933–39." *Vierteljahrschrift für Sozial- und Wirtschaftsgeschichte* 66 (1979): 466–499.

Gillmann, Helmut. "Beitrag zum Problem der Unterernährung aus den Erfahrungen einer ärztlichen Prüfstelle an Hand von 123,425 Fällen." *Ärztliche Wochenschrift* 7/8 (February 1948): 120–124.

Gilman, Sander. *Fat: A Cultural History of Obesity*. Cambridge: Polity Press, 2008.

Glatzel, Hans. *Nahrung und Ernährung; Altbekanntes und Neuerforschtes vom Essen*. Berlin: J. Springer, 1939.

Gold, Bela. *Wartime Economic Planning in Agriculture: A Study in the Allocation of Resources*. New York: Columbia University Press, 1949.

Goldberg, David Theo. "Racial States." In *A Companion to Racial and Ethnic Studies*, edited by David Theo Goldberg and John Solomos, 233–258. Oxford: Blackwell, 2002.

Goldring, Douglas. *What the Army Thinks of the Blockade: Summary of Reports by British Officers on the Condition of Affairs in Germany and the Effect of the Allies' Naval Blockade*. London: Fight the Famine Council, 1919.

Gollancz, Victor. *Is It Nothing to You? Photographs of Starving German Children*. London: V. Gollancz, 1945.

Gollancz, Victor. *Leaving Them to Their Fate: The Ethics of Starvation*. London: V. Gollancz, 1946.

Gräfe, Heinrich-Karl. *Richtige Ernährung, gesunde Menschen. Nahrungsbedarf, Ernährungsweise u. Kostpläne unter verschiedenen Lebens- u. Arbeitsbedingungen*. Leipzig: Fachbuchverlag, 1967.

Gräfe, Heinrich-Karl. *Vollwertige Gemeinschaftsverpflegung nach den drei Werkessenstufen I, II, III. Zugleich ein Ratgeber neuzeitlicher Mittagessengestaltung in Heim u. Familie*. Berlin: Verl. Technik, 1955.

Gries, Rainer. *Die Rationen-Gesellschaft: Versorgungskampf und Vergleichsmentalität: Leipzig, München und Köln nach dem Kriege*. Münster: Westfälisches Dampfboot, 1991.

Gries, Reiner. "Geschmack der Heimat." *Deutschland-Archiv* 27 (October 1994): 1041–1058.

Grossmann, Atina. "Grams, Calories, and Food: Languages of Victimization, Entitlement, and Human Rights in Occupied Germany, 1945–1949." In *The Human Rights Revolution: An International History*, edited by Petra Goedde, William Hitchcock, and Akira Iriye, 113–132. Oxford: Oxford University Press, 2012.

Grossmann, Atina. *Jews, Germans, and Allies: Close Encounters in Occupied Germany*. Princeton, NJ: Princeton University Press, 2007.

Grossmann, Atina. *Reforming Sex: The German Movement for Birth Control and Abortion Reform, 1920–1950*. New York: Oxford University Press, 1995.

Grünbacher, Armin. *The Making of German Democracy: West Germany in the Adenauer Era, 1945–65*. Manchester: Manchester University Press, 2010.

Grundfragen unserer Ernährungswirtschaft im Zweijahresplan. Berlin: Deutscher Bauern-Verlag, 1948.

Gumbert, Heather. *Envisioning Socialism: Television and the Cold War in the German Democratic Republic*. Ann Arbor: University of Michigan Press, 2014.

Günther, S. "Sozialmedizinische Bedeutung der Fettsucht." *Medizinische Welt* 6 (February 10, 1968): 386–392.

Gutezeit, G. "Rückwirkungen der Schulverpflegung auf das Elternhaus." In *Internationale Arbeitstagung Schulverpflegung*, edited by Günter Schlierf, 177–193. Frankfurt: DGE, 1976.

Guthman, Julie. *Weighing In: Obesity, Food Justice, and the Limits of Capitalism*. Berkeley: University of California Press, 2011.

Gysi, Jutta, and Dagmar Meyer. "Leitbild: berufstätige Mutter—DDR-Frauen in Familie, Partnerschaft und Ehe." In *Frauen in Deutschland 1945–1990*, edited by G. Helwig and H. M. Nickel, 139–165. Berlin: Akademie, 1993.

Gysi, Jutta. *Familienleben in der DDR. Zum Alltag von Familien mit Kindern*. Berlin: Akademie, 1989.

Haas, Sigmund Franz. "Veränderungen in der deutschen Volksernährung, ihre Ursachen und die Neugestaltung der von diesen Veränderungen betroffenen Teile der deutschen Ernährungswissenschaft durch die nationalsozialistische Gesetzgebung." PhD diss., Heidelberg University, 1937.

Haase-Nothnagel, Margarethe. *Harmonische Ernährung für wenig Geld durch gesunde Kost.* Krailling: Müller, 1958.

Haenel, H., M. Zobel, and M. Möhr. "Probleme der gesellschaftlichen Speisenwirtschaft in der DDR." *Ernährungsforschung* 15, no. 2 (1970): 33–43.

Hajek, Hans. "Für und wider den großen Topf." *Das Großküchen-Magazin* 1, no. 3 (1949): 1.

Hambach, Richard. *Wie das Strichmännlein den Kobold Huckedack besiegte.* Dresden: Deutsches Hygiene-Museum, 1965.

Harsch, Donna. *Revenge of the Domestic: Women, the Family, and Communism in the German Democratic Republic.* Princeton, NJ: Princeton University Press, 2007.

Härtel, Christian. "Ostdeusche Bestimmungen für den Paketverkehr im Spiegel westdeutscher Markblätter." In *Das Westpaket: Geschenksendung, Keine Handelsware*, edited by Christian Härtel and Petra Kabus, 45–56. Berlin: Ch. Links, 2000.

Haselmayr, Luise. *Einkaufen will gelernt sein.* Munich: BLV Verlagsgesellschaft, 1962.

Haskerl, Liane. "Verbraucherausschußarbeit im Dienste der Hausfrau." In *Die Macht der Hausfrau: Eine ernährungswirtschaftliche Fibel für den Verbraucher*, edited by Liane Haskerl and Wolfgang Clauss, 19–21. Kiel: Kieler Druckerei, 1952.

Haskarl, Liane, and Wolfgang Clauss. *Die Macht der Hausfrau. Eine ernährungswirtschaftliche Fibel für den Verbraucher.* Kiel: Verl. d. Kieler Druckerei, 1952.

Heim, Susanne. *Plant Breeding and Agrarian Research in Kaiser-Wilhelm-Institutes 1933–1945: Calories, Caoutchouc, Careers.* Göttingen: Wallstein, 2003.

Heinzelmann, Ursula. *Beyond Bratwurst: A History of Food in Germany.* London: Reaktion, 2014.

Hell, Andreas. *How Do People Live in the GDR? Living Standards and Way of Life under Socialism.* Berlin: Panorama DDR, 1974.

Helweg-Larsen, Per. *Famine Disease in German Concentration Camps: Complications and Sequels.* Copenhagen: Andelsbogtr, 1952.

Hendriks, Gisela. "The Politics of Food: The Case of Germany." *Food Policy* 12, no. 2 (1987): 35–45.

Hertwig, Hugo. *Richtige Ernährung, eine Lebensfrage.* Berlin: Gersbach & Sohn, 1938.

Herwig, Holger. "Total Rhetoric, Limited War: Germanys U-boat Campaign 1917–1918." In *Great War, Total War: Combat and Mobilization on the Western Front, 1914–1918*, edited by Roger Chickering and Stig Forster, 189–206. Cambridge: Cambridge University Press, 2000.

Heyll, Ulrich. "Der Kampf ums Eiweissminimum. Zum Konflikt zwischen wissenschaftlicher Ernährungslehre und Ernährungsreform in Deutschland im 19. und 20. Jahrhundert." *Deutsche medizinische Wochenschrift* 132, no. 51 (2007): 2768–2773.

Higgins, Benjamin. "Germany's Bid for Agricultural Self Sufficiency." *Journal of Farm Economics* 21, no. 2 (1939): 435–461.

"Hinter glänzender Fassade: Hunger!" *Gemeinschaftsverpflegung mit Volksernährung* 4 (February 1944): 74.

Hionidou, Violetta. *Famine and Death in Occupied Greece, 1941–1944.* Cambridge: Cambridge University Press, 2006.

Hirschmann, Ira. *The Embers Still Burn: An Eye-Witness View of the Postwar Ferment in Europe and the Middle East and Our Disastrous Get-Soft-with-Germany Policy.* New York: Simon and Schuster, 1949.

Hitler, Adolf. *Mein Kampf.* Boston: Reynal & Hitchcock, 1940.

Hitler, Adolf. *Speeches and Proclamations, 1932–1945.* Edited by Max Domarus. Wauconda, IL: Bolchazy-Carducci, 1990.

Hoffmann, Stefan-Ludwig. "Introduction: Genealogies of Human Rights." In *Human Rights in the Twentieth Century*, edited by Stefan-Ludwig Hoffmann, 1–26. Cambridge: Cambridge University Press, 2010.

Höfler-Waag, Martin. *Die Arbeits- und Leistungsmedizin im Nationalsozialismus.* Husum: Matthiesen, 1994.
Holcomb, Rodney, John Park, and Oral Capps. "Revisiting Engel's Law: Examining Expenditure Patterns for Food at Home and Away from Home." *Journal of Food Distribution Research* 26, no. 2 (1995): 1–8.
Holtmeier, H. J. "Ernährungsprobleme der Gegenwart." *Die Agnes Karl-Schwester, Der Krankenpfleger* 21, no. 8 (1967): 309–312.
Hoover, Herbert. *Can Europe's Children Be Saved? Herbert Hoover Appeals for the Lives of 40,000,000 Starving Women and Children.* Washington, DC: US Government Printing Office, 1941.
Hoover, Herbert. *Food in War.* London: W. H. Smith & Son, 1918.
Hoover, Herbert. *No Reconstruction without Food: A Remedy for Near Starvation in Germany.* New York: Common Cause, 1948.
Hoover, Herbert. "The Weapon of Food." *National Geographic Magazine,* September 1917, 197–212.
Hoover, Herbert. *We'll Have to Feed the World Again.* New York: Colliers, 1942.
Horn, Erna. *Der Eintopf: Das deutsche Spargericht.* Munich: Siegismund & Volkening, 1933.
Horne, John, and Alan Kramer. *German Atrocities, 1914: A History of Denial.* New Haven, CT: Yale University Press, 2002.
Hottinger, Adolf. *Hungerkrankheit, Hungerödem, Hungertuberkulose; historische, klinische, pathophysiologische und pathologisch-anatomische Studien und Beobachtungen an ehemaligen Insassen aus Konzentrationslagern.* Basel: B. Schwabe, 1948.
Howard, N. P. "The Social and Political Consequences of the Allied Food Blockade of Germany, 1918–19." *German History* 11, no. 2 (April 1993): 161–188.
Hübner, Peter. "Arbeiterklasse als Inszenierung: Arbeiter und Gesellschaftspolitik in der SBZ/DDR." In *Die Grenzen der Diktatur: Staat und Gesellschaft in der DDR,* edited by Richard Bessel and Ralph Jessen, 199–223. Göttingen: Vandenhoeck & Ruprecht, 1996.
Hübner, Peter. *Konsens, Konflikt und Kompromiss: Soziale Arbeiterinteressen und Sozialpolitik in der SBZ/DDR 1945–1970.* Berlin: Akademie, 1995.
Hueppe, F. *Unser täglich Brot in Krieg und Frieden.* Dresden: T. Steinkopff, 1918.
Hull, Isabel. *Absolute Destruction: Military Culture and the Practices of War in Imperial Germany.* Ithaca, NY: Cornell University Press, 2005.
Hull, Isabel. *A Scrap of Paper: Breaking and Making International Law during the Great War.* Ithaca, NY: Cornell University Press, 2014.
"Hungersnot: Wie Gewöhnlich." *Gemeinschaftsverpflegung* 3, no. 1 (February 1944): 50.
Ingimundarson, Valur. "The Eisenhower Administration, the Adenauer Government, and the Political Uses of the East German Uprising in 1953." *Diplomatic History* 20, no. 3 (1996): 381–410.
Irving, David John. *Der Morgenthau-Plan: 1944–45.* Bremen: Wieland Soyka, 1986.
Jachertz, Ruth, and Alexander Nützenadel. "Coping with Hunger? Visions of a Global Food System, 1930–1960." *Journal of Global History* 6 (2011): 99–119.
Jacobeit, Wolfgang, and Christoph Kopke. *Die biologisch-dynamische Wirtschaftsweise im KZ: die Güter der 'Deutschen Versuchsanstalt für Ernährung und Verpflegung' der SS von 1939 bis 1945.* Berlin: Trafo-Verlag Weist, 1999.
James, Robert Rhodes, ed. *Winston S. Churchill: His Complete Speeches 1897–1963.* Vol. 7: *1943–1949.* New York: Chelsea House, 1974.
Jarausch, Konrad. "Beyond the National Narrative: Implications of Reunification for Recent German History." *Historical Social Research. Supplement.* 24, no. 4 (2012): 498–514.
Jensen, Borge. *The "World-Food-Shortage": A Communist-Zionist Plot.* Aberfeldy, UK: W. L. Richardson, 1947.
Joice, Arthur. *CRALOG, Council of Relief Agencies Licensed for Operation in Germany; a Brief Historical Description.* CRALOG, 1949.
Jones, Grinnell. "Nitrogen: Its Fixation, Its Uses in Peace and War." *Quarterly Journal of Economics* 34, no. 3 (May 1920): 391–431.

Jourdain, Margaret. "Air Raid Reprisals and Starvation by Blockade." *International Journal of Ethics* 28, no. 4 (July 1918): 542–553.
Junker, Reinhold. *Die Lage der Mütter in der Bundesrepublik Deutschland: ein Forschungsbericht.* Frankfurt: Eigenverlag des deutschen Vereins für öffentliche und private Fürsorge, 1965.
"Kakao, Schokolade, Pralinen." *Die Ernährungswirtschaft* 9 (1957): 155.
Kaminsky, Annette. *Wohlstand, Schönheit, Glück: Kleine Konsumgeschichte der DDR.* Munich: Beck, 2001.
Kavanaugh, Sarah. *ORT, the Second World War and the Rehabilitation of Holocaust Survivors.* London: Vallentine Mitchell, 2008.
Kay, Alex. "Germany's Staatssekretäre, Mass Starvation and the Meeting of 2 May 1941." *Journal of Contemporary History* 41 (2006): 685–700.
Kerr-Boyle, Neula. "Orders of Eating and Eating Disorders: Food, Bodies and Anorexia Nervosa in the German Democratic Republic, 1949–90." PhD diss., University College London, 2012.
Kertzer, David, and Marzio Barbagli, eds. *History of the European Family.* Vol. 2: *Family Life in the Long Nineteenth Century, 1789–1913.* New Haven, CT: Yale University Press, 2003.
Ketz, Hans-Albrecht. "Der Beitrag der Gesellschaft für Ernährung in der DDR zur Förderung einer gesunden Ernährung der Bevölkerung der DDR." *Zeitung für die gesamten Hygiene und ihre Grenzgebiete* 26, no. 12 (1980): 924–927.
Ketz, Hans-Albrecht, and Hans Eichhorn. *Schlank aber wie?* Berlin: Verlag Volk und Gesundheit, 1987.
Kimball, Warren. *Swords or Ploughshares? The Morgenthau Plan for Defeated Nazi Germany, 1943–1946.* Philadelphia: Lippincott, 1976.
Klatt, Werner. "Food and Farming in Germany: I. Food and Nutrition." *International Affairs* 26, no. 1 (1950): 45–58.
Klee, Ernst. *Deutsche Medizin im Dritten Reich: Karrieren vor und nach 1945.* Frankfurt: S. Fischer, 2001.
Klemann, Hein, and Sergei Kudryashov. *Occupied Economies: An Economic History of Nazi-Occupied Europe, 1939–1945.* London: Berg, 2012.
Klosterkötter, W. "Hygenische und sozialhygienische Gesichtspunkte zur betrieblichen Gemeinschaftsverpflegung." *Zeitschrift für Allgemeimmedizin, der Landarzt* 48, no. 16 (1972): 783–786.
Kluge, Ulrich. "Kriegs- und Mangelernährung im Nationalsozialismus." *Beiträge zur historischen Sozialkunde* 15 (1985): 67–73.
Knight, Eric, and Paul Rotha. *World of Plenty: The Book of the Film.* London: Nicholson & Watson, 1945.
Knoch, Habbo. *Die Tat als Bild: Fotografien des Holocaust in der deutschen Erinnerungskultur.* Hamburg: Hamburger Edition, 2001.
Koistinen, Paul. *Mobilizing for Modern War: The Political Economy of American Warfare, 1865–1919.* Lawrence: University Press of Kansas, 1997.
Kolinsky, Eva. *Women in 20th century Germany: A Reader.* Manchester, UK: Manchester University Press, 1995.
Körner, Norbert. "Die Rolle der staatlichen Gaststätten beim Aufbau des Sozialismus." *Die neuzeitliche Gaststätte* 5, no. 8 (1957): 2–3.
Köstlin, Konrad. "Der Eintopf der Deutschen. Das Zusammengekochte als Kultessen." In *Tübinger Beiträge zur Volkskultur*, edited by Utz Jeggle and Hermann Bausinger, 220–241. Tübingen: Tübinger Vereinigung für Volkskunde, 1986.
Kraft, Wilhelm. *Wahrheiten über das Brot, unter besonderer Berücksichtigung des Knäckebrotes.* Frankfurt: Salle, 1938.
Kramer, Alan. *Dynamic of Destruction: Culture and Mass Killing in the First World War.* Oxford: Oxford University Press, 2007.
Krause, Andrea. "Mobile Beratung und Information über Ernährung des AID-Verbraucherdienstes." In *Ernährung in Deutschland nach der Wende: Veränderungen in Haushalt, Beruf und Gemeinschaftsverpflegung*, edited by Thomas Kutsch and Sigrid Weggemann, 251–262. Witterschlick: M. Wehle, 1996.

Krauß, Herbert. *Gesunde Küche: Anleitung zu einer gesundheitsfördernden Ernährung*. Berlin: Verlag Volk und Gesundheit, 1960.

Kraut, Heinrich. "Ernährungsphysiologie als Grundlage der Ernährungswirtschaft." *Ernährung und Verpflegung* 1, no. 4–6 (1949): 77–80.

Kraut, Heinrich, and Willy Wirths. *Mehr Wissen um Ernährung. Berichte über Studienreisen im Rahmen der Auslandshilfe der USA*. Frankfurt: Verlag Kommentator, 1955.

Kruse, Walter, and Kurt Hintze. *Sparsame Ernährung nach Erhebungen im Krieg und Frieden*. Dresden: Dt. Hygiene-Museums, 1922.

Kucher, E. "Fettsucht: bei ambulanter Therapie doch heilbar?" *Münchner medizinische Wochenschrift* 120, no. 48 (1978): 1589.

Kuhn, Gerd. *Wohnkultur und kommunale Wohnungspolitik in Frankfurt am Main 1880 bis 1930: auf dem Wege zu einer pluralen Gesellschaft der Individuen*. Bonn: Dietz, 1998.

Kühnau, J. "Die Frau als Hüterin der Ernährung." In *Die Frau und ihre Ernährung*, edited by Deutsche Gesellschaft für Ernährung, 5–10. Frankfurt: Franz Jos. Henrich, 1959.

Kühnau, J. "Ernährungsphysiologische Gesichtspunkte bei der Verwendung von Gefrierprodukten." In *Probleme der Ernährung durch Gefrierkost*, edited by Deutsche Gesellschaft für Ernährung. Darmstadt: Steinkopff, 1964.

Kühne, Thomas. *Belonging and Genocide: Hitler's Community, 1918–1945*. New Haven, CT: Yale University Press, 2010.

Kunz, Norbert. "Das Beispiel Charkow: Eine Stadtbevölkerung als Opfer der deutschen Hungerstrategie 1941/42." In *Verbrechen der Wehrmacht: Bilanz einer Debatte*, edited by Christian Hartmann, Johannes Hürter, and Ulrike Jureit, 136–144. Munich: Beck, 2005.

Kury, Patrick. *Der überforderte Mensch: eine Wissensgeschichte vom Stress zum Burnout*. Frankfurt: Campus, 2012.

Landsman, Mark. *Dictatorship and Demand: the Politics of Consumerism in East Germany*. Cambridge, MA: Harvard University Press, 2005.

Langer, William. *The Famine in Germany*. Washington, DC: US Government Printing Office, 1946.

League of Nations. "The Economic Depression and Public Health: Memorandum Prepared by the Health Section." *Quarterly Bulletin of the Health Organisation* 1 (1932): 425–476.

League of Nations. "The Most Suitable Methods of Detecting Malnutrition due to the Economic Depression." *Quarterly Bulletin of the Health Organisation* 2 (1933): 116–129.

LeBesco, Kathleen. *Revolting Bodies? The Struggle to Redefine Fat Identity*. Amherst: University of Massachusetts Press, 2004.

Lefevre, Andrea. "Lebensmittelunruhen in Berlin 1920–1923." In *Der Kampf um das tägliche Brot: Nahrungsmangel, Versorgungspolitik und Protest, 1770–1990*, edited by Manfred Gailus and Heinrich Volkmann, 346–360. Opladen: Westdeutscher, 1994.

Lévi-Strauss, Claude. *The Raw and the Cooked*. New York: Harper & Row, 1969.

Lippki, Erika, Antje Lode, and Anna Teut. *Essen in der Arbeitswelt: Tatsachen, Ursachen, Hypotheken, Hypothesen*. Berlin: Internationales Design Zentrum, 1973.

Lipscomb, F. "Medical Aspects of Belsen Concentration Camp." *Lancet* (August 9, 1945): 313–315.

Liulevicius, Vejas Gabriel. *War Land on the Eastern Front: Culture, National Identity and German Occupation in World War I*. Cambridge: Cambridge University Press, 2000.

Loehlin, Jennifer Ann. *From Rugs to Riches: Housework, Consumption and Modernity in Germany*. Oxford: Berg, 1999.

Logemann, Jan. *Trams or Tailfins: Public and Private Prosperity in Postwar West Germany*. Chicago: University of Chicago Press, 2012.

Lüdtke, Alf. "Hunger in der Großen Depression: Hungererfahrung und Hungerpolitik am Ende der Weimarer Republik." *Archiv für Sozialgeschichte* 27 (1987): 145–176.

Lummel, Peter. "Food Provisioning in the German Army of the First World War." In *Food and War in Twentieth Century Europe*, edited by Ina Zweiniger-Bargielowska, Rachel Duffett, and Alain Drouard, 13–26. Farnham, UK: Ashgate, 2011.

Lutz, Julie. *Eintopf-Gerichte von Julie Lutz: eine leicht fassliche Schilderung aller Kochvorgänge, die es jeden, auch dem gänzlich Unerfahrenen ermöglicht, ohne weitere Anleitung gute und billige Eintopf-Gerichte herzustellen*. Bramenburg a.J: Lutz, 1933.

Macdonald, Dwight. *Shall Europe Starve?* New York: Politics, 1945.
Madarasz, Jeanette. *Working in East Germany: Normality in a Socialist Dictatorship 1961–79.* Basingstoke, UK: Palgrave Macmillan, 2006.
Maier, Charles. "Between Taylorism and Technocracy: European Ideologies and the Vision of Industrial Productivity in the 1920s." *Journal of Contemporary History* 5, no. 2 (1970): 27–61.
Maier, Charles. *Leviathan 2.0: Inventing Modern Statehood.* Cambridge, MA: Belknap Press, 2014.
Major, Patrick. *Behind the Berlin Wall: East Germany and the Frontiers of Power.* Oxford: Oxford University Press, 2010.
Marcusson, Hildegard. *Das Wachstum von Kindern und Jugendlichen in der Deutschen Demokratischen Republik: Grösse, Gewicht und Brustumfang nach Untersuchungen in den Jahren 1956–1958.* Berlin: Akademie, 1961.
Marx Ferree, Myra. "Rise and Fall of 'Mommy Politics': Feminism and Unification in (East) Germany." *Feminist Studies* 19, no. 1 (1993): 89–115.
Marx, Karl. *The German Ideology.* New York: Prometheus, 1976.
Matheja-Thaeker, Mechthild. *Alternative Emanzipationsvorstellungen in der DDR-Frauenliteratur 1971–1989.* Stuttgart: Verlag Hans-Dieter Heinz, 1996.
Mathias, Middell, and Felix Wemheuer, eds. *Hunger, Nutrition and Rationing under State Socialism, 1917–2006.* Leipzig: University of Leipzig Press, 2010.
Mattes, Monika. *Das Projekt Ganztagsschule: Aufbrüche, Reformen und Krisen in der Bundesrepublik Deutschland 1955–1982.* Köln: Böhlau, 2015.
May, Elaine Tyler. *Homeward Bound: American Families in the Cold War Era.* New York: Basic Books, 2008.
Mazower, Mark. "The Strange Triumph of Human Rights, 1933–1950." *Historical Journal* 47 no. 2 (2004): 379–398.
Mecklinger, Ludwig. "Aspekte der Prophylaxe und Therapie ernährungsabhängiger und ernährungsbeeinflussbarer Erkrankungen." In *Die Kooperation bei der Herausbildung eines Systems der gesunden Ernährung in der DDR*, edited by Werner Fiebiger, 50–57. Berlin: GBH, 1971.
Melillo, Edward. "The First Green Revolution: Debt Peonage and the Making of the Nitrogen Fertilizer Trade, 1840–1930." *American Historical Review* 117, no. 4 (2012): 1028–1060.
Melzer, Jörg. *Vollwerternährung: Diätetik, Naturheilkunde, Nationalsozialismus, sozialer Anspruch.* Stuttgart: Franz Steiner, 2003.
Menne, Bernhard. *Armistice and Germany's Food Supply, 1918–19: A Study of Conditional Surrender.* London: Hutchinson & Co., 1944.
Mensink, G. B. M., and R. Beitz. "Food and Nutrient Intake in East and West Germany, 8 Years after the Reunification: The German Nutrition Survey 1998." *European Journal of Clinical Nutrition* 58 (2004): 1000–1010.
Merkel, Ina. "Changing Meanings in East German Consumer Culture." In *The Making of the Consumer: Knowledge, Power and Identity in the Modern World*, edited by Frank Trentmann, 249–270. Oxford: Berg, 2005.
Merkel, Ina. *Wunderwirtschaft: DDR-Konsumkultur in den 60er Jahren.* Köln: Bohlau, 1996.
Meyer, Konrad. *Bodenordnung als volkspolitische Aufgabe und Zielsetzung nationalsozialistischen Ordnungswillens: Festrede am Leibniztag der Preußischen Akademie der Wissenschaften am 27.6.1940 gehalten.* Berlin: de Gruyter, 1940.
Meyer, Konrad. "Drei Jahre Forschungsdienst." In *Forschung für Volk und Nahrungsfreiheit*, edited by Konrad Meyer, 1–8. Berlin: Verlag J. Neumann-Neudamm, 1938.
Miller, James. "Pre-War Nazi Agrarian Policy." *Agricultural History* 4 (1941): 175–181.
Miller, Susanne, Heinrich Potthoff, and Erich Matthias, eds. *Die Regierung der Volksbeauftragten 1918/19.* Düsseldorf: Droste, 1969.
Mintz, Sidney. *Sweetness and Power: The Place of Sugar in Modern History.* New York: Viking, 1985.
Moeller, Robert. "Dimensions of Social Conflict in the Great War: The View from the German Countryside." *Central European History* 14, no. 2 (1981): 142–168.
Moeller, Robert. *Protecting Motherhood: Women and the Family in the Politics of Postwar West Germany.* Berkeley: University of California Press, 1993.

Möhr, Manfred. *Zur Ernähungssituation in der DDR*. Berlin: Gesellschaft für Betreibsberatung des Handels, 1971.
Mollison, P. L. "Observations of Cases of Starvation at Belsen." *British Medical Journal* (January 5, 1946): 4–8.
Monger, David. *Patriotism and Propaganda in First World War Britain: The National War Aims Committee and Civilian Morale*. Liverpool: Liverpool University Press, 2012.
Mouton, Michelle. *From Nurturing the Nation to Purifying the Volk: Weimar and Nazi Family Policy, 1918–1945*. Cambridge: Cambridge University Press, 2007.
Müller, Friedrich. "Nationale und internationale Ernährungsprobleme aus medizinischer Sicht." In *Die Kooperation bei der Herausbildung eines Systems der gesunden Ernährung in der DDR*, edited by Werner Fiebiger, 32–49. Berlin: GBH, 1971.
Müller, Friedrich. "Zur Verbreitung der Fettsucht in der Deutschen Demokratischen Republik." *Zeitschrift für die gesamte innere Medizin und ihre Grenzgebiete* 22 (November 15, 1970): 1001–1009.
Müller, Rolf-Dieter. "Stalingrad: Was wir an Hunger ausstehen müssen, könnt Ihr euch gar nicht denken: Eine Armee verhungert." In *Stalingrad: Mythos und Wirklichkeit einer Schlacht*, edited by Wolfram Wette and Sabine R. Arnold, 131–145. Frankfurt: Fischer-Taschenbuch, 1993.
Müller, Wenzel. *Leben in der Platte: Alltagskultur der DDR der 70er und 80er Jahre*. Vienna: Selbstverlag, 1999.
Münzenberg, Willi. *Über Grösse, Ursache und Bekämpfung der Hungersnot in Deutschland*. Berlin: Zentralkomitee d. Internat. Arbeiterhilfe, 1923.
Murray, R. O. "Recovery from Starvation." *Lancet*, April 19, 1947, 507–511.
Nally, David. "The Biopolitics of Food Provisioning." *Transactions of the Institute of British Geographers* 36, no. 1 (2011): 37–53.
Nathan, Otto, and Milton Fried. *The Nazi Economic System: Germany's Mobilization for War*. Durham, NC: Duke University Press, 1944.
Nelson, Heinrich. *ABC des langen Lebens*. Dresden: Dt. Verl. für Volkswohlfahrt, 1936.
Neuloh, Otto, and Hans-Jürgen Teuteberg. *Ernährungsfehlverhalten im Wohlstand: Ergebnisse einer empirisch-soziologischen Untersuchung in heutigen Familien-haushalten*. Paderborn: Schoeningh, 1979.
Neumann, Alexander. "Nutritional Physiology in the 'Third Reich,' 1933–1945." In *Man, Medicine, and the State: The Human Body as an Object of Government Sponsored Medical Research in the 20th Century*, edited by Wolfgang Eckart, 49–60. Stuttgart: Franz Steiner, 2006.
Neve, Monica. *Sold! Advertising and the Bourgeois Female Consumer in Munich 1900–1914*. Stuttgart: Franz Steiner, 2010.
Nicosia, Francis. "Jewish Farmers in Hitler's Germany: Zionist Occupational Retraining and Nazi 'Jewish Policy.'" *Holocaust and Genocide Studies* 19, no. 3 (Winter 2005): 365–389.
Nitti, Francesco. "The Food and Labour-Power of Nations." *Economic Journal* 6, no. 21 (March 1896): 30–63.
Niven, Bill, ed. *Germans as Victims: Remembering the Past in Contemporary Germany*. New York: Palgrave, 2006.
Nolan, Mary. *Visions of Modernity: American Business and the Modernization of Germany*. New York: Oxford University Press, 1994.
Nothnagel, Margarethe. *Harmonische Ernährung für wenig Geld durch gesunde Kost*. Dresden: Müllersche Verlagshaus, 1939.
Nützenadel, Alexander. "A World without Famine. Internationale Ernährungspolitik in Zeitalter der Weltkriege." *Comparativ. Zeitschrift für Globalgeschichte und vergleichende Gesellschaftsforschung* 17, no. 3 (2007): 12–28.
Obenaus, Herbert. "Hunger und Überleben in den nationalsozialistischen Konzentrationslagern." In *Der Kampf um das tägliche Brot: Nahrungsmangel, Versorgungspolitik und Protest, 1770–1990*, edited by Manfred Gailus and Heinrich Volkmann, 361–376. Opladen: Westdeutscher, 1994.

Obens, Heinz-Udo. *Wir hatten viel Hunger: Fremdarbeiter, Ostarbeiter, Zwangsarbeiter: die Standard-Metallwerke zu Werl und ihre ausländischen Arbeitskräfte im Zweiten Weltkrieg.* Werl: Stein, 2003.

OECD Committee for Agriculture, ed. *Prospects for Agricultural Production and Trade in Eastern Europe: 1. Poland, German Democratic Republic, Hungary.* Paris: Organisation for Economic Co-operation and Development, 1981.

Offer, Avner. "The Blockade of Germany and the Strategy of Starvation, 1914–1918." In *Great War, Total War: Combat and Mobilization on the Western Front, 1914–1918*, edited by Roger Chickering and Stig Forster, 169–188. Cambridge: Cambridge University Press, 2000), 183.

Offer, Avner. *The First World War: An Agrarian Interpretation.* Oxford: Oxford University Press, 1991.

OMGUS. *German Understanding of the Reasons for the Food Shortage.* Berlin: ICD Opinion Surveys: 1947.

Orland, Barbara. *Wäsche Waschen: Technik- und Sozialgeschichte der häuslichen Wäschepflege.* Munich: Deutsches Museum, 1991.

Orlopp, Josef. *Im Kampf gegen den Hunger.* Berlin: SED Landesverband Gross-Berlin, 1947.

Otzen, Barbara, and Hans Otzen. *DDR-Backbuch.* Köln: Komet, 2005.

Parrish, Thomas. *Berlin in the Balance, 1945–1949: The Blockade, the Airlift, the First Major Battle of the Cold War.* Reading, MA: Addison-Wesley, 1998.

Patel, Raj. *Stuffed and Starved: The Hidden Battle for the World Food System.* New York: Melville House, 2012.

Pence, Katherine. "'You as a Woman Will Understand': Consumption, Gender, and the Relationship between State and Citizenry in the GDR's Crisis of 17 June 1953." *German History* 19, no. 2 (2001): 218–252.

Pence, Katherine, and Paul Betts, eds. *Socialist Modern: East German Everyday Culture and Politics.* Ann Arbor: University of Michigan Press, 2008.

Peppler, E., and H. D. Cremer. "Fragen der modernen Gemeinschaftsverpflegung." *Deutsches medizinisches Journal* 15 (1964): 313–320.

Pfau-Effinger, Birgit. "Der soziologische Mythos von der Hausfrauenehe—sozio-historische Entwicklungspfade der Familie." *Soziale Welt* 2 (1998): 167–182.

Pfeil, Elisabeth. *Die Berufstätigkeit von Müttern; eine empirisch-soziologische Erhebung an 900 Müttern aus vollständigen Familien.* Tübingen: Mohr, 1961.

Pietsch, Dorothea. "Möglichkeiten und Erfahrungen der Ernährungsberatung." PhD diss., Justus Liebig-Universität Giessen, 1969.

Pranke, E. J. "The Cyanamid Industry: World Status." *American Fertilizer Handbook*, April 1916, 79–82.

Price, Hoyt, and Carl E. Schorske. *The Problem of Germany.* New York: Council on Foreign Relations, 1947.

Prinz, Michael. *Der Sozialstaat hinter dem Haus. Wirtschaftliche Zukunftserwartungen, Selbstversorgung und regionale Vorbilder: Westfalen und Südwestdeutschland 1920–1960.* Paderborn: Ferdinand Schöningh, 2012.

Raup, Philip. "Postwar Recovery of Western German Agriculture." *Journal of Farm Economics* 32, no. 1 (February 1950): 1–14.

Reagin, Nancy. "*Marktordnung* and Autarkic Housekeeping: Housewives and Private Consumption under the Four-Year Plan, 1936–1939." *German History* 19, no. 2 (2001): 162–184.

Reagin, Nancy. *Sweeping the German Nation: Domesticity and National Identity in Germany, 1870–1945.* Cambridge: Cambridge University Press, 2007.

Reichsausschuß für Volkswirtschaftliche Aufklärung. *Ernährungspolitik und Schule.* Berlin: Verlag für volkswirtschaftliche Aufklärung, 1938.

Richert, Annie Juliane. *Bereite dein Eintopf-Gericht aus deutschem Gemüse und Obst, dann hilfst Du doppelt.* Berlin: Büchereien d. dt. Gartenbaus, 1935.

Richter, Lina. *Family Life in Germany under the Blockade.* London: National Labour Press, 1919.

Robertson, Thomas. *The Malthusian Moment: Global Population Growth and the Birth of American Environmentalism*. New Brunswick, NJ: Rutgers University Press, 2012.
Rodgers, Marvin. "Herbert Hoover and American Relief: A Study of the Relationship between Hoover's American Relief Program and Bolshevism in Europe in 1919." MA thesis. Fresno State College, 1966.
Roerkohl, Anne. *Hungerblockade und Heimatfront: die kommunale Lebensmittel-Versorgung in Westfalen während des Ersten Weltkrieges*. Stuttgart: F. Steiner, 1991.
Rösch, Rudolf. *Hausfrauen, jetzt verwendet, was die Scholle spendet! Nahrhafte, gesunde Kost aus heimischer Scholle*. Munich: Reinhardt, 1940.
Rostalski, Margarethe. "Fortschritte in der Behandlung der Fettsucht." *Die medizinische Welt* 33–34 (1954): 1110–1112.
Rothenberg, Gunther Erich. *The Art of Warfare in the Age of Napoleon*. Bloomington: Indiana University Press, 1980.
Rothenberger, Karl-Heinz. *Die Hungerjahre nach dem Zweiten Weltkrieg: Ernährungs- u. Landwirtschaft in Rheinland-Pfalz 1945–1950*. Boppard: Boldt, 1980.
Rubmann, Max. *Hunger! Wirkungen moderner Kriegsmethoden*. Berlin: Reimer, 1919.
Rubner, Max et al. *Hauptbericht der freien wissenschaftlichen Kommission zum Studium der jetzigen Ernährungsverhältnisse in Deutschland: abgeschlossen 27. Dezember 1918*. Berlin: 1919.
Ruhl, Klaus-Jörg. *Frauen in der Nachkriegszeit 1945–1963*. Munich: Deutscher Taschenbuch, 1988.
Ruhl, Klaus-Jörg. *Verordnete Unterordnung: Berüfstätige Frauen zwischen Wirtschaftswachstum und konservativer Ideologie in der Nachkriegszeit. 1945–1963*. Munich: R. Oldenbourg, 1994.
Russell, Edmund. *War and Nature: Fighting Humans and Insects with Chemicals from World War I to Silent Spring*. Cambridge: Cambridge University Press, 2001.
Ruttan, Vernon. *Why Food Aid?* Baltimore: Johns Hopkins University Press, 1993.
Salaman, Redcliffe. *The History and Social Influence of the Potato*. Cambridge: Cambridge University Press, 1985.
Saller, Karl. *Kampf dem Hunger: eine Aussprache*. Stuttgart: Hippokrates, 1948.
Saul, Dr. "Die Ernährung im Dienst der Gesundheitserziehung in der Familie." In *Gesundheit aus eigener Verantwortung*, edited by Hans Hoske. Freiburg/Breisgau: Tries, 1956.
Sayre, Francis. "Rebuilding a War-Torn World." In *The Postwar World*, edited by Hastings Eells, 87–103. New York: Abingdon-Cokesbury Press, 1945.
Scarpellini, Emanuela. *Material Nation: A Consumer's History of Modern Italy*. Oxford: Oxford University Press, 2011.
Schaeffer, Werner. *War against Women and Children: England's Hunger Blockade against Germany 1914–1920*. Berlin: German Information Service, 1940.
Schäfer, Annette. *Zwangsarbeiter und NS Rassenpolitik: russische und polnische Arbeitskräfte in Württemberg 1939–1945*. Stuttgart: Kohlhammer, 2000.
Schaffner, Bertram. *Father Land: A Study of Authoritarianism in the German Family*. New York: Columbia University Press, 1948.
Schall, Thomas. *Relief for the Distressed and Starving Women and Children of Germany*. Washington, DC: US Government Printing Office, 1924.
Scharfenberg, Horst. *Kochbuch für die Hausfrau von Heute: über 600 Rezepte mit genauen Angaben f. d. Zubereitung mit elektr. Küchenmaschinen*. Weil der Stadt: Hädecke, 1974.
Scheffler, Ute. *Alles Soljanka oder wie? Das ultimative DDR-Kochbuch 1949–1989*. Leipzig, BuchVerlag für die Frau, 2000.
Schelsky, Helmut. *Wandlungen der deutschen Familie in der Gegenwart*. Dortmund: Helmut Ardey, 1953.
Scheunert, Arthur. *Ernährungsprobleme der Gegenwart*. Leipzig: Hirzel, 1952.
Schevardo, Jennifer. *Vom Wert des Notwendigen: Preispolitik und Lebensstandard in der DDR*. Stuttgart: Steiner, 2006.
Schildt, Axel, and Arnold Sywottek. "'Reconstruction' and 'Modernization': West German Social History during the 1950s." In *West Germany under Construction: Politics, Society, and Culture*

in the Adenauer Era, edited by Robert Moeller, 413–440. Ann Arbor: University of Michigan Press, 1997.

Schissler, Hanna. "Social Democratic Gender Policies, the Working-Class Milieu and the Culture of Domesticity in West Germany in the 1950s and 1960s." In *Between Reform and Revolution: German Socialism and Communism from 1840 to 1990*, edited by David Barclay and Eric Weitz, 507–529. New York: Berghahn, 1998.

Schmidt, Hubert. "Postwar Developments in West German Agriculture, 1945–1953." *Agricultural History* 29, no. 4 (October 1955): 147–159.

Schnabel, Dr. "Die Gemeinschaftsverpflegung für den Betrieb." In *Gemeinschaftsverpflegung im Betrieb und Krankenhaus*, edited by Deutsche Gesellschaft für Ernährung, 40–44. Frankfurt: DGE, 1966.

Schneider, Lothar. *Die Ernährung in ihrer Bedeutung für Haus- und Volkswirtschaft*. Köln: Bundesaussschuß für Volkswirtschaftliche Aufklärung, 1968.

Schneider, Norbert. *Familie und private Lebensführung in West- und Ostdeutschland. Eine vergleichende Analyse des Familienlebens 1970–1992*. Stuttgart: Ferdinand Enke, 1994.

Schubert, Friedel. *Die Frau in der DDR: Ideologie und konzeptionelle Ausgestaltung ihrer Stellung in Beruf und Familie*. Opladen: Leske + Budrich, 1980.

Schubuth, Alwine. *Schmackhafter Eintopf, frohe Esser: 30 bekömml. Eintopfgerichte d. süddt. u. sudetendt. Küche*. Reichenberg: Sollors, 1939.

Schultz, Theodore. *Food for the World*. Chicago: University of Chicago Press, 1945.

Schulze, Rainer. *Unruhige Zeiten: Erlebnisberichte aus dem Landkreis Celle 1945–1949*. Munich: R. Oldenbourg, 1990.

Schumacher, Martin. *Land und Politik. Eine Untersuchung über politische Parteien und agrarische Interessen 1914–1923*. Düsseldorf: Droste, 1978.

Schumann, Dirk. *Political Violence in the Weimar Republic, 1918–1933: Fight for the Streets and Fear of Civil War*. New York: Berghahn, 2009.

Schwartzer, Alice. *Lohn, Liebe: zum Wert der Frauenarbeit*. Frankfurt: Suhrkamp, 1985.

Seeßlen, Georg. "Die Banane. Ein mythopolitischer Bericht." In *Mauer-Show: das Ende der DDR, die deutsche Einheit und die Medien*, edited by Rainer Bohn, Knut Hickethier, and Eggo Müller, 55–69. Berlin: Ed. Sigma, 1992.

Sell, Werner. "Die Arbeitsgemeinschaft 'die moderne Küche' und ihre Ziele." *Die moderne Küche* 39 (1966): 11–12.

Selmeczi, Anna. "'… we are being left to burn because we do not count': Biopolitics, Abandonment, and Resistance." In *Foucault and International Relations: New Critical Engagements*, edited by Nicholas Kiersey and Doug Stokes, 157–176. New York: Routledge, 2013.

Semmler, Lore. *Gesunde Ernährung. Informations- und Argumentationsmaterial zur Gesundheitserziehung*. Dresden: Institut für Gesundheitserziehung, 1974.

Sheffer, Edith. *Burned Bridge: How East and West Germans Made the Iron Curtain*. Oxford: Oxford University Press, 2008.

Shub, Boris. *Starvation over Europe: Made in Germany*. New York: Institute of Jewish Affairs, 1943.

Sich, Bauer Claus. "Die Macht der Hausfrau." In *Die Macht der Hausfrau: Eine ernährungswirtschaftliche Fibel für den Verbraucher*, edited by Liane Haskerl and Wolfgang Clauss, 3–4. Kiel: Kieler Druckerei, 1952.

Simmons, Dana. "Starvation Science: From Colonies to Metropole." In *Food and Globalization: Consumption, Markets and Politics in the Modern World*, edited by Alexander Nützenadel and Frank Trentmann, 173–192. Oxford: Berg, 2008.

Simmons, G. "Rasse und Ernährung." *Kraft und Schönheit: Zeitschrift für Vernünft* 4 (1904): 156–159.

Smith, Charles. *Food in Wartime*. London: Fabian Society, 1940.

Smith, Munroe. *German Land Hunger and Other Underlying Causes of the War*. New York: Knickerbocker Press, 1918.

Snyder, Timothy. *Black Earth: The Holocaust as History and Warning*. New York: Tim Duggan, 2015.

Snyder, Timothy. *Bloodlands: Europe between Hitler and Stalin*. New York: Basic Books, 2010.
"So sollte eine Werkküche geplant und eingerichtet werden." *Die neuzeitliche Gaststätte* 6 (1956): 19–21.
Soluri, John. *Banana Cultures: Agriculture, Consumption, and Environmental Change in Honduras and the United States*. Austin: University of Texas Press, 2005.
Sonnemann, Theodor. "Was darf die Ernährungsindustrie vom kommenden Jahr erwarten?" *Die Ernährungswirtschaft* 2 (1954): 40–41.
Sozialistische Einheitspartei Deutschlands. *Protokoll der Verhandlungen des VI Parteitages der SED*. Vol. 1. Berlin: Dietz, 1963.
Spiekermann, Uwe. "Pfade in die Zukunft? Entwicklungslinien der Ernährungswissenschaft im 19. und 20. Jahrhundert." In *Die Zukunft der Ernährungswissenschaft*, edited by Gesa Schönberger, 23–46. Berlin: Springer, 2000.
Spiekermann, Uwe. "Vollkornbrot in Deutschland. Regionalisierende und nationalisierende Deutungen und Praktiken während der NS-Zeit." *Comparativ* 11 (2001): 27–50.
Spindler, Sonja, and Rainer Horbelt. *Tante Linas Kriegskochbuch: Erlebnisse, Kochrezepte, Dokumente: Rezepte einer ungewöhnlichen Frau, in schlechten Zeiten zu überleben*. Frankfurt: Eichborn, 1982.
Starling, Ernest. *Report on Food Conditions in Germany*. London: H.M.S.O., 1919.
Steege, Paul. *Black Market, Cold War: Everyday Life in Berlin, 1946–1949*. New York: Cambridge University Press, 2007.
Steiner, André. *The Plans That Failed: An Economic History of the GDR*. New York: Berghahn, 2010.
Steinert, Johannes-Dieter. *Nach Holocaust und Zwangsarbeit. Britische humanitäre Hilfe in Deutschland: die Helfer, die Befreiten und die Deutschen*. Osnabruck: Secolo, 2007.
Steller, Werner. *Zwischenmahlzeiten ausser Haus, Pausenbrot für Erwachsene?* Bonn: Mühlenstelle, 1976.
Stolper, Gustav. *German Realities*. New York: Reynal & Hitchcock, 1948.
Stone, Lawrence. *The Family, Sex and Marriage in England, 1500–1800*. New York: Harper & Row, 1977.
Strasser, Susan, Charles McGovern, and Matthias Judt, eds. *Getting and Spending: European and American Consumer Societies in the Twentieth Century*. Cambridge: Cambridge University Press, 1998.
Stregel, Tobias, and Fabian Tweder. *Deutsche kulinarische Republik: Szenen, Berichte und Rezepte aus dem Osten*. Frankfurt: Eichborn, 1998.
Strickland, Charles. "American Aid to Germany, 1919 to 1921." *Wisconsin Magazine of History* 45, no. 4 (Summer 1962): 256–270.
Strotdrees, Gisbert. *Höfe, Bauern, Hungerjahre: aus der Geschichte der westfälischen Landwirtschaft 1890–1950*. Münster: Landwirtschaftsverlag, 1991.
Stuart, Richard, and Barbara Davis. *Slim Chance in a Fat World*. Champaign, IL: Research Press, 1972.
Stübler, E. "Entwicklungstendenzen der Ernährung und ihre Auswirkungen auf die Hauswirtschaft." In *Entwicklungstendenzen der Ernährung*, edited by Forschungsrat für Ernährung, Landwirtschaft und Forsten, 59–66. Munich: BLV-Verlagsgesellschaft München, 1962.
Surface, Frank, and Raymond Bland. *American Food in the World War and Reconstruction Period*. Stanford, CA: Stanford University Press, 1931.
Tanner, Jakob. *Fabrikmahlzeit. Ernährungswissenschaft, Industriearbeit und Volksernährung in der Schweiz 1890–1950*. Zürich: Chronos, 1999.
Ten Dyke, Elizabeth. "Tulips in December: Space, Time and Consumption before and after the End of German Socialism." *German History* 19 (2001): 253–276.
Teuteberg, Hans-Jürgen. "Food Provisioning on the German Home Front." In *Food and War in Twentieth Century Europe*, edited by Ina Zweiniger-Bargielowska, Rachel Duffett, and Alain Drouard, 59–72. Farnham, UK: Ashgate, 2011.
Thoms, Ulrike. "Einbruch, Aufbruch, Durchbruch? Strukturen und Netzwerke der deutschen Ernährungsforschung vor und nach 1945." In *Kontinuitäten und Diskontinuitäten in*

der Wissenschaftsgeschichte, edited by Rüdiger vom Bruch and Uta Gerhardt, 111–130. Stuttgart: Steiner, 2006.

Thoms, Ulrike. "Industrial Canteens in Germany, 1850–1950." In *Eating out in Europe since the Late Middle Ages: Picnics, Gourmet Dining and Snacks since the Late Eighteenth Century*, edited by Peter Scholliers and Marc Jacobs, 351–372. Oxford: Berg, 2003.

Thoms, Ulrike. "The Innovative Power of War: The Army, Food Sciences, and the Food Industry in Germany in the Twentieth Century." In *Food and War in Twentieth Century Europe*, edited by Ina Zweiniger-Bargielowska, Rachel Duffett, and Alain Drouard. Farnham, UK: Ashgate, 2011.

Thoms, Ulrike. "Separated, but Sharing a Health Problem: Obesity in East and West Germany, 1945–1989." In *The Rise of Obesity in Europe: A Twentieth-Century Food History*, edited by Derek J. Oddy, Peter Atkins, and Virginie Amilien, 207–222. London: Ashgate, 2009.

Thrall, Charles. "The Conservative Use of Modern Household Technology." *Technology and Culture* 23 (1982): 175–194.

Thurnwald, Hilde. *Gegenwartsprobleme Berliner Familien; eine soziologische Untersuchung an 498 Familien*. Berlin: Weidmann, 1948.

Tieke, Wilhelm. *Nach der Stunde Null. Not und Hungerjahre im Oberbergischen 1945–49*. Gummersbach: Gronenberg, 1987.

Tooze, Adam. *The Deluge: The Great War and the Remaking of Global Order 1916–1931*. New York: Penguin, 2014.

Tooze, Adam. *The Wages of Destruction: The Making and Breaking of the Nazi Economy*. New York: Viking, 2007.

Torp, Claudius. *Konsum und Politik in der Weimarer Republik*. Göttingen: Vandenhoeck & Ruprecht, 2011.

Treitel, Corinna. "Max Rubner and the Biopolitics of Rational Nutrition." *Central European History* 41 (2008): 1–25.

Trittel, Günter. *Hunger und Politik: Die Ernährungskrise in der Bizone, 1945–1949*. Frankfurt: Campus Verlag, 1990.

Tropp, Casper. *Ernähren Sie sich richtig, Herr Direktor?* Munich: Verlag Moderne Industrie, 1965.

United Nations Conference on Food and Agriculture. *United Nations Conference on Food and Agriculture; text of the final act. Draft agreement for United Nations Relief and Rehabilitation Administration. Address by the Honorable Herbert H. Lehman, June 17, 1943*. New York: Carnegie Endowment for International Peace, Division of Intercourse and Education, 1943.

United States Agency for International Development. *Celebrating Food for Peace, 1954–2004: Bringing Hope to the Hungry*. Washington, DC: US Agency for International Development, 2004. Accessed online on December 7, 2016. http://pdf.usaid.gov/pdf_docs/Pdabz818.pdf.

United States Congress, Senate Committee on Appropriations, *Foodstuffs and Supplies for Europe, 1919*. Washington, DC: Government Printing Office, 1919.

United States Department of Agriculture. *Food for Freedom: Informational Handbook, 1943*. Washington, DC: US Department of Agriculture, 1942.

University of Cambridge. *Studies of Undernutrition, Wuppertal, 1946–9*. London: H. M. Stationery Office, 1951.

"Unnötige Angstkäufe bei Kartoffeln! Sonderbericht der Preisberichtsstelle beim Reichsnährstand." *Zeitschrift für Volksernährung* 14 (1934): 169.

Unsere Ernährung: die brennenste Frage. Berlin, 1946.

"Unsere Ernährungslage." *Die Ernährungsdienst* 7 (September 1935): 8–10.

US-British Bipartite Food and Agriculture Panel. *Food and Agriculture: U.S.–U.K. Zones of Germany*. Berlin: OMGUS, 1947.

Van der Kloot, William. "Ernest Starling's Analysis of the Energy Balance of the German People during the Blockade, 1914–19." *Notes and Records of the Royal Society of London* 57, no. 2 (May 2003): 185–193.

Veit, Helen. *Modern Food, Moral Food: Self-Control, Science, and the Rise of Modern American Eating in the Early Twentieth Century*. Chapel Hill: University of North Carolina Press, 2013.

"Verbraucher-Gewohnheiten wandelbar." *Hauswirtschaft und Volksernährung: Fachzeitschrift für rationelle Haushaltsführung* 2 (1969): 18–19.

Verhey, Jeffrey. *The Spirit of 1914: Militarism, Myth, and Mobilization in Germany*. Cambridge: Cambridge University Press, 2006.

Vernon, James. *Hunger: A Modern History*. Cambridge, MA: Belknap Press, 2007.

"Viele Hausfrauen ernähren sich falsch." *Die Ernährung* 14, no. 5 (1961): 143.

"Viele Köche verderben (nicht) den Brei. Ein Blick in die Henkel-Küche." *Rationelle Hauswirtschaft: Fachblatt für die hauswirtschafliche Führungskräfte* 8, no. 7 (1971): 4–6.

Voglis, Polymeris. "Surviving Hunger: Life in the Cities and the Countryside during the Occupation." In *Surviving Hitler and Mussolini: Daily Life in Occupied Europe*, edited by Robert Gildea, Anette Warring, and Olivier Wieviorka, 16–41. New York: Berg, 2007.

Voigt, Dr. "Sie kauft nur das Teuerste. Eine Betrachtrung zur Physiologie des Alltags." *Verbraucherdienst* (January 1959): 6–7.

Voit, K. "Leitsymptom: Fettsucht." *Münchener medizinische Wochenschrift* 92, no. 27–28 (1950): 1106–1113.

"Vom Borschtsch und Schtschi. Die Verpflegung der Ostarbeiter und Ostarbeiterinnen." *Gemeinschaftsverpflegung und Kochwissenschaft* 1 (January 1943): 5.

von François, Hermann. *Deutschlands Hungersnot: Wodurch entstand sie? Wie ist sie zu beseitigen?* Berlin: Scherl, 1919.

von Wendt, Georg. *Kost und Kultur: ein Buch über Ernährung, Gesundheit und Widerstandskraft*. Leipzig: Thieme, 1936.

"Vorboten der Lebensmittelrationierung in den USA." *Gemeinschaftsverpflegung mit Volksernährung* 3 (November 1942): 80.

Voß, P. "Wie erreichen wir den Bürger? Überlegungen aus der Sicht des Deutschen Hygiene Museums in der DDR." In *Ernährung—Gesundheit—Genuss: Praxis u. Wissenschaft*, edited by Arbeitsgruppe Ernährung des Nationales Komitees für Gesundheitserziehung, 64–67. Karl-Marx-Stadt: Warenverzeichnenverband Diätetische Erzeugnisse, 1986.

Vrints, Antoon. "Beyond Victimization: Contentious Food Politics in Belgium during World War I." *European History Quarterly* 45, no. 1 (January 2015): 83–107.

Wagemann, Ernst. *Die Nahrungswirtschaft des Auslandes*. Berlin: Beiträge zur Kriegswirtschaft, 1917.

Wange, Udo. "Die Anforderungen der gesunden Ernährung an die Lebensmittelindustrie." In *Die Kooperation bei der Herausbildung eines Systems der gesunden Ernährung in der DDR*, edited by Werner Fiebiger, 58–63. Berlin: GBH, 1971.

Watenpaugh, Keith David. *Bread from Stones: The Middle East and the Making of Modern Humanitarianism*. Berkeley: University of California Press, 2015.

Watts, Michael. "Heart of Darkness: Reflections on Famine and Starvation in Africa." In *The Political Economy of African Famine*, edited by R. E. Downs, Donna O. Kerner, and Stephen P. Reyna, 1–68. Philadelphia: Gordon and Breach Science Publishers, 1991.

Webster, Wendy. "From Nazi Legacy to Cold War: British Perceptions of European Identity 1945–64." In *European Identity and the Second World War*, edited by Michael Wintle and M. Spiering, 92–110. Houndmills, UK: Palgrave Macmillan, 2011.

Weggemann, Sigrid. "Entwicklung des Ernährungsverhaltens der Bevölkerung der Bundesrepublik Deutschland von 1950–1990." In *Ernährung in Deutschland nach der Wende: Veränderungen in Haushalt, Beruf und Gemeinschaftsverpflegung*, edited by Thomas Kutsch and Sigrid Weggemann, 21–48. Witterschlick: M. Wehle, 1996.

Weichardt, Herma. *101 Eintopf-Gerichte*. Munich: Einhorn, 1933.

Weinreb, Alice. "Hot Lunches in the Cold War: The Politics of School Lunches in Postwar Divided Germany." In *Gender and the Long Postwar: The United States and the Two Germanys, 1945–1989*, edited by Karen Hagemann and Sonya Michel, 227–252. Washington, DC: Woodrow Wilson Center Press, 2014.

Werdelmann, Hans. *Der Marschbefehl des Gaues Kurmark für den Kampf gegen Hunger und Kälte im Winter 1935/36*. Berlin: Amt für Volkswohlfahrt bei der Gauleitung Kurmark, 1936.
Werner, Ruth. "Schulverpflegung in der Bundesrepublik Deutschland, wo und wie?" In *Internationale Arbeitstagung Schulverpflegung*, edited by Günter Schlierf, 136–148. Frankfurt: DGE, 1976.
Werner, Wolfgang Franz. *"Bleib Übrig!" Deutsche Arbeiter in der nationalsozialistischen Kriegswirtschaft*. Düsseldorf: Schwann, 1983.
Wieloch, Elisabeth. *Gesund durch Gemüse, Roh und Gekocht*. Leipzig: Fachbuchverlag, 1964.
Wierlacher, Alois. *Vom Essen in der deutschen Literatur: Mahlzeiten in Erzähltexten von Goethe bis Grass*. Stuttgart: W. Kohlhammer, 1987.
Wiesen, Jonathan. "Overcoming Nazism: Big Business, Public Relations, and the Politics of Memory, 1945–50." *Central European History* 29, no. 2 (1996): 201–226.
Wildenthal, Lora. *The Language of Human Rights in West Germany*. Philadelphia: University of Pennsylvania Press, 2012.
Wildt, Michael. *Am Beginn der "Konsumgesellschaft": Mangelerfahrung, Lebenshaltung, Wohlstandshoffnung in Westdeutschland in den Fünfziger Jahren*. Hamburg: Ergebnisse, 1995.
Wildt, Michael. "Changes in Consumption as Social Practice in West Germany during the 1950s." In *Getting and Spending: European and American Consumer Societies in the Twentieth Century*, edited by Susan Strasser, Charles McGovern, and Matthias Judt, 301–316. Cambridge: Cambridge University Press, 1998.
Wilmenrod, Clemens. *Es Liegt Mir auf der Zunge*. Hamburg: Hoffmann und Campe, 1954.
Winckel, Max. "Hunger und Politik." *Zeitschrift für Volksernährung* 10 (May 20, 1937).
Winckel, Max. *Nahrung und Zubereitung. Wissen um Küche und Kochen*. Weimar: Schmidt & Thelow, 1948.
Winckel, Max. "Zukunftsprobleme der deutschen Volksernährung." *Volksernährung und Kochwissenschaft* 19, no. 9 (May 1944): 56–58.
Winkler, G., S. Brasche, and J. Heinrich. "Trends in Food Intake in Adults from the City of Erfurt before and after the German Reunification." *Annals of Nutrition and Metabolism* 41, no. 5 (1997): 283–290.
Winnington, Ursula. *Rationelles Kochen, gesunde Ernährung*. Leipzig: Verlag für d. Frau, 1975.
Wnuck, F. "Gemeinschaftsverpflegung muß vollwertig sein." *Die neuzeitliche Gaststätte* 11 (1955): 327.
Wölfer, Theodor. *Der deutsche Mensch in der Landwirtschaft als Arbeitgeber, Unternehmer, Staatsbürger u. Persönlichkeit*. Berlin: Deutsche Verlagsgesellschaft, 1935.
Wright, Jan, and Valerie Harwood, eds. *Biopolitics and the "Obesity Epidemic": Governing Bodies*. New York: Routledge, 2009.
Wulff, Birgit. *Arbeitslosigkeit und Arbeitsbeschaffungsmassnahmen in Hamburg 1933–1939: Eine Untersuchung zur nationalsozialistischen Wirtschafts- und Sozialpolitik*. Frankfurt: P. Lang, 1986.
Wunderlich, Frieda. *Farmer and Farm Labor in the Soviet Zone of Germany*. New York: Twayne, 1958.
Wurm, Max, Mathilde Mann, and Heinrich Barthel, *Hunger in Deutschland*. Berlin: Malik-Verlag, 1923.
Young, Brigitte. *Triumph of the Fatherland: German Unification and the Marginalization of Women*. Ann Arbor: University of Michigan Press, 1999.
Zaretsky, Eli. *Capitalism, the Family and Personal Life*. New York: Harper and Row, 1976.
Ziegelmayer, Wilhelm. *Neue Nahrungsquellen. Kommunalpolitische Aufgaben zur Sicherung der deutschen Volksernährung*. Berlin: Heymann, 1949.
Zietze, Hans-Joachim. *Gelenkte Ernährung. Die DDR auf dem Weg zur gesellschaftlichen Ernährung*. Frankfurt: Peter Lang, 1989.
Zischka, Anton. *Brot für Zwei Milliarden Menschen*. Leipzig: W. Goldmann, 1938.
Zobel, Martin. "Ernährungswissenschaftlich und technologisch begründete Prognose über die Entwicklung der Gemeinschaftsverpflegung in der Deutschen Demokratischen Republik." Habilitation, Humboldt-Universität Berlin, 1967.

Zobel, Martin. *Zur Gemeinschaftsverpflegung Werktätiger.* Dresden: Deutsches Hygiene-Museum in der DDR, 1984.
Zolling, Peter. *Zwischen Integration und Segregation. Sozialpolitik im "Dritten Reich" am Beispiel der "Nationalsozialistischen Volkswohlfahrt"(NSV) in Hamburg.* Frankfurt: P. Lang, 1986.
Zweig, Ronald. "Feeding the Camps: Allied Blockade Policy and the Relief of Concentration Camps in Germany, 1944–1945." *Historical Journal* 41, no. 3 (September 1998): 825–851.
Zweiniger-Bargielowska, Ina. *Austerity in Britain: Rationing, Controls, and Consumption, 1939–1955.* Oxford: Oxford University Press, 2000.

INDEX

Adenauer, Konrad, 145, 162, 237–38
advertising
  in East Germany, 226, 229–30
  grocery shopping and, 147, 150, 155
  weight loss and, 226, 230–32
  in West Germany, 147, 150, 230–33
Advisory Board for Collective Feeding (West Germany), 137–38
Agricultural Trade Development and Assistance Act; PL 480 (United States), 120
agriculture
  in East Germany, 129, 243
  fertilizer and, 22, 62, 86, 123, 145
  First World War and, 13, 20, 22–24, 37, 39
  globalization of trade in, 9, 13–14, 57–59
  imperialism and, 13–14
  Jews and, 67
  munitions and, 14
  in Nazi Germany, 49–50, 57–58, 62–64, 66–68, 73, 80–81, 86
  in occupied Germany, 98–99, 123
  prisoners of war and, 81
  racial conceptions of, 63, 66–69, 80–81
  in the Soviet Union, 117–18
  in the United States, 21, 31, 33, 89, 120
  in Weimar Germany, 39, 49
  in West Germany, 145
  women's work in, 20, 22, 73
Allied Powers. *See also specific countries*
  Berlin Airlift and, 114–19
  European reconstruction after Second World War and, 88–89, 92–93, 107, 120
  German occupation after Second World War by, 10, 93–102, 104, 106–9, 112–19, 121–23, 127, 185–86
  liberation of concentration camps by, 89–91, 109

  Nazi propaganda regarding, 45, 48, 73–74, 102, 117
  Potsdam Conference and, 93–94
  propaganda in Nazi Germany by, 73
  rationing policies of, 74, 87, 94–102, 104, 106–7, 109–10, 112–15, 123, 143, 185–86
Alston, Philip, 120–21
American Committee for the Relief of German Children (Children's Fund), 255n111
American Jewish Joint Distribution Committee, 104
American Relief Administration (ARA), 33, 35, 38
American zone of occupation (1945–49)
  Berlin Airlift and, 114–15
  coal production in, 123
  currency reform (1948) and, 143
  displaced persons (DPs) in, 104, 262n82
  former forced laborers in, 103
  former Nazis in, 102
  productivity in, 123
  rationing policies in, 94, 97–98, 102, 104, 109, 112, 123, 143, 185–86, 262n82
anthropology, 50–51
anti-Semitism. *See also* The Holocaust; Jews
  agricultural labor and, 67
  food shortages and, 262n78
  Nazi Party laws and, 64, 76, 78, 80, 86
  Nazi Party rhetoric and, 44–45, 50–52, 57–58, 60, 62, 67, 87, 103, 105
  in occupied Germany, 103–4
ANUGA (*Allgemeine Nahrungs-und Genussmittelausstellung*; General Food and Drink Trade Fair), 145–46, 168
Arbeitsgemeinschaft für die moderne Küche (AgmK; Working Group for the Modern Kitchen), 170

Arendt, Hannah, 118, 135
artificial sweeteners, 224–25, 232–33
Aryan racial ideology. *See also* race and racism
  agriculture and, 81
  bread and, 62
  collective meals and, 79
  hunger rhetoric and, 67–68
  Lebensraum ("living space") doctrine and, 68
  nutrition and, 56, 65–66
  rationing policies and, 76–80, 83
Atkins Diet, 214
Austria, 33, 37, 67, 70
autarchy
  Weimar Germany and, 47
  Nazi Germany and, 56, 59–60, 66, 80, 86

Backe, Herbert, 67–68, 73–74
bananas, 225, 237–40
Baten, Jörg, 87
Batocki-Friede, Adolf von, 24
"the battle for rye," 66
Baumgartner, Josef, 103
Bavaria, 45, 103
behavior-modification therapy, 210–11
Belarus, 68, 72
Belgium
  First World War and, 30–31, 33, 47, 89
  food aid to, 30–31, 33, 37
  German atrocities in, 30, 47
  Second World War and, 71, 74, 89
Bergen-Belsen concentration camp, 90–91, 103–4, 109
Berlin. *See also* East Berlin; West Berlin
  airlift (1948–49) in, 114–20, 244
  Allied bombing of, 117
  canteens in, 136
  construction of Berlin Wall (1961) in, 6, 134, 160, 244
  fall of Berlin Wall (1989) in, 2, 237, 239
  grocery shopping in, 151–52, 160, 244
  hunger in, 109, 115–16, 118–19
Berlin Medical Association, 28
Berning, Heinrich, 126
Bethmann-Hollweg, Theodor von, 47
Beveridge, Sir William, 18
biopolitics
  food aid and, 120
  Foucault on, 4, 15
  hunger and, 4–5, 7–8
  industrial food production and, 4, 243
  obesity and, 247
  occupied Germany's economic reconstruction and, 10
  race and, 50
Bismarck, Otto von, 199
black markets
  in East Germany, 158
  in occupied Germany, 99, 106–7
  Second World War and, 73–74
  in Weimar Germany, 28, 39
  in Wilhelmine Germany, 20–21, 23–24
Blockade and the Civilian Population (Beveridge), 18
blood and soil (*Blut und Boden*) rhetoric, 5, 62–63, 67
Boer War, 16
Bolshevik Revolution (1917), 36–37
Bolshevism, 36–38, 42–44
Bourdieu, Pierre, 234
Boym, Svetlana, 242
Brack, Gustav, 128
Brailsford, Henry, 36
Brandt, Karl, 106
Brandt, Willi, 196
Brauksiepe, Aenne, 176
Brecht, Bertolt, 121
Brest-Litovsk Treaty (1918), 25, 40
Brigitte-Diet, 212
British Blockade (First World War). *See* Hunger Blockade
British zone of occupation (1945–49)
  Berlin Airlift (1948–49) and, 114–15
  displaced persons (DPs) in, 98, 104, 262n82
  food imports to, 98
  food protests in, 112
  liberated concentration camps in, 90, 109
  rationing policies in, 97–98, 109, 112, 123, 143, 262n82
Buchenwald concentration camp, 106, 109
Burchardt, Lochar, 69
Burgfrieden (Fortress Peace), 24

cafeterias. *See* canteens
canteens
  Advisory Board for Collective Feeding (West Germany) and, 137–38
  chefs and, 133
  consumerism and, 131–33, 136, 139–40, 142, 218–19
  in East Germany, 11, 125, 127–35, 137–38, 141–43, 153, 156, 159–61, 163, 178–79, 187–90, 193–94, 204–6, 213, 217–18, 243
  economic productivity and, 124–25, 127–28, 133, 135–36, 138
  at factories, 53, 79, 124–36, 139–42, 178–79
  fatness and, 217–19
  food-borne illnesses and, 134–35
  forced laborers and, 81
  gender and, 125, 127
  middle-class culture and, 138–42
  as model for home cooking, 178–79
  in Nazi Germany, 52–53, 56, 78–79, 81, 126–27
  nutrition and, 127, 130, 132, 134, 142, 178–79, 189, 218–19

in occupied Germany, 97, 128, 136
Order 234 and, 128–29
participation rates at, 128, 130–32, 134, 136, 142
prices at, 130, 132, 141
in reunified Germany, 240, 246, 248
at schools, 188–90, 240, 248
Second World War and, 125–26
weight loss programs and, 208, 217–20
in West Germany, 11, 125, 127, 131, 135–43, 218–20
in Wilhelmine Germany, 125
Card V (Soviet occupation zone rations card), 96
Carter, Erica, 125
casserole Sunday (*Eintopfsonntag*), 53–54
Central Committee for International Workers' Aid, 41
Central Institute for Nutrition (East German), 130, 158, 180, 214
chocolate
　in East Germany, 226
　Second World War and, 73
　weight loss and, 231
　in West Germany, 116–17, 145, 231
Christian Democratic Party, 144, 176, 196
Churchill, Winston, 27, 93, 164
Clauß, Wolfgang, 50
Clay, Lucius, 112, 123
Cohen, Lizabeth, 246
Cold War
　Berlin Airlift and, 114–20, 244
　body images during, 2
　consumerism and, 117
　end of, 12, 243
　food aid and, 112–13, 120, 244–45
　human rights and, 111–12
　hunger and, 6, 118, 121, 245
　kitchens and, 164, 167
　occupied Germany and, 92, 109, 111, 114–17, 121
collective meals. *See also* canteens; school lunches
　Aryan racial ideology and, 79
　in East Germany, 129–35, 137, 142, 188, 217, 235
　in Nazi Germany, 79, 126–27
　nutrition and, 217
　in reunified Germany, 248
　in West Germany, 135–42, 217
Committee for the Relief of Belgium (CRB), 30–31
Communists. *See* German Communist Party (KPD)
concentration camps. *See also* The Holocaust; *specific camps*
　Allied soldiers' liberation of, 89–91, 109
　Boer War and, 16
　forced labor at, 81–83

hunger at, 65, 80, 89–91, 233
medical experimentation at, 65, 126,
occupied Germany compared to, 106–7, 109, 121
prisoner of war camps compared to, 109–10
racial classification systems at, 52, 76, 79–80, 82
rations at, 65, 79–80, 82, 91, 106–7
consumerism
　canteens and, 131–33, 136, 139–40, 142, 218–19
　Cold War and, 117
　in East Germany, 131–33, 158, 162, 183, 196, 218, 223–24, 226–28, 247
　grocery shopping and, 124, 143, 145, 149–53, 158, 245–46
　kitchens and, 170, 183
　obesity and, 199, 220–22, 226, 228–32
　occupied Germany and, 148
　public education efforts regarding, 148–52
　in reunified Germany, 240, 245
　supermarkets and, 124, 147–48, 153, 157
　in West Germany, 139–40, 142, 145–46, 149–53, 162, 165, 170, 183, 199, 206, 222, 230–33, 247
cookbooks
　in East Germany, 178, 180–81, 183
　Eintopf (casserole) and, 53
　gender and, 167–70, 178, 180–82
　kitchen technology and, 170, 173
　in Nazi Germany, 53, 56
　in occupied Germany, 118–19, 245
　Ostalgie and, 242
　in reunified Germany, 242
　socialist cooking and, 179–81
　weight loss and, 201, 213–14
　in Weimar Germany, 45–46
　in West Germany, 167–70, 173, 180, 201, 238
cooking. *See* home cooking; kitchens
Cooperative for American Remittances to Europe (CARE), 112–13, 116–17
Council of Relief Agencies Licensed to Operate in Germany (CRALOG), 113
Cremer, Hans-Dietrich, 137, 140
currency reform (occupied Germany, 1948)
　dietary changes following, 198
　inflation following, 143, 186
　Soviet responses to, 114
　West German prosperity following, 145
cyclamate, 232–33
Czechoslovakia, 71

Darré, Walther, 57–58, 63
Davis, Mike, 3
Deutsche Forschungsgemeinschaft (German Research Foundation, DFG), 64
diabetes, 207, 222, 224, 228

dieting. *See also* weight loss
  artificial sweeteners and, 232–33
  behavior-modification therapy and, 210–11
  diet pills and, 232
  in East Germany, 214–16
  fads and, 211–12, 215
  gender dynamics and, 212, 216
  media programs promoting, 211–12
  in the United States, 214
  in West Germany, 198, 210–12, 232–33
diseases of civilization (*Zivilizationskrankheit*), 201–2, 206
displaced persons (DPs), 95, 98, 103–4, 262n82
"the double burden," 181, 188, 192–95
Dresden Hygiene Museum, 156, 180, 214, 216, 222, 236

East Berlin
  Berlin Airlift and, 115
  East German food distribution system and, 225
  fall of the Berlin Wall (1989) and, 237
  grocery shopping in, 151–52, 160
East German Central Institute for Nutrition, 130, 158, 180, 214
East Germany (1949–89)
  advertising in, 226, 229–30
  agriculture in, 129, 243
  black markets in, 158
  butter consumption levels in, 206
  caloric intake levels in, 203, 205, 224
  canteens in, 11, 125, 127–35, 137–38, 141–43, 153, 156, 159–61, 163, 178–79, 187–90, 193–94, 204–6, 213, 217–18, 243
  consumerism in, 131–33, 158, 162, 183, 196, 218, 223–24, 226–28, 247
  cookbooks in, 178, 180–81, 183
  diabetes in, 207, 228
  economic growth and reconstruction in, 2, 125, 127, 131–32, 166
  establishment of, 122
  family meals in, 166, 205
  fatness in, 11, 195–97, 203–8, 213–14, 216–17, 220–22, 226–27, 234–36, 244, 247
  food aid to, 244–45
  food prices in, 156–59, 161, 207, 226–27
  food shortages in, 129, 159–60, 224–28, 235, 244
  fruit and vegetable supply in, 225, 228, 237
  gender politics in, 182, 185, 194, 247
  grocery shopping in, 143, 151–59, 161, 163, 193, 222, 227–28, 247
  home cooking in, 159–60, 163, 177–87, 189–90, 194–95, 217, 247
  housewives in, 157–58, 177, 182–84, 188–90, 193
  hunger and, 243–44
  June 17 Workers' Uprising (1953) in, 129–30, 156, 244
  nutrition in, 126–27, 130, 132, 155–56, 158–59, 177–81, 183–84, 188–89, 195, 203–7, 213–17, 222, 224, 226, 228–29, 235
  obesity in, 11, 195–97, 204–5, 207–8, 213–14, 216–17, 221–22, 226, 234–35, 244, 247
  processed food in, 183–84
  rations in, 128–29, 157, 162, 187, 203
  school lunches in, 129, 166, 185–90, 193–94, 216–17, 248–49
  Soviet aid to, 122
  subsidies in, 157–58, 226, 235
  supermarkets in, 11, 124–25, 153, 161, 225
  weight loss and, 203–4, 207–8, 213–18, 220–27, 229, 235
  West German food shipments to, 160, 235, 244
  women's wage labor in, 11, 127, 154–55, 158–59, 166, 177–79, 181–88, 194, 216, 247–48
Ebert, Friedrich, 27
Edkins, Jenny, 10
Ehrenberg, Paul, 47
Ehrlich, Paul, 196
Eintopfsonntag (casserole Sunday), 53–54
Eisenhower, Dwight, 120
Engel's Law, 146
Erhard, Ludwig, 138–39, 144, 170, 200
Erntedankfest (annual harvest festival), 62
ersatz foods, 21, 40, 64–65
Ertl, Joseph, 230, 234
eugenics, 50–51, 82
European Children's Fund, 37
European Community (EC), 238, 240

factory canteens. *See* canteens
family meals. *See also* home cooking
  collective meals compared to, 133, 136–37
  in East Germany, 166, 205
  housewives and, 136, 165
  nuclear family ideal and, 165, 168–69, 195
  school lunches and, 166, 189
  in West Germany, 166, 168–69, 202, 208–9
  women's labor power and, 11, 195
Famine Emergency Committee, 109, 112
famines. *See also* starvation
  imperialism and, 3, 8, 30
  in the late Victorian era, 3, 30
  post–First World War Europe and, 33, 36
  post–Second World War Europe and, 89, 196
  in the Soviet Union, 44–45, 71
farming. *See* agriculture
fatness. *See also* obesity; weight loss
  behavior modification therapy and, 210–11
  canteens and, 217–19
  children and, 209–10, 216–17, 235, 246
  class dynamics and, 201–2, 220
  consumerism and, 199, 220–22, 226, 228–32

in East Germany, 11, 195–97, 203–8, 213–14, 216–17, 220–22, 226–27, 234–36, 244, 247
economic growth and, 200–201
free markets and, 234
gender and, 200–202, 204, 208, 220
in reunified Germany, 1, 241, 246, 249
in West Germany, 11, 199–203, 205, 208–10, 216, 218–20, 230–36, 247
Federal Center for Health Education (*Bundeszentrale für gesundheitliche Aufklärung*, BZgA), 208, 219
Federal Republic of Germany (FRG). *See* West Germany
Feldman, Gerald, 28
feminism, 175, 192
fertilizer
 agriculture and, 22, 62, 86, 123, 145
 Marshall Plan and, 120
 nitrogen and, 17–18, 24, 39
Finland, 71, 74, 89
First World War. *See also* Wilhelmine Germany
 agriculture and, 13, 20, 22–24, 37, 39
 civilians' dietary changes during, 20–23
 food aid and, 13–15, 30–31, 113, 121
 food protests in, 14–15, 24, 79, 239
 food shortages and, 5, 8, 23–26, 28
 German veterans of, 53–54
 Hindenburg Program and, 125
 hunger and, 1, 14–17, 24–25, 30–31, 41, 43–44
 Hunger Blockade of Germany during, 5, 10, 14–17, 30, 44–46, 51, 57, 87, 89
 munitions in, 10, 14, 17–19, 21
 nitrogen and, 17–18, 39, 253n24
 prisoners of war (POWs) in, 22, 25
 propaganda in, 23–24
 rations in, 15, 17, 20, 23–25, 28, 41, 43, 55, 99
 soup kitchens in, 138
 starvation and, 13
 as "total war," 14, 18–19, 29
 trench warfare in, 17, 19–20
 tuberculosis and, 29
 women's work during, 20
Fishburn, Howard, 75
food aid
 to Belgium, 30–31, 33, 37
 Berlin Airlift and, 114–20
 biopolitics and, 120
 Cold War and, 112–13, 120, 244–45
 to East Germany, 244–45
 First World War and, 13–15, 30–31, 113, 121
 "Hunger Map of Europe" and, 31–33
 Marshall Plan and, 120
 in occupied Germany, 2, 10, 112–19, 141, 185–86
 to Poland, 34, 89, 120
 to the Soviet Union, 38

from the United Kingdom, 30–31, 36, 89, 114–15
from the United States, 2, 14, 29–39, 42, 46, 73, 89, 112–20, 244–45, 255n111
to Weimar Germany, 2, 29–30, 35–39, 41–42, 46, 185, 255n111
to West Germany, 116–17
Food and Agricultural Organization (FAO; United Nations agency), 89
"Food for Peace" (U.S. Agricultural Trade Development and Assistance Act), 120
food protests
 First World War and, 14–15, 24, 79, 239
 industrial capitalism and, 9
 in occupied Germany, 100–101, 112
 in Weimar Germany, 15, 39, 43
 in Wilhelmine Germany, 24, 41, 79
 women's role in, 5, 79
Food Relief Program (U.S. initiative in East Germany), 244–45
food shortages. *See also* famine; hunger
 anti-Semitism and, 262n78
 in East Germany, 129, 159–60, 224–28, 235, 244
 in the First World War, 5, 8, 23–26, 28
 in Nazi Germany, 8, 57, 75
 in occupied Germany, 8, 98, 106, 243
 in post–Second World War Europe, 2, 92, 94–95, 196, 262n78
 in the Second World War, 8, 70
 in Weimar Germany, 15, 39–40, 46, 156
 in Wilhelmine Germany, 5, 8, 15, 23–26, 28, 254n67
forced laborers. *See also* prisoners of war (POWs)
 canteens and, 81
 labor and health conditions among, 82–83
 in Nazi Germany, 79, 81–84
 rations and, 82–84
 stranded in occupied Germany, 95, 103
Foucault, Michel
 biopolitics and, 4, 15
 on hunger and nation-states, 4, 15, 251n13
 on industrial food production, 4
 on neoliberalism and occupied Germany, 10
 on West German economic growth and the state, 135
France
 First World War and, 25, 30, 33, 46
 occupation zone in Germany administered by, 97–98, 106
 post–Second World War period in, 112, 238
 rations in, 71, 98
 Second World War and, 70–71, 74, 84, 89, 98
 Versailles Treaty and, 28
François, Hermann von, 44
French zone of occupation (1945–49), 97–98, 106

Fresswelle ("eating wave" in West Germany), 145, 198–99, 236, 240
Friedmann, Harriet, 120
frozen foods, 151, 170–71, 184. *See also* processed foods

gardens, 56, 75, 144–45, 241
Gellately, Robert, 78
gender
   canteens and, 125, 127
   cookbooks and, 167–70, 178, 180–82
   dieting and, 212, 216
   East German norms regarding, 182, 185, 194, 247
   fatness and, 200–202, 204, 208, 220
   grocery shopping and, 125, 247
   home cooking and, 165, 168–69, 177, 179, 181
   kitchens and, 166, 168, 171–72
   obesity and, 200–202, 208, 220
   rationing policies and, 76, 95
   reunified Germany and, 247, 249
   weight loss and, 203, 208, 212, 216, 232
German Communist Party (KPD)
   on German militarism, 110–11
   Great Depression and, 48
   hunger rhetoric and, 41–42, 110
   in occupied Germany, 96, 98, 110–12
   in Weimar Germany, 40–44, 47–48
German Democratic Republic (GDR). *See* East Germany
German Nutritional Society (*Deutsche Gesellschaft für Ernährung*; DGE)
   Advisory Board for Collective Feeding and, 137–38
   consumer education programs and, 148–49
   former Nazis working in, 126
   National Nutritional Report (1976), 142, 218–19
   weight loss programs and, 209–10, 212
Germany. *See* East Germany; Nazi Germany; reunified Germany; Weimar Germany; West Germany; Wilhelmine Germany
Glatzel, Hans, 59
globalization
   agriculture and, 9, 13–14, 57–59
   hunger and, 3
   interdependence of food supply and, 3, 6, 8, 13–14
glycerin, 18–19
Goebbels, Joseph, 67, 73
Goldberg, David Theo, 52
Gollancz, Victor, 107–8
Good Bye Lenin (film), 242
Göring, Hermann, 60, 62, 73, 84
governmentality, 4–5, 7, 234, 251n13
Gräfe, Heinrich, 158
Grazia, Victoria de, 153
Great Britain. *See* United Kingdom

Great Depression, 47–49
Greece, 71, 74, 89
Gries, Rainer, 245
grocery shopping. *See also* supermarkets
   advertising and, 147, 150, 155
   consumerism and, 124, 143, 145, 149–53, 158, 245–46
   in East Germany, 143, 151–59, 161, 163, 193, 222, 227–28, 247
   educational efforts regarding, 149–50
   food availability and, 134, 227–28
   housewives and, 125, 143–44, 146–53, 157–58, 170–71, 208, 231–32
   in Nazi Germany, 52, 57, 75, 78–79
   in occupied Germany, 99, 143–44
   prices and, 151–52, 156–59, 161
   in reunified Germany, 237, 239, 245–46
   weight loss and, 208–9, 227
   in West Germany, 125, 143, 145–53, 160, 163, 170–71, 193, 199, 208–9, 239, 244, 247
   in Wilhemine Germany, 20–21
   women's wage labor and, 154–55, 158–59
Gropius, Walter, 166
Grossmann, Atina, 101, 165
Grotewohl, Otto, 177
Grüne Woche (Green Week), 57–58, 241, 244
guest workers *(Gastarbeiter)*, 135, 201
Gutezeit, G., 191
Gypsies, 80, 87, 103

Haber, Fritz, 17–18, 64, 253n24
Haenel, Helmut, 132, 227, 229–30
Hahnemann, Helga, 204
Handelsorganisationen (HO) products, 152
Harsch, Donna, 96
Hertwig, Hugo, 55, 66
Himmler, Heinrich, 65
Hindenburg Program, 125
Hirschmann, Ira, 93
Hitler, Adolf. *See also* Nazi Party
   agricultural policies and, 49–50, 66, 80
   Allied propaganda regarding, 73
   on casserole Sunday *(Eintopfsonntag)*, 53
   elections (1933) and, 49, 62, 100
   hunger rhetoric of, 44, 48–50, 53
   racial ideologies of, 63, 76
   vegetarianism of, 55
Höcherl, Hermann, 148, 230
Hofer, Adolf, 40
The Holocaust
   Allied soldiers' encounters with, 89–91, 109
   concentration camps and, 16, 52, 65, 76, 79–83, 89–91, 106–7, 109–10, 233
   occupied Germany compared to, 107–9, 245
   survivors of, 104, 262n82
Holtmeier, H., 200
home cooking. *See also* family meals
   canteens as model for, 178–79

in East Germany, 159–60, 163, 177–87, 189–90, 194–95, 217, 247
housewives and, 167–68, 171–77, 183, 189–90, 208–9, 238
in Nazi Germany, 56
nuclear family ideals and, 165, 168–69, 172–73, 247
nutrition and, 173, 176–80
in reunified Germany, 248–49
in West Germany, 163, 167, 169, 171–76, 178, 190–95, 208–9, 218, 235, 247
women's wage labor and, 163, 166, 172–79, 181–82
home economics programs, 180–81
Honecker, Erich, 188, 196, 206, 222
Hoover, Herbert
  Committee for the Relief of Belgium and, 30–31
  Famine Emergency Committee and, 109, 112
  food aid in First World War–era Europe and, 13, 29–33, 36–39, 46
  food aid in Russian Civil War by, 38
  food aid in Second World War–era Europe and, 89, 109, 112–14, 185
  Germans' personal appeals to, 113–14
  Hunger Map of Europe and, 31–33
  National Committee on Food for the Small Democracies and, 89
Hot Springs Conference (1943), 88, 125–26
housewives
  Catholic Church views regarding, 173
  in East Germany, 157–58, 177, 182–84, 188–90, 193
  efforts to establish wages for, 176
  family meals and, 136, 165
  grocery shopping and, 125, 143–44, 146–53, 157–58, 170–71, 208, 231–32
  home cooking and, 167–68, 171–77, 183, 189–90, 208–9, 238
  in Nazi Germany, 54, 56–57, 69, 78–79, 167
  in occupied Germany, 96, 143–44, 149
  public education efforts geared toward, 148–52
  public opinion regarding, 174–75
  rationing policies and, 78–79, 149
  in reunified Germany, 249
  weight loss and, 211–13
  in West Germany, 116, 125, 144, 146–53, 162, 167, 170–76, 191–92, 208–9, 211–13, 231, 238, 247–48
  in Wilhelmine Germany, 18, 20
Huber, Antje, 219
Hull, Isabell, 15
humanitarianism
  Berlin Airlift and, 114, 120
  Cold War and, 120
  focus on women and children in, 31, 35, 37, 107
  food aid during First World War era and, 15, 29–31, 35, 37–39, 121

food aid in Second World War era and, 88, 100, 107, 114, 120
human rights
  Cold War and, 111–12
  food access and, 10, 91, 100, 105, 107, 111, 120–21, 125–26
  occupied Germany and, 91–92, 107, 111–12
  post–Second World War Europe and, 91–92, 105
  Universal Declaration of Human Rights (1948) and, 91
hunger. *See also* starvation
  in Berlin, 109, 115–16, 118–19
  biopolitics and, 4–5, 7–8
  Cold War and, 6, 118, 121, 245
  at concentration camps, 65, 80, 89–91, 233
  in East Germany, 243–44
  First World War and, 1, 14–17, 24–25, 30–31, 41, 43–44
  German Communist Party rhetoric and, 41–42, 110
  modernization and, 3, 9, 14
  in Nazi Germany, 55, 72–73, 85–87, 102–3, 144
  Nazi Party rhetoric and, 44–45, 48–50, 53, 57–58, 66–68, 75, 87, 105
  in occupied Germany, 87, 94, 98–101, 104–13, 117–18, 121–22, 124, 136
  post–First World War Europe and, 31–33
  post–Second World War Europe and, 88–90, 92
  prisoners of war and, 25, 65, 85, 109–10, 199–200
  race and, 50–52
  Second World War and, 1–2, 70, 87
  in the Soviet Union, 37–38, 72, 84
  in Weimar Germany, 10, 14–15, 27–28, 33–37, 39–48, 51–52
  in Wilhelmine Germany, 10, 14–15, 24–25, 30, 41, 43–44, 99
Hunger Blockade (First World War)
  continuation after war of, 27–29, 35, 39, 47
  data regarding deaths from, 28, 46
  food shortages and malnourishment during, 5, 51, 87, 89, 254n67
  nitrogen supplies and, 17
Hunger Map of Europe, 31–33
Hunger Plan (Nazi Germany's policies toward Soviet POWs), 84
"Hunger Years" (*Hungerjahre*, 1945–49). *See* occupied Germany
Hygiene Museum. *See* Dresden Hygiene Museum

imperial Germany. *See* Wilhelmine Germany
imperialism
  famines and, 3, 8, 30
  racism and, 50–51
  resource extraction and, 13–14, 59
  United Kingdom and, 8, 16

Imperial Naval Command (Wilhelmine Germany), 27
Independent Social Democratic Party, 40
influenza epidemic (1918), 29
Institute for Nutrition and Food Science, 128
Iron Curtain speech (Churchill, 1946), 164
Italy, 70–71, 74

Jews
  agricultural labor and, 67
  German anthropology and, 50
  German suffering compared to suffering of, 102–3
  The Holocaust and, 52, 70, 90, 104, 107–9
  Nazi Germany's laws regarding, 64, 76, 78, 80, 86
  Nazi Party rhetoric regarding, 44, 50–52, 57–58, 60, 62, 67, 87, 103, 105
  in occupied Germany, 96, 103–5
  rationing policies and, 71, 76–78, 80, 83, 96, 104
  in the US armed forces, 103
Jourdain, Margaret, 16
June 17 Workers' Uprising (East Germany, 1953), 129–30, 156, 244

Kharkiv (Ukraine), 72
Kiel Mutiny (1918), 27
Kiev (Ukraine), 71–72
kitchens
  architectural design of, 166–67, 182–83, 269n11
  in canteens, 132–33, 141
  Cold War and, 164, 167
  consumerism and, 170, 183
  in East Germany, 165, 182–84, 193–94
  housewives and, 164, 172, 183, 193
  in Nazi Germany, 167
  P2 model kitchen and, 183
  soup kitchens and, 7, 20, 138
  technology and modernization in, 164–65, 169–70, 173, 183–84
  in Weimar Germany, 166
  in West Germany, 165, 167–70, 172–73, 183
Klatt, Werner, 144
Koczian, Johanna von, 192
Koistinen, Paul, 14
Krauss, Herbert, 233
Kraut, Heinrich, 126, 264n21
Kriegsbrot (K-Brot; whole-grain bread in Wilhelmine Germany), 20–21
Kühnau, Joachim, 136, 169
Künast, Renate, 246

Langer, William, 108
Lebensraum (Nazi doctrine of "living space"), 67–68, 243

LeBesco, Kathleen, 247
Leningrad siege (1941–44), 71
Ley, Robert, 126
Locarno Treaty (1925), 46
Lüdtke, Alf, 41

Mabry, Hannalore, 176
Maier, Charles, 124
malnourishment
  at concentration camps, 90
  First World War and, 2
  Hunger Blockade and, 5, 51, 87, 89
  in Nazi Germany, 73, 84
  in occupied Germany, 107, 143
  prisoners of war and, 84
  Second World War and, 2, 90
  in Weimar Germany, 15, 40–41, 43, 49
  in Wilhelmine Germany, 15
Manager's Disease *(Managerkrankheit)*, 200–201
Marshall Plan, 120, 122, 145
Marx, Karl, 9
Mauthausen concentration camp, 65, 109
Mazower, Mark, 92
McDonald, Dwight, 109
Menne, Bernhard, 48
Meyer, Erna, 166
Meyer, Konrad, 58–59
milk
  in East Germany, 229–30
  munitions and, 34
  subsidized distribution of, 186
  in West Germany, 153, 186, 230–31
Moeller, Robert, 118
Monowitz concentration camp, 106
Morgenthau Plan, 93, 261n34
Müller-Armack, Alfred, 170

Nally, David, 3
National Committee for Communal Feeding (Nazi Germany), 126
National Committee on Food for the Small Democracies, 89
National Nutritional Report (West Germany, 1976), 142, 218–19
National Socialist Party (Nationalsozialistische Deutsche Arbeiterpartei; NSDAP). *See* Nazi Party
National Workgroup for Healthy Living and Health Education (East Germany), 205–6
Nazi Germany (1933–45). *See also* Nazi Party
  agriculture in, 49–50, 57–58, 62–64, 66–68, 73, 80–81, 86
  anti-Jewish laws in, 64, 76, 78, 80, 86
  autarchy and, 56, 59–60, 66, 80, 86
  bread in, 52, 55–56, 60–62, 66–67
  canteens in, 52–53, 56, 78–79, 81, 126–27
  elections (1933) in, 49, 62, 100

Index

food imports to, 56, 58, 62, 86
food shortages in, 8, 57, 75
forced laborers in, 79, 81–84
grocery shopping in, 52, 57, 75, 78–79
The Holocaust and, 70, 90, 104, 107–9, 245
housewives in, 54, 56–57, 69, 78–79, 167
hunger in, 55, 72–73, 85–87, 102–3, 144
Lebensraum (living space) ideology in, 67–68, 243
malnourishment in, 73, 84
nutrition in, 54, 57, 59–65, 73–74, 80, 82
Poland invaded and occupied (1939–44) by, 52, 67–71, 75, 80
prisoners of war from, 72–73, 94, 109–11
prisoners of war in, 65, 81–85, 126
propaganda in, 49, 51, 57, 63, 73–74, 87, 102, 117
racism and racial identity in, 10, 50–60, 62–63, 65–69, 71, 75–87, 105, 126
rationing policies in, 69–86, 97, 100, 106
Reich Farm Inheritance Law (1933) in, 62–63
Reichsnährstand (National Food Estate) in, 49–50
Soviet Union invaded and occupied (1941–44) by, 52, 67–72, 83–84
starvation in, 2, 72, 79–80, 84–85, 87, 93
Volksgemeinschaft (people's community) concept in, 52, 54, 56, 75, 79, 91, 102
Winterhilfswerk (winter charity drive) in, 53–54, 86
Nazi Party. *See also* Nazi Germany
anti-Semitic rhetoric of, 44, 50–52, 57–58, 60, 62, 67, 87, 103, 105
blood and soil rhetoric of, 5, 62–63, 67
hunger rhetoric of, 44–45, 48–50, 53, 57–58, 66–68, 75, 87, 105
postwar treatment of members of, 96, 99, 101–2, 113–14
rise of, 48
rural support for, 49, 62
The Netherlands, 70–71, 74, 89
News Agency for Food Questions (*Nachrichtendienst für Ernährungsfragen*), 23
Niemann, Kai, 242
Niemöller, Martin, 106
Nitrate Commission (Wilhelmine Germany), 17
nitrogen, 17–18, 24, 39, 64, 253n24
Nitti, Francesco, 124
Norway, 71, 74, 89
nostalgia. *See Ostalgie*
nutrition. *See also* malnourishment
anthropology and, 50–51
Aryan racial ideology and, 56, 65–66
canteens and, 127, 130, 132, 134, 142, 178–79, 189, 218–19
East Germany and, 126–27, 130, 132, 155–56, 158–59, 177–81, 183–84, 188–89, 195, 203–7, 213–17, 222, 224, 226, 228–29, 235

economic productivity and, 136, 179
education programs regarding, 56, 148–49, 209–10, 216–17, 229, 233
home cooking and, 173, 176–80
modern nation-states' efforts to promote, 3–4
Nazi Germany and, 54, 57, 59–65, 73–74, 80, 82
in occupied Germany, 105–6
in reunified Germany, 245–46, 248
school lunches and, 189, 191–92
in Weimar Germany, 45–47, 49
West Germany and, 123–24, 126, 148–49, 171, 173, 176, 191–92, 195, 202, 208–10, 213, 218–19, 230–31, 233, 235
in Wilhelmine Germany, 22–23

obesity. *See also* fatness; weight loss
canteens and, 218
children and, 209–10, 216–17, 235
class dynamics and, 201, 220, 234
in East Germany, 11, 195–97, 204–5, 207–8, 213–14, 216–17, 221–22, 226, 234–35, 244, 247
economic costs associated with, 202–3, 207, 234–35
gender and, 200–202, 208, 220
health problems associated with, 202–3, 207–8
modern lifestyles and, 197, 200, 202–3
in reunified Germany, 1, 246, 249
school lunches and, 216–17
in the United States, 1, 197, 210, 246
in West Germany, 11, 195–203, 208–10, 218, 220, 230–36, 247
occupied Germany (1945–49). *See also specific zones*
agriculture in, 98–99, 123
Berlin Airlift and, 114–20
black markets in, 99, 106–7
canteens in, 97, 128, 136
Cold War and, 92, 109, 111, 114–17, 121
concentration camps compared to, 106–7, 109, 121
Cooperative for American Remittances to Europe aid to, 112–13
currency reform (1948) and, 143, 244
displaced persons (DPs) in, 95, 103–4, 262n82
ethnic Germans expelled to, 95, 99
food aid to, 2, 10, 112–19, 141, 185–86
food protests in, 100–101, 112
food shortages in, 8, 98, 106, 243
former Nazis in, 96, 99, 101–2, 113–14
German Communist Party in, 96, 98, 110–12
grocery shopping in, 99, 143–44
The Holocaust compared to, 107–9, 245
housewives in, 96, 143–44, 149
human rights rhetoric and, 91–92, 107, 111–12

occupied Germany (1945–49) (*Cont.*)
  hunger in, 87, 94, 98–101, 104–13, 117–18, 121–22, 124, 136
  Jews in, 96, 103–5
  productivity in, 123–24
  rations in, 94–102, 104–15, 122–24, 127, 143, 148–49, 185–86, 262n82
  school lunches in, 185–86
oil crisis (1973), 142, 201
Opfer des Fascismus (victim of fascism; OdF), 96
optimized food (*optimierte Nahrung*) program (East Germany), 222–24, 226
Order No. 234 (East Germany), 128–29
Orr, John Boyd, 88
Ostalgie (nostalgia for the East), 241–43
Ostarbeiter (workers from the East in Second World War), 83
overweight. *See* fatness; obesity
Oxford Famine Relief Committee (Oxfam), 89

P2 model kitchen, 183
Pfeil, Elisabeth, 174
pig murder (*Schweinemord*), 23, 58
Poland
  Brest-Litovsk Treaty (1918) and, 25
  First World War and, 30
  food aid to, 34, 89, 120
  former forced laborers from, 103
  German invasion and occupation (1939–44) of, 52, 67–71, 75, 80
  prisoners of war from, 22, 81–82
  rations in, 80
Potsdam Conference (1945), 93–94
Price, Hoyt, 107
prisoners of war (POWs)
  concentration camps compared to plight of, 109–10
  First World War and, 22, 25
  forced labor by, 22, 81, 83–84
  hunger among, 25, 65, 85, 109–10, 126, 199–200
  from Nazi Germany, 72–73, 94, 109–11
  in Nazi Germany, 65, 81–85, 126
  from the Soviet Union, 65, 72, 81–82, 84–85, 126
  in the Soviet Union, 109–11
  in Wilhelmine Germany, 22
processed foods, 145–47, 183–84. *See also* frozen foods
Pross, Helge, 192

Quakers, 37, 42, 101, 185

race and racism
  agriculture and, 63, 66–69, 80–81
  anthropology and, 50–51
  concentration camps and, 52, 76, 79–80, 82
  imperialism and, 50–51
  modern food economy and, 53–56
  in Nazi Germany, 10, 50–60, 62–63, 65–69, 71, 75–87, 105, 126
  obesity and, 246
  rationing policies and, 70–71, 75–85
  in reunified Germany, 246
  in the United States, 50, 260n25
rape, 102, 118
rations
  at concentration camps, 65, 79–80, 82, 91, 106–7
  in East Germany, 128–29, 157, 162, 187, 203
  First World War and, 15, 17, 20, 23–25, 28, 41, 43, 55, 99
  foreign workers in Nazi Germany and, 82–84
  former Nazis and, 96, 99, 101–2, 113–14
  in German-occupied territories during Second World War, 71, 74
  Holocaust survivors and, 104, 262n82
  housewives and, 78–79, 149
  in Nazi Germany, 69–86, 97, 100, 106
  in occupied Germany, 94–102, 104–15, 122–24, 127, 143, 148–49, 185–86, 262n82
  racism and, 70–71, 75–85
  Second World War and, 70–71, 74–77
  in the United Kingdom, 17, 94–95, 98
  in the United States, 95
  in West Germany, 144
  in Wilhelmine Germany, 20–25, 28, 41, 43, 55, 76, 99, 145
Reich Farm Inheritance Law (1933), 62–63
Reichsnährstand (National Food Estate), 49–50
reparations, 27, 43, 46, 122
restaurants, 53, 136-137, 142, 214, 218
Reumann, Kurt, 248
reunified Germany (1990–)
  canteens in, 240, 246, 248
  eastern German eating habits in, 240–41, 243
  fatness in, 1, 241, 246, 249
  gender and, 247, 249
  grocery shopping in, 237, 239, 245–46
  housewives in, 249
  Ostalgie and, 241–43
  school lunches in, 186, 248–49
  women's wage labor in, 247–49
Reuter, Ernst, 116
Robertson, Brian, 123
Roma and Sinti. *See* Gypsies
Roosevelt, Franklin, 93
Rubmann, Max, 42–43
Russenbrot (Russian bread), 65, 84
Russia, 13, 18, 25. *See also* Soviet Union
rye bread, 20–21, 60, 62, 67, 217

Schenck, Ernst-Günther, 126
Scheunert, Arthur, 64, 126, 177

Index

Schiller, Karl, 148
school cafeterias. *See* school lunches
school lunches
 in East Germany, 129, 166, 185–90, 193–94, 216–17, 248–49
 international food aid and, 185
 nutrition and, 189, 191–92
 obesity and, 216–17
 in occupied Germany, 185–86
 parents' responses to, 186–87, 192, 249
 participation rates in, 186–89, 216–17
 in reunified Germany, 186, 248–49
 in West Germany, 166, 186, 190–93, 272n138
Schorske, Carl, 107
Schuette-Lihotzky, Margarete, 166, 269n11
Schultz, Theodore, 88
Schwartzer, Alice, 176, 192
Schweinemord (pig murder), 23, 58
second-wave feminism, 192
Second World War. *See also* Nazi Germany
 black markets and, 73–74
 food shortages during, 8, 70
 German demography changed by, 165
 German invasion and occupation of Poland (1939–44) and, 52, 67–71, 75, 80
 German invasion and occupation of the Soviet Union (1941–44) and, 52, 67–73, 83–84
 mass rapes in, 102, 118
 rations and, 70–71, 74–77
 starvation and, 5, 69–71, 85, 92
shopping. *See* grocery shopping
Shub, Boris, 52, 70–71
Siemens, 83, 139–41
Slavs, 67–69, 83, 85–86, 103
Social Democratic Party of Germany (Sozialdemokratische Partei Deutschlands; SPD)
 canteens and, 129
 hunger rhetoric and, 41
 in Weimar Germany, 27, 40–41, 46
 in West Germany, 135
Socialist Unity Party (Sozialistische Einheitspartei Deutschlands, SED)
 canteens and, 129
 food industry regulations and, 223
 food provisioning policies and, 157
 school lunch programs and, 186–88
 women's workforce participation and, 186–87
soup kitchens, 7, 20, 138
Soviet Union
 agriculture in, 117–18
 Berlin Airlift and, 114–15
 Bolshevik Revolution (1917) and, 36–37
 Cold War tensions with United States and, 94, 111–12, 118, 122, 164
 Eastern bloc states and, 162, 243
 famines in, 44–45, 71

food aid to, 38
 former forced laborers from, 103
 German invasion and occupation (1941–44) of, 52, 67–73, 83–84
 hunger in, 37–38, 72, 84
 occupation zone in Germany administered by, 96–97, 110, 115–16, 118, 128, 244
 prisoners of war from, 65, 72, 81–82, 84–85, 126
 prisoners of war in, 109–11
 Stalingrad, battle (1942–43) of, 72, 100
 starvation in, 69, 71–72, 83–84
Soviet zone of occupation (1945–49)
 Berlin Airlift and, 115–16
 canteens in, 97, 128
 former Nazis in, 96, 102, 113–14
 hunger and, 244
 rationing policies in, 94, 96–98, 102, 110, 112–15, 185
Spartacist uprising (1919), 38
"stab in the back" myth, 43–44
Stalingrad, battle (1942–43) of, 72, 100
starvation. *See also* famine; hunger
 at concentration camps, 80, 89–91
 in Nazi Germany, 2, 72, 79–80, 84–85, 87, 93
 in occupied Germany, 98, 107–9
 in post–First World War Europe, 36
 in post–Second World War Europe, 88
 prisoners of war and, 84–85, 109–10, 126
 Second World War and, 5, 69–71, 85, 92
 in the Soviet Union, 69, 71–72, 83–84
Steege, Paul, 116
Stolper, Gustav, 107
supermarkets. *See also* grocery shopping
 canteens compared to, 124–25, 153
 in East Germany, 11, 124–25, 153, 161, 225
 in reunified Germany, 245
 self-service markets and, 124, 153, 155, 158
 in West Germany, 11, 124–25, 149, 153, 162

Teuteberg, Hans-Jürgen, 202–3, 234
Third Reich. *See* Nazi Germany
Thompson, E. P., 9
Tilly, Charles, 9
Trademark Association for Dietetic Products (*Warenzeichenverbandes diätetische Erzeugnisse*), 213, 222
Truman, Harry, 94, 112
Turnip Winter (Germany, 1916–17), 23–24, 29

U-boat attacks (First World War), 17, 31
Ukraine
 Brest-Litovsk Treaty (1918) and, 25–26
 collectivization and famine in, 71
 Nazi invasion and occupation (1941–44) of, 52, 68, 85
Ulbricht, Walter, 129, 196, 207, 236

United Kingdom
  Berlin Airlift and, 114–15
  Committee for the Relief of Belgium (CRB) and, 30
  First World War and, 5, 10, 14–19, 30, 33–34, 39, 44, 46
  food aid and, 30–31, 36, 89, 114–15
  Hunger Blockade in Wilhemine and Weimar Germany by, 5, 10, 14–17, 22–23, 27–30, 35, 44–46, 51, 57, 87, 89
  imperialism and, 8, 16
  occupation zone in Germany administered by, 90–92, 97–98, 104, 109, 112, 118, 123, 143
  rations in, 17, 94–95, 98
  Second World War and, 73, 94–95, 109, 117
  U-boat campaign against, 17
United Nations Relief and Rehabilitation Administration (UNRRA), 74, 88, 104, 112
United States
  agriculture in, 21, 31, 33, 89, 120
  Berlin airlift and, 114–20
  Cold War tensions with Soviet Union and, 94, 111–12, 118, 122, 164
  Committee for the Relief of Belgium (CRB) and, 30–31
  First World War and, 13–14, 17–18, 21, 31
  food aid from, 2, 14, 29–39, 42, 46, 73, 89, 112–20, 244–45, 255n111
  food exports from, 17, 33
  Marshall Plan and, 120
  Morgenthau Plan proposal and, 93, 261n34
  obesity in, 1, 197, 210, 246
  occupation zone in Germany administered by, 92, 97–98, 103–4, 108–9, 112, 118, 123, 143, 185–86
  racism and segregation in, 50, 260n25
  reconstruction of post–Second World War Europe and, 93, 107, 120
  Second World War and, 73, 109, 117
Universal Declaration of Human Rights (1948), 91

vegetarianism, 55, 100
Veit, Helen, 33
Vernon, James, 9
Versailles Treaty (1919), 27, 36, 39, 45, 47
Volksgemeinschaft (people's community), 52, 54, 56, 75, 79, 91, 102
Vollkornbrot (whole grain or rye bread), 60, 65, 77, 225

Wagemann, Ernst, 13
War Food Office *(Reichsernährungsamt)*, 22–24, 43
Wartime Raw Materials Department *(Kriegsrohstoffabteilung, KRA)*, 21, 23
Watts, Michael, 4

weight loss. *See also* fatness; obesity
  advertising and, 226, 230–32
  artificial sweeteners and, 225
  behavior-modification therapy and, 210–11
  canteens and, 208, 217–20
  children and, 216
  commercial products designed to promote, 199–200, 222–23, 232
  cookbooks and, 201, 213–14
  dieting and, 198, 210–16, 232–33
  East Germany and, 203–4, 207–8, 213–18, 220–27, 229, 235
  gender and, 203, 208, 212, 216, 232
  housewives and, 211–13
  low-calorie foods and, 222, 224, 226, 232
  nutrition and, 204, 206–10, 213–14, 217
  public education campaigns regarding, 208–11, 213–14, 219–20, 235
  West Germany and, 198–201, 208–12, 219–20, 230–33, 235
Weimar Germany (1918–1933)
  agriculture in, 39, 49
  black markets in, 28, 39
  Bolshevism seen as threat to, 41–44
  cookbooks in, 45–46
  food aid to, 2, 29–30, 35–39, 41–42, 46, 185, 255n111
  food protests in, 15, 39, 43
  food shortages in, 15, 39–40, 46, 156
  German Communist Party (KPD) in, 40–44, 47–48
  Great Depression and, 47–48
  Hunger Blockade and, 27–29, 35
  hunger in, 10, 14–15, 27–28, 33–37, 39–48, 51–52
  hyperinflation in, 37, 40–41, 43
  influenza epidemic (1918) and, 29
  kitchens in, 166
  nutrition and, 45–47, 49
  political radicalization in, 14, 38, 40, 43–44, 46–48
  reparations from First World War and, 27, 43, 46
  Social Democratic Party and, 27, 40–41, 46
  "stab in the back" myth and, 43–44
  Versailles Treaty and, 27–28, 39, 45, 47
Wende ("the Turn"; East German term for reunification), 243, 246–48
West Berlin
  Berlin Airlift and, 114–18
  canteens in, 136
  grocery shopping in, 151–52, 160, 244
  Soviet offers of food aid to, 115–17
West Germany (1949–89)
  advertising in, 147, 150, 230–33
  African famine relief and, 279n37
  agriculture in, 145

canteens in, 11, 125, 127, 131, 135–43, 218–20
CARE packages to, 112
collective meals in, 135–42, 217
consumerism and, 139–40, 142, 145–46, 149–53, 162, 165, 170, 183, 199, 206, 222, 230–33, 247
cookbooks in, 167–70, 173, 180, 201, 238
currency reform (1948) and, 114, 143, 145, 186, 198, 244
dieting in, 198, 210–12, 232–33
economic growth and reconstruction in, 2, 11, 120, 125, 135–36, 138, 145–47, 166–70, 194, 200–201, 243
establishment of, 122
family meals in, 166, 168–69, 202, 208–9
fatness in, 11, 199–203, 205, 208–10, 216, 218–20, 230–36, 247
food aid to, 116–17
food imports to, 145
food prices in, 151–53, 157
food processing in, 145–47
Fresswelle ("eating wave") in, 145, 198–99, 236, 240
grocery shopping in, 125, 143, 145–53, 160, 163, 170–71, 193, 199, 208–9, 239, 244, 247
guest workers (*Gastarbeiter*) in, 135, 201
home cooking in, 163, 167, 169, 171–76, 178, 190–95, 208–9, 218, 235, 247
housewives in, 116, 125, 144, 146–53, 162, 167, 170–76, 191–92, 208–9, 211–13, 231, 238, 247–48
kitchens in, 165, 167–70, 172–73, 183
Marshall Plan and, 120, 122, 145
middle-class society in, 135–36, 138–42, 144, 162
nutrition in, 123–24, 126, 148–49, 171, 173, 176, 191–92, 195, 202, 208–10, 213, 218–19, 230–31, 233, 235
obesity in, 11, 195–203, 208–10, 218, 220, 230–36, 247
oil crisis (1973) and, 142, 152–53, 201
price controls in, 144
rations in, 144
school lunches in, 166, 186, 190–93, 272n138
supermarkets in, 11, 124–25, 149, 153, 162
weight loss programs in, 198–201, 208–12, 219–20, 230–33, 235
women's wage labor in, 11, 166, 174–75, 191, 247–48
Westpäckchen ("West packages"), 235
whole grain bread
  in East Germany, 227–28
  in Nazi Germany, 56, 60–62, 66–67
  in Wilhelmine Germany, 20–21
Whole-Grain Bread Committee (*Reichsvollkornbrotausschuss*), 67
Wilhelmine Germany (1890–1918)

black markets in, 20–21, 23–24
Burgfrieden (Fortress Peace) agreement between political parties in, 24
canteens in, 125
Committee for the Relief of Belgium and, 30
ersatz food production in, 21
food imports to, 16, 18
food protests and, 24, 41, 79
food shortages in, 5, 8, 15, 23–26, 28, 254n67
grocery shopping in, 20–21
Hindenburg Program and, 125
housewives and, 18, 20
Hunger Blockade against, 5, 10, 14–17, 22–23, 27, 30, 44–46, 51, 57, 87, 89
hunger in, 10, 14–15, 24–25, 30, 41, 43–44, 99
influenza epidemic (1918) in, 29
News Agency for Food Questions in, 23
nutrition in, 22–23
price controls in, 21–22
prisoners of war in, 22
propaganda in, 23–24
rations in, 20–25, 28, 41, 43, 55, 76, 99
Schweinemord (pig murder) and, 23, 58
soup kitchens in, 138
Turnip Winter (1916–17) and, 23–24, 29
U-boat warfare and, 17
War Food Office in, 22–24, 43
Wartime Raw Materials Department and, 21, 23
Wilmenrod, Clemens, 167
Wilson, Woodrow, 31, 33–34, 37–38
Winckel, Max, 60, 66
Winterhilfswerk (Nazi Germany winter charity drive), 53–54, 86
Wirz, Franz, 67
women. *See also* gender; housewives
  agricultural work by, 20, 22, 73
  Catholic Church views regarding, 173
  "the double burden" and, 181, 188, 192–95
  wage labor by, 11, 20, 127, 154–55, 158–59, 163, 166, 172–79, 181–88, 191, 194, 216, 247–49
  West German law regarding employment of, 11, 173
World War I. *See* First World War
World War II. *See* Second World War
Wunderlich, Frieda, 243
Wurm, Emanuel, 29
Wurm, Max, 41

Yugoslavia, 95, 120

Ziegelmayer, Wilhelm, 180
Zischka, Anton, 63
Zobel, Martin, 132
Zonen-Gabi (Gabi from the Eastern zone), 237–39
Zulagen (supplements to rations in occupied Germany), 97

www.ingramcontent.com/pod-product-compliance
Ingram Content Group UK Ltd.
Pitfield, Milton Keynes, MK11 3LW, UK
UKHW041307180426
11947UKWH00009B/738